Knowledge-based Decision Support Systems

Knowledge-based Decision Support Systems With Applications in Business

MICHEL R. KLEIN
LEIF B. METHLIE

JOHN WILEY & SONS
Chichester • New York • Brisbane • Toronto • Singapore

First edition published as *Expert Systems: A Decision Support Approach* by Addison-Wesley Publishers Ltd 1990.

This edition Copyright ©1995 by John Wiley & Sons Ltd,
  Baffins Lane,
  Chichester,
  West Sussex PO19 1UD, England

  National   01243 779777
  International   (+44) 1243 779777

Other Wiley Editorial Offices

John Wiley & Sons, Inc., 605 Third Avenue, New York, NY 10158-0012, USA

Jacaranda Wiley Ltd, 33 Park Road, Milton, Queensland 4064, Australia

John Wiley & Sons (Canada) Ltd, 22 Worcester Road Rexdale, Ontario M9W 1LI, Canada

John Wiley & Sons (SEA) Pte Ltd, 37 Jalan Pemimpin #05-04, Block B, Union Industrial Building, Singapore 2057

Library of Congress Cataloging-in-Publication Data

Klein, Michel, 1942–
    Knowledge based decision support systems : with applications in business / Michel R. Klein, Leif B. Methlie.
        p. cm.
    Rev. ed. of: Experts systems. 1990.
    Includes bibliographical references (p.   ) and index.
    ISBN 0-471-95295-8
    1. Business enterprises—Finance—Data processing. 2. Finance – -Decision making—Data processing. 3. Decision support systems. 4. Expert systems (Computer science) I. Methlie, Leif B., 1939– . II. Klein, R. Michel, 1942–   Expert systems. III. Title.
    HG4012.5.K56 1995
    658.4'03'0285—dc20   94—36750
                                                               CIP

British Library Cataloguing in Publication Data

A catalogue record for this book is available from the British Library

ISBN 0-471-95295-8

Typeset in 10/12pt Palatino by Dobbie Typesetting Ltd, Tavistock, Devon
Printed and bound in Great Britain by Biddles Ltd, Guildford, Surrey

Contents

Preface to the First Edition

Rationale for the book

An exciting application area is emerging from the field of artificial intelligence – expert systems. In the early 1980s we became aware of the signficance of this new technology to business, and ways in which it could change business and improve decision making. However, early research on applying this technology to managerial problems, and financial problems in particular, demonstrated some shortcomings. Firstly, expert systems are reasoning systems. They are not particularly good at dealing with numbers and performing numeric computations. Secondly, they are problem solving systems and are not easily integrated into a decision making environment dealing with ill-structured decisions. Therefore, both of us saw opportunities in integrating the expert systems technology with the decision support systems technology. The new framework resulting from this we have called knowledge-based decision support systems. The paradigm of decision support systems (DSS) remains: to support decision making in ill-structured situations. The system architecture, however, consists of components from DSS and expert systems.

To our knowledge, the idea of such a framework was presented for the first time at a NATO conference 'Decision Support Systems: Theory and Applications' held in Maratea, Italy in 1985. In the Spring semester of 1986 Leif B. Methlie was on sabbatical leave to work with Michel Klein at Centre HEC-ISA, near Paris, on applying this framework to problems in management control and finance. The idea of this book was then created.

Both of us have more than 15 years of experience in academic teaching, research and consulting in the field of DSS. We have taught expert systems and DSS in business schools and in executive seminars for a number of years. In particular, together with Professor Paolo Mottura at SDA Bocconi, Italy, we have organized and run seminars on expert systems and DSS in banks and financial institutions for managers and analysts since 1986. In 1988, seminars of this kind were organized in five different countries in Europe. In our teaching and consulting activities we have felt a need for a comprehensive text on expert systems and problem solving that could deal with these topics from a business perspective. Most textbooks on expert systems take their examples from other fields, such as medicine, science and engineering. This makes the reading rather hard for business students and managers, due to the unfamiliar domain vocabularies that they are confronted with in these examples. After having worked on development tools, prototypes for several financial tasks, and more recently on implementation of such systems in business organizations, we felt that we had enough material to make a comprehensive text on knowledge-based decision support systems for a business-oriented audience.

Readership

This book is particularly designed for students on courses covering DSS, expert systems, or knowledge-based DSS, in a business administration curriculum, in management, in finance, or in information systems. The book gives full coverage of technical aspects together with examples and cases from business.

We think that it is also important for executives and managers, particularly managers of financial institutions, to know about knowledge-based systems, the importance of these systems to their business, and how they can be developed. Business managers may choose to avoid the more fundamental issues developed in Chapters 2–4 as well as the more specific aspects of knowledge modeling described in Chapter 8, and testing and evaluation in Chapter 10. Thus, we recommend business managers to read Chapters 1, 5–7, 9 and 11–13.

For the training of systems personnel in knowledge engineering for business problems, this book should be particularly helpful. In this case, we recommend the reader to study the chapters in the order in which they are presented.

We have presented a comprehensive framework of knowledge-based DSS and shown these concepts partly implemented. Still much has to be done to fully implement this framework. Tool designers and researchers should find this book challenging in this respect.

Acknowledgements

In developing this book over a number of years, we have benefited from discussions with many people.

Michel Klein wishes to thank all the members of the development team on OPTRANS EXPERT at the company SIG. In particular, Alain Manteau for his work on the mainframe version, Pierre Monnier for his work on the PC version, J. L. Dussartre and F. Despoux, Marc Kossa and T. Martin for their work on the expert subsystem, and D. Dollé for his work on the database subsystem.

Michel Klein also wishes to thank: Alain Manteau who made the initial transfer of the FINSIM model under OPTRANS EXPERT, Thierry Villedieu for his work on FINSIM, Eric Briys from the Finance Department of the Groupe HEC for his advice on a first prototype knowledge base. Mr Cabanac and Mr Nicol from the Caisse Régionale du Crédit Agricole de Toulouse for their work on one of the FINSIM knowledge base, Mr J. J. Burgun from the SOREFI Champagne Ardenne for his work on another FINSIM knowledge base. Mr Derksen (SOREFI Champagne) and Mr Renaudin (CRCAM Toulouse) for their encouragement. Dr Brita Shwartz from the Stockholm School of Economics Research Center for her comments on Chapter 3.

Dr Jacques Pezier for his comments on the rational decision analysis section of Chapter 3. Professor A. Lux from LIFIA-ENSIMAG for his advice on the integration of AI in OPTRANS. Pierre Rosenthiel who encouraged my initial work in this field.

My former professors at the Tuck School of Dartmouth College, Peter Williamson, C. Bower, Vic McGee and W. Carleton who gave me the taste for decision support systems in finance.

My colleagues from the IFIP Working Group 8.3 and 8.1, in particular, Professor R. Traunmuller (J. Kepler Universitat, Linz) and Professor V. Rajkovic (J. Stefan Institute, Ljubljana) with whom I had many discussions in many wonderful European cities.

My partners in the IKB/DSS ESPRIT project, in particular, Dr F. Schmidt (IKE, Universitat, Stuttgart), Professor M. Milanese (Politecnico di Torino), Professor P. Vincke (Université Libre de Bruxelles) with whom I had many discussions on second generation KB-DSS. Hopefully, this project which gave us the opportunity to discuss ideas and collaborate is now financed by the company SIG.

My colleagues from the Information and Decision Support System Department at the Groupe HEC.

Dominique de Saint Aubert, Chantal Boeffard, Micheline Rico and Elisabeth Sartiaux for typing the manuscript.

Leif B. Methlie wishes to thank members of the research team on financial expert systems: Svien O. Båtnes, Heidi Følstad, Per B. Lyngstad, and Helge Lilletvedt and Gunnar A. Dahl, a partner with Ernst and Young in Norway, for making his expertise on financial analysis available for the project. Also he wants to extend his gratitude to the Royal Norwegian Council for Science and Industrial Research for financial support. Furthermore, he wants to thank his colleagues for valuable comments: Gunnar Christensen, A. M. Fuglseth, Knut Ims and Linda Lai, and, finally, Wenche Mørch for typing and organizing the text.

Both authors wish to thank Professor Paolo Mottura with SDA Bocconi, Italy for valuable collaboration in organizing seminars for financial institutions in Europe.

Michel R. Klein
Leif B. Methlie
February 1990

Preface to the Second Edition

The second edition of this book is to be published five years after the first one. We are extremely pleased to have the opportunity to build on the first edition and take into account what has been learned during the last five years with respect to using the book for teaching and to incorporate the progress made in knowledge-based DSS and related fields.

As a consequence, the changes which have been made concern the ordering of the chapters as well as the content of the book.

We have had many discussions with colleagues who have used the book. Chapter 2 on cognitive processes and problem solving is now more focused on how the human mind solves problems and makes decisions effectively, known in cognitive psychololgy and AI as *human problem solving*. The chapter is, like in the previous edition, focused on production systems and the information processing paradigm of cognitive psychology. However, the chapter is extended with developments in cognitive theories in the 1980s, in particular, the development of the SOAR and ACT* theories of cognition. The chapter should give a good introduction to cognitive psychology necessary to understand the theoretical basis and new developments in expert systems and knowledge acquisition. Theories of behavioral decision making in organizations are no longer dealt with since these theories or frameworks were not used in latter parts of the book dealing with systems developments.

The second change is our decision to merge the chapter on AI and the chapter on expert systems and to place the chapter on expert systems after the chapter on DSS. The reason is simply that we are only interested here in presenting the AI concepts necessary to understand the expert system conceptual framework. It makes, we believe, more sense to present the DSS conceptual framework after the first four chapters since by then all the concepts needed will have been introduced. However we have kept the chapter on expert systems where it is logically needed, that is to say, before the introduction of the knowledge-based DSS conceptual framework.

We have decided to abandon the description of FINSIM KB-DSS application. We have also decided to abandon the chapter on organizational impacts of the KB-DSS technology. The reason for this decision is that we wish to concentrate on methodology rather than descriptive knowledge in order to keep the book to a reasonable size.

With respect to the content several changes have been made.

We have updated the chapter on cognitive science with developments in production systems such as SOAR and ACT*. These are both cognitive theories. With respect to SOAR, this theory has been turned into AI systems. These systems are, however, still at an experimental stage. If the book is used as text in a more practical and applied course on DSS, this chapter may be skipped. In a more research-oriented course these topics are, however, mandatory.

The chapter on DSS has been almost entirely rewritten and the chapter on KB-DSS has been rewritten in part. The reason is that very important results have been achieved during the last five years which have led to a second generation of DSS and KB-DSS. These results concern mainly the design and use of specific graphical interfaces for DSS and KB-DSS and the structure of KB-DSS development environments. In particular, the separation of the user interface from the other resources of the system (data bases, decision models, reports, knowledge bases) has been achieved. Also important improvements have been obtained on certain classical functions such as report generation and the connection with heterogeneous data bases.

Also the development of programming technology, in particular object-oriented programming languages and operating systems, has improved the software quality of KB-DSS development environments.

The consequence has been the possibility to support the development of more powerful applications much more easily than before.

Acknowledgements to the second edition

Since the publication of the first edition we have benefited from discussions with many people.

Michel Klein wishes to thank Mike Uschold for constructive criticism on the first edition, Professor R. Traunmüller (J. Kepler Universität, Linz) for valuable comments concerning the user-interface of KB-DSS while he was staying at the HEC School of Management for joint research work, Professor A. Lux from LIFIA-ENSIMAG for his continuous help concerning the research projects conducted at DECISION SYSTEMS RESEARCH and related to OPTRANS Object, Professor M. Levasseur and Y. Simon for their encouragement.

Mr. C. Danes and D. Besnier from DECISION SYSTEMS RESEARCH for programming, Mr. Y. Garandeau and H. Guibert for their work on the report generator, Mr. T. Villedieu from SIG for his suggestions on OPTRANS and Professor V. Hargreaves for stylistic advice.

The French State for its contribution to the partial funding of the OPTRANS Object research project.

Availability of the KB-DSS software

Since the appearance of first edition of this book a major investment was made concerning OPTRANS. The system was entirely redesigned and reprogrammed in C and C + +. The new version called OPTRANS Object has an object oriented graphical user interface and provides a complete separation between the user interface and global logic of the application and the other resources (models, reports, knowledge bases, data bases . . .).

The OPTRANS Object development environment is available from the company Decision Systems Research (DSR). FINSIM EXPERT and BANKER are available from the company SIG.

OPTRANS Object is available in English and French. FINSIM is available in French, however, at the time of writing adaptation to other accounting systems is planned. BANKER is in its current version available in OPTRANS Expert only. It will be converted to OPTRANS Object. OPTRANS Object is available under MS/DOS and Windows.

All enquiries concerning the OPTRANS, FINSIM and BANKER software should be sent to: SIG; 4 bis, rue de la libération, 78350 Jouy-en-Josas, FRANCE Fax (33) 1 39 56 57 42.

Michel R. Klein
Leif B. Methlie
March 1995

1
Introduction

1.1 FROM DECISION SUPPORT SYSTEM TO KNOWLEDGE-BASED DECISION SUPPORT SYSTEM

This is a book about decision making – about understanding how people solve problems and make decisions, and about how they can improve their problem-solving and decision-making capabilities by the use of computers. We shall deal with problems that are characterized as ill-structured because no procedure or algorithm can be prescribed for their solutions. Therefore, there exists no computerized choice procedure. These problems can only be solved by a cooperation between man and computer.

Computer systems for problem solving and decision making have been developed since around the end of the Second World War, when computers became available for non-military tasks. Also, they have been the target of research and application from a multitude of disciplines. Over time, systems have been built on different principles and with different aims. Therefore, investigation of this field, is not a study of one homogeneous area. Despite the diversity of the field, it should be possible to explain continuities and changes and to recognize lines of descent, that is, the genealogy of issues and related concepts and tools.

One concept is central to this book: Decision Support Systems (DSS). This concept is built on the paradigm of *support*. That is, a computer system is placed at the disposal of the decision maker, who may use data or models to recognize, understand, and formulate a problem, and make use of analytical aids to evaluate alternatives. In the complex world in which managerial decision making takes place, we think that this is the only paradigm of computer decision systems that is operational.

The term 'decision support system' was coined at the beginning of the 1970s to denote a computer program that could support a manager in making decisions when facing ill-structured problems. This concept is a result of research in two areas: theoretical studies of human problem solving and decision making done at the Carnegie Institute of Technology during the 1950s and 1960s, and the work on interactive computer systems at the Massachusetts Institute of Technology in the 1960s. As time-sharing systems became available, several business schools in the USA and Europe started to work on computer systems for decision support. At first, this area was dominated by demonstrating the applicability of this new concept to managerial decision making. This was then followed by a great interest in software development. New tools, DSS generators, for easier building of such systems were created. With the introduction of microcomputers, developments in DSS speeded up. Today, software for supporting decision making is available for almost any financial problem. Chapter 4 describes the DSS technology and why it was immediately useful. Emphasis in the DSS concept is put on information access and display, and on numeric computations by analytical models.

A second important concept to our body of knowledge of computer systems for problem solving and decision making, is the concept of expert systems. Interestingly enough, this concept was created almost at the same time as the DSS concept, with the DENDRAL project at Stanford University in the late 1960s. During the 1970s several research projects were launched in artificial intelligence laboratories. The commercial use of expert systems started at the beginning of the 1980s, but widespread commercial use came with the more powerful microcomputers and cheaper software. Recently, both the cost and the risk of using this technology have been dramatically reduced. This technology is here to be utilized now. Management in general and the financial domain, in particular, is expected to be an important target area of this technology. Chapter 5 discusses the concept of expert systems and shows how it can be applied to a credit decision. Two fundamental results were derived from research on expert systems:

(1) that it is possible to simulate expert problem solving; and
(2) that this problem solving can be explained by the system.

When expert systems technology was first applied to management problems, and finance problems in particular, it fell short in several respects. The main problem was that, this technology was not capable of handling the classical DSS functions which are more computational than logical. Also, problem solving in managerial domains is not solely symbolic reasoning, which is the predominant problem solving method of expert systems. It is not due to just data retrieval and numeric calculations either; which are the functions found in a traditional DSS. What is needed is a system which can process data and numeric relationships and, by reasoning, transform this data into opinions, judgment, evaluations and advice. It turns out that it is not just a matter of interconnecting the existing software tools from the DSS and the expert system areas. Therefore, we shall develop a new framework which is based on the paradigm of decision support, but which also enables us to incorporate specialized knowledge and expertise into the system. This will add the capability of reasoning to the functionality of the DSS and will enable it to give advice on specific problems. We shall call these systems *Knowledge-based Decision Support Systems* (KB-DSS). This new framework, and the new development tools which come out of this framework, will be described in Chapter 6.

1.2 THE SCIENTIFIC BACKGROUND

Decision support systems grew out of the experience of applying quantitative models to management. It became apparent that an *understanding* of the decision situation was a prerequisite to any proposal for improvements. Therefore, in the DSS concept two major scientific developments in the study of decisions merged: the descriptive, behavioral theories, and the prescriptive, rationalistic theories.

To understand how decision making is actually done, we can draw on a body of knowledge developed by psychologists and management researchers. Psychologists have studied human cognition and problem solving. A major contribution on these topics has come from the Carnegie school by researchers such as Herbert Simon and Allan Newell. From empirical studies they developed a theory of the cognitive architecture of the mind – what they call the Human Information Processor System (HIPS). The key characteristic of this theory is that cognitive systems are symbol systems with mental operations on symbol structures which can be in different states (long- and short-term memories). Their theory has methodological consequences for the study of problem solving processes (thinking-aloud protocols). They also gave a description of the problem solving process that holds for a wide range of activities. Problem solving proceeds by *heuristic search* through a large set of possibilities. Heuristics are used to guide the search and in selecting the steps towards the goal. Along with the development of expert systems technology there has been an increase into the research of expert problem solving. What constitutes a good expert system, primarily, is the large amounts of domain knowledge that are stored in memory to which access is gained by pattern recognition.

Also, psychologists have studied decisions by the process used to arrive at a choice. Again, the Carnegie school is central to this research, and to the development of a behavioral theory of decision making. A central concept for designing decision support systems is Simon's description of the *decision making process* – the intelligence-design-choice phases. Simon's work has caused further research on behavioral decision making to be carried out, also by management researchers. We shall report on a framework developed by Mintzberg and some of his colleagues which is conceptually richer than Simon's description of the decision making process. Another central concept developed by Simon is that of *bounded rationality*. In a situation of incomplete, imprecise and inconsistent knowledge, the decision maker satisfies rather than optimizes in the choice of a decision. This framework is described in Chapter 4.

In the opening sentence of this chapter we assume that the quality of decision making can be improved. The next issue is 'how can this be accomplished?' Here, we shall rely on the prescriptive decision theories. These are theories that have their roots in economics and mathematical logic. Central to this body of theories is the *utility theory*. It is a formally axiomatized statement of what it means for an agent to behave in a consistent, rational manner. To be rational means to act in a way that is consistent with rules that we have adopted, and to which our actions should conform. The utility theory has been further developed to deal with choice under uncertainty – and the calculus that is used most often to encode uncertainty is the *probability* theory. Furthermore, probability is a subjective concept; it is an individual's perception of uncertainty. Thus, we arrive at a new normative criterion: the subjective, expected utility maximization.

The subjective, expected utility theory is the basis for most of the methods and techniques of modern operations research. Modeling and optimization are the key issues here. Operations research techniques are concerned with choice and they use the assumptions of the subjected, expected utility theory. These techniques work well for decision problems that are relatively well structured.

However, methods have been developed to apply this decision theory to complex, practical situations. These methods include the statistical decision theory, the decision analysis school, and the multi-criteria decision making and preference modeling school. We shall use the term decision methodology to describe the body of techniques that are available for effectively performing analysis of a decision situation. They include: how to structure a problem, and how to model that problem once structured, how to develop an analysis, and how to elicit subjective probabilities and preferences. Normative decision theories are dealt with in Chapter 3. Our objective is to give readers an understanding of the tools (methods and techniques) that are available, and to provide sufficient references to the literature for further studies.

In the spirit of the descriptive tradition and the cognitive studies of human problem solving, the field of artificial intelligence (AI) has been developed. A number of techniques have been developed to imitate intelligent behavior using computers. Today, these computer programmes can perform difficult tasks at the same level as professionally-trained humans. These AI programs are usually called expert systems. A description of a typical expert system will closely resemble the typical description given to human problem solving, in other words, that of symbolic reasoning and heuristic search. An expert system will rely on the storage and computing power of the machine, while the human being will have a richer set of heuristics, even though the aim is to represent as much heuristics as possible in the computer system. Many AI-techniques have been developed for knowledge representation, reasoning and heuristic search using this computer power. In Chapter 4 we shall deal with these techniques before dealing with the expert system architecture.

The scientific background and the developments that have led to the definitions of the two system concepts, expert systems and DSS are shown, diagramatically, in Figure 1.1. Also, we have shown some key concepts that characterize each major scientific development.

1.3   DEVELOPMENT METHODOLOGY

This book is about applying computer technology to decision making in business organizations. Therefore, we must provide the necessary methods and techniques to put the technology to work in a management environment. The theories on decisions and decision making constitute the conceptual frameworks by which decisions can be studied and understood, and by which improvements can be analyzed and proposed. From what has already been said it seems plausible that a development methodology has to be centered on decisions. The first papers on the design of DSS, for instance that by Gerrity (1971), argue strongly for replacing a data-centered approach

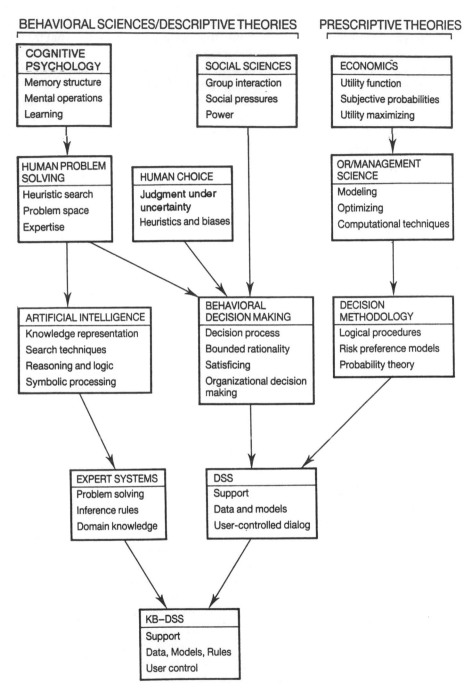

Figure 1.1 *The scientific background*

with that of a decision-centered approach. However, in the DSS field there is some controversy about the decision-centered approach. The argument against it is that it is not compatible with the actual nature of managerial work. Management researchers, like Mintzberg (1973), claim that managers seldom make decisions as part of a deliberate, coherent and continuous decision making process. Instead, managerial work is characterized by brevity, variety and fragmentation. Moreover, managers are much more than decision makers; they play a multitude of roles in particular motivating people.

The complexity of the decision making context is also taken as an argument against decision or task analysis. 'Designers literally "cannot get to the first base" because no one, least of all the decision maker or user, can define in advance, what the functional requirements of the system should be' (Sprague and Carlson (1982) p. 15). Adaptive design and prototyping have been the key words. Development has been focused on computer representations and program design. By means of powerful development tools, the so-called DSS generators and expert system shells, rapid prototyping has been the predominating approach. Skill in using these tools has had a greater emphasis than that of methodological competence in performing task analysis. This process can be characterized as a technology-driven process.

Here, we shall adhere to the view that evolutionary design and prototyping are important elements in a development methodology for knowledge-based DSS. They are important in reducing context complexity by performing successive redefinitions of the functionality of the computer system. However, although difficult to identify, decision making must be *understood and described before it can be improved*. We shall, therefore, provide a decision-centered methodology for task analysis. This decision-centered methodology includes descriptive and normative aspects as well as knowledge engineering to develop expert problem solving models. A design methodology that we think is needed within the knowledge-based DSS (KB-DSS) conceptual framework is presented in Chapter 8. Since knowledge-based functions will be part of this new framework, in Chapter 7, we shall provide a methodology, based on a cognitive approach, to the building of knowledge bases in financial domains. Testing and evaluation of knowledge bases impose problems of validation and verification. These problems will be dealt with in Chapter 9.

1.4 APPLICATION OF THE KB-DSS TECHNOLOGY

How can decision making take advantage of this new technology? Improved performance can be accomplished by more efficient processes or by better outcomes of decisions. Today, business is, generally, more complex than it was in the past. Almost all sectors of industry experience greater competition, more complex production technology, and more sophisticated market demand. In the financial sector, the environment is even more complex due to deregulation. The result of this is growing diversification and accelerated innovation. The service component of delivered products is increasing, and, in general, service activities are characterized by high-intensity decision making. Supply and demand are more closely interconnected. The gap between production and customers diminishes. More decisions must be made at the front line, and more people are involved in decision making. With a growing number of products to deliver, increased product complexity, more demanding customers, and also greater competition, this puts a heavy burden on the front-line decision makers. Decision making needs to be decentralized, but at the same time, controlled. However, diversification and innovation of the corporation's portfolio of products may lead to rapid obsolescence of front-line knowledge and a problem of specialization. This results in a deterioration of services to customers, a growing risk of ineffective management of customer relationships and lack of control of peripheral decisions.

The technology offered by DSS, expert systems, and KB-DSS may improve the situation. Knowledge-based systems can improve quality of decision making throughout the whole organization by making expertise available at the customer level. They can also support decision making which is consistent and in compliance with the rules set by the organization, and can provide a stable service to customers due to easier maintenance of knowledge.

In general, the KB-DSS technology described in this book can be applied to decision making in any organization. However, we have particularly approached the domains of management control and finance. Throughout this book, research, cases, and applications in these areas are reported. To a great extent we are relying on our own research carried out during the last ten years, and in almost every chapter we use this research and our practical experience to illustrate concepts and methods. But we are also using selected research and practice from the literature to broaden the scope of the book.

We believe that business opportunities of the KB-DSS framework are infinite. To show this we have surveyed the applications of knowledge-based systems in finance and marketing. This survey is presented in Chapter 10. The systems we have found are primarily expert systems. The survey is by no means comprehensive, however it should give the reader ideas about where to find adequate application domains for this technology. In systematizing this search and in describing these systems we have used a classification scheme based on three major subject types: corporations, individuals, banks and financial institutions. Within each subject category we have defined financial functions, each of which is described, and known systems are presented.

In Chapter 11 we make a survey of present research and developments in this field to see what we can expect to be on the market in the future. This chapter presents some of these expected developments: the second generation of KB-DSS.

1.5   TEACHING ADVICE

This book can be used as a textbook in a business administration curriculum at the undergraduate or postgraduate level. The text is intended to be covered in a single-semester course of about 40 lecture hours. The chapters develop the field in a fairly systematic manner from the underlying theories, through an evolution of system concepts, to development and implementation methodologies.

This book can be used in courses on DSS, expert systems, and information systems for management. It should also fit well into more general courses in management and finance as a supplementary text. It should also appeal to specialists, particularly for in-service training courses, for instance, in banks and financial institutions.

A course on knowledge-based decision support systems must, in addition to the study of basic concepts, also include some practical experience in the application of these concepts. Also, it must include the use of a KB-DSS development tool to implement small applications, in order to master the concepts in an operational way. In the appendix we have described a course outline for a single-semester course intended to cover DSS, expert systems, and KB-DSS. In addition to the material covered in this book, the course includes a lecture on the use of a development tool, OPTRANS object. Therefore, references are given to the manual of this software product.

Our experience with this course has been that it is difficult to succeed, in a single semester, to get across a thorough understanding of the basic concepts, together with the satisfactory skills that are needed to master the software tool. Therefore, our recommendation is that this text should be supplemented with a project-oriented course, where the students are asked to develop a major application.

2
Cognitive Processes and Problem Solving

2.1 INTRODUCTION

2.1.1 Problem Solving and Decision Making

Problem solving and decision making are important tasks in all intelligent activities, and so are of great concern to researchers in a multitude of scientific disciplines. Mathematicians have studied the implications of the axioms of decision theory; statisticians have been concerned with decision making in the face of uncertainty; economists have studied how human decision making determines economic activity. In the behavioral sciences several areas of decision making study can be found: cognitive psychologists study human problem solving; social psychologists study how decisions are reached in organizations; and political scientists study how political processes result in decisions.

The usual image of a decision maker is of someone who evaluates and chooses between decisions. Problem solving, on the other hand, is concerned with the intelligent activities that are performed by a person who is confronted with a situation in which there is a gap between what is desired (the goal) and what is given (the initial state), and in which the steps that need to be taken to reach this goal are unknown. Problem solving has been the concern of cognitive psychologists, some of whom have a managerial perspective. We shall deal with problem solving in the broadest sense taking the definition given above as the basis. This is how it is dealt with in artificial intelligence and expert systems. But we shall also deal with problem solving as part of decision making. This is of concern in decision support systems.

In this book we shall use the term 'decision making' to include all stages of problem solving such as: recognizing situations that call for actions, formulating problems, designing actions and setting goals, as well as final evaluation and choice. We call these tasks the *decision making process*.

Two scientific approaches to the studies can be identified:

(1) the *normative* approach which prescribes optimal behavior, that is, how decisions should be made, and;
(2) the *descriptive* (or behavioral) approach which is concerned with understanding how people actually behave when solving problems and making decisions.

At the heart of the normative approach lies the rational, 'economic man' decision model. It was first developed in economics and was later applied to management through the fields of operation research and management science. Normative theories are based on a rationality paradigm where rational behavior is prescribed by a formally axiomatized statement. Therefore, normative models of decision making are also called formal models. They define conditions for perfect utility maximization. The decision maker, the economic man, behaves rationally towards this goal by calculating the consequences for each relevant alternative decision, ranking these consequences according to preference, and finally computing the optimal decision, that is, finding the alternative that will maximize utility.

Normative theories are concerned only with how to choose from a set of alternatives. Therefore, we may call them *theories of choice*. They say nothing about how to frame problems, develop alternatives, set goals, or implement decisions.

Rational choice implies that future consequences of current actions are predicted and that guesses are made, about the future preferences for those consequences. Neither prediction is easy. Theories of choice have also been developed to handle uncertainties, usually by assigning probability distributions to the consequences of alternative decisions. In Chapter 3 we shall deal with several methods or schools within this normative tradition of decision making. We shall do this because developing computer aids that are implicit to decision makers implies a normative perspective, in other words, using a DSS makes decision making more effective. Normative theories enable us to analyze the structure of a decision.

However, even though the normative theories are significant in optimizing a decision under certain conditions, they fall short in dealing with the complexity of most real-world decision making. Empirical research carried out on how people make decisions shows that actual human behavior deviates from what should be expected in view of the rationalistic tradition. Simon (1960) by himself, and in collaboration with others, March and Simon (1958) and Newell and Simon (1972), observed that actual decision making is performed under conditions such as:

- lack of information on several aspects such as problem formulation, alternatives and consequences;
- time and cost constraints that inhibit comprehensive search;
- imperfections in perceiving information.

Simon introduced the concept of *bounded* rationality to describe decision making under these conditions. His idea was that the list of technical constraints imposed by the rational models of choice should include the properties of human beings as processors of information and as problem solvers. Bounded rationality is a sensible explanation of the human efforts being undertaken in order to achieve rational information gathering and processing. The theory takes into account the costs of intelligence and information processing. Intelligence is selective; the decision of a situation is oversimplified or subjective; the choices are biased and so on. Simon coined the term 'satisficing' for decision procedures under the bounded rationality paradigm. He made no distinction between individual and organizational decision making. This distinction, however, was made some years later by Cyert and March (1963) in their behavioral theory of the firm.

The theory of bounded rationality is still a rational model. It is based on decision making as a sequential process. A problem has to be decided upon, and there has to be an argument for the alternative chosen. Informational and computational costs are evaluated in light of the benefits that can be achieved. It is assumed that the decision maker will make a rational evaluation of these costs, and thus, bounded rationality still applies, at least as a quasi-rational decision.

Other researchers in organizational decision making have gone even further than Simon in relaxing the rather strong requirements of rational behavior. Lindblom (1959), for instance, argues that, far from making rational decisions, organizations proceed by 'muddling-through'. He explains this decision making behavior as one in which the decision maker moves incrementally, searching for alternatives which are only slightly different from existing situations. Lindblom studied policy making in governmental organizations. His later thoughts on this topic were presented in a paper, after 20 years of discussion of his idea (Lindblom, 1979). He still believes that, as a sensible guide for organizational decision making, incrementalism has much to offer.

So far, we have been primarily concerned with the first implication of rational choice: predicting future consequences. We have assumed that future preferences are exogenous, stable, and are known with enough precision to make the decisions unambiguous. In the beginning of the 1970s researchers started to challenge these assumptions. In the case of collective decision making there is the problem of conflicting objectives that represent the values of different participants. In addition, individual preferences often appear to be fuzzy and inconsistent, and preferences appear to change over time due partly, at least, as a consequence of the actions that were taken (March, 1978). Cohen *et al.* introduced the notion of the 'garbage can' as a model for explaining decision making in organizations (Cohen *et al.*, 1972). This model describes situations in terms of 'anarchy', consisting of four loosely-coupled elements: choice opportunities, problems, solutions, and participants. Decisions are made under conditions of ambiguity, that is, situations where goals are vague, problematic, inconsistent or unstable.

Also, social psychologists have studied how decisions are reached in organizations. Janis and Mann (1977) give a good review of the research in this area. They identified the phenomenon of 'group think' that can lead to defective decision making as it inadequately researches the alternative courses of action. It can also lead to a bias in processing the available information. Also, social psychologists have studied how social pressure affects decision making. Two such pressures which have been identified by Janis and Mann (1977) are:

(1) anticipatory regret, our tendency to worry how disappointed we, and others, might feel after the event, if we take the wrong decision; and
(2) threats, or constraints, imposed by others.

Finally, we shall mention the study of decision making in the field of political sciences. A subject which is of great interest to political scientists is the way in which the political process results in decisions (see, for instance, Hall and Quinn (1983)). The political science model sees organizational decision making as a result of the interplay of pressure groups who have different views and different powers. The outcome of a decision is determined by negotiation among groups of people, and the exploitation of the influence and power that they have at their command.

Empirical research carried out on actual decision making behavior has modified the classical, formal model in two ways: it has revealed the effects of real-world complexity on rational behavior, and it has shown that most organizational processes cannot be interpreted in the rational framework. The understanding we have gained about decision making behavior is collected in a set of descriptive theories under the label of *behavioral theories of decision making*. These theories are concerned with the process of reaching solutions. Both the behavioral and normative theories are important for recommending better methods and for offering advice on the improvement of decision processes. These theories are the basis for the design of computer aids to be used in decision making.

Simon and his colleagues developed their behavioral theories of decision making into the more general theories of *problem solving*. Rather than concentrating on the kinds of decisions that managers make, psychologists study tasks that can be viewed as problems of choice within a range of alternatives. Human problem solving is usually studied in laboratory settings, using problems that can be solved in relatively short periods of time (theorem proving, puzzles, and so on). From empirical studies, a description can be given of the problem solving process that holds for a rather wide range of activities.

One of the accomplishments of the theory of problem solving has been the understanding of complex problems, and to develop strategies and intellegent processes to deal with them. In the field of artificial intelligence these strategies are developed into formal methods and are computerized. More recently, these methods have been employed in expert systems.

Above, we have given a brief exposé of the fundamentals behind human problem solving and decision making. We shall structure this part into two chapters. First, in this chapter we will look at the cognitive theories governing human thinking and problem solving. The next chapter takes a more rational view on decision making, the normative view. Here, properties other than preferences of the agent, the decision maker, are not considered. The basis for this view is economics and operation research.

2.1.2　What is this Chapter About?

As stated in the opening of this chapter, problem solving and decision making have been extensively studied from a number of perspectives.

Above, we have described the main avenues of this research. In what follows, we will pursue these lines of thought in more depth. The aim of this chapter is to present the theoretical frameworks necessary to develop decision aids to increase effectiveness of managerial work. As stated in Chapter 1, our interest lies with computerized decision aids: decision support systems, expert systems, and knowledge-based decision support systems where we combine the two technologies. These systems concepts have very different scientific foundations. Central to decision support systems are data access and analytic modeling; central to expert systems are knowledge representation and reasoning. However, they share a common feature. They are both anchored in the behavioral approach of decision making, an approach that puts emphasis on compatibility between the computer systems and the problem solving activities of the human user.

This chapter starts with a discussion of problem solving on the cognitive level of experts problem solving. Our paradigm and theoretical framework is the *information processing view*, which defines the architecture of the mind, the fundamental cognitive processes, and the process model known as production systems; the latter being the fundamental building block behind rule based expert systems. Two lines of research in the general field of cognitive science in the last decade are described, both based on production systems: the SOAR and the ACT* systems.

Furthermore, some characteristics of expertise are described. In relation to expert systems, interest in expertise and expert performance have gained increased attention. Expert systems have stored representations of problem solving knowledge. This knowledge can be viewed as cognitive processes that individual experts perform to solve their problems. The theory of human problem solving shows that this is heuristic in nature and that it is possible to trace the elementary cognitive processes used in actual problem solving. These theories are the basis for the methodology needed in order to elicit and represent procedural knowledge.

2.2 THE COGNITIVE 'REVOLUTION'

The information technology as developed in the 1940s, plays a vital role in the dramatic change in perspective in psychology that took place in the 1950s. Previous to this change, behaviorism dominated the academic research in psychology. In this perspective behavior is controlled by observable stimuli. The organism executing the behavior has no significant role. The new war technologies like radar, however, put new requirements on the operator – the human. Why are some people better than others? In the behavioristic perspective this can not be explained. The concept of man-machine system is introduced to describe the interaction between operator and technology. The engineers working with the technology use terms like input, output, information channel, channel capacity, etc. The psychologists lack a vocabulary for the human part. Psychological studies that followed started to concentrate more on the information processing capacities of the operators in these contexts.

In 1956 G. A. Miller presented his psychological studies in the work: *The Magical Number Seven, Plus or Minus Two* (Miller, 1956). This work became one of the most important contributions to the cognitive 'revolution' and the establishment of the field of cognitive psychology. Miller observed that the working memory (short-term memory) had a limited capacity. However, this capacity was not limited by standard language measures like syllables, words or sentences or by communication measures like bits. In terms of these measures there seems to be an extreme variability among people. Miller introduced the term *chunk* to describe the units stored in the working memory. A chunk is a semantic entity – an organized unit of information. The brain's capacity to handle information is limited by the number of chunks in the receiving stimulus. Miller contended that subjects remembered approximately seven chunks. He also showed that stimuli received are organized into chunks according to previous experience. Experts learn to organize more information into a chunk than do novices. Miller's findings show that a person does mental activities – *information processing* – in receiving a stimuli. This was a change from the behavioral tradition that looked at the brain as a black box. The term *information* became a central concept in the new theory of cognitive psychology, which also became known as the information processing psychology after the Miller article. Later, in 1960, Miller together with Galanter and Pribram published the book *Plans and the Structure of Behavior* (Miller *et al.*, 1960) where they claimed that behavior is generated by a set of mental processes and tests on the environment rather than tied to an environmental stimulus as claimed by the behaviorism. The cognitive revolution was started.

Another significant contribution to the field of cognitive psychology came from linguistics. Noam Chomsky showed in the beginning of the 1950s the limitation of the behavioristic perspective in psychology to language understanding. This shift was spearheaded by *Syntactic Structure* (Chomsky, 1957), a book that provided for a cognitive analysis of language behavior.

At the same time Allan Newell and Herbert Simon, two researchers at Carnegie-Mellon University, studied problem solving by humans and by computers. Computers could do many things that humans did – store and manipulate information as well as use language, solve problems and reason. Like a computer that controls its behavior by an internally stored program, a human controls its mental activities also by an internal program. Computer programs and programming languages played a significant role in the psychological theories they developed. They use theories from computer science in formulating their psychological theories of human problem solving. They developed the first high-level, list processing computer language IPL. The results of their research on human problem solving was documented in the significant work *Human Problem Solving* (Newell and Simon, 1972).

By 1967 there was enough research literature for Neisser to produce a textbook called *Cognitive Psychology*. The theoretical contribution of Neisser's book was to posit a general information processing model consisting of memory stores and processes and to show that it is possible to study internal mental processes by the tools of cognitive psychology.

An important event for establishing this field was the Dartmouth conference in 1956. Here Miller and Chomsky presented their works and Newell presented the first version of the 'Logic Theorist', a computer program capable of doing theorem proving. At this conference the term *artificial intelligence* (AI) was coined for computer programs that display intelligent behavior. AI is at the intersection of computer science and cognitive psychology. More recently the term *cognitive science* has been used for the integrated field of cognitive psychology, philosophy, linguistics and AI. The first journal *Cognitive Science*, appeared in 1976.

2.3   NEWELL AND SIMON'S THEORY OF PROBLEM SOLVING

2.3.1   The Information Processing View

Cognitive psychology is the scientific analysis of human mental processes and memory structures in order to understand human behavior. Cognitive psychology studies what is going on inside a person's head while performing a task, i.e. how people collect, store and use information. The general theoretical framework underlying cognitive psychology is the *information processing model*. This framework views all mental activities performed by humans as information processing and the human mind as an information processing system. Information comes in through our sense receptors, we apply a mental operation to it and thus change it, until we have an output ready to be stored or used to generate some behavior. The performance of a cognitive task involves a sequence of mental operations (cognitive processes) on mental objects (cognitive structures).

The central hypothesis of the information processing view is that human thinking is governed by programs that organize myriad of simple information processes into orderly, complex sequences. These programs can best be understood by the analogy to computers. Winograd and Flores have summarized the assumptions behind this view in the following:

(1) All cognitive systems are symbol systems. They achieve their intelligence by symbolizing external and internal situations and events, and by manipulating those symbols.

(2) All cognitive systems share a basic underlying set of symbol manipulation processes.

(3) A theory of cognition can be couched as a program in an appropriate symbolic formalism such that the program when run in the appropriate environment will produce the observed behavior (Winograd and Flores, 1986, p. 25).

The information processing view is central to Newell and Simon's theory of problem solving. They define an information processing system (IPS) consisting of the four main components: memory, processor, effectors and receptors. The memory is the component that stores and retrieves symbolic structures. In the Newell and Simon's theory there are two memories: the short-term and long-term memory. The processor executes the information processes. Symbol structures are taken as input to the processor and new structure symbols are produced as output. The information processes are made of elementary information processes (EIP) which the processor can handle. These components in the human mind are dealt with not in terms of the physiology of the nervous system and neuroscience, but rather in terms of their functionality.

To build the internal system structures in memory is referred to as *reading*. The opposite operation, i.e. to act on an internal structure is to *write*. An IPS communicates with its environment by means of receptors and effectors. The behavior of the IPS is based on the execution of EIPs. By executing sequences of EIPs the IPS can solve complex problems.

In addition to the general information processing model there are more specific techniques for representing what is going on in a person's head while performing a task. These techniques concern cognitive processes, symbol structures and strategies. By analyzing the cognitive processes involved in problem solving, the *procedural knowledge* that a person uses can be described in terms of a process model. We shall also use the term *performance model* for this (cf. Chapter 7). Knowledge about facts is represented by the symbol structures and is called *declarative knowledge*. Finally, people use cognitive strategies to *control* the various pieces of knowledge they want to apply. We shall look into these techniques below.

Computers offer an interesting analogy with which to build a functional model of the brain. Due to their ability to interpret, in their memory, sequences of symbols as instructions to perform more complex operations, they are considered to be general-purpose information processing systems. A cognitive theory should be like a computer program. That is, it should be a precise specification of the behavior, but offered in sufficiently abstract terms to provide a conceptually tractable framework for understanding the phenomenon (Anderson, 1985).

Thus, we shall build a model of the human mind that has properties equivalent to real human problem solving. This model defines the functionality of the mind. We call it the architecture of the mind. The model gives an insight into the limitations of human information processing, and of the specific strategies that people develop in order to deal with complex problems.

2.3.2   The Cognitive Architecture of the Mind

The cognitive architecture of the human mind can be described as consisting of:

- *Long-term memory*, which for all practical purposes, has unlimited capacity, permanent storage, instant retrieval times, but fairly long write times. Storing of knowledge in the memory is meaning-based, i.e. it is the meaning of a sentence and not its wording that is stored (and remembered). Central to this is the understanding of what a concept is and how it is defined. Furthermore, to unveil human problem solving knowledge means to describe the conceptual structure (sometimes the term 'mental model' is used) for the problem solver. We shall deal with several meaning-based representation formalisms for conceptual structures below such as proposition and schemas.
- *Short-term memory*, or working memory, provides instantaneous access and storage, but has a very limited size. Information can only

be processed when it is in short-term memory (in an active state). Knowledge in short-term memory is not thought of as being in a different location than long-term memory, but rather as being in a special active state. For a long time cognitive psychologists have considered the capacity of the short-term memory to be the bottleneck in human information processing. Miller (1956), as we have seen, introduced the term chunk to describe the units and capacity of the human memory. These chunks are located in long-term memory but are placed in an active state in which they can be used by the processor. Spread of activation is one important topic of cognitive psychology.

- *Mental operations*, or the cognitive processor, which is a serial mechanism capable of executing only a handful of so-called elementary processes, such as retrieving symbols, comparing two symbols and so on. Recent psychological studies have drawn the distinction between *controlled* and *automated* processes. Controlled processes are mental processes that require conscious attention in order to be performed. They can be compared to the interpretative processes that occur in computers. In the same way that an interpretative programming language is able to perform specific data processing on an input statement, controlled processes in the human mind are able to interpret and perform information processing on propositional representations (cf. 2.4.1). Automated processes, on the other hand, require no interpretation. Rather, they perform information processing directly. They can be compared to compiled programs in computers (Stillings *et al.*, 1987). Automated processes have some key characteristics: they make no demands on working memory; they are automatically triggered by patterns in currently activated information; they are parallel and independent in nature; and they speed up gradually as the automatic sequence is learnt.

2.4 UNDERSTANDING OF CONCEPTS AND THEIR REPRESENTATIONS IN MEMORY

It is now well accepted in the field of cognitive psychology that the memory representation of information is meaning-based rather than language-based. In other words, it is the meaning of a sentence that is stored in memory rather than its grammatical form. How then is meaning represented? *Propositional representations* are supported by experimental evidence.

2.4.1 Propositions and Propositional Networks

The concept of *proposition* is borrowed from logic and linguistics and is the simplest complete unit of information. It is complete in the sense that it can be judged to be either true or false. Consider the following sentence:

Smith, who is a lawyer, sold his car to his colleague Clark

It can be seen that this sentence is composed of the following simpler sentences, each one represented by a proposition:

(1) Smith is a lawyer
(2) Clark is a colleague of Smith
(3) Smith owns a car
(4) Smith sold this car to Clark

Typically, propositions capture *relations* such as 'sold', that holds between *arguments* such as 'Smith', 'car' and 'Clark'.

A collection of propositions can be represented graphically by a *propositional network* as shown in Figure 2.1. In the propositional network each proposition is a unique structural unit built around a node denoted by a circle with a number inside it. Relational nodes are denoted by capital letters and argument nodes by lower case words in angled brackets.

We can think of the nodes in the network as ideas and the links between nodes as associations between ideas. A propostional network then becomes an associated structure that determines the tendency of one idea to lead to another. The closer the concepts in the network are, the better cues they are for each other's recall. Propositional networks are sometimes called *semantic networks* (see Chapter 5).

2.4.2 Schemas

Propositions are fine for representing small units of information, for instance a fact. A fact arises when we attach an attribute to an object, for instance when we attach the attribute 'owning a car' to the object 'Smith'. We can build a concept by listing such facts. However, listing simple facts about an object does not capture the interrelationships between the facts–the configuration of features. For instance, we have a general concept of a car: it has generally four wheels, an engine, is driven on roads, carries people, is used for transportation and so on. These general facts can be represented in a propositional network. The cluster of general propositions attached to a concept node forms

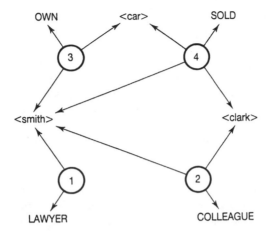

Figure 2.1   *Propositional network*

a conceptual schema for that concept. So we have the following partial
schema representation of a car.

Car
Belongs to: vehicle
has: engine and four wheels
function: transport people and goods
driven on: roads

In this list terms like 'belongs to' or 'function' are *attributes* and 'vehicle'
or 'roads' are *values*. Real world objects can be perceived at several
levels of abstraction, for example vehicle or car. In some other contexts
the car may be perceived as an asset or even a fixed asset. Human
memory for concepts appears to be organized in a kind of hierarchical
fashion (Rosch *et al.*, 1976). Hierarchical organization of object
categories can be described by 'is-a-kind-of' relationships. A knowledge
representation formalism that implements schemas is called frames and
will be dealt with in Chapter 5.

2.4.3   Concepts and Categories

Schemas, as described in the previous section, are useful because they
represent generalizations about the world that allow us to categorize
objects, events, situations and actions. For these categorizations we
need concepts.

The classical theory is the *definitional theory*. This theory states that the information content of a concept is a definition that gives the necessary and sufficient conditions that an object must meet in order to fall under the concept (Stillings *et al.*, 1987). For some concepts it may be straightforward to define these necessary and sufficient conditions. For example, a mother would be a female person who has at least one child. However for most concepts it is hard to find a set of necessary and sufficient conditions that uniquely define them. Take for instance the concept 'car'. As we have seen already, we can describe a car by a set of propositions. Each of these propositions are necessary, but is the schema as a whole sufficient. Does the schema discriminate a car from a bus or a truck? Hardly. And this is the case with most concepts of everyday life. For the Canadian census, database designers found thorny problems with basic terms like 'building' and 'dwelling'. Since the number of possible forms was so large, they did not even attempt to give a definition (Sowa, 1984). For most ordinary concepts we do not think in terms of necessary and sufficient conditions. When we have to describe things we use features that are *typical*, rather than necessary and sufficient, and we think of typical instances of a concept.

The difficulties encountered with the definitional theory of concepts have led philosophers to look for alternative theories. Ludwig Wittgenstein, an Austrian philosopher, developed in his later work a new view on concept definitions which was based on *family resemblance*. When viewed in terms of family resemblance, the instances of a concept resemble each other in the way that members of a family do. Some members of a conceptual family will be very typical because they share many features with many other family members. If we think of birds, for instance, most birds, but not all, can fly. A typical feature (a family feature) of a bird, therefore, is that it can fly. We can use the theory of family resemblance to knowledge representation. We define a *prototype* of a concept which consists of all the typical features. The prototypical description of a bird will have all of the most common features of a bird. In the prototype theory a concept is defined by an example or prototype if an object, which is an instant of a particular concept, resembles the characteristic prototype of this concept more closely than the prototypes of other concepts (Smith and Medin, 1981).

In developing the knowledge base for an expert system a recurrent problem is the level of generalization. In financial analysis, for instance, we have a general formula for debt–equity ratio. However, this single measure is not enough to interpret the solidity. A hotel has different requirements than a real estate company. Furthermore, a hotel with high seasonal demand has need for more equity than a city hotel with a more stable demand. We may define *patterns* that describe family-like companies. A pattern can identify what type of company we are dealing with and provide the necessary framework for interpretation of the equity needed for satisfactory solidity. To avoid ending up with one pattern for each specific company that the knowledge base can deal with, we can organize our knowledge into hierarchies where the more atypical a feature is for the general concept, the lower it is located in the hierarchy.

In modeling procedural knowledge for expert systems, two important tasks must be performed: elicitation of expert knowledge and analysis and structuring the knowledge for implementation on a computer. Elicitation requires that we know what to look for. Analysis requires that we have a conceptual framework to represent what we have been looking for. In this section on the cognitive architecture of the mind we have provided this conceptual framework. In Chapter 7 we will present the methodology for knowledge elicitation and modeling based on this framework.

2.5 HUMAN PROBLEM SOLVING

Problem solving is an intelligent activity performed by a person who is confronted with a situation where there is a gap between what is desired (the goal) and what is given as the initial state. In performing this activity, people employ information processing.

Research has been carried out to explain human behavior in performing poorly-structured tasks and to explain how individuals acquire cognitive skill in a particular domain.

In their theory of human problem solving, Allan Newell and Herbert Simon (1972) developed some key concepts, such as problem space and heuristic search, which we will describe in the next two sections.

2.5.1 The Problem Space and the Task Environment

Newell and Simon make an important distinction between the two concepts: *problem space* and *task environment*. The problem space is a person's internal (mental) representation of a problem, and the place where the problem-solving activity takes place. The task environment, on the other hand, is the physical and social environment in which problem solving takes place. It contains the task as it exists. The reason for introducing this distinction is that individual behavior influences problem solving; this influence is greater the less structured the task is.

An example may clarify the distinction between the two concepts. A class of business students studying financial statement analysis is given a class assignment to perform a loan evaluation of a company that is asking for a loan. The task is the credit evaluation. The task environment is made up of all the information given about the circumstances of the loan application. That is, financial statements of the company, market information and so on. Thus, everybody in the class has the same assignment and the same information. The task environment is general across all individuals.

Assuming that the class has not been given a strict, analytical procedure for this task, we can assume that the task is perceived as poorly structured. Consequently, we expect variances in the individual approaches that are taken in order to perform the task. Monitoring the individual problem solvers gives an insight to the problem space; that is, which data from the material provided is used?; in which sequence is it used?; how is new information computed from old?; and so on. All of this is done in the problem space.

Situations which do not influence individual behavior can be studied by only analyzing the task environment. For instance, fetching a glass of milk from the refrigerator can be predicted by studying the task environment, that is, the location of the person wanting the milk in relation to the location of the refrigerator. Also, in some modern sciences, for instance, economics, the scientific theory is based on the task environment only, assuming that humans are always motivated to maximize their utility. They behave rationally towards this goal, the economic man, and everything of importance for decision making is given by the task environment (even values and preferences of the performer). Therefore, economics is a science about the structure of the task environment.

We know, however, from empirical findings that behavioral aspects of decision making are closely related to the decision maker and not to the task environment. Decision makers seldom or never behave according to the economic man model. We have to look inside the decision maker's mind to explain this behavior. Therefore, it is of great importance in studying problem solving to analyze the task environment as well as the internal representation of the problem, that is, the problem space.

Newell and Simon (1972) say that examination of behavior leads to two kinds of knowledge: task knowledge and knowledge of the problem space. Task knowledge is obtained if the observed behavior is precisely what is called for by the situation. Knowledge of the problem space is obtained if the observed behavior departs from perfect rationality. Then we gain knowledge about the internal mechanisms for problem solving. The distinction between the task environment and the internal representation in the problem space leads to a study of two complementary aspects of human problem solving:

(1) the demands of the task environment, and;
(2) the problem solving behavior in that task environment.

Obviously, there is a close relationship between the task environment and the problem space. We have already mentioned that certain problem situations demand the same behavior (see the milk example above). In other situations, however, the individual's behavior plays a greater role, leading to very different individual problem solving behavior when performing a specific task. It is likely that the degree to which individuals are different is assumed to be a function of the structuredness of the task environment. Highly-structured environments, in which motivation is not a question, will demand similar behavior among performers. Highly unstructured environments, on the other hand, are more open for individual behavior.

According to the theory of human problem solving, the structure of the task environment determines the structure of the problem space, and the structure of the problem space determines the possible programs (strategies) for problem solving. In other words, we see the influence of the task environment on problem solving behavior. Therefore, we must analyze the structure of the task environment as well as the cognitive performance of human problem solvers in order to be able to model and computerize human problem solving.

Given these properties of the task environment and the problem space we will expect problem solving behavior to be very similar among individual performers within domains that deal with fairly well-structured problems.

We shall call the model of the task environment a task model and the model of the problem space a performance model. In reality, they represent two kinds of knowledge.

A *task model* represents generalized concepts (objects, relations, processes and strategies). This model describes a typical high-level problem solving strategy within a domain. It represents an abstract, stereotyped performer within this domain. Task models are sometimes called *epistemological* (Wielinga and Breuker, 1984) or *competence* (Laske, 1986) models.

A *performance* model is a model of the problem space and represents the problem solving behavior of one person who is performing a specific task. Knowledge elicitation by verbal, thinking-aloud protocols leads to performance models. Verbal protocols are discussed in Chapter 7.

Performance models, alone, do not give adequate knowledge for systems development, since they are constrained to a single performer and a single problem. Thus, we are faced with an induction problem: that is, to generalize problem solving behavior from individual cases (performers and problems). Furthermore, elements of performance that are found in protocols do not necessarily reflect the demands of the task environment. Therefore, both task models and performance models are required to enable problem solving behavior to be properly modeled within a specific domain.

To summarize, the cognitive architecture of the mind helps us to understand how problem solving is performed and how we can use this understanding to acquire knowledge of human problem solving behavior. Also, the distinction between the task environment and the problem space helps us to understand and explain individual behavior and how to interpret individual behavior in a broader context, the task environment.

2.5.2 Heuristic Problem Solving

The theory of human problem solving behavior illustrates the fact that people apply very few general, formal principles and they violate normative rules. Yet, they seem to progress successfully. The answer seems to be that human problem solving is *heuristic*. That is, people employ procedures that are efficient and that work most of the time, even though they sometimes lead to errors. This becomes more apparent as the complexity, that is, the unstructuredness of the task, increases. In highly structured task environments, general, formal principles that are independent of any particular context, for instance, linear programming, can solve problems very effectively. However, in this section we shall describe how people handle ill-structured problems.

Problem solving, as we have seen, is a process of transforming an initial situation into a desired situation, the goal. Problem solving takes place in the problem space, a subjective model of the task is built. Due to the bounded rationality of humans, normally, the problem space is a very simplified model of the task. Problem solving proceeds by a selective search within the problem space, using rules of thumb (heuristics) to guide the search. For most problems, only a selective search will lead to the goal within the time available. We see that problem solving can be described as a *search* for a solution within the problem space. The elements of the space consist of knowledge states.

The first step in solving a problem is that the problem solver must make a representation of the task within the problem space. However, this representation is not trivial. It may turn the problem solving onto an obvious, easy, obscure, difficult or unsolvable task depending on the way that the task is represented. The same task may be represented in many different ways by different individuals, depending on experience, values and situations. Different representations may have a large impact on the problem solving process, as well as the situations that are arrived at.

The second step, following the problem representation, is the selection of a particular problem solving method. Much of the theory of problem solving is concerned with identifying the principles that govern people's search through the problem space. The most general method is called *generate-and-test*.

It consists of two processes:

(1) *generate* a set of new knowledge states, from a preceding state;
(2) *test* if one of the generated states is a member of the goal state.
    If yes stop.

The efficiency of the method will depend on the time to generate states of the problem space, the size of the problem space and the time to test whether a candidate state satisfies the goal state.

Using information about the problem to select states in the problem space to be expanded by the generation process has been known as *heuristic search*. The fundamental heuristic method identified by Newell and Simon is *means-ends* analysis. The available operators or legal moves are the means that will achieve the goal, in other words, the end. The basic prinicple for operator selection is *difference reduction*; that is, operators are selected that will reduce the difference between the current state of the problem and the goal. Typically, the process is performed as a series of subprocesses where subgoals are subsequently achieved.

Heuristic search by means-ends analysis is a great improvement over general generate-and-test methods (exhaustive search). Means-ends analysis makes heavy demands on controlled processing. The subgoals that are relevant at that time, and the possible states of the problem being considered must be maintained in an active state. Heuristic search as a formal method for problem solving will be dealt with in more detail in Chapter 5.

So far, we have implicitly assumed that our problem solving method starts with the initial state and proceeds through a generate-and-test procedure working towards the goal state. However, an alternative method can be proposed, that of working backwards. Here, the goal (problem) is decomposed into sub-goals (or sub-problems). The problem solver can then focus on each sub-goal or problem which may either be solved or decomposed further. This procedure is also called problem reduction and is dealt with in Chapter 5.

2.6   PRODUCTION SYSTEMS

2.6.1   The Concept

A central component of the information processing model in cognitive psychology is the concept of production systems. The basic claim is that human cognition is a set of condition-action pairs called *productions* and that programs controlling human behavior are organized as production systems (PS). The production system is an effective way of representing goal structures and search in such structures.

In a production, that is a condition-action pair, the condition clause specifies some data patterns, and if elements matching these patterns are in working memory (STM), then the production can apply. The action specifies what to do in that state. The basic action is to add new data elements to working memory.

A production rule may look like:

IF person A is the mother of person B and person B is the mother of person C THEN person A is the grandmother of person C

If the following two symbol structures, 'Mary is the mother of Alice' and Alice is the mother of Carol', are active in working memory, then the following new symbol structure can be inferred by applying the production: 'Mary is the grandmother of Carol'. This new symbol structure will be deposited in working memory. New symbol structures in working memory can activate new productions. Thus a sequence of productions can be executed during a problem solving task.

Modern production systems began with Newell's work at Carnegie-Mellon in the early sixties. Right from the start production systems had a dual purpose, being both a psychological theory and a programming formalism in computer science. The latter purpose has been extended to include other formalisms under the broader term *pattern-directed systems* (see Waterman and Hayes-Roth, 1978).

2.6.2   The Water Jug Problem

An example of a production system that performs a specific task will be useful for illustrating the concept. The water jug problem is a well known problem from many textbooks in AI. The problem is, given two jugs, one four gallon and one three gallon jug, neither has any measuring markers on it, to get exactly two gallons of water in the four gallon jug. There is a pump that can be used to fill the jugs with water.

A solution of the problem is the appropriate sequence of moves taken to reach the (goal) state. First, we need a symbolic representation of the problem. We represent the content of the four gallon jug by x and the three gallon jug by y. The set of ordered pairs (x,y) represents the state at any time. The set of all ordered pairs is called the *state space* of the problem. It can be described as follows:

$$\text{State space: } (x,y) \text{ where } x=0,1,2,3,4$$

$$y=0,1,2,3$$

The initial state with two empty jugs is represented by the ordered pair $(0,0)$ and the goal state as $(2,y)$ where y can be any permissible number since the content of the three gallon jug is irrelevant to the way the problem is stated. We can now specify the productions that will apply in this problem. These productions are as we have seen condition-action pairs, also called *production rules*. An action will change the state of the system. This action can only be applied if the state space of the system matches with the condition clause of that production. For instance, we can only fill up the four gallon jug if there is less than four gallons in the jug. This can be formulated as the following production rule:

IF there are less than four gallons in the four gallon jug
THEN fill the four gallon jug

Instead of specifying the action we can in the action clause specify the conclusion of the action, i.e. in our example the conclusion will be that the four gallon jug is filled up. We can formalize the rule in the following manner:

$$\text{IF } (x,y) \text{ where } x<4 \text{ THEN } (4,y)$$

The formalized set of production rules that generate legal moves in the water jug problems is listed below:

(P1) IF $(x,y \mid x<4)$ THEN $(4,y)$
(P2) IF $(x,y \mid y<3)$ THEN $(x,3)$
(P3) IF $(x,y \mid x>0)$ THEN $(0,y)$
(P4) IF $(x,y \mid y>0)$ THEN $(x,0)$
(P5) IF $(x,y \mid x+y\geqslant4 \wedge y>0 \wedge x<4)$ THEN $(4, y-(4-x))$
(P6) IF $(x,y \mid x+y\geqslant3 \wedge x>0 \wedge y<3)$ THEN $(x-(3-y), 3)$
(P7) IF $(x,y \mid x+y\leqslant4 \wedge y>0)$ THEN $(x+y,0)$
(P8) IF $(x,y \mid x+y\leqslant3 \wedge y>0)$ THEN $(0, x,y)$

We start our problem solving with two empty jugs (0,0). Applying the set of production rules to this state reveals two rules that are applicable: P1 and P2. Both of these rules have conditions that match with the state (0,0). The production P1 sets the new state to (4,0). At this point productions P2, P3 and P6 apply. P2 results in the state (4,3). P3 will return the state to the previous state (0,0) while P6 will result in a new state (1,3).

As can be seen, in a certain state several production rules may have their conditions matched. But only a single production can apply at a time. We are then left with a problem of how to select rules from this set of applicable rules. The criteria by which rules are selected are known as *conflict resolution principles*. One such principle could be simply the ordering of the rules. We try the rules in the order they are specified and the first applicable is executed. Other principles, which may be used alone or in combinations, are for example recency and specificity. Recency selects the production that matches the state most recently generated. Specificity refers to the number of condition clauses in the condition part of the rule. More specified condition elements give higher executing priority.

Generating new states by these production rules and testing if the goal state has been reached is known as *search*. Selecting rules (the conflict resolution principle) and keeping track of sequences of rules that have already been tried and the states produced by them constitute what is called the control or search strategy. The search strategy repeatedly applies rules to states until the goal state is reached. When this happens the search process is terminated and the problem is solved.

Production systems are particularly general in that they claim to be *computationally universal*, that is capable of modeling all cognitive activity. One consequence of this is that a production system can accomplish the same task in a number of different ways. According to Anderson (1983, p. 13) this is a point in favor of production systems, because we know that people are capable of performing a single task in various ways. If the task is complex different people will do it differently, and the same person will even behave differently on different occasions. Although persons can perform tasks in many ways, one or a few methods are usually preferred. It is reasonable to ask why a person performs a task as he or she does. We shall later in this chapter look at how people develop expertise.

As noted above, modern production systems began with Newell's work at Carnegie-Mellon. Lenat and Harris (1978) has called the Newell system 'neoclassical' architecture. The neoclassical systems place a heavy emphasis on simplicity: a set of production rules, a working memory and simple rules of conflict resolution. The neoclassical production systems emphasize modular productions, in which each production is independent of the others and capable of being added, deleted, or separately modified.

2.6.3 The Architecture of Production Systems

The major components of the production system can then be defined as follows:

(1) A *working memory* which holds the symbol structure chosen to represent the states of the problem space. In our example above (4,0) is an example of such structure. Working memory, which can hold a limited number of such elements, orders them according to recency. As new elements are entered, old ones are pushed out. The original limit of working memory was taken to be on the order of seven elements.
(2) A *production memory* which in the neoclassical architecture is regarded as the only long-term memory. The production memory holds the production rules.
(3) A *control strategy* that directs the search in the problem space by selecting the sequence of rules to be applied.

The production system architecture employs a three-phase *control cycle*. Here, each rule is a separate entity which can be viewed as a small process that monitors the workspace continuously and changes the content of the workspace when it is allowed to execute or 'fire' as it is also called. Execution of a rule requires a *match* between the preconditions of the rule and the content of the workspace. When a pattern of data structures in the workspace matches the preconditions the rule is said to be *applicable*. A pattern-matching facility that can recognize a pattern and modify it is a central feature of the production system. As we have seen above, one particular state of the workspace may match several rules, thus making several rules applicable. We need, therefore, a selection strategy, also called *conflict resolution*, to choose one rule for execution. Executing a rule means to apply the action part, that is, the workspace is *acted* upon and the content is changed. The new state of the workspace gives rise to new patterns and new matches, that is, rules that are eligible for execution. The three-phase control cycle; matching, conflict resolution, and action, is used in most rule-based systems. It is also called the recognize-act cycle (see Figure 2.2).

The recognize-act-control cycle is general. However, particular conflict resolution schemes or search strategies may be employed under the

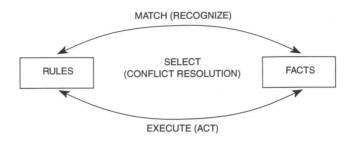

Figure 2.2   *The recognize-act cycle of production systems*

control of the general recognize-act cycle. We shall describe specific strategies in more detail in Section 5.4. Three things are worth noticing about the production system:

(1) The *contents* of the workspace determine which production rules are candidates for execution. Which rule to select first is determined by the search strategy applied.
(2) *Each* rule is an independent entity which constantly surveys the entire workspace. (In practical applications this may be modified by segmenting the workspace in order to increase search efficiency.)
(3) A rule *activates* itself when the contents of the workspace match the conditions of the rule.

The production system is a good way to model intelligent problem solving behavior. No pre-specified procedure is necessary as in traditional programming. The behavior of the system is determined by the content of the database. Therefore, for a given rule set, alterations in the database will change the behavior of the system. Since each rule is an independent entity and all communication is via patterns in the database, new rules can easily be added to account for new situations without disturbing the rest of the system.

2.7   RECENT DEVELOPMENTS IN PRODUCTION SYSTEMS

2.7.1   The SOAR System

The SOAR architecture (Laird *et al*,1987) is a further development of the production systems described above by researchers such as John E. Laird, Allen Newell and Paul Rosenbloom. The SOAR architecture is a computer simulation model of the human cognitive system with powerful generic problem solving and learning methods. It is one of the many AI systems that have attempted to provide an appropriate organization for general intelligent action. SOAR is to be compared with ACT*, a system also engaged in problem solving and learning, and to be described below. In SOAR, the main components in the architecture are long-term memory, working memory, sensors and receptors.

SOAR is a *problem solving system*. It works on symbolic representations of a problem in a problem space. The problem is solved by finding a desired state, the goal state, in this problem space.

Problem spaces for formulating tasks.   SOAR formulates all its tasks as problem spaces. Every system must somehow represent to itself the task it is going to work on. This representation provides the framework within which knowledge is brought to bear and in which the task is accomplished. This is done by searching the problem space for the desired state. When operating in a problem space, the system is always located at some current state. In the water jug problem described above, this may be the initial state (0,0). It can apply any of the operators (the production rules) of the problem space to the current state. Operating in the problem space requires knowledge to guide the problem search. This knowledge is held in the long-term memory of the system and brought to bear on the current state. A search for this knowledge (the knowledge search) is made through long-term memory (the production rules), whereas the problem space search generates states one by one, so only a single state exists physically at any one time, e.g. (4,0). The primitive functions of SOAR are as follows:

- select a problem space
- select a state from those directly available
- select an operator
- apply the operator to obtain new state

Production systems for long-term memory.   The second feature of the SOAR cognitive architecture is that it has a single uniform long-term memory constructed as a production system. The same memory structure, that of productions, is used for any kind of knowledge, procedural as well as declarative. This is probably the most controversial feature of SOAR in AI and cognitive science (cf. also the ACT* architecture below in which one argues strongly for two separate memories, one for procedural and one for declarative knowledge). One of the key features of SOAR is that the action part of the production contains a preference element.

Accumulation of preferences for decisions. The way SOAR resolves conflicts and determines which action to take is through preferences attached to the action part of the production rules. When SOAR has evaluated all operators that apply in the current state (this is called the elaboration phase), then a decision procedure determines on the basis of the preferences which operator to fire. The decision procedure uses a small set of preference values: acceptable, reject, better (worse), best (worst), and indifferent. For an operator to fire, the decision must be acceptable.

Impasses and subgoals. SOAR creates a goal–subgoal hierarchy dynamically as it runs into *impasses*. An impasse occurs when the decision procedure is prevented from choosing a unique decision. For instance, in the water jug problem, in the current state (0,0) there are three operators that can apply (P2, P3, and P6). We have no information on which one is the best. In the SOAR terminology this is a tie impasse. When this happens SOAR creates a subgoal to resolve the impasse. Thus, subgoals arise dynamically. There are four ways that impasses can arise:

(1) a tie impasse;
(2) a no-change impasse;
(3) a reject impasse; and
(4) a conflict impasse.

Chunking. Chunking is SOAR's learning capability. Chunking is a way to create new productions during the problem solving that are added to the production memory. Chunking occurs when the problem solving process encounters an impasse. When the impasse is resolved by SOAR, a new production (the chunk) is created. By tracing backwards to the state just prior to the impasse, the elements of this state are picked up and become the conditions of the new production (the chunk). Thus, the next time the process passes through this state the system has learned how to proceed without going through a long process of impasses and resolutions. Chunking applies to all subgoals.

Above, we have described the central cognitive structure of SOAR. The reader is referred to Newell (1990) for more detail about this cognitive system.

Applications of the SOAR Architecture

The SOAR architecture has been applied to a large variety of tasks, from small knowledge-lean tasks typically found in the AI literature such as blocks world, eight puzzle, etc., to more knowledge-intensive tasks usually tackled by expert systems like R1 (XCON), Neomycin and others.

R1 is an expert system developed at Carnegie-Mellon University jointly with Digital Equipment Corporation (DEC). R1 has become one of the most commercially successful expert systems. R1 configures a VAX computer system from a sales order. Configuration is a simple type of design task and not quite a typical expert system task. Most expert systems perform diagnostic tasks. However, R1 is one of the largest expert systems developed.

Newell (1990) describes the behavior of R1-SOAR on a small configuration task in order to demonstrate its capability of dealing with real knowledge-intensive tasks. The system is developed from a base case without heuristic knowledge to a full system with the same heuristics as R1. Then learning is turned on and the system builds its chunks. Considerable improvements in performance are achieved through these steps.

Summary on SOAR

- The SOAR architecture is realized within the physical symbol system paradigm and general intelligent behavior is attained by a symbolic goal structure.
- A uniform memory structure based on production system accommodates for all kinds of long-term knowledge. This creates flexibility in the problem solving process.
- SOAR is capable of creating subgoals dynamically during a problem solving process. All goals arise in response to impasses and are generated automatically by the architecture.
- Impasses are resolved by a decision procedure and are dependent on preference assertions.
- The SOAR architecture is fully responsive to learning, through its built-in chunking mechanisms.

2.7.2 The ACT* System

John Anderson is a cognitive scientist whose work is also based on the concept of production systems. He has developed a cognitive framework which is called *Adaptive Control of Thought (ACT)* of which ACT* is the final version in this framework. Here, we shall follow the description of the ACT* system given by Anderson (1983).

Anderson started his cognitive work by developing a semantic memory model HAM (Human Associative Memory) together with Gordon Brower (Anderson and Bower, 1973). In this model, declarative knowledge is represented as semantic nets. However, to be able to use this knowledge, Anderson needed procedural knowledge and chose production systems as the basis for the ACT* cognitive frameworks.

Anderson shares the view of Newell and Simon of a unified theory of cognition and considers ACT* as a theory of human cognitive architecture. It specifies the memory and processing structures that underlie human performance in all tasks. Figure 2.3 illustrates the main components of the ACT* architecture.

As shown in Figure 2.3, an ACT* production system consists of three memories: working, declarative, and production. As can be seen from this figure, most of the processes involve the working memory. Encoding processes deposit information about the outside world into working memory; performance processes convert commands in working memory into behavior. The storage process can create permanent information in declarative memory of the contents of working memory and can increase the strength of existing information

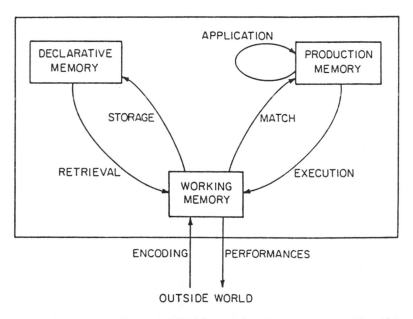

Figure 2.3 *A general framework for the ACT production system, identifying the major structural components and their interlinking processes. From Anderson (1983)*

in declarative memory. In the match process, data in working memory are put in correspondence with the conditions of productions. The execution process deposits the actions of productions in working memory. The whole process of production matching followed by execution is referred to as production application. Note that the loop denoted application cycles back. This reflects the learning capabilities of the ACT* system.

Working memory contains the information that the system can currently access, consisting of information retrieved from long-term declarative memory as well as temporary structures deposited by encoding processes and the action of productions. Basically, working memory refers to declarative knowledge that is in an active state.

The *declarative memory* is a long-term memory in the form of a semantic net. Knowledge comes in chunks or cognitive units as they are called in ACT*. Cognitive units can be of three basic data types: propositions, strings or spatial images. They come in no more than five elements (cf. Miller's finding as described above in Section 2.2). More complex structures are organized in hierarchies.

There is a long-term *procedural memory* in the form of productions. Each production has a set of conditions on the declarative memory and a set of actions that create new nodes or associations in the declarative memory.

The ACT* system has an *activation* process that defines the working memory and productions can match only knowledge that is currently active. A production's level of activation determines the probability of matching, thus making the ACT* system a probabilistic system.

Each production has a *strength* associated with it. This strength will increase with every successful application of the production, that is, stronger productions will succeed in matching its conditions more often than weaker. Pattern matching is the mechanism that decides which productions will apply. Goal structures can be built into the production system, thus achieving a goal-directed processing behavior.

The major difference between ACT* and SOAR is the distinction between declarative and procedural knowledge. This means that the process of retrieving data from declarative memory does not have to compete with the productions that perform the task. Anderson finds empirical evidence for this distinction in the time it takes to store declarative versus procedural information. A fact may be committed to memory after a few seconds. Furthermore, the pattern matching mechanism used makes ACT* a probabilistic system compared to the deterministic SOAR system.

Allen Newell in his book *Unified Theories of Cognition* (Newell, 1990) describes and comments on the ACT* system. He says that ACT* is, in his opinion, the first unified theory of cognition. However, he is critical of ACT*'s complexity. Only for a few very simple applications has this theory been applied. ACT* does not exist as a coherent operational computer system producing explanations.

Exercises

2.1   Define *normative* and *descriptive* as they apply to decision making.

2.2   What is the difference between *problem solving* and *decision making?*

2.3   Explain what is meant by a *symbol system*. Give examples of physical symbol systems. Explain why all cognitive systems are symbol systems in Newell and Simon's theory of cognition.

2.4   What is the significance of Miller's findings about mental information processing

2.5   Describe the cognitive architecture of the human mind as a symbol system.

2.6   Concepts can be defined in different ways. Explain:

(a) the classical way

(b) by means of family resemblance.

2.7   In their problem solving theories, Newell and Simon define two basic concepts: *task environment* and *problem space*. Explain these two concepts.

2.8   A foreigner is lost in Paris. He had started to walk from his hotel in the direction he thought would take him to the Louvre, but the streets have become unfamiliar. Looking at the map, he observes that it cannot be far away. He could ask the way, but his French is limited and would probably take him a few streets at a time. From his present position he can see a taxi station and a subway station. Define:

(a) the task environment

(b) the problem space

2.9   Why do people use heuristics in problem solving? Give examples. Why are heuristics more acceptable to managers than algorithms?

2.10 How can expertise be explained in terms of mental processes?

2.11 What are the major components of the production system architecture, and what are their functions?

2.12 List advantages of production systems compared to procedural programs

2.13 SOAR and ACT* are two general problem solving systems. Explain the main differences.

3
The Normative View of Decision Making

3.1 THE IMPORTANCE OF THE NORMATIVE VIEW OF DECISION MAKING

In chapter 2 problem solving and decision making were described from a cognitive perspective. A descriptive analysis of a problem solving and decision making situation is the starting point for improvements and for the application of prescriptive methods. Indeed, one of the first means of improvement might be to increase efficiency in the decision process, that is, to provide support for some of the sub-processes by means of DSS.

However, the literature on DSS has always had an emphasis on increased effectiveness of decision making, that is, an increase in *quality* of the decision, as the main benefit of a DSS. This is why it is important to study what has been written on *what is a good decision* and how such a decision should be made.

Also, we should keep in mind that if we contend that it is possible to use computers to assist in problem solving performance and decision making we must be able to demonstrate *why* this support should lead to *better decisions*. So we must have a *normative* view to explain why a supported decision is better than an unsupported one. It is interesting to note that the normative point of view, as a guide in designing DSS, is now appearing, once again, in the recent literature on DSS (see, for example, the *Nato Advanced Study Institute Program on Mathematical Models for Decision Support*, held in Val d'Isere, France in 1987).

A designer of a DSS should have design methodologies that include normative methods. Generally, decision makers do not master normative principles for several reasons:

- the presentation is too abstract and complex;
- there is a lack of satisfactory and easy to use software with which to support the method;
- they do not match the real problem that the user has.

However, as we shall see in Chapter 4, a good DSS environment *improves* the decision making process, by *speeding up the learning process* of the user and *providing reliable methods*.

We have frequently observed that the user, once he or she has performed the first step (which usually involves performing a task more efficiently than before), will start requesting a more *rigorous* and *effective methodology* as he or she becomes *more conscious* of the weaknesses of the present solution. This behavior is observed in domains where there is a motivation to improve results (such as profit in business), where the value system of the user and/or the organization is in favor of rewarding professional development, or in the search for truth and in the spirit of inquiry found in the scientific field.

Another reason for studying the normative point of view is that as shown in Chapter 5, it is now much easier to build systems which include *methodological* knowledge and, as a consequence, can provide normative assistance to the user. This possibility is made available through expert system technology.

As a consequence, the decision maker will increasingly look for decision support tools which will provide him or her with a *normative assistance* as and when he or she wishes to use such tools. It is worth noting at this point that, here, we make two important assumptions: firstly that decision making can be studied and secondly that it can be improved. This has been considered to be obvious by most people in the Western world since The Renaissance, but as Howard has pointed out this is not the case in Eastern philosophy. The type of systems we wish to build are used to provide arguments in favor of a course of action for decision makers, who have a value system which implies:

- that they are responsible for their own actions;
- that improved decisions can help them to reach their own goals or the goals of their organization.

Even in the Western world some thinkers argue that:

- free will is an illusion (our actions are motivated mainly by biological and/sociological laws or are in the hands of God);

- our motivations are often unconscious (note, however, that the work of Freud and the psychoanalysis school was to explain rationally apparently irrational behavior).

If there is no free will and our future is in the hands of God then there is not much motivation for improving decisions! If important decisions are motivated by unconscious impulsions then developing rational arguments may be a loss of time to convince someone. However this does not mean that we should not take a rational decision when facing what may appear to be irrational behavior.

Before the name DSS was coined, a lot of high quality work had been carried out under the name of Operations Research and Management Science. We have found it useful to recall the point of view of these movements and, also, to study the kinds of problems they have been able to solve for managers. Also in this chapter we shall give a brief review of the quantitative decision methodologies, as they are used in the main schools in this field. We shall end the chapter with a description of the decision analysis cycle which seems to give the most comprehensive normative view.

3.1.1   The Difficulty of Decision Making and the Meaning of Rationality

In everyday life we usually think of decision making as being good if it is rational, so it will be important to specify the concept of rationality. Each one of us has many examples of decisions that are usually considered to be bad.

It will be argued in this chapter that we should distinguish between the *decision making process* and the *outcome* of the decision. It is quite possible for the outcome that results from a chosen alternative to be good, even though the decision making process is bad and vice versa. Clearly, decisions can be made which are bad, both in process and outcome. One of the usual reasons for this situation occurring is the complexity of the decision. Management problems are full of complex decisions with far-reaching consequences. As we have seen in Chapter 2, there are limitations on a person's ability to take all of the important factors into account. Bad decision making may result from the decision maker's inability to incorporate all of the important factors into his or her thoughts. One of these important factors is uncertainty, and decision making is often difficult just because of the many uncertainties involved.

Another factor which has increased the difficulty of decision problems is the increasingly large number of people involved in a decision. This characteristic may be related to the growing number and size of organizations over the last 50 years.

As a consequence, the people involved in a decision often have different views on the relative importance of various objectives. In the face of complexity, uncertainty, conflicting objectives and multiple decision-makers, the Western culture has developed a rational decision making process. We seek a *rational framework* to help us think through our decisions. The first intuitive approach is to define a good decision as a rational one, which implies the need to clarify this concept of rationality. One of the key characteristics of rationality is, it seems, *consistency*.

For example, if we declare that *A* implies *B*, and also that *B* implies *C*, then we shall, presumably, declare that *A* implies *C*. It would be considered irrational to do otherwise. What we have been doing was just making *inferences* that accord to the classical principle of logic that inferences should be transitive. We would be considered to be inconsistent with this principle if we assert that *A* does not imply *C* in this example. Similarly, we might state, as a principle, that our preferences should display transitivity. If we declare that *X* is preferred to *Y*, and *Y* to *Z* but we do not prefer *X* to *Z*, then we may be accused of irrationality. The accusation is probably based on the assumption that we wish our preferences to be consistent.

We notice that, in both these examples, the demonstration of irrationality depended on the *presence of a rule and showing that the statements were inconsistent with that rule*. In other words, we shall make the assumption that the decision maker is willing to make choices that are based on a consistent line of reasoning. We are rational when, having adopted rules which our statements or actions should conform to, we act in a way that is consistent with them. It is to be noted that this definition allows many different kinds of rules to be adopted in complex decision making situations. We can then satisfy our need for rationality by conforming to those rules. It is also important to note that for a formal decision methodology to be useful in solving real problems its conclusions must, ultimately, make intuitive sense to the decision maker.

As stated by Holtzman (1989) 'the decision maker must develop an intuitive understanding of the validity of any successful recommendation for action, even if he does not have detailed knowledge of the underlying information that led to the recommendation'.

The concept of rational action has always been a subject of philosophical debate. One important point is the difference between a reason for doing something and a cause of an event. A human being may clearly have a reason for acting in a given way, but is this reason equivalent to the cause which is found in physical phenomena? The most systematic analysis of this question in contemporary philosophy is probably that of Donald Davidson (1982), who has formulated a general theory of the interpretation of belief and rational action. Davidson defends a causal conception of action according to which an action *A* is intentional only if:

(1) one can say that the person committing *A* had reasons to do so (beliefs, desire, intention);
(2) there is at least one reason of *A* which is the cause of it.

Many philosophers including Wittgenstein consider that (2) is false since a cause implies that there is a law like in physical science. Some philosophers consider that there are no mental laws. Reasons are only rationalizations explaining actions in the light of objectives (goals) of a human being (teleological principle) which cannot be assimilated with causality as found in physical science.

This debate is related to the understanding of causality between two events. A cause is an event which produces an other event which is its effect, independently of the way it is described. The interested reader can refer to Davidson (1982).

We shall see in Chapter 11 that when developing systems which present artificial intelligent behavior one of the rules which is followed is known as the 'principle of rationality'. This principle states that 'an intelligent system will take the actions that according to its knowledge, will lead to the achievement of its goals' (Van de Velde 1993).

It should be pointed out that rationality is not only a matter of logic. For example a task of financial analysis may be seen as different from another because of differences in the environment (static or dynamic, size, complexity, and time limitation different from another similar task . . .).

The task may also be seen different from another due to differences in the decision maker interacting with the task who may impose additional restrictions (quality level, specificity of the solution to be achieved . . .;).

Practical limitations of the environment may imply limits to the level of knowledge of a variable, or the exhaustive character of alternatives. In other words an *adequate* behavior may be the result of *rational* behavior taking into account *practical* constraints.

Section 3.3 is devoted to describing the rules of decision analysis, and we shall argue that they constitute a sensible set of rules to follow.

3.1.2   The Nature of Formal Decision Methods and their Validity Conditions

A formal decision method must provide concepts and a formalism to describe the context of the decision (that is, a formal description of a decision situation, including decision maker's preferences, information and alternatives). The definition of a formal decision method must also include at least one prescriptive axiom (McCarthy 1984) which Holtzman (1989) calls the *action axiom*.

The formal method used to describe the context of a decision is not normative. On the other hand, the action axiom defines a set of conditions that are sufficient for action. The action axiom, being a statement about real action in the terms of a formal system, is an act of faith. In other words, we can give arguments according to which an action axiom such as maximizing expected utility is a valid (that is, sensible) axiom to act upon in the world, but this *cannot be proved*. This raises the problem of validity conditions for formal decision methods. Holtzman (1989) points out that a formal decision method must satisfy two domain-specific conditions: it must be *locally correct*, and capable of *extrapolation*. Local correctness means that the method must yield solutions that are intuitively correct to a representative class of toy problems, that is, simple situations that are solvable 'by inspection' and to which the formal technique is applicable.

'When a formal decision method is both locally correct and extrapolable with respect to a decision domain, the method's solutions to large, unintuitive problems can be considered superior to intuitive (and possible conflicting) alternative solutions, although this superiority can never be proved. In particular, formally derived solutions are superior because there is nothing in a sound formal method (aside from computational limitations) that is adversely affected by the complexity and size of the problem. This cannot be said of intuitive methods, which are subject to our bounded rationality (Simon, 1976, 1982)'. Holtzman, 1989.

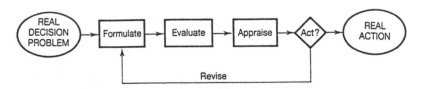

Figure 3.1 *Closed-loop decision process. (Reproduced from Howard R. (1988). Decision Analysis: practice and promise.* Management Science, **34**(6), 679–695)

3.1.3 Methodology for using a Formal Decision Method

The purpose of a formal decision method is to tell the decision maker something that, in principle, is already known, in the sense that if the decision maker believes that the model represents his or her decision problem, then he or she should act according to the recommendations of the method's conclusion. In practice, using formal decision methods requires that we formally capture the decision context as a decision model and that we interpret the formal recommendation that results from applying the decision method to the model.

As a consequence, the practical use of formal decision methods is a three-stage process (See Figure 3.1): formulation (that is, development of the formal decision model) evaluation and appraisal (that is, interpretation of the formal recommendation). If a formally derived prescription is unacceptable then a feedback loop is included to remind us that the decision maker should react to any surprising element of the formal prescription by re-evaluating and possibly modifying his or her formulation. Alternatively, if after developing enough insight the decision maker agrees with the suggested strategy or, if he or she determines that his or her disagreements result solely from logical error, he or she may choose to follow the formal prescription.

3.2 THE HISTORY OF QUANTITATIVE DECISION MAKING

The French mathematician and philosopher Pascal was probably the first to use a logical and mathematical method, that is, a scientific method, to solve decision problems that were met in games. To apply a scientific method means, according to the Austrian philosopher Karl Popper (1934), to construct a hypothesis about the way the world works, and to collect data to try to falsify this hypothesis. In the absence of such falsification, the hypothesis may be used to explain phenomena.

Operations Research is often presented as the first large-scale organized activity having, as a goal, the scientific analysis of decisions. However, to be scientific is one thing, to be rational is another. To be rational means to take the procedures of science as the rules with which we want to conform. The application of scientific rationality to management of organizations is known as Operations Research (OR).

The early OR studies were done in the military during the Second World War. Most of the decisions that were studied were repetitive problems. Certain researchers concluded that the only management problems that could be dealt with, using a scientific approach, were repetitive problems.

It is clear that the focus on repetitive problems led researchers also in civilian organizations to concentrate on operation management. Rarely have higher-level management problems been studied. Many critical contributions started flourishing in the OR literature, some of them written by well-known pioneers in the field, such as Ackoff (1979a,b), Quade (1975, 1984), Tomlinson and Kiss (1984). The problem was that OR methods were no longer providing the same noticeable improvements to management problems as had been seen in the early years. Now, it is usually recognized that the mind set of the OR approach, while appropriate for solving logistics problems, is inadequate for solving higher-level management problems.

Checkland (1981) demonstrated that many OR scientists were more concerned with how to achieve a given end most *efficiently*, rather than with what that end should be in the first place. The inadequacies in the attempts to apply the scientific rationality of OR to management have been summarized by Watson and Buede (1987) to be: failure to involve the decision-maker in the experimental and iterative nature of analysis; failure to appreciate the organizational and personal context of decision making; and failure to explore ends as well as means.

In the mid 1950s operations research gave birth to the *Management Science* movement. The aim of this movement was to apply scientific methods to management problems. However, people applying the management science approach were, just as the OR people, quickly accused of having much more interest in problems susceptible to mathematically elegant solutions, than to the real problems of managers, in particular high-level managers.

Since the OR/management science approach did not provide the adequate methodology for solving management decisions, new approaches began to appear in the 1970s. These new approaches tried to fulfill the basic properties necessary to support managerial decision making. These approaches included aspects of rationality, values, preferences and perceptions, rationality in the face of uncertainty, and a language (calculus) in which the decision problem could be formulated (cf. Watson and Buede, 1987). A new discipline, called *rational decision analysis*, emerged. It will be dealt with in the next section.

3.3   RATIONAL DECISION ANALYSIS

Several main directions appeared at the beginning of 1970, roughly at the same time as the DSS concept appeared: the statistical decision theory school, the decision analysis school at Stanford, and the multicriteria school in Europe are some of the most well-known examples.

We shall first describe, in this section, the main concepts used by these schools, then the differences in emphasis of each one of these schools will be discussed, followed by a description of the *decision analysis cycle* which seems, to us, to be the most comprehensive of these approaches, and, finally, we shall raise some questions about the normative point of view. We shall follow closely, in this section, the ideas of Watson and Buede (1987).

3.3.1 The Problem of Conflicting Objectives

We make personal decisions all the time, however, when it comes to 'important' decisions such as which job to choose, or where to live, the stakes at risk are significant, and we find ourselves using more effort to ensure that we choose correctly.

When we have responsibility for decisions that affect many other people we are highly motivated to make the correct decision. It may be the choice between different locations for a factory, the choice of which investments to make, the recruiting of a new employee and so on. In such circumstances we check that the choice we make is consistent with our own beliefs and values, as well as the values of the organization that we serve.

The practical role of the rational decision theory is to provide a framework that assists people in achieving such consistency. In such decisions two important factors can usually be pointed out:

(1) there exist conflicts between objectives,
(2) there is uncertainty about the outcomes.

We shall see how the decision theory can provide a framework for thinking about these two factors at once. We shall first see how to handle conflicting objectives when we have no uncertainty about the outcome of our decision making.

Utility and Value

Choice is simple if we have only one criterion. For example, if we can buy the same product in several different shops, we usually use cost as the single criterion and we buy the product in the shop where the price is lowest.

If we have several criteria and can establish a single numerical measure which takes all of these criteria into account, then our choice procedure, would again, be straightforward. The difficulty is how to construct such a measure.

The concept of a numerical measure to describe the value of alternative choices has come to be referred to as the *utility theory*, with the *utility function* being the numerical measure itself. The utility theory appears to have been first discussed by the French mathematician Daniel Bernouilli in 1738 when solving a gambling problem. Bernouilli's explanation was that money was not an appropriate measure of value. Instead, he suggested that the *worth*, or the utility of money for each individual, was non-linear and had a decreasing slope; marginal utility decreased as wealth increased.

In the 1940s and 1950s the concept was used again, and was made more precise in game theory. Game theory was developed both to describe how people behave when engaged with others in conflicting goals, and to describe how rational people ought to behave in such situations. The game theory was developed by the mathematician John von Neumann and the economist Oskar Morgenstern. In their book *The Theory of Games and Economic Behavior* (1944), they found the need to develop a cardinal theory of utility to describe how people should evaluate options about which they were uncertain.

Decision analysts have made the distinction between two types of utility, which can be characterized as the distinction between value and risk preference. *Value preferences* are made between competing objectives or attributes when *no uncertainty is present*. *Risk preference* addresses the decision maker's aversion to, indifference to, or desire for *risk taking*.

Value Functions

We can only recall here the key elements of the value function theory. The reader is referred to Keeney and Raiffa (1976) for an authoritative presentation of this theory. Here, we shall only deal with the properties that a value function should have and why we want to construct one. The problem under consideration can be defined as follows: a set of alternatives has been defined. We assume that we know the attributes (criteria) which discriminate among these alternatives. For example, if the problem is to choose among cars, the alternatives could be: Volvo, Ford, Peugeot, BMW, Mercedes; and the attributes: power, purchase price, mileage, comfort, aesthetics, reliability, maintenance costs and so on. We suppose that there are n such attributes, named X_1, X_2, . . . X_n and that it is possible to provide a numerical score for each alternative with respect to each attribute. This set of scores will be represented by a vector $x = (x_1, x_2, . . . x_n)$. The problem is to decide which vector score is most attractive.

Although, at first sight, the formalization above may seem to be a reasonable abstraction, real problems are rarely like this. It is often the case that the set of alternatives is not completely known, or that all the possible alternatives have not been identified. Assuming that this difficulty can be overcome, we introduce the concept of value functions.

A value function $v(.)$ is defined using real numbers that have the following properties:

- $v(x^A) > v(x^B)$ if, and only if, the option whose score vector is x^A is preferred to another with score vector x^B
- $v(x^A) = v(x^B)$ if, and only if, there is indifference to the choice between x^A and x^B.

The choice between these alternatives is simple: we choose the alternative with the score vector x for which $v(x)$ is largest. The difficulty will be in constructing this function $v(.)$. If the only way to do so were to elicit from the decision maker his or her relative preferences for all the possible score vectors, then we would not have achieved anything by trying to construct a value function. The choice problem would have been answered by direct intuition.

Fortunately, there are ways of computing $v(.)$ that rely on *general properties* of our preferences structure and just a few simple comparative judgments. As Watson and Buede (1987) point out, the power of the method is that if our preferences obey certain conditions (and they often do) we can synthesize $v(.)$ from an analysis of only part of our set of preferences. In certain cases, we do not even need to completely specify $v(.)$. This is the case when we have *dominance* of one alternative over another. An alternative, A is said to dominate another alternative, B if, for all $i, 1 \leqslant i \leqslant n, x_i^A \geqslant x_i^B$ and for at least one $i, x_i^A > x_i^B$. If one alternative dominates all the others, it is rational to choose it. Clearly, dominance rarely occurs with problems that are complex enough to require analysis, and we need to develop a method for those problems.

Since a partial ordering of our preferences can be inferred from any set of decisions we make, the interest of creating a value function is that it will help us construct preferences between score vectors which we find difficult to compare directly. The problem, then, is to construct our preferences within, and across, the attributes x_i of x in such a way that we have a complete ordering of all vectors x. This theory is *normative*, in that it shows us how we should behave if we want to be rational, rather than being a description of how we actually behave.

'The idea is to use value function theory to construct preferences which we find difficult to articulate directly, using only those preferences that we can express easily and adopting the principle of complete transitivity for all our preferences.' (Watson and Buede, 1987)

Once we have assumed the existence of $v(.)$ we now have to measure it. It should be noted that there is no reason to suppose that $v(.)$ will not change from problem to problem or as a function of time. Fortunately, there are properties that our *preference structure* often has that lead to special forms of the value function which can be elicited more easily.

Additive value functions

The most common form of the value function is the additive one:

$$v(x) = \sum_{i=1}^{a} v_i(x_i)$$

This form has the advantage of being very simple, and allows each attribute to be worked on separately. However, it is quite possible for a particular preference structure to lead to a non-additive value function.

We now have to recall what the conditions on our preferences have to be to justify additivity. The essential condition is that of *preference independence*. A pair of attributes X_1, X_2 is said to be preference independent of all the other attributes $\{X_i, i=3, \ldots n\}$ if preferences between different combinations of X_1, X_2 with the level of all other attributes, being held at constant value, do not depend on what these constant values are.

For example, when buying a car if we say that cost and mileage are preference independent from reliability it means that we prefer a car with cost c_1, mileage m_1, and reliability r to one with cost c_2 mileage m_2 and reliability r, then we prefer a car with cost c_1, mileage m_1, and reliability r' to one with cost c_2 mileage m_2 and reliability r' no matter what r is. This should hold for all possible c_1, c_2, m_1 and m_2.

Clearly, this condition does not hold in certain cases, however, additive value functions can be useful in many circumstances. Several authors have discussed multiplicative or other forms. The reader is referred to Keeney and Raiffa (1976) for an expansion of these functions.

3.3.2   Encoding Uncertainty

In the preceding section, we analyzed the problem of choosing between alternatives when objectives are in conflict. We assumed that we knew, with certainty, what the results of choosing an alternative would be, so that the only problem was how to cope with the conflict between our objectives.

It is clear that in the problem of choosing which car to buy, to ignore uncertainty is not unreasonable, however, the certainty assumption is obviously unrealistic for most real decision problems. According to authors such as Howard and Matheson (1968) uncertainty is the central problem of decision making.

Description of Uncertainty

If we are to incorporate uncertainty into our theories of choice, then a calculus for handling uncertainty must be developed. The theory that is most commonly employed for this purpose is that of probability. Probability theory is not very old, and is usually dated back to the French mathematicians and philosophers, Pascal, Bernoulli and Laplace. In fact, contrary to what one may think, there has been considerable controversy about the meaning of probability, and, in particular, its relation to real-world phenomena. The interested reader is referred to Weatherford (1982) and Hacking (1975).

Three main theories of probabilities can be identified. They were developed by their authors to incorporate a satisfactory method for measuring probabilities, and they are: the logical theories of Keynes (1921) and Carnap (1950), the relative frequency theories of Venn, Von Mises (1957) and Reichenbach, and the subjective probabilities theories of Ramsey (1931), de Finetti (1974), and Savage (1954).

The most important conflict has been between the relative frequency theory and the subjective probability theory. The relative frequency theory states that the probability of an event is the *long run frequency* with which the event occurs in an infinite repetition of an experiment, thus, it is seen as an objective property of the real world. The subjective theory presents probability as the *degree of belief* which an individual has in a proposition. This is a property of the individual's subjective perception (or state of knowledge) of the real world. The former theory has dominated scientific thinking for many years because it has the appearance of conforming to the empirical objectivity which science is sometimes claimed to need and possess. The relative frequency theory will not be adequate, however, as a theory for helping an individual to model his or her perception of uncertainty when making decisions.

The interpretation of probability which must be adopted for the application of decision theory has to be the subjective probability theory. Alternatives to the probability theory are the subject of much discussion:

'interpreting the parameters of nonprobabilistic measures of uncertainty with respect to reality has received much less attention than the interpretation of probabilities' (de Finetti, 1974). These parameters are, at best, poorly defined and essentially unassessable with any degree of reliability. Therefore, although they cannot be completely ruled out, non-probabilistic measures of uncertainty are inferior to probability measures for decision-making.' (Holtzman, 1989).

Events and Probability

Probability theory is an obvious construct for describing perceived uncertainty, and has been applied with success during the last fifty years. When we wish to apply this calculus to decision problems we need a set of assumptions about an individual's judgments. This leads us to infer that a set of numbers must exist which describe that individual's perception of uncertainty that is related to a set of possible events and that these numbers should be combined using the rules of probability calculus to infer what numbers should be used to describe other uncertainties.

Numerical Estimation of Probabilities

The question which has to be raised now is how in the real world, we can set the numerical value of certain probabilities; for example, the probabilities of elementary events need to be set in order that we can compute non-elementary events.

The problem of how to measure probabilities is a practical one which is different from the theoretical problem of their coherence. There are two well-known methods to set the numerical values of probabilities: 'subjective' estimation and experimental estimation. With respect to the experimental method we shall recall, here, the so-called 'law of great numbers': if an event is produced by a process a large number of times, then the relative frequency of event A of probability $p(A)$, converges towards $p(A)$. As a consequence, the observed frequency of occurrence of the event can be used as an estimation for $p(A)$.

As we have pointed out above the interpretation of probability which must be adopted for the application of decision theory has to be the subjective one. The reader should be aware, however, that all scholars are not ready to accept this theory. If the subjective theory of probability is not adopted, the intellectual justification for the procedure of decision analysis is much weakened.

Theoretical Background to Subjective Probabilities

Probability theory is an obvious construct for describing subjectively perceived uncertainty. To apply this calculus in other situations and, in particular, in decision problems requires more than an act of faith. What is required is a set of assumptions about an individual's judgment which, if they are satisfied, lead us to infer that a set of numbers must exist which describe that individual perception of uncertainty, and, moreover, that these numbers should be combined using the rules of the probability calculus to infer what numbers should be used to describe other uncertainties. This work was successfully undertaken by Ramsey (1931), Savage (1954) and most extensively by de Finetti (1974). The behavioral suppositions are set up as axioms as shown in Figure 3.2. The first axiom expresses the idea that given two uncertain events, a person can say which is more likely, or whether they are equally likely. Axioms (2), (3) and (4) are quite easy to accept. Axiom (5) supposes the existence of a set of events which acts as a standard in probability judgment.

With these behavioral assumptions, it can be proved (de Groot, 1970) that a set of numbers exists which correspond to the judgments of relative likelihood, in the sense that if, for two events A and B, A is judged to be more likely than B, then the number for A is larger than the number for B. Furthermore, these numbers must, collectively, satisfy the properties of probabilities such as:

$$0 \leqslant p(A) \leqslant 1$$
$$p(A \text{ or } B) = p(A) + p(B) - p(A \text{ and } B)$$
$$p(A \text{ and } B) = p(A) \, p(B|A)$$

with $p(B|A)$ being the probability of B occurring given A.

Despite these results, many scholars reject the notion of subjective probability. They argue that the first assumption (that we can compare the relative likelihood of any two events) is untrue and since the premise is false, the conclusion is false.

However, one of the objectives of developing decision theory is to establish a *framework* to guide rational behavior. For Watson and Buede (1987) the question is whether we choose to behave in such a way that our judgments either have this property or not. What the theory we have described tells us is that if we would like all our judgments of relative likelihood to exist and to exhibit transitivity then subjective probabilities should be used.

Axioms for probability

(1) For any two uncertain events, A is more likely than B, or B is more likely than A, or they are equally likely.

(2) If A_1 and A_2 are any two mutually exclusive events, and B_1 and B_2 are any other mutually exclusive events; and if A_1 is not more likely than B_1, and A_2 is not more likely than B_2; then $(A_1$ and $A_2)$ is not more likely than $(B_1$ and $B_2)$. Further, if either A_1 is less likely than B_1 or A_2 is less likely than B_2, then $(A_1$ and $A_2)$ is less likely than $(B_1$ and $B_2)$.

(3) A possible event cannot be less likely than an impossible event.

(4) Suppose A_1, A_2, ...A_i is an infinite decreasing sequence of events; that is, if A_i occurs, then A_1 occurs, for any i. Suppose further that each A_i is not less likely than some other event B, again for any i. Then the occurrence of all the infinite set of events $A*i = 1, ..., \infty$, is not less likely than B.

(5) There is an experiment, with a numerical outcome, such that each possible value of that outcome, in a given range, is equally likely.

Exhibit 3.1 If an individual is able to, or wishes to, express his or her judgments of likelihood according to these axioms, then numbers must exist which describe his or her perceptions of the uncertainty of any event which satisfy the rules of the probability calculus. Conformity to these rules is our definition of what it means to be rational in evaluating uncertainty.

Figure 3.2 *Rationality in evaluating uncertainty. (Reproduced from Watson S.R. and Buede D.M. (1987)* Decision Synthesis: The Principles and Practice of Decision Analysis. *Cambridge University Press)*

Using Probabilities

If we accept the idea that our judgment on uncertainty is to be represented by numbers, and that these numbers must satisfy the rules of probability then a question is raised as to how to elicit these numbers in specific cases. Probability elicitation is a difficult problem and much work has been done on this process, for example, by Spetzler and Stael von Holstein (1975), Seaver *et al.* (1978).

Subjective probabilities have to obey the laws of probability. For example, if we assess the probabilities of events X, Y, X given Y, Y given X (written as, $p(X)$, $p(Y)$, $p(X|Y)$, $p(Y|X)$) are assessed, we have seen that we must have:

$$p(X).\ p(Y|X) = p(Y).\ p(X|Y)$$

since both must be equal to the probability that $(X$ and $Y)$ occur. If this relationship is not satisfied with the elicited numbers, then one or more of the four numbers must be changed.

One of the reasons for the observed phenomenon of incoherence in a set of probability estimates may be that the person is suffering from cognitive biases (Hogarth 1980, Kahneman *et al.* 1982). There seems to be considerable evidence that in assessing perception of uncertainty (Section 3.7.4), people are often subject to biases in cases where a norm for comparison exists.

The issue of how to correct biases when accessing subjective probabilities has been explored in the literature about the calibration of probability appraisers. But the literature is controversial, and no general conclusion can yet be derived about the possibilities of correcting for biases. We should also remember that to use probabilities in decision analysis implies familiarity with probability theory. In particular, the following concepts are needed:

- random variables (discrete and continuous);
- cumulative probabilities, probability density functions;
- moments of distributions, means, variances;
- conditional joint and marginal probabilities, independence;
- distribution functions of random variables.

These concepts are classical and the reader should consult one of the many standard instruction texts about probability theory. However, we would like to point out here that since we shall see in Chapter 6 that it is possible to embed methodological knowledge in a computer system, it is possible to design systems which will take care of most of the tasks of applying the laws of probabilities.

3.3.3 Structuring a Problem using a Decision Tree and Risk Preference

Since we know how to describe subjectively perceived uncertainty in numerical terms, we have to now describe how this formalism can be used to aid decision makers who face alternative courses of action, each involving uncertainty.

The Problem and its Representations

The XYZ company has produced a new cosmetic product. Unfortunately, the production cost of this product is 50% higher than ordinary cosmetic products of the same kind. The marketing division of the XYZ company is discussing the potential market share of the product. After discussion, the marketing expert of XYZ came to the conclusion that two results are possible.

Table 3.1 *Predicted profit ($000) for a new product*

	R1	R2
A1	800	– 300
A2	0	0

R1. The product very quickly reaches a 10% market share and stays at this level.
R2. Total failure.

After careful analysis, the management of the company came to the conclusion that there are two possible courses of action. Either:

A1. Invest in a production unit able to supply 10% of the market.
A2. Abandon this product immediately.

The predicted profit (in thousand of dollars) which can be obtained from these operations is presented in Table 3.1. The management of the company is rather pessimistic, and uncertain about the future of this product. The marketing manager estimated that there is a 30% chance of gaining 10% of the market, but that this estimation could be wrong. The marketing manager also pointed out that if a market test was done, the uncertainty associated with this choice could be reduced, and hence, the decision would be improved. For $50 000 (the cost of the market test and corresponding delays), the marketing manager thought that it would be possible to identify a good market with 60% probability, or a bad market with 80% probability. If we call $I1$ and $I2$ the two possible indications of the market test with respect to a good market ($R1$) or a bad market ($R2$), then:

$$p(I1/R1)=0.6$$
$$p(I2/R2)=0.8$$

Where $P(I1/R1)$ denotes the probability of having a test indication of a good market, and the market is good ($R1$), and $P(I2/R2)$ denotes the probability of having a test indicating a bad market, and the market is bad ($R2$).

Figure 3.3 illustrates the situation that the manager faces. Such a diagram is referred to as a *decision tree*. It has proved to be useful in describing decision problems. Indeed, merely describing a problem in this way can often lead to an appreciation of what the best option ought to be. Three different kinds of nodes can be distinguished in a decision tree:

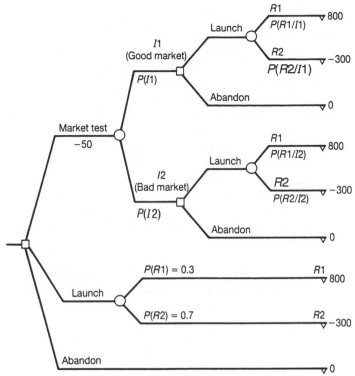

Figure 3.3 *A decision tree corresponding to the new product problem*

(1) decision nodes, denoted by a square ($\square$);
(2) chance nodes, denoted by a circle ($\bigcirc$);
(3) terminal nodes (outcomes), denoted by a triangle ($\triangledown$).

and two kinds of branches:

(1) alternative branches;
(2) outcome branches.

Emanating from each decision node is a set of branches, each branch representing one of the alternatives available for selection at the corresponding decision node. Each chance node is followed by a set of outcome branches, one branch for each possible outcome that may happen following that chance node. Probabilities of occurrence and values are assigned to each of these outcomes. Costs (resource allocation) are assigned to each decision alternative. Looking at Figure 3.3. we see that the first node (starting with the root of the tree) is a decision node, which represents the three alternatives that are open to the management of the company: (1) abandon, (2) launch, (3) perform a market test.

(1) If we abandon the product (bottom branch) we come directly to an outcome branch, the end value of which is zero.
(2) If we launch the product we come to a second node where we have two branches $R1$ and $R2$ corresponding to the two possible conditions of the market (good and bad). At this point, the decision maker can not change anything; he or she can only estimate the probability to move in the direction of each alternative. This is a probabilistic (or chance) node.
(3) Finally, if the management decides to perform a market test, it will, first of all, be necessary to finance this test (we can consider this cost as a fee the decision maker must pay to move along this branch). Then the decision maker finds his or her self facing a chance node corresponding to possible results from the test. He or she can control the situation again by deciding to launch or abandon the product.

The probability of coming to each of the branches of the tree are not directly known. They depend on the reliability of the market test and can be computed using Bayes's theorem:

$$P(R1|I1) \;=\; \frac{P(R1)\,P(I1|R1)}{P(I1)} \;=\; \frac{(0.3)\,(0.6)}{P(I1)}$$

$$P(R1|I2) \;=\; \frac{P(R1)\,P(I2|R1)}{P(I2)} \;=\; \frac{(0.3)\,(0.4)}{P(I2)}$$

$$
\begin{aligned}
\text{with } P(I1) &= P(I1|R2)\,P(R1) + P(I1)\,P(R2)\\
&= (0.6)\,(0.3) + (0.2)\,(0.7)\\
&= 0.32\\
\text{and } P(I2) &= 1 - P(I1) = 0.68
\end{aligned}
$$

Thus: $P(R1|I1) = \dfrac{18}{32}$ $P(R2|I1) = \dfrac{14}{32}$

$\qquad\quad P(R1|I2) = \dfrac{12}{68}$ $P(R2|I2) = \dfrac{56}{68}$

The Evaluation Method

We now seek some way to evaluate the uncertain options (or *lotteries* or *gambles* as we shall refer to them) facing a decision maker.

We want to construct an evaluation method such that, once a problem has been specified, its *decision tree* drawn, and the uncertainties measured using probabilities, we will be able to compute a number that

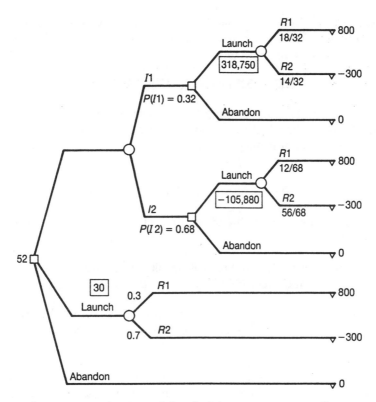

Figure 3.4 *Evaluation of the decision tree corresponding to the new product problem*

represents its actual value to the decision maker, in a way that is consistent with his or her judgment.

The simplest and most common evaluation method, at least in problems where the only important attribute is money, is the *expected monetary* value for the option. We multiply the probability of a particular future set of events by the final asset position if that future occurs, and sum it over all possible futures. This method was first explored by Daniel Bernouilli (1738).

The method starts at the end of the branches and moves to the left from node to node. At each chance node, we shall compute the expected value of the tree to the right of the current node. At each decision node we shall select the branch leading to the *maximum expected value*. In our case, the immediate launching of the product leads to an expected value of:

$$800\,(0.3) \; -300\,(0.7) = \$30\,000$$

which is better than immediately abandoning it (value=0). Similarly, if the result of the market test is favorable (I1), the launching of the product leads to an expected value of:

$$800(18/32)+(-300)(14/32)=\$318\,750$$

which is much better than abandoning the project.

On the other hand, if the result of the market test is unfavorable, it is better to abandon the product than to launch it, since the expected value of a launch in this case is:

$$800(12/68)+(-300)(56/68)=\$105\,880$$

Finally, the expected value of the project if we make the market test is equal to:

$$\$318\,750(0.32)+0(0.68)=\$102\,000 \text{ minus the cost of}$$
the market test ($\$50\,000$) which equals $\$52\,000$.

A recording to the criteria of maximum expected value the last strategy is to make a market test since the expected value of this strategy is $\$52\,000$ against $\$30\,000$ for immediate launching and zero for immediately abandoning it.

Therefore, this method suggests launching the product if the result of the market test is favorable, and abandoning the product if the result of the market test is unfavorable.

Lottery of the Project

The expected global value of the project that we have evaluated ($\$52\,000$) is just a way to summarize all of the possible consequences when following the best strategy. The details of the consequences take the form of a lottery among the possible outcomes associated with their respective probabilities. In our example, if we follow the best strategy that the company can take then the data shown in Table 3.2 holds.

To understand this lottery, we just have to recall that the best strategy is to make a market test before launching the product (highest expected

Table 3.2 *Various probabilities and values for the product.*

Probability	Value ($)
0.18	750 000
0.68	− 50 000
0.14	− 350 000

value), and to launch the product if the market test is good and to abandon if the market test is bad. If, after launch, the market is good, we obtain an outcome of:

$$800\,000 - 50\,000 = \$750\,000 \text{ with a probability of } \frac{18}{32} \times 0.32 = 0.18$$

If, after launch, the market is bad: we obtain an outcome of

$$-300\,000 - 50\,000 = \$ -350\,000 \text{ with a probability of } \frac{14}{32} \times 0.32 = 0.14$$

If the market test was bad then we abandon the project, the outcome is $-50\,000. With a probability of 0.68.

In general, *a decision will be the choice between several lotteries.* The method used above is to replace each lottery by an expected value and to choose the lottery with the highest expected value. This simple rule does not satisfy many people and we must introduce the concept of utility to compare lotteries.

Utility Theory

Daniel Bernouilli was the first person to introduce the concept of utility. The *Bernouilli solution* argued that the value (to the individual) of money was not a linear function (Bernouilli suggested that it was a logarithm). However, early writers in this area made no distinction between attitudes towards value differences and attitudes towards risk. It was with the publication of Von Neumann and Morgenstern's theory of games and economic behavior (1944) that modern utility theory can be said to have begun.

The idea behind this theory is to define the utility of an outcome as equal to the probability of winning a given prize in a gamble, such that the individual is indifferent to the choice between receiving the outcome for certain, and accepting the gamble.

We will start by exploring utility for money in a defined range, although the concept can be extended to any amount of money, and also to any non-monetary attribute. A lottery refers to a set of prizes or prospects with probabilities attached, as shown on Figure 3.5. The monetary values are H (high) and L (low). We have assumed that $L < X < H$. Using the symbol $\sim$ to denote the indifference of the decision maker between the options before him or her, we have:

$$X \sim \{L, H; u(X)\}$$

Theory

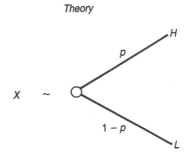

Figure 3.5 *The concept of certain equivalence. For any outcome X which is preferable to L and not as good as H, there is some probability p such that the decision maker is indifferent between X for sure, and a gamble, giving a chance p of getting H and 1−p of getting L*

as the definition of the utility function u (.) using a standard notation. We introduce the concept of certain equivalent (X). The certain equivalent is the amount of money that the decision maker is willing to exchange for this lottery.

Application of the Utility Theory

The utility concept is now applied to the example of the XYZ company. The management of this company may consider that a probability of 0.3 for a gain of $800 000 and a probability of 0.7 for a loss of $300 000 constitute too risky a prospect to launch the product. On the other hand, if the abandonment had the consequence of leading to a loss of $100 000, the company may still prefer to launch the product.

Their certainty equivalent for this project is somewhere between $0 and $−100 000. Where exactly? At −$50 000 if they are obliged to produce an accurate estimate?

One can imagine that instead of computing the expected value we analyze the decision tree by replacing a lottery by a certain equivalent each time it is needed. The advantage of this method over a purely arbitrary method is, perhaps, not very convincing if we are obliged to introduce very subjective and intuitive preferences.

We shall point out, however, that we have reduced the global problem to a series of much simpler smaller experiences and the gain will be more important as the initial problem becomes more complex. In fact, by using some natural coherence axioms, we can define a systematic method to translate our attitude towards any lottery, as complex as it may be, as we had decided to use the expected value of the lottery. The method consists of replacing monetary value by utility for which we shall have to compute an expected value.

In other words, it is possible to demonstrate that utility functions can be built for a decision maker if he or she accepts the following axioms:

U1 Orderability axiom. The decision maker can tell if he or she prefers *A* to *B*, or *B* to *A*, or is indifferent. This preference must be transitive, that is, if *A* is preferred to *B*, and *B* to *C*, the *A* must be preferred to *C*.

U2 Monotonicity axiom. If *A* is preferred to *B*, a decision must be made between two lotteries for which the outcomes are *A* and *B* with different probabilities, then the lottery giving *A* with the maximum probability must be preferred.

U3 Decomposability axiom. A superlottery, the outcomes of which are themselves lotteries, is equivalent to a lottery offering the ultimate outcomes with the probabilities computed according to the calculus of probability.

U4 Continuity axiom. If *A* is preferred to *B*, and *B* to *C*, there must be a probability *p* such that *B* is the certain equivalent of the lottery giving outcome *A* with the probability *p*, and *C* with a probability $1-p$.

U5 Substitutability axiom. It is always possible to replace a lottery by its certain equivalent.

One of the examples of such axiomatization and, perhaps, the most comprehensive one, was done by Savage (1954) who proved that an individual who acts in accordance with these five axioms possesses a utility function that has two important properties:

(1) He or she can compute the utility for any lottery by computing the utility of each prize, multiplying by the probability of that prize and then summing over all prizes (that is, using the maximum expected utility rule as the action axiom).

(2) If one lottery is preferred to another, then the utility for it will be higher.

In addition to logic and probability the decision theory requires that the decision maker accepts the set of the five axioms of utility theory, which together imply the Maximum Expected Utility (MEU) action axiom. Thus, MEU is not really an axiom but rather a theorem within the utility theory.

Given our previous discussion (Section 3.1.2) on the validity of formal methods for real decision making, we need to verify that the MEU axiom satisfies the conditions of local correctness and extrapolability in terms of personal decision making.

The orderability axiom (U1) states that the decision maker can consistently and completely rank all of the possible outcomes that could be received as a result of his or her decision. This axiom implicitly requires the decision maker to have a well-defined set of outcomes to consider. By well defined, we mean that the decision maker has successfully circumscribed his or her decision context in order to make the definition of each outcome clear.

Given the many kinds of ignorance we may face, Holtzman (1989) has an interesting classification of types of ignorance, our ability to circumscribe real decision problems is a mixed blessing. One argument to show the local correctness of axiom U1 is known as the 'money pump argument' (Raiffa 1968; Howard *et al.* 1983). This argument demonstrates that a transitive ordering of the decision maker's preferences over the outcome set is a direct consequence of the reasonable desire of most decision makers not to voluntarily engage in sure-loss action.

The decomposability axiom (U3) states that the decision maker derives no pleasure (or displeasure) from breaking down an uncertain event into a set of components that together, yield a compound event which has probability of occurring that is equal to that of the original.

The continuity axiom (U4) is the only utility theory axiom subject to controversy. Much of the axiom controversy focused on people's inability to visualize uncertainty effectively (Kahneman *et al.*, 1982). Several areas of research have arisen in response to the difficulty of assessing probabilities in practice.

Extrapolability of the MEU Action Axiom

The argument here is that the MEU action can be extrapolated to any decision problem which can be represented by a set of well-defined variables (controllable as well as uncertain), by an explicit set of dependence relations between these variables and by a comprehensive utility function. One practical limitation of decision-theoretic calculations is the amount of computation inherent in the methodology. With only rare exceptions, probabilistic descriptions grow exponentially with the number of variables in a problem. As we shall see in Chapter 6 one way to reduce the computational burden is to introduce domain-specific knowledge into the methodology in return for a loss of generality.

Extensive professional experience using decision analysis provides powerful reasons to believe that algorithms based on MEU can be used to solve complex real decision problems (Matheson 1970; Howard 1980, 1983, 1988).

Comparing risky alternatives

Let us imagine that the management of the XYZ company accepts the axioms; let us see how it can take into account its preference for risk and revise the solution to its problem. Let us take two extreme outcomes such as $1 000 000 and $-500 000 and let us suppose that, after an interview with the management, we have established the following equivalents shown in Figure 3.6.

We can now replace the end branches by a lottery between $1 000 000 and $-500 000. For example, the immediate launching of the new product has the equivalent shown in Figure 3.7. The immediate abandonment has the equivalent shown in Figure 3.8. and this seems preferable. The reader can check that the market test leads to the lottery (as shown in Figure 3.9). This is still slightly less satisfactory than immediate abandonment. These answers translate the risk behavior

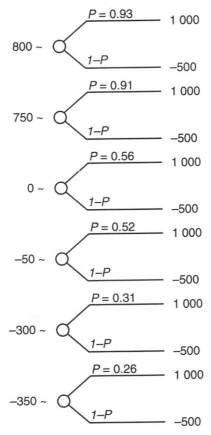

Figure 3.6 *The certain equivalents for the management of the XYZ company*

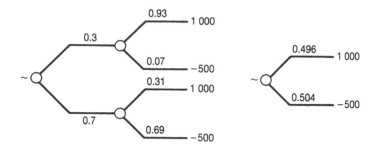

Figure 3.7   *Replacing the direct launching alternative*

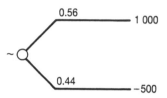

Figure 3.8   *Replacing the direct abandon by a lottery*

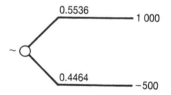

Figure 3.9   *Replacing the market test alternative by a lottery*

of the company facing certain lotteries. We could have asked other questions and plotted the probability, p of the lottery as a function of its certain equivalent x.

We shall denote utility $u(y)$ as the probability p corresponding to a monetary value y. The utility of a lottery will be obtained by computing the weighted mean of utilities of each outcome and the certain equivalent is the monetary value corresponding to this mean utility:

$$u(y_{CE}) = \Sigma\, p_i u(y_i)$$

with y_{CE}= certain equivalent

y_i= ith outcome

p_i= probability to obtain the ith outcome.

Implications of the Utility Theory and Use of a Utility Curve

There are at least three ways to use a utility curve: as a descriptive tool, as a forecasting tool, or as a normative tool. The points obtained when plotting the answers that an individual gives to a series of choices among various lotteries show both the risk behavior and the coherence of the risk behavior. If the points are on a straight line it will imply a general indifference towards risk, a strong curvature indicates an aversion toward risk.

On the contrary, a convex curve will denote the behavior of a player for whom the certain equivalent of a lottery is always greater than its expected value. It is very rare to see a company showing a convex curve. Dispersion of points around a mean curve shows a variability in the decision maker's preference.

We know that for an individual who accepts the five axioms the utility curve must be an increasing monotonous function of monetary outcomes. A person (or a company), having established his or her mean utility curve will be able to delegate his or her decision making power or analyze risks systematically by using just this curve. However, it is common to observe that once this curve is established it turns out to be a normative instrument. The decision maker will reduce the dispersion in this cluster of points answer so as to conform better to the axioms of the theory. Then he or she will try to reduce irregularities in the shape of the curve. From time to time even, he or she will be willing to accept new axioms which will reduce the utility curves to a limited number of reasonable classes of curves. As an example, the following additivity axiom is used in many applications:

Additivity axiom

If all prizes in the lottery are increased by the same amount Δ, then the certain equivalent of the lottery is increased by Δ.

This additional axiom seems quite reasonable, since no matter which prize in the lottery is won, an additional amount of Δ will be won, therefore, the new lottery should be worth more than the original lottery. The counter argument is that having an amount Δ available whatever happens, changes the wealth of the decision maker, and, as a consequence, his or her risk aversion. This axiom is very powerful since it reduces the possible utility curves to exponential functions of the form:

$$u(x) = (1 - e^{-cx})/c$$

Where c is a coefficient called the risk aversion. Figure 3.10 represents three utility functions of the exponential family for positive, null or negative values of the c coefficient, that is, for a risk averse, an indifferent to risk, or a risk-prone person. To understand the meaning of the coefficient, we can note that:

- the asymptote to the utility curve is given for $1/c$ on the utility axis, that is, no profit (no loss) can go beyond the utility of $1/c$ for such a decision maker
- the certain equivalent of a profit distribution following a normal law with mean m and standard error σ is:

$$CE = m - 1/2c\ \sigma^2$$

We can point out here that any utility function is such that $u'(x) = au(x) + b$ is equivalent to $u(x)$.

The reader is referred to Howard (1968) and Spetzler (1968) for a more detailed analysis of properties of utility curves and for an example of utility curves used by a company as an element of its policy.

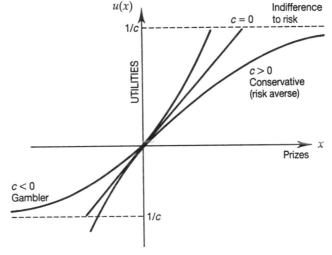

Figure 3.10 *Three utility functions of the exponential family*

Stochastic dominance

A utility curve gives an answer to any problem of choice between lotteries, and enables us to compute, for each one, a certain equivalent. However, many problems of choice between lotteries can be solved more simply if circumstances are favorable. For example, we have to choose between the two lotteries L1 and L2 that are described in Table 3.3.

Let us draw the cumulative distribution of the outcomes of the two lotteries that is, the function $F(x)=$ probability for the outcome to be less or equal to x, this is shown in Figure 3.11. As can be seen, the cumulative distribution of lottery L1 (solid line) is always above and on the left of L2 (dashed line). This means that for any sum x, the probability to obtain this outcome with lottery L2 is superior or equal to the corresponding probability for L1. We say that there is stochastic dominance of lottery L2 over lottery L1. In these conditions, whatever the user's utility curve, he or she will have to prefer lottery L2 to lottery L1. Let us emphasize the point that this type of dominance is not absolute but stochastic; it is always possible to win 200 when playing L1 or lose 50 when playing L2.

Value of Information

We shall now introduce the concept called 'value of information' using the XYZ company case. We shall do this by analyzing the value of the information given by the market test, its origin and its limits.

Table 3.3 *Outcomes and probabilities for two lotteries*

| | Probabilities | |
Outcomes (dollars)	L1	L2
−50	0.25	0.20
0	0.40	0.45
100	0.25	0.20
200	0.10	0.15

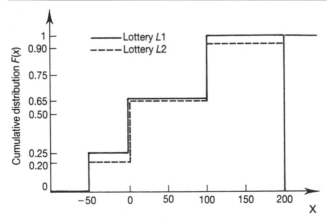

Figure 3.11 *Stochastic dominance*

First, let us assume that the market test is made in the hope that it will reassure the management. However, due to time constraints it is decided, in advance, to launch the product anyway. The expected value of the project is then:

$$\$318\,750\ (0.32)-\$105\,880\ (0.68)=\$30\,000$$

exactly what could have been expected 'a priori' (which is obvious since):

$$
\begin{aligned}
&[800\,000\ (18/32)-300\,000\ (14/32)]\ (0.32)\\
&+[800\,000\ (12/68)-300\,000\ (56/68)]\ (0.68)\\
&=800\,000\ (0.18+0.12)-300\,000\ (0.14+0.56)\\
&=800\,000\ (0.3)-300\,000\ (0.7)\\
&=30\,000
\end{aligned}
$$

A piece of information which is not capable of modifying a decision has always a *null value* in the framework of a decision problem. It is also possible to verify that the value of our market test: $\$102\,000-\$30\,000=\$72\,000$ is exactly equal to the probable loss that we avoid by abandoning the project (in opposition to the 'a priori' decision) if the market test is unfavorable $=-105\,880$ $(0.68)=\$72\,000$. It is this Expected Value of Information (EVI) which, compared to its cost (here $\$50\,000$), enables the decision maker to decide if it is worthwhile to acquire it or not.

In certain problems, the expected value of a given kind of information can be difficult or costly to compute. In this case, it is useful to use the concept of Expected Value of Perfect Information (EVPI). This quantity is rather easy to compute, and gives a superior limit to the cost of information. In our example, a perfect market test would produce the exact answer to the question: is the market good or bad? (that is, R1 or R2). With a probability of 0.3 the answer will be 'good', and the project will have a value of $\$800\,000$. With a probability of 0.7 the answer will be 'bad', and the project will be abandoned (value 0) the expected value of such a perfect information is:

$$
\begin{aligned}
\mathrm{EVPI}&=800\,000\ (0.3)+0\ (0.7)-[800\,000\ (0.3)-300\,000\ (0.7)]\\
&=210\,000
\end{aligned}
$$

No market test, however good it might be, should be undertaken for a cost above this amount.

3.3.4   Risk Preference and Conflicting Objectives

So far we have seen how to construct a calculus for evaluating decision options when the decision maker has conflicting objectives and no uncertainty, or a single objective but considerable uncertainty.

Real decision problems usually involve both. For example, in the problem of choosing which car to buy, it is clear that the characteristics of the cars are uncertain. We shall only really know the cost of maintenance of the car once we have bought it!

If we have to choose vacation destination, we would include more attributes than just the cost of accommodation.

Most problems, which may at first sight appear to be single attributed, may turn out to be better formulated as multi-attribute problems.

All finance courses teach criteria for choice of investment such as net present value, internal rate of return and so on. When studying a new investment, a manager will search to estimate the cash outflows (initial investment, costs and so on) and cash inflows (sales of the product and so on) associated with the investment. Apparently, the outcomes can be measured in monetary terms, so the method of discounting cash flow to obtain a single attribute such as net present value seems appropriate.

It is true that this approach is often a sensible one in commercial organizations, but sometimes it will be useful to use other criteria as well, such as market share or company image, which will be better expressed as separated variables, rather than attempting to give a monetary equivalent for them at the beginning of the analysis. Thus, uncertainty and conflicting attributes need to be handled at the same time. It is possible to extend the single-attribute utility theory, developed in the last section, to the multi-attribute case.

The main difficulty of this approach is its practicability. While there are non-trivial problems in determining satisfactory single-attribute utility functions, these problems are magnified when dealing with multiple attributes.

Part of the power of decision analysis lies in the replacement of complex judgmental tasks by simple ones. Several approaches have been suggested for coping with this difficulty and we will recall two of them in the next sections.

Keeney's Approach

The idea initially described by Keeney (1969) in his thesis and in Keeney and Raiffa (1976) is that the assessment of a multi-attribute utility function would be much simplified if it could be written as a simple function of single-attribute utility functions. Then it would be possible to assess the single-attribute functions without reference to the other attributes and, as a consequence, reduce the complexity of the utility assessment task to manageable proportions.

An additive form of the multi-attribute function is the most simple structure which comes to mind. The conditions that would justify using the additive form were a subject of active research for some time, and Keeney has given the conditions for a multi-attribute utility function to have a simple form which is slightly more general than the additive one but which gives additivity in a special case. The conditions stated by Keeney are the following:

- preference independence (see Section 3.3.1)
- utility independence.

An attribute X is said to be utility independent of other attributes Y, Z and so on, if the decision maker's preference between lotteries on X do not depend on the actual level of the other attributes.

Much work was done on this approach for the multi-attribute problem over the last fifteen years, and there have been many reports of its use on practical problems. (See Kirkwood, 1982 or Bell, 1979a as just two among many examples.)

The Stanford Approach

The application of decision analysis has a different flavor in different schools of practice. The problem of constructing multi-attribute utility functions which properly reflect risk preference occurs whenever decision theory is applied to a practical problem. Yet it appears that the Stanford school, in which the key figure has been R. A. Howard, has not perceived the need to follow the procedures of Keeney's approach. The procedures followed by the Stanford school are best explained in a series of papers published by Howard *et al*. (1983).

As a conclusion, we see that there is a theoretically sound definition for the utility of multi-attribute consequences which may be used in the maximization of expected utility. It is difficult to assess this directly, however, and various approaches exist to assist a decision maker in indirect assessment.

Other Normative Approaches

The methods which have been presented above are based on what many individuals consider to be reasonable behavioral postulates, these postulates being the preference judgments that the axiomatic development of decision analysis requires. This means that many people consider the framework as a sensible one to adopt when one *unique* decision maker is confronting uncertainty and conflicting objectives. Many applications satisfy this requirement. However, this approach is not the only normative one. The other most well-known normative methodologies are: the cost-benefit analysis, and the multi-criteria decision making methods.

Cost-benefit analysis

This technique is a special case of the search for a multi-attribute value function. This method was mainly used for the evaluation of social projects. In the method, all factors of importance are identified, outcomes are measured and a price is determined for each factor, and all the resulting costs are added up. In so doing, an additive multi-attribute value function is constructed. Prices may be interpreted as weight, and the net cost is simply a weighted sum.

The main difference with what we have seen above is that if cost-benefit analysis is used then *society as a whole* will be better off as a result of undertaking the project. In the preceding section we were studying the behavior of an *individual* decision maker. In fact, cost benefit analysis was developed as a tool for the analysis of social desirability of public projects. However, some writers consider that the method can be criticized in the way that it handles equity and the assumption of additivity (see Fischoff, 1981).

Multi-criteria decision making

Multi-criteria decision making can be broken down into three families of methods:

- multi-attribute utility theory
- interactive multi-criteria programming
- outranking multi-criteria programming

We have introduced multi-attribute utility theory in Section 3.3.1 and above. We shall now say a few words of the two other methods.

Interactive multi-criteria programming. The origin of the ideas behind this method can be found in Zeleny's (1982) work. The idea is to use mathematical programming and, in particular, linear programming to solve the multi-criteria problem. The method is usually suited to problems where there is a continuum of options rather than a set of discrete alternatives.

The most important contribution seems to be interactive multi-criterial programming. As we have seen in Section 3.3.1 in applying multi-attribute value theory to a problem, it is necessary to compute weights before the value function can be used. Some people believe that this can be done effectively only when facing real decision options and not hypothetical situations. The interactive versions of multi-criteria programming software are not subject to this criticism since they enable the decision maker to inter-actively explore the set of good options. In such software, once several conflicting objectives have been presented as (usually linear) objective functions, the interactive system will explore the Pareto optimal boundary, allowing the direction of search to be specified at each stage by the decision maker who is using the system.

Outranking. The multi-attribute utility theory considers that a multi-criteria decision problem can always be reduced to a unique criterion eliminating any incomparability. On the contrary the 'outranking methodology' accepts incomparability. The outranking method initially introduced by B. Roy at the University of Paris Dauphine and developed by P. Vincke and J.P. Brans aims at first to build a relation called an outranking relation, which represents the decision maker's strongly established preference given the information at hand. The latter relation is therefore neither complete nor transitive. The second step will consist in exploiting the outranking relation in order to help the decision maker solve his or her problem.

A good survey of these methods can be found in Roy and Vincke (1981, 1984) and in Brans *et al.* (1986). The method assumes that a well-defined set of alternatives exists, and that each alternative can be unambiguously defined in terms of a set of attributes with respect to which each option can be measured. The best summary of these methods to our knowledge is made in the book *Multicriteria Decision Aids* (P. Vincke, 1992).

3.3.5 Influence Diagrams

This section introduces the concept of influence diagrams and gives a brief description of them. To conduct a decision analysis, we need an effective means of structuring and representing decision problems. A formal representation of a decision problem is a task that reflects someone's perception of the world.

The best known representation language for decision problems is the decision tree. As we have seen in Section 3.3.3 the decision tree representation requires that each decision and each uncertain variable must be made explicit. Also, the end nodes of a decision tree give the value of each of the possible outcomes. However, there are several known drawbacks to using decision trees as a representation language for decision problems:

- They do not allow independence relations to be exploited (as a consequence, they lead the decision maker to describe highly symmetrical structures).
- They grow exponentially with problem size and, as a consequence, can only be used to represent very small problems.
- They lead the decision maker to think in a forward direction about the decision at hand.

It is now accepted that influence diagrams (Howard and Matheson, 1983a) have significant theoretical and practical advantages over decision trees (Owen, 1978; Olmsted, 1982). Figure 3.12 (from Holtzman, 1989) gives a comparison between a decision tree and an equivalent influence diagram. The aleatory (uncertain) variables A and B are independent. The distribution of the outcome of B does not depend on the outcome of A–this is not apparent from the tree structure. It is necessary to examine the numerical distribution to discover the independence. Figure 3.12(b) is much simpler than the decision tree shown in Figure 3.12(a). The absence of an arrow between chance nodes A and B in Figure 3.12(b) indicates, explicitly, their (conditional) independence.

We find in influence diagrams two types of nodes: *decision* and *chance* and two types of arrows *conditioning* and *informational* and typically (although not necessarily) a single sink node of type chance.

'The acyclic, singly connected nature of influence diagrams implies that sets such as predecessors, successors, direct (or immediate) predecessors, and direct (or immediate) successors of a node are defined in the usual manner. Furthermore, for an influence diagram to represent a decision problem for a single decision-maker who does not intentionally forget information (known as the no-forgetting condition), the set of decision nodes in the diagram must be fully ordered, and the direct predecessors of any decision must be direct predecessors of all subsequent decisions.' (Holtzman, 1989)

The decision nodes, in an influence diagram closely resemble those in decision trees, they denote variables under the decision maker's control. Chance nodes usually represented by a circle (or oval), denote probabilistic variables.

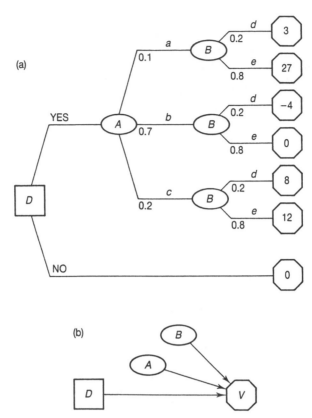

Figure 3.12 *Comparing decision trees and influence diagrams. (a) Sample decision tree. (b) Equivalent influence diagram. (Reproduced from Holtzman S. (1989).* Intelligent Decision Systems. *Addison-Wesley)*

Arrows in an influence diagram have a different meaning to the branches in a decision tree. *Conditioning arrows* are always directed towards a chance node and denote probabilist dependence. The aleatory variable represented by a chance node is modeled as being probabilistically dependent on the variables (decision or aleatory) represented by its set of direct predecessors. *Informational arrows*, however, are always directed toward a decision node and denote available information. A decision is assumed to be made using knowledge of the outcomes of its direct predecessors. Furthermore, the no-forgetting condition mentioned above implies that the direct predecessor of a decision that is itself a predecessor (direct or not) of another decision, must also be direct predecessors of the latter decision. In an influence diagram, informational arrows imply a chronological order, where as conditioning ones do not.

'An influence diagram can represent a decision problem completely, not just in terms of its structure. A full description of a decision problem requires that the diagram contain at least one decision node influencing a value node and that consistent, detailed specifications exist for each node in the diagram. For decision nodes, the set of possible outcomes corresponds to the set of decision alternatives; for chance nodes, this set of outcomes corresponds to the sample space of the variable being represented. Furthermore, for chance nodes, a detailed description should also include a probability measure over the set of possible outcomes. An important, yet subtle, fact about probabilistic specifications of chance nodes is that they must be consistent with the set of direct predecessors of the node and their respective outcomes. In addition to containing a list of its direct predecessors (or successors), a node's description should include its name and a label for each of its possible outcomes. Furthermore, because influence diagrams are likely to be implemented in a computer-based environment, it is useful to include a short statement describing each variable being represented.' (Holtzman, 1989)

Manipulating and Evaluating Influence Diagrams

As shown by Olmsted (1982) once a Well-Formed Influence Diagram (WFID) has been defined, we can manipulate it by performing four key elementary operations: reversing an influence, merging two nodes, splitting a node and removing a node and still preserving the state of information embodied in the original WFID.

'Operations that preserve this state of information are very useful, particularly when the WFID includes at least one decision node directly or indirectly influencing a value node; such a diagram is referred to as a well-formed decision influence diagram (WFDID). Since WFDID fully define decision problem in the language of decision theory, the diagram logically entails a recommendation for action.' (Holtzman, 1989)

The important contribution of Olmsted was to propose a procedure for solving probabilistic inferences and decision problems directly from an influence diagram. The procedure requires that we represent certain equivalent for decision problems on the diagram. Olmsted introduces a new symbol (the $\diamond$ diamond) and shows how to modify the diagram transformation when it is present.

Goal-Directed Generation of Influence Diagrams

The generation of an influence diagram should be viewed as an attempt to represent formally real decision in a progressive manner. As the development proceeds, the diagram will become an increasingly accurate statement about the decision maker's perception of reality.

An important feature of the progressive nature of influence diagram generation is that the structural aspect of the diagram is often generated first. Once the structure is reasonably stable, the diagram is defined further in more detail. Using Holtzman's terminology a node which has been fully specified is called an assessed node and a node not fully specified is an unassessed node. An unassessed node is assessable if the decision maker feels that an actual assessment of a corresponding probability distribution is obtainable with reasonable effort.

> 'If an outcome space and, in the case of a chance node, an unconditional probability distribution are specified, then the node is said to be directly assessed. It is also possible for a node to be indirectly assessed if, instead of directly specifying an outcome space (and for a chance node, an unconditional probability distribution), a conditional assessment function is given that maps every possible combination of outcomes of its set of direct predecessor variables to a unique outcome space (and for a chance node, a corresponding conditional probability measure) for the node.' (Holtzman, 1989)

An important case of indirect assessment occurs when the assessment function is deterministic. Deterministic assessment functions map sets of direct predecessor values to outcome spaces with a single element that bears the full mass of the associated probability measure (that is, it occurs with unit probability).

We consider the conceptual tool called the influence diagram as one of the most helplful for extracting information in a technically useful form. We shall discuss, in Chapter 11, recent research on delivering this methodology with intelligent software.

Much of the research on representation and inferencing with influence diagrams has focused on specialization of influence diagrams that contain only chance nodes (Cooper 1990, Kim and Pearl 1983, Pearl 1986) but these specialized representation exclusively express probabilistic relationships among states of the world without explicit consideration of decision and values.

We must now describe the way to implement the decision analysis methodology. This process is called the decision analysis cycle.

3.3.6   The Decision Analysis Cycle

Our objective in this section is to present the process of applying analysis. We shall use and follow very closely the original presentation made by Howard and Matheson in 1968, which is, in our opinion, the best introduction for managers. The more mathematically-inclined reader is referred to Howard's (1968) paper *Foundation of Decision*

Analysis. Decision analysis as a procedure for analyzing a decision is described in Figure 3.13. This procedure is a means of ensuring that the essential steps have been consciously considered.

The procedure is iterative and comprises three phases. The first is the *deterministic phase*, during this phase 'the variables affecting the decision are defined and related, values are assigned, and the importance of the variables is measured without any consideration of uncertainty' (Howard and Matheson, 1968).

During the second, or *probabilistic phase*, the decision analyst introduces probability assignments on the important variables and derives associated probability assignments on values. This phase also introduces the assignment of risk preference, which provides the solution to take into account uncertainty.

The third, or *informational phase*, 'reviews the result of the last two phases to determine the economic value of eliminating uncertainty in each of the important variables in the problem' (Howard and Matheson, 1968). The third phase is very important because it shows just what it would cost in dollars not to have *perfect information*, a concept which we introduced in Section 3.3.3

A comparison of the value of information with its costs determines whether additional information should be collected. This is, as we have seen, a very important methodological result because it gives a manager who is facing a decision a guideline on two fundamental questions:

(1) Is it useful to gather additional information?
(2) What is the maximum amount of money I should spend in order to acquire this information?

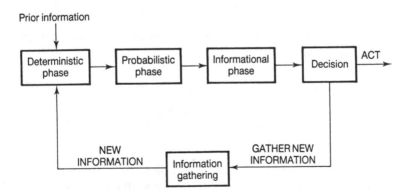

Figure 3.13 *The decision analysis cycle. (Reproduced from Howard R.A. and Matheson J.E. (1968).* An Introduction to Decision Analysis. *Stanford Research Institute)*

'If there are (profitable) further sources of information, then the decision should be to gather information rather than to make the primary decision at this time. Thereupon will follow the design and execution of the information gathering program, whether it be a market survey, a laboratory test or a military field trial.' (Howard and Matheson, 1968)

The information that results from this program may change the model and the probability assignments on important variables.

'Therefore, the original three phases must be performed once more. However, the additive work required to incorporate the modifications should be slight and the evaluation rapid. At the decision point, it may again be profitable to gather new information and repeat the cycle or it may be more advisable to act. Eventually the value of new analysis and information gathering will be less than its costs and the decision to act will then be made.' (Howard and Matheson, 1968)

The Deterministic Phase

The deterministic phase usually starts with a systematic analysis of the problem. Within this phase, we can distinguish efforts devoted to modeling from efforts devoted to analysis.

Modeling

'Modeling is the process of representing the various relationships of the problem in formal, mathematical terms. The first step in modeling is to *bound the decision*, to specify precisely just *what decision must be made*. This requires listing in detail the perceived alternatives. Identification of the alternatives will separate an actual decision problem from a worry.' (Howard and Matheson, 1968)

The next step: finding *new alternatives*, is the most creative part of decision analysis.

'New alternatives can spring from radically new concepts; more often they may be careful combinations of existing alternatives. Discovering new alternatives can never make the problem less attractive to the decision maker; it can only enhance it or leave it unchanged.' (Howard and Matheson, 1968)

Often, the difficulty of a decision problem disappears when a new alternative is generated. Then the decision maker must specify the various *outcomes* that the set of alternatives could produce. These outcomes are the subsequent events that will determine the ultimate desirability of the whole issue. In an investment (a new product introduction, for example) the outcomes might be specified by sales levels and cost of production, or even more simply by yearly profits, computed from the forecasted income statement of the product.

One of the most challenging processes is the selection of the system *variables* for the analysis. System variables are all those variables on which the outcome depends. One could start by having only outcome variables as system variables, but most of the time it is difficult to think directly in terms of outcome variables. In Klein (1988) we described a deterministic model FINSIM that is used to generate financial alternatives for a company. An example of outcome variables a financial manager would consider each year for a given horizon can be:

- the profit level or a measure of return, such as return on assets;
- the debt/equity ratio or another measure of risk.

The direct estimate of these outcomes is difficult. Most of the time it is easier to use other system variables such as level of sales, the growth rate of sales, level of expenses, ratio of expenses to sales, inventory level, ratio of inventory to sales and so on, to compute the profit and the debt/equity ratio.

> 'The selection of system variables is a process of successive refinement, wherein the generation of new system variables is curtailed by considering the importance of the problem and the contribution of the variables.' (Howard and Matheson, 1968)

Once the selection of system variables is done, the next step is the classification of these variables into *decision* variables and *state* (or environmental) variables. A decision variable is a variable which is under the control of the decision maker, and the selection of an alternative in a decision problem can be defined as the specification of the setting of the decision variables. A state variable is a variable determined by the environment of the problem. Although state variables may have a very important effect on the outcomes, they are autonomous and beyond the control of the decision maker. For example, in the forecast of the sales of a software product marketed by a software company, the increase in the number of computers on which the software products runs, and the number of competitors' software and their associated marketing expenses are state variables.

> 'The next step (of the modeling process) is to specify the relationships among the system variables. This is the heart of the modeling process, that is, the creation of a structural model that captures the essential interdependances of the problem. This model should be expressed in the

language of logical mathematics–typically, by a set of equations relating the system variables.' (Howard and Matheson, 1968)

The decision maker will want to assign values to system variables. In general he or she has a *nominal value* and a *range* of values that the variable may take on. In the case of state variables, the nominal value and range reflects the uncertainty assigned to the variables.

'For convenience, we often think of the nominal value of a state variable as its expected value, in the mathematical sense, and of the range as the 10th percentile and 90th percentile points of the probability distribution.' (Howard and Matheson, 1968)

An important methodological point is that, at this stage, it is better to include a variable that will later prove to be unimportant than to eliminate a variable prematurely. For most decisions of professional interest, the equations will be used to create a computer program that represents the model. It is interesting to note here the importance of defining a *deterministic decision model* as the first step of the decision analysis.

The next step for the decision maker is, as we have seen in Section 3.3.1, to assign *utility values* to the outcomes. (This distinction between utility of an outcome and the outcome itself is fundamental in decision analysis.)

The final step in the deterministic model is to specify the *time preference* of the decision maker. Howard and Matheson are thus using the classical theory of value to relate interest (discount) rate and present value. The market value today of *x* dollars delivered in period *n* is called the net 'present value' or worth of the deferred payment.

$$NPV = \frac{x}{(1+r)^a}$$

where *r* is the interest (discount) rate. The important point here is that, according to decision analysis, we need a mechanism for describing the time preference of the decision maker, a mechanism that reduces any time stream of money to a single number called worth (*NPV*).

In the deterministic model the *state variables* are called S_i and the *decision variables* d_i. The state variables can be visualized as a set of knobs, the value of which is set by nature. The decision variables are set by the decision maker (each configuration of these knobs constitutes an alternative). For example, in the case of the FINSIM model (Klein, 1989) used by a credit analyst to decide if a loan will or will not be granted to a company (see Figure 3.14), the state variables

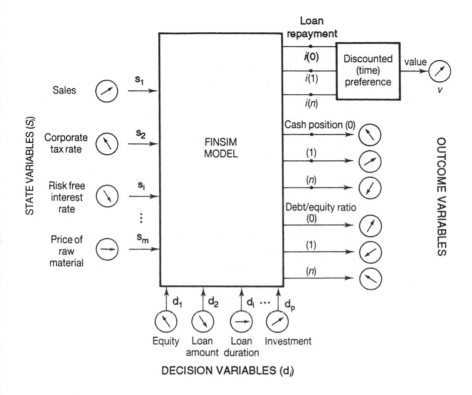

Figure 3.14 *Deterministic model for a long-term loan within the FINSIM application*

(S_i) could be the value, over the lending period of the loan, of the activity level of the company (sales of goods, sales of services and so on), the risk free interest rate, the income tax rate and so on. The decision variables (d_i) are the characteristics of the loan: the loan amount, duration, repayment schedule, interest level and so on. The *outcome* variables are the self-financing capacity of the company to repay the loan (something like the future stream of profit plus depreciation), the flow of interest paid to the bank, the debt to equity ratio at the end of each period (a global measure of risk for the banker), the cash position of the company at the end of each period and so on.

The values developed over time by the model (for example, a stream of interest or profits) are transformed by the time preference function to produce a present value (or worth) v, which is displayed on a present value meter.

Analysis

The analysis which is performed on a deterministic model has several goals:

- To refine the formulation of the problem.
- To generate alternatives and compute criteria for evaluation (values of outcomes) transformed by preference over time, that is, worth.

The analysis is based on the observation of changes in worth due to changes in variables. This type of analysis is well known under the name of *sensitivity analysis*.

The first type of sensitivity analysis is performed on decision variables. The decision maker sets the state variables at their nominal value and then allows one of the decision variables to move in its assigned range and observes how its worth changes. If a particular decision variable has a major effect, then the decision maker knows he or she was correct in including it in the original formulation. On the contrary, if a decision variable has little or no effect, the decision maker is justified in removing it as a decision variable.

The second type of sensitivity analysis is performed on state variables, which are considered to be uncertain by the decision maker, and over which he or she has no control. All other system variables being at their nominal value, the change in worth is observed while sweeping one state variable over its range. If a state variable has a major effect, then the uncertainty in the variable deserves special attention. Such variables are called *aleatory variables*. However, if varying a state variable over its range produces only a minor change in worth, then that variable might well be fixed at its nominal value. The state variable has become a fixated variable.

> 'A state variable may become fixated either because it has an important influence on the worth per unit of its range, but an extremely small range, or because it has little influence on the worth per unit of its range, even though it has a broad range.' (Howard and Matheson, 1968)

There is no reason to conclude that a fixated variable is unimportant in an absolute sense. The corporate tax rate, for example, can be regarded as a fixated variable because the decision maker has no reason to believe it will change over the time period that is considered. Yet, it is possible that a change in government policy could lead to a large change in this variable, which would transform a favorable venture into an unfavorable one.

One difficult problem is raised by *simultaneous* changes in state variables, since the possibility of jointly changing state variables grows rapidly with the number of state variables.

We can suggest how this methodology can be used in the case of a long-term loan decision that is made by the loan officer in a bank. Our hypothesis here is that the loan is issued to the company in order to increase its production capacity. We shall use the FINSIM model (Klein, 1989) but we shall not describe in detail all of the system variables which are represented by that model.

The basic idea of the model is that it should support the decision process of the loan officer by helping him or her to compute the future values of the variable such as: the cash position, over the duration of the loan, of the company that is asking for a loan (*cash t*), the discounted amount of interest paid by the company to the bank for the duration of the loan, the debt equity ratio and so on. The cash position can be computed utilizing a uses and sources of funds statement which gives the cash flow for the period.

The decision for the loan officer is whether he or she should grant a loan or not: in other words, should the investment be financed or not. In fact, the number of alternatives can be much larger if we wish to consider different types of loans, we shall, for the sake of simplification, consider here only one type. The alternatives facing the loan officer can be generated using the FINSIM model. If the loan is granted, the state variables have to be fixed in accordance with this alternative (in particular, the value of the sales variable and of expense variables have to be coherent with the investment which, in our case, is expected to increase the sales). The decision variables are fixed at their nominal amount. The model will then be used to compute the outcomes of interest for the decision maker which are:

- The loan repayment schedule (interest + plus capital) received by the bank over the duration of the loan.
- The cash position of the company at the end of each period.
- The debt/equity ratio of the company at the end of each period.

The loan repayment schedule will be discounted using a time preference model since it is an important decision criterion for the loan officer. The bank should earn a return for the loan which is higher than the return the bank would receive from an investment in a risk-free asset (government bonds, for example). The cash position of the company is a fundamental outcome. The credit officer wants to check that this variable is positive over the duration of the loan. If it is not, then there is a risk of the company defaulting in its payments. Other important outcomes for the loan officer are the level of debt to equity ratio, if he or she wishes to make a global measure of risk and, also, a 'quick' ratio if he or she wishes to make a short-term measure of risk. The loan officer may not want the debt/equity ratio to go beyond a certain limit, since beyond that limit there is an increase in global risk which he or she may not want to take. The loan officer can now perform a sensitivity analysis. He or she can consider that the estimates of the sales projections, which have been given to him by the company, to be the best known estimates, and the value of the three main outcomes can be completed: the discounted flow of interest, the cash position over the duration of the loan, the global debt/equity rates. The loan can be granted if the following decision rules hold:

- The discounted value of cash flow associated with the loan should be positive.
- The cash position should be positive at the end of each period.
- The debt/equity ratio should be below one over the duration of the loan.

If the loan officer is uncertain about the values of the sales estimates, it will be easy to make sensitivity analyses on the sales growth rate given the investment that is to be undertaken. If the above criteria are fulfilled, and the sales growth rate goes down to 10% instead of the 20% which was expected by the company, as a first hypothesis, and the loan officer has good reason to consider that a growth rate of less than 10% has a probability of almost nil, then the decision is, clearly, to make the loan. In the case where one of the outcomes does not fulfill the conditions fixed in the decision rules when the sensitivity analysis is performed on sales growth rate, then a conclusion cannot be reached without going to the next phase, which is the probabilistic phase.

The Probabilistic Phase

The purpose of the deterministic sensitivity analysis on the state variables is to divide them into aleatory and fixated classes, and to determine which state variables are the most critical in causing an alternative to be preferred to another. The probabilistic phase determines the uncertainty in value and worth due to the aleatory variables.

Modeling probability distribution

'The first modeling step in the probabilistic phase is the assignment of probability distributions to the aleatory (stochastic) variables. Either the decision-maker or someone that he or she designates must assign the probability that each aleatory variable will exceed any given value. If any set of aleatory variables is dependent, in the sense that knowledge of one would provide information about the others, then the probability assignment on any one variable must be conditional on the value of the others.' (Howard and Matheson, 1968)

Analysis

Since the deterministic model gives the relation between worth and the state variables, and since we have assigned probability distributions to aleatory variables, it is possible to compute the probability distribution of worth for any setting of the decision variables. This probability distribution is called the 'worth lottery'.

> 'The worth lottery describes the uncertainty in worth that results from the probability assignments to the aleatory variables for any given alternative (setting of decision variables). Of course the values of the fixated variables are never changed.' (Howard and Matheson, 1968)

To select a course of action, the analyst will generate a worth lottery for each alternative and then select the one that is the more desirable.

Howard uses the bracket notation $\{\vartheta | \vec{d}, \varsigma\}$ to denote a probability distribution of value ϑ given the decision vector $\vec{d}$ and the prior state of information ς. The brackets are also used for the probability assignments to the state variables.

Modeling risk preference

If stochastic dominance has not determined the best alternative, the decision analyst must formalize the risk preference of the decision maker. Decision methodology will then request that we encode the risk preference. Decision analysis uses, at this point, the theory of cardinal utility which we have outlined in Section 3.3.3.

The risk preference of the decision maker can be represented as a utility curve as shown on Figure 3.10. This curve assigns a utility to any value of worth. As we have seen, the utility curve provides a practical method of incorporating risk preference into the model. When faced with a choice between two alternatives whose worth lotteries do not exhibit stochastic dominance, the analyst computes the expected utility of each and chooses the one with the highest expected utility. By using the utility curve, the analyst can see what worth corresponds to this expected utility. This quantity is called the 'certain equivalent worth of the worth lottery'. The name 'certain equivalent' comes from the idea that the certain equivalent worth of any lottery is the amount of worth received for certain, so that the decision maker is indifferent between receiving this worth or participating in the lottery (see Figure 3.5). The best alternative is the one whose lottery has the highest certain equivalent worth (see the MEU action axiom in Section 3.3.3).

Analysis

The first step is to compute the certain equivalent worth of each of the alternatives. Then the alternative with the highest certain equivalent worth is selected. In fact, Howard and Matheson (1968) point out that a careful analyst would not stop there, but would perform sensitivity analysis on:

- decision variables,
- aleatory (stochastic) variables,
- risk.

By setting all of the decision variables but one at their nominal values, and then sweeping this one decision variable through its range, the analyst may find that although this variation changes the worth lottery it does not significantly change the certain equivalent worth. Then the decision variable would be fixed at its nominal value.

Aleatory variables receive the same sensitivity analysis by setting one of the aleatory variables to a trial value within its range, and the other aleatory variables have the appropriate conditional joint probability distribution when all decision variables are set to their nominal value. The model will then give a certain equivalent worth for the trial value. By sweeping the trial value of the stochastic variable over its range the analyst can observe the change in the certain equivalent worth. If this change is small, there is evidence that this aleatory variable can be changed to a fixated variable. This procedure is called measurement of *stochastic sensitivity*. According to Howard and Matheson (1968) the decision to remove variables from aleatory status on the basis of deterministic sensitivity might be reviewed by measurement of stochastic sensitivity. He also points out that it is possible to test sensitivity of many variables simultaneously. Measurement of stochastic sensitivity appears in the methodology as a powerful tool for locating important variables of a problem and, as a consequence, as a method to focus attention and to validate the model.

The last kind of sensitivity analysis available at this point of analysis of the problem is *risk sensitivity*. As we have seen in Section 3.3.3 it is possible to characterize the utility curve by a single number: which is called the risk aversion constant. When this is possible, the risk aversion constant measures the willingness of the decision maker to accept a risk.

If two people share the responsibility for a decision, the less risk tolerant will assign a lower certainty equivalent worth for any given worth lottery than the other will.

'The measurement of risk sensitivity determines how the certainty equivalent worths of the most favorable alternative depends on the risk aversion constant.' (Howard and Matheson, 1968)

An example of application of the analysis methodology to the FINSIM model is given in Figure 3.15. The environmental variables are: sales growth rate, risk free interest rate, raw material price. The decision variables are: the equity financing the amount of the loan, the duration of the loan, the interest rate and the amount of the investment. A distribution of the environmental variable is encoded by the decision maker. FINSIM will then produce distributions for the decision variables: interest on loan, cash position, debt/equity ratio.

As can be seen, the best alternative in the problem is derived from the combination of:

- the problem structure,
- the set of alternatives generated,
- the probability assignments to aleatory variables,
- the value assessments,
- the time preference assessment,
- the risk preference.

The overall procedure is presented in Figure 3.16 (from Howard and Matheson, 1968)

Informational Phase

The goal of this phase is to help the decision maker decide if it is worthwhile to engage in a possibly expensive information gathering activity before making a decision. One possible result of this experimental design procedure is the decision to perform no experiment at all.

Analysis

The fundamental idea in the information phase is that of placing a monetary value on additional information. The concept used here is the idea of perfect information which Howard and Matheson (1968) call 'clairvoyance'. The decision analyst assumes that he can get from a 'clairvoyant' the value of a given aleatory variable. The question is: how much should be paid in order to get this information? To answer this question, recall that the discussion of stochastic sensitivity described how to compute the certain equivalent worth given that an

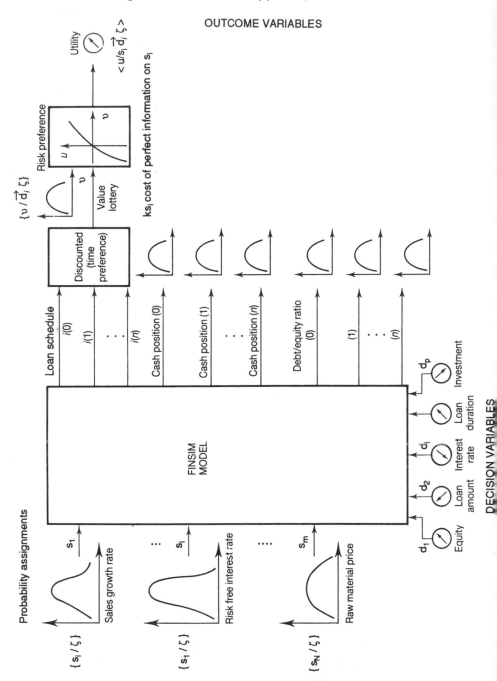

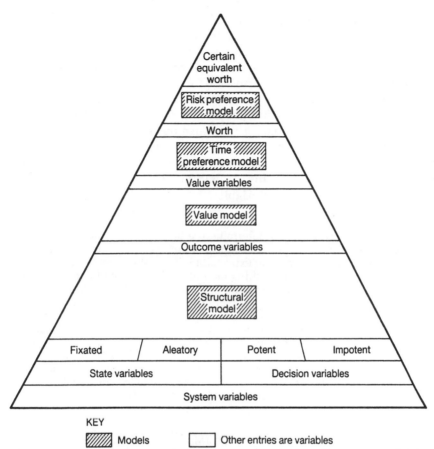

Figure 3.16 *The decision analysis hierarchy. (Reproduced from Howard R.A. and Matheson J.E. (1968).* An Introduction to Decision Analysis. *Stanford Research Institute)*

aleatory variable took on a value say, *s* in this case. In that procedure, the decision variables were set equal to their best values from the probabilistic phase. Suppose now that we engage the clairvoyant at a cost *k*, and then he or she tells us that the aleatory variable will take on the value *s*.

First of all, we would set the decision variables to take best advantage of this information. However, since the other aleatory variables are still uncertain, they would be described by the appropriate distributions, given the available information. The computer program would then determine the expected utility of the entire decision problem including the payment to the clairvoyant, which are all conditional on him or her reporting the value of *s*.

The process of measuring the value of perfect information is called the measurement of *economic sensitivity*. Clearly, if an aleatory variable exhibits high economic sensitivity, it is a good candidate for an information gathering program. Information gathering programs seldom provide perfect information, so we should not use them for the value of perfect information. An experimental program will provide only a new probability distribution for the aleatory variable under study. In the FINSIM case, it may turn out that the cash position is very sensitive to the price of raw material, or to the sales growth rate, in which case the loan analyst can decide to see if he or she can obtain information to improve his or her knowledge of the probability distribution of these two variables.

'The analyst would then determine the best decision, given this new information, and compute the expected utility of the decision problem. He would next multiply the expected utility by the probability that the experimental program would come out in this way and sum over all possible outcomes of the experimental program. The result would be the expected utility of the experimental program at a given cost. The cost that would make the expected utility just equal to the expected utility of the problem without the experimental program would be the value of the experimental program. If the value is positive, it represents the maximum that one should pay for the program. If the value is negative, it means that the experimental program is expected to be unprofitable. Consequently, even though it would provide useful information, it would not be conducted.' (Howard and Matheson, 1968)

Modeling

At this stage, the decision maker and the decision analyst must identify the relevant information gathering alternatives, from survey to laboratory experiment, and find which, if any, are expected to make a profitable contribution to the decision problem.

It is important in considering alternatives for information gathering to take into account the negative effect of delay in making the primary decision. In the FINSIM case, if the banker is an investment banker and is studying whether or not he or she should take a partnership in the company, he or she may want to carry out a market study in order to check how the new product that he or she might finance is going to perform. But by doing this time may be lost and the probability of competing products improving their market share will increase.

When the preferred information gathering program is performed, it will lead, at least, to new probability assignments on the aleatory variables; it might also result in the structure of the model being changed. Still studying the FINSIM case, it may turn out that sales cannot be analyzed properly unless they are broken down by main lines of product, which will mean that the analyst must include new variables.

When all of the changes implied by the information program have been incorporated into the model, the deterministic and probabilistic phases are repeated to check sensitivity. So the decision analyst inserts loops in the process and, at some point, the cost of gathering further information will be more than its worth and the alternative which currently has the highest certain equivalent worth should be selected.

3.3.7 Recent Progress with the Decision Analysis Cycle

In a TIMS/ORSA address in 1986 Ronald Howard presented a paper later published in *Management Science* (Howard, 1988) where he introduced a revised version of the decision analysis cycle. This process taken up by Holtzman is presented in Fig 3.1. We have seen in Section 3.1.3 that this process has three steps. The first step is the description of a formal model of the decision maker real decision situation which Howard calls the 'decision basis'.

The second step is the evaluation of the decision situation by a computation procedure which produces the alternative that is logically consistent with the basis and is therefore recommended.

The last step is the appraisal of the analysis to gain insight into the recommended alternative and check that the recommended alternative is not only correct but clearly persuasive.

In his paper Howard introduced the concept of decision quality to evaluate any decision process. The criteria of decision quality are the following:

- decision framing
- decision basis
- integration and evaluation with logic
- balance of basis
- commitment to action.

Decision framing is related with the fundamental question of knowing if the proper problem is being analyzed. Decision basis is considering three main questions. What is the quality of the information we base our decision upon? Do we consider significantly different alternatives? Are our values clearly stated?

The pertinence and difference between alternatives is a question of creativity. The question of value is a fundamental one.

Ralph Keeney shows in his book *Value Focus Thinking* (Keeney, 1993) the importance of values for:

- guiding strategic thinking
- uncovering hidden objectives
- identifying decision opportunities
- creating alternatives.

Integration and evaluation with logic has been the most explored question. The problem is to avoid logical errors and to follow the correct procedure to select the right alternative.

The 'balance of basis' step studies the allocation of efforts between: improving the quality of information, spending time generating new alternatives or thinking about values.

Finally we wish to make sure that the right course of action is sufficiently clearly indicated and communicated to the decision maker so that he develops a clear commitment to action. In case the decision maker cannot make up his or her mind to act then it can only be a problem of lack of will and not a lack of clear and persuasive recommendation.

Two last interesting points of R. Howard in this paper are that he considers that the combination of decision tree methodology and spread sheet would be an important progress and that he suggests the development of 'Intelligent Decision Support System' following the idea of Holtzman. We shall deal more with this question in Chapter 11.

3.4 DSS FOR SUPPORTING THE NORMATIVE POINT OF VIEW

3.4.1 Decision Tree Compilers

Decision analysts have developed several systems to automate part of the decision analysis process. The first such software were decision tree 'compilers' such as SUPERTREE© (Olmsted, 1982; McNamee and Celona, 1987), ARBRE© (Pezier and Klein, 1973). Then software systems to support the task of defining, checking and evaluating influence diagrams were developed (Korsan and Matheson, 1978; Merkchofer and Leof, 1981) and Holtzman (1989). We shall see in Chapter 6 that the methodology of decision analysis can take advantage of recent developments in the field of expert systems to give birth to a new kind of decision support environment, including a better support of the normative point of view. This point will be expanded in Chapter 11.

3.4.2 Interactive Influence Diagram Formulation and Solving

Holtzman (1989) describes a development environment for 'goal-directed generation' of an influence diagram. The influence diagram is considered as an evolving model whose progress reflects changes in how the decision maker perceives the world. Two tendencies are always present in this process, on the one hand the decision maker wishes to *expand* the diagram in order to increase the accuracy and comprehensiveness of the representation that embodies. On the other hand, the decision maker wishes to *reduce* the diagram to make it more intuitively appealing and more computationally manageable. The other functions must be able to:

- *check* the diagram for mathematical correctness as the development effort proceeds;
- *evaluate* the influence diagram as it progresses.

Once a formal decision model has been defined, and an evaluation algorithm is available, it is possible to compute a strategy. As seen in Section 3.1.3 such a strategy needs to be appraised (that is, interpreted in terms of reality). To appraise a strategy we need to ask two types of questions about the features of the model and about how the model was developed. As we have seen important features of the model are: sensitivity to model variables, profit lotteries and value of information measurement on its uncertain variables. Holtzman calls obtaining information about these features 'mining the model'.

The question about how the model was developed is related to the reasoning that led to the specific model being used. In order to develop an intuitive understanding of a model's recommendation, a decision maker needs to *justify* that model.

> 'Justifying a model differs from mining it in that the desired information is extralogical (that is, not contained within the model itself). The information needed to justify a model lies primarily in the methodological decisions and trade-offs made to construct it and in the theory (if any) that underlies the methodology.' (Holtzman, 1989)

The development environment proposed by Holtzman to promote the construction of a valid decision model consists of an interactive composition of six tasks: expansion, reduction, checking, evaluation, mining and justification. Holtzman stresses the point that no rigid order should be imposed on applying these tasks within the formulation process. Apart from the environment available at the company Strategic Decision Group (SDG), other belief net compilors are now on the market. The ERGO software from Noetic Systems is an other example.

3.5 THE RELEVANCE OF THE NORMATIVE POINT OF VIEW IN DSS

A very strong argument in favor of the normative point of view is that it gives the decision maker a methodology: that is, a series of steps to follow, as a guide, to reaching a decision. This methodology is very useful at the *conceptual* level but also as a guide in *designing* computerized decision support systems. Outcome variables, value functions, value variables, time preference functions, worth (utility of money, present value of money), risk preference functions (utility functions) and certain equivalent are all important concepts. The decision analysis cycle is a very fundamental process to guide the decision maker from the certainty model to the probabilistic one, as well as to guide him or her in the methodology of preference and knowledge encoding.

The central concept of the decision methodology maybe is the concept of a decision maker maximizing his or her Subjective Expected Utility (the SEU theory). The major intellectual achievement of the SEU theory is that it provides a formally axiomatized statement of what it means for an individual to behave in a consistent, rational manner.

With respect to the design of a computerized decision support development environment it is clear that the environment should provide:

- A language to structure a problem in the form of a deterministic model.
- A possibility to make different sensitivity analyses on the variables of the model.
- The possibility to convert deterministic variables into probabilistic ones (to move from deterministic to a probabilistic model).
- The possibility to perform probability calculus (Bayes's theorem).
- A language to structure a problem in the form of a decision tree or, better, an influence diagram.
- Software to encode risk and time preference for multi-attribute functions.
- Software to encode knowledge on variables (probability elicitation).
- A solver to evaluate the influence diagram or decision tree and select the best alternative.

3.6 NORMATIVE THEORIES FOR GROUP DECISION MAKING

Attempts have been made to apply decision theory to organizations. As we have seen, the decision methodology requires that the decision maker expresses a preference order on alternatives and encode his or her knowledge in the form of probabilities. When dealing with organizations and, as a consequence with groups, it is much more difficult to define what the group preferences are. The immediate answer is the method of majority voting. Unfortunately, the majority rule does not lead to a clear-cut group preference as shown originally by the French mathematician Condorcet (1785).

If we consider a group of three people, Michael, Frances and Emma, and they all wish to go on vacation together, there are three alternatives: to go to the mountains (m), to the seaside (s) or on a cruise (c). Their preferences can be displayed as:

$$\text{Michael } m > s > c$$
$$\text{Frances } s > c > m$$
$$\text{Emma } c > m > s$$

If a decision is taken by a vote we can have the following results: Frances and Emma vote in favor of a cruise over a holiday in the mountains, Michael and Frances vote to choose between the seaside and a cruise, and they are two to one in favor of the seaside. Michael, who is not very pleased with this result, suggests that a vote should be made in order to choose between the seaside and the mountains.

The vote on this last alternative results in a majority for the mountains, which were ruled out at first. Thus, by using majority voting the group prefers the mountains to the seaside, the seaside to a cruise but also a cruise to the mountains.

This result, known as the 'Condorcet paradox', shows that if each member of a group displays consistent views, it is perfectly possible for the decisions of the group to be inconsistent. In the above case, majority voting leads to a non-transitive set of preferences.

Since majority voting is not a satisfactory method for determining group preference, it is natural to ask 'what method is satisfactory then?'. This question was studied by Arrow (1951) and the answer came in an astonishing theorem known as 'Arrow's impossibility theorem': there is no satisfactory method.

Arrow established four reasonable conditions that he felt would be fulfilled by a procedure for determining a group's preferences between a set of options, as a function of the preferences of the group members. Arrow's conditions can be stated as follows:†

(1) Whatever the preferences of the group members, the method must produce a group preference order for the options being compared.

† (Reproduced from *Social Choice and Individual Values* by Arrow K.J. © 1951, reprinted by permission of John Wiley & Sons, Inc.)

(2) If every member of the group prefers option *A* to option *B*, then the group must also prefer *A* to *B*.
(3) The group choice between two options, *A* and *B*, depends only on the preferences of the group members between *A* and *B*, and not on their preferences between *A* and *B* and any other option.
(4) There is no dictator; no individual always gets his way.

Arrow proved that there is no aggregation procedure which satisfies these four conditions. It should be noted, however, that Arrow's result is concerned with the combination of preference orders, and does not use the intensity of preferences of individuals nor interpersonal comparisons of utility. The interested reader can consult Harsanyi (1977) for an in depth treatment of interpersonal comparisons of intensity of preference into account.

As a conclusion we can say that there is still no satisfactory quantitative method for determining group preferences by some mathematical operation on the expressed preferences of individuals.

3.7 CRITICISM OF THE NORMATIVE POINT OF VIEW

As we have seen in the preceding sections, the body of prescriptive knowledge about decision making is well developed. This chapter is a summary of the main concepts and the associated methodology, but anybody who has had a look through the literature on this subject is likely to be impressed by the quality and generality of the concepts and methods associated with decision analysis.

If we start looking for applications of this decision methodology we find interesting cases, such as the ones described by Howard *et al*. (1983) for strategic management decisions, by Tribus (1969) for engineering decisions and by Holtzman (1989) for medical decisions and so on, but it would be difficult to argue that the methodology is in widespread use in organizations, nearly twenty years after it was worked out. There are several reasons why this situation has arisen:

(1) The concepts are not easy to grasp and to put to work.
(2) There is no adequate low-cost support software to help implement the methodology.
(3) The concepts themselves are not consistent with reality.

3.7.1 Refinement and Complexity of the Concepts of Decision Analysis

The decision maker who is willing to use decision analysis must have mastered the following concepts:

- Model building (the relation between system variables and outcomes).
- Transforming outcomes into values.
- Subjective and objective probability distribution (simple and marginal).
- Updating prior probability with new information (Bayes's theorem).
- Preference function (for risk and time).
- The concept of a lottery to encode risk preference.

It is clear that such a methodology is not for people who have difficulty in formalizing things! A good understanding of the difference between outcome and value, of the Bayes's theorem and so on, implies that the decision maker has some education and an ability to think in rigorous and abstract terms. We have to recognize that these concepts are not well known by the immense majority of decision makers, even after they have been introduced in the curriculum of many graduate Business Schools.

3.7.2 Inexistence of Low-cost Support Software to Implement the Methodology.

We have seen in Section 3.5 that the implementation of the decision analysis methodology requires computer programs. There have been several attempts to market software, such as decision tree or influence diagram compilers. However, this software has been rather expensive and has only sold in limited numbers. It is interesting to note that we have seen, with the personal computer, a wide distribution of simple decision support software, mainly used for deterministic modeling (such as the spreadsheet, or DSS development tools), but there is no wide distribution of decision analysis software, the only exception maybe of multi-criteria methods. We shall see in Chapters 6 and 11 that these attempts may be developed further in the near future.

3.7.3 Pertinence of the Theory

The descriptive view of decision making (Chapter 2) demonstrates that people solve problems by 'selective, heuristic search through large problem spaces and large data bases, using means-ends analysis as a principal technique for guiding the search' (Simon *et al.*, 1987). In other words, the empirical research puts the emphasis on the limit of human rationality.

'These limits are imposed by the complexity of the world in which we live, the incompleteness and inadequacy of human knowledge, the inconsistency of individual preference and belief, the conflicts of value among people and groups of people, and the inadequacy of the computation we can run out.' (Simon *et al.*, 1987)

On the other hand, the normative view assumes that:

'A decision maker possessed a utility function (an ordering by preference among all the possible outcomes of choice), that all the alternatives among which choice could be made were known, and that the consequences of choosing each alternative could be ascertained (or, in the version of the theory that treats of choice under uncertainty, it assumed that a subjective or objective probability distribution of consequences was associated with each alternative).' (Simon *et al.*, 1987)

3.7.4   Limits of Rationality and Biases in Human Decision Making

The decision analysis methodology makes a high demand on information. In the FINSIM model described above, we must compute the consequences for each alternative. These consequences are variables associated with a probability distribution. These probability distributions (value lotteries) have to be transformed into utilities. We have then, in the case of a multi-attribute decision problem, to convert the utilities into a single number through a multi-attribute utility function. Also, we have exogenous variables to be given probability assessments. To perform the complete cycle of formal decision analysis is a formidable task that most people do not have the skill, the computational power or the time to do.

After the normative theories of decisions had been developed, psychologists began asking whether human decision making conformed to these theories. Could they be used as descriptive theories? Several experiments were performed and we shall recapitulate the results of these studies in three important areas: the perception of uncertainty, subjective expected utility, and judgment. In so doing, we shall follow closely the review of Watson and Buede (1987).

Uncertainty

In 1971, Amos Tversky and Daniel Kahneman published the first of a series of papers on biases that they observed in peoples' judgment of uncertainty (see Kahneman *et al.* 1987). Their studies show that people rely on a limited number of heuristic principles, which reduce the complex task of assessing probabilities. However, these simple heuristics sometimes lead to systematic and severe errors. Here are three heuristic strategies that people commonly use in judgment and decision making (see Kahneman *et al.* 1982):

Representativeness heuristic.   Many of the probabilistic questions with which people are concerned belong to one of the following types: What is the probability that object *A* belongs to class *B*, or that the event *A* originates from process *B*? In answering such questions people rely on representativeness heuristics, in which probabilities are evaluated by the degree to which *A* is *representative* of *B*.

Availability heuristic.   There are situations in which people assess the frequency of a class by the ease with which instances can be brought to mind.

Adjustment and anchoring heuristic.   People make estimates by starting from an initial value that is adjusted to yield the final answer. There is a systematic tendency to underestimate adjustments and to be biased toward the initial value. This tendency is called *anchoring*.

Heuristics are necessary for efficient human problem solving as we have seen in Section 2.5.2. We have to be careful in applying heuristics and to avoid heuristics that violate normative theories. These findings demonstrate a fundamental failure in human judgmental abilities. However, considerable criticism has been raised about the generalization of the results (Edwards, 1983).

Subjective Expected Utility

Central to the normative theories of decision making has been the concept of *subjective expected utility*. Therefore, the next question that attracted the psychologists' interest was: do decision makers maximize expected utility when they face uncertainty? The answer is no; we do not conform to the principle of subjective expected utility. All of the experiments that have been performed show that people prefer to gamble on options for which probabilities are more clearly established (Shoemaker, 1980). Tversky and Kahneman (1981), in yet another sequence of experiments, demonstrated that choices between uncertain options can depend on the way that the problem is *framed*. The decision maker will need aids to overcome biases in evaluating uncertain options, in the same way as for the biases in the perception of uncertainty.

Judgment

Does our representation of preferences or value judgment follow the prescriptions of the normative theories? Does real decision making conform to multi-attribute value theory? Again, the answer is no. In buying a car, for instance, one may first look for candidates within a certain price range, and then use other criteria, in sequence, to discriminate among these candidates until the final choice is made. In other words, one concentrates on one attribute only, and only brings others into play if the options are equally good with respect to that attribute. This is the *satisficing choice* behavior described by Simon (1960). It is easy to see that it is not possible to create a value function that is consistent with this choice behavior. For further discussion on this topic, see Hogarth (1980) and Fischoff *et al.* (1982).

3.7.5   Limited Rationality in Economic Theory

Empirical studies which we have described in Chapter 2 point out that managers are trying to achieve the firm's market share in the industry, rather than trying to maximize profit. New work is being done which still assumes that decision makers seek to maximize utility, but within limits imposed by the incompleteness and uncertainty of the information available to them. In other words, decision makers are seeking to reach specified aspiration levels (satisficing) for goals instead of maximizing them. Empirical studies also seem to point out that economic agents do not follow assumptions made in the decision methodology theory. For example, decision makers tend to overreact to new information in violation of Bayes's rule. The same idea is conveyed by recent studies which tend to demonstrate that stock prices fluctuate up and down more rapidly and violently than they would if the market were purely rational.

However, we should be careful to acknowledge that a promoter of decision analysis would argue that his or her main task is not just to clarify a decision as a function of the decision maker's criteria and preferences, but also to guide him or her towards more rigorous thinking. In other words, if empirical studies point out that decision makers are not coherent in certain situations, it does not mean that they should not be helped to become conscious of these incoherences in the hope that they will change their mind.

3.7.6   Time Constraints

Time is involved in decision making in many ways. Usually through the time preference of a decision maker. However, the subjective expected utility theory assumes a fixed and consistent utility function. It is known that preference changes with time. The answer of the decision analyst should be fairly easy: nothing prevents him or her from updating the risk aversion parameter, for example, as it changes with time.

A much more difficult problem arises when decisions have to be taken within time constraints. In such cases, it may not be possible to go through the complete decision analysis cycle. The decision maker may need rules which will help very bad outcomes to be avoided or help him or her to reach a level which he or she considers satisfactory but which is far from maximizing the expected utility. We shall see, in Chapter 6, how such an approach can be implemented.

3.7.7 The Ethical Point of View

We would like here to point out that it is usually recognized that there are two types of answers to the question of what the most reasonable course of action is.

- One type is made of theories about *economic rationality*, (maximizing subjective expected utility).
- The other is made of *moral* or *ethical* theories.

The problem is that when we apply these two classes of theories to some given decisions, we often have different answers (we all know that a sound economic decision may be a moral disaster), so we have to decide which theory we wish to follow or how we can take ethical principles into account in any rationally taken decision.

Three main factors are usually considered in order to determine how we look at human conduct from the moral or ethical point of view. The first factor is that we are not alone, but we live in a society and, as a consequence, are confronted by other people who have their own aims and goals, as we do. The second factor is that we live in a world of scarcity. Theft and waste do not matter if there is no limit to the goods available. The third factor is inequality. Even if the division of goods and services was made with perfect equality, in a few days trade, bargaining and different rates of consumption and waste will produce inequality. The problem is to make certain that the unequal distribution of goods and services is not unfair. Equal opportunity to gain advantages is, therefore, a natural provision that must be sought and built into the principle that governs ethical decision making.

The characteristic of a person who looks at his or her life from the moral point of view is that he or she regards him or herself as morally responsible, a creature who is responsible for their actions. Two extreme types of moral behavior can be observed. The first is the nihilist who abdicates all responsibilities on the grounds that nothing matters – we are all in the hands of Fate or God and we have no control over anything, not even our own conduct. Such a person cannot perform any ethical decision making (nor any rational decision making). The other extreme type is the bureaucrat, who dodges responsibility, wherever possible, by acting so that someone else determines how he or she acts and also determines the reasoning for his or her behavior.

The basic problem for ethical decision making is to ensure fair treatment of all concerned, given the fact that there is an irreducible plurality of independent persons to be considered with distinctive and occasionally conflicting and competing interest and rights, situated in a world between extreme scarcity (in which no one's needs could be satisfied) and unlimited resources (in which everyone's whims could be satisfied). So, when a person makes a decision on the grounds of ethics it means that ethical principles are used, and that had he or she not relied on such ethical principles the reason for deciding upon something different would have been due to some other principle such as business efficiency, self interest and so on.

One example of such ethical principle is the following: 'everything possible must be done to avoid causing the innocent to suffer even in a just cause'.

One important question is clearly the objectivity of ethics. 'Are some ethical judgments true and others false?' Most ethical philosophers deny the fact that ethical judgment is a matter of personal preference, opinion or test. They are more likely to claim that ethical decision making can be a rational and objective discipline. This assumption is very important since, if this assumption is not granted, then ethical decision making becomes impossible, or arbitrary, or it turns into something else, such as self interest. The interest in ethics as a discipline is derived from the assumption that not all moral principles and ethical judgments are equally sound.

One very interesting point for us is the following. It seems that people who follow their self interest can be led to contradiction. We would like to refer, here, to the work of philosophers such as Derek Parfit. In his book *Reasons and Persons* (1968) Parfit defines the self interest theory, or *S*, in the following way:

> S: for each person, there is one supremely rational ultimate aim: that life goes for him or her as well as possible.

As can be noticed, the *S* theory is about rationality. Then Parfit introduces the self defeating idea. This idea is that a theory which fails, even in its own terms and thus condemns itself, is self defeating. Parfit shows that some of the best-known self interest theories are, in certain ways, self defeating.

Exercises

3.1   What does it mean to be rational?

3.2   What methodology is useful for utilizing formal decision methods?

3.3   What are the reasons for studying formal decision methods when designing DSS?

3.4   What are the validity conditions of a formal decision method?

3.5   What is the role of an 'action axiom' in a formal decision method?

3.6   Frances has a job decision to take. She has been offered four jobs. The criteria she is considering are: starting salary, promotion opportunity, location and interest of the job. She is following a course in decision analysis and has structured her decision with the criteria, values and weights shown in Table 3.4.

   (a) Assuming that all pairs of criteria are preference independent of the other criteria, which job maximizes Frances's value function?

   (b) If Frances changes her weight for the criteria so that starting salary has a weight of 0.2 and promotion opportunity a weight of 0.4, does the job with the highest value change?

   (c) Do either of these results change if job C is removed from the list?

Table 3.4   *Table of criteria, values and weights for a job decision*

Job	Starting salary	Promotion opportunity	Location	Interest of the job
A	100	0	20	60
B	65	100	0	40
C	30	65	100	0
D	0	25	75	100
Weights	0.4	0.2	0.1	0.3

3.7   Select a decision problem of concern to you, such as the choice of a job, or of a vacation destination, and apply the method of multi-attribute analysis to help you think through it (from Watson and Buede).

3.8 We have two bags containing red and blue marbles. One bag contains 70 red marbles and 30 blue marbles, the other bag contains 70 blue marbles and 30 red ones. You select, at random, one bag (it is not possible to distinguish their content) and you pick 12 marbles (putting them back each time), eight red marbles and four blue marbles are picked.

What is the probability for this bag to be the one with 70 red marbles and 30 blue ones? (direct application of the Bayes's theorem).

3.9 In the new cosmetic product case should we consider the proposal made by a market research company who are offering to conduct a more thorough market study: at a cost of $100 000?

$$p(I_i/R_1)=0.8$$
$$p(I_2/R_2)=0.9$$

Study the sensitivity of the strategy to change in the 'a priori' probability to obtain a good market.

3.10 Show that the additivity axiom implies the use of an exponential utility curve

4
Decision Support Systems

4.1 REQUIREMENT FOR DECISION SUPPORT

4.1.1 Origin of DSS Research: Ill-structured Decision Processes and Man–machine Cooperation in Problem Solving

The origin of DSS as a domain of study and research can be traced back to the end of the 1960s. Historically the field of DSS seems to have emerged from the study of ill-structured problems which we have described in Chapter 2. Initial research work was published by researchers at the Sloan School of Management at the Massachusetts Institute of Technology, the Harvard Business School in the USA, and at the Business School HEC in France.

The concept of a 'management decision system' was described by Scott Morton (1971) in his thesis entitled 'Management decision systems: computer based support for decision making'.

Several professors of the marketing department of the Sloan School published, at the end of the 1960s, some important papers that viewed DSS applied to marketing from a conceptual point of view. The well-known paper of John D. C. Little (1970) on decision calculus was important, with respect to the DSS approach, to solving management decision problems. The concept of DSS, as applied to marketing, was developed by Little and his ideas published several years later (Little, 1979). Even earlier, David B. Montgomery and Glen L. Urban in their book *Management Science in Marketing* (1969), had introduced the concept of decision information systems within a framework including a data bank, a model bank, and a statistical bank, and had stressed the importance of the man–system interaction. However, these works were mainly concerned with marketing information systems and marketing models and not with the design of DSS software itself.

Another interesting work of the same period was the thesis of Gerrity (1970) which concentrated on the design of man–machine decision systems. The methodology developed was applied to portfolio management as described in Gerrity (1971).

At approximately the same time, work was also going on at the Tuck School of Business Administration of Dartmouth College. Several interesting interactive models had been developed by professors of the Finance Department, mainly in financial planning (Carleton, 1970), portfolio performance measurement, Bower (1969) and Williamson (1970), and bank management.

A study of the origin of DSS has still to be written. It seems that the first DSS papers were published by PhD students or professors in business schools, who had access to the first time-sharing computer system: Project MAC at the Sloan School, the Dartmouth Time Sharing Systems at the Tuck School. In France, HEC was the first French business school to have a time-sharing system (installed in 1967), and the first DSS papers were published by professors of the School in 1970.

The term SIAD ('Système Interactif d'Aide à la Décision' the French term for DSS) and the concept of DSS were developed independently in France, in several articles by professors of HEC working on the SCARABÉE project which started in 1969 and ended in 1974. The concept of DSS and a design and implementation strategy for these systems are described in several papers related to this project, Klein and Tixier (1971), Klein (1971), Klein and Girault (1971).

4.1.2 The Objective of DSS

A DSS can be defined as:

A computer program that provides information in a given domain of application by means of analytical decision models and access to databases, in order to support a decision maker in making decisions effectively in complex and ill-structured (non-programmable) tasks.

DSS are useful when a fixed goal exists but there is no algorithmic solution. The solutions paths can be numerous and user-dependent (Klein and Tixier, 1971). In other words, the goal of a DSS is to improve a decision by better understanding and preparation of the tasks leading towards evaluation and choosing (collectively called the decision making process – see Section 4.1.4).

The concept of *ill (or semi) structured* problems as opposed to those that are *well structured* is a key concept here. In the literature (Newell & Simon, 1972, Simon, 1973) the latter usually refers to decision making processes that are routine and repetitive, the former to situations where there is no known and clear method of solution because the problem arises for the first time, or because the nature of the problem itself is complex and unclear. The situation is, in fact, slightly more complex. A financial analysis problem which will lead to the decision to grant a loan or not is, for the credit analyst, a *routine task*. However, it is not usually possible to fully automatize the information processing which will be used to reach the conclusion. If an information processing method can be stated as an algorithm then the decision process is structured, and can be incorporated in a computer program. The solution to the problem is then *automated*. The way that the DSS will accommodate the unstructuredness of the problem is expressed by Bonczek *et al.* (1981) in the following way:

> 'The human investigates in the decision-making process and during this investigation the computer supports the process by furnishing pertinent information, thus creating a human–computer decision making system.'

Unstructuredness is accommodated in:

(1) the nature of and sequencing of requests made on the DSS,
(2) the manner in which DSS responses are utilized,
(3) the DSS recognition of alternative methods for satisfying a given request.

Structured problems are routine and repetitive, because they are unambiguous (since each such problem has a single solution method). A less structured problem has more alternative solution methods, and the solutions may not be equivalent. A completely 'unstructured' problem has unknown solution methods or too many solution methods to evaluate effectively.

The number of situations where decisions have to be taken and where the problem is non-programmable is very large in management. In finance, which will be our application domain, we can point out: financial analysis, credit analysis, financial planning and engineering, management control, capital budgeting, investment advising, portfolio management, performance evaluation and so on.

The end users of a DSS application are not always known during its development, but the decisions which it is designed to support must have something in common. A credit analysis DSS such as FINSIM which we present in (Klein, 1989) is designed to support a given decision class. The support provided can include decision methodology support (see Chapter 6).

The economic importance of research and development in the field of DSS is directly related to the pervasiveness of ill-structured problems in management, and the need to provide DSS support to all these decision classes. The development of AI technology has widened the spectrum of application of these systems.

4.1.3 Characteristics of Ill-structured Problems

Characteristics of situations where the DSS approach is useful are known (Klein and Tixier, 1971). We have defined them above as ill-structured decision problems, in such situations:

- The preferences, judgments, intuition and experience of the decision maker are essential.
- The search for a solution implies a mixture of:
  - search for information,
  - formalization, or problem definition and structuring (system modeling),
  - computation,
  - data manipulation.
- The sequence of the above operations is not known in advance since:
  - it can be a function of data,
  - it can be modified, given partial results,
  - it can be a function of the user preferences.
- Criteria for the decision are numerous, in conflict, and highly dependent on the perception of the user (user modeling).
- The solution must be achieved in limited time.
- The problem evolves rapidly.

As can be noticed from the above description one of the key characteristics of situations where DSS are useful is that modeling of the decision problem (and user) is needed. One of the most obvious examples of time constraint can be found in dealer rooms. Traders working on the money or the stock-market must be able, in certain cases, to make decisions in a few seconds. Here, DSS are a prerequisite. Very often the problem has to be solved in limited time. In such a situation it is crucial to be able to implement a DSS application which provides a first satisfactory solution and which can be improved as time permits.

4.1.4 The Decision Making Process

The successful manager is one who is able to choose the right actions at the right time. Thus, our usual image of a decision maker is of a person who makes the right choices. However, a choice is just the final result of a complex process of exploration, analysis and evaluation. This process we call the *decision making process*.

The decision making process can be described by models which form a continuum from the rational models at one end, to irrational models at the other end. Bounded rationality and satisficing are found towards the rational end, while 'garbage can' and ambiguous decisions are located towards the irrational end. The difference is very much determined by the way that the decision maker or the decision making body (in the case of a group) is treated. Rational models regard the decision making body as homogeneous. That is, a person or a group of persons with consistent and non-conflicting objectives. The irrational or anarchistic models, on the other hand, regard the decision making body as an heterogeneous group of people. That is, people have changing and conflicting preferences. We have already seen a great impact of DSS upon unstructured and semi-structured decisions, these are decisions which can be described within the rationality paradigm of decision making, and for which a structure of the decision process can be identified. In this section we shall, therefore, describe in more detail a framework that describes the unstructured decision processes.

Perhaps the most well-known framework for studying decisions by the process is Simon's intelligence–design–choice trichotomy (Simon, 1960). This conceptual framework has been taken as a basis for much of the work that has been carried out on decision support systems (see, for example, Sprague and Carlson, 1982). Simon's framework consists of three phases:

(1) Searching the environment for conditions that call for a decision – the *intelligence* activity
(2) Inventing, developing and analyzing possible courses of action – the *design* activity
(3) Selecting a particular course of action from those available – the *choice* activity.

Generally speaking, intelligence activity precedes design, and design precedes choice. The cycle of phases is, however, interwoven. It is believed that human beings cannot gather information without, in some way, simultaneously developing alternatives. They cannot avoid evaluating these alternatives immediately, and in doing this they are forced to a decision (Witte, 1972).

Herbert Simon introduced the concept of bounded rationality in order to describe decision making in an environment of incomplete and inconsistent information. Under these circumstances a decision maker 'satisfices' – he or she looks for a course of action that is 'good enough' rather than one that is optimal. What techniques are available for decision making under satisficing behavior? Simon makes the distinction between *programmed* and *non-programmed* decisions. A task that is programmed is one for which clear rules can be defined. A non-programmed decision, on the other hand, is one for which there is no cut and dried method for handling the problem, and one for which judgment, is essential in reaching a solution. However, Newell and Simon's research on human problem solving showed that, when faced with complex, unprogrammed situations, a problem solver seeks to reduce the problem into subproblems to which he or she applies general-purpose procedures or routines (Newell and Simon, 1972). In other words, a decision maker deals with unstructured situations by factoring them into familiar, structurable elements.

Mintzberg *et al.* (1976) conclude from this that decision processes are programmable even if they are not in fact programmed. Although the processes used are not predetermined and explicit, there is strong evidence that a basic logic or structure underlies what the decision maker does and that this structure can be described by systematic study of this behavior. The behavior that Mintzberg *et al.* studied is that of decision makers dealing with strategic decisions. They developed a decision process model that resembles Simon's model but which is conceptually richer. The model describes the phases slightly differently and uses different terms: identification, development, and selection. Furthermore, these three phases are described in terms of seven activities, called central routines. In addition, three supporting routines: decision control, communication, and political, as well as six sets of dynamic factors that help to explain the relationships among the central and supporting routines, are defined. Figure 4.1 depicts the decision process as envisaged by Mintzberg *et al.*

There are seven central routines within the three phases of the decision process which are now to be discussed.

The identification phase.   This phase comprises two routines: decision recognition and diagnosis. *Recognition* evokes a decisional activity. This activity can be triggered by a problem or an opportunity identified in the profusion of information that the decision maker receives. A problem is identified as the difference between 'what it is' and 'what it

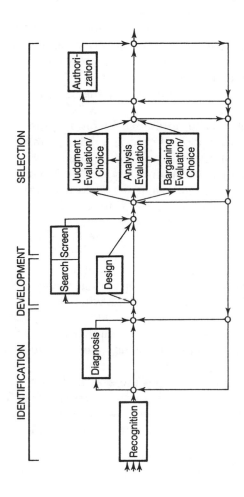

Figure 4.1 *A model of the decision process. (Reprinted from 'The structure of the "unstructured" decision process' by Mintzberg, H. et al. published in* Administrative Science Quarterly, **21**(2) (June 1976) by permission of Administrative Science Quarterly.)

ought to be'; between the actual situation and a desired situation. Once a cumulation of stimuli reaches a threshold level, a decision process is initiated. In the *diagnosis* routine, further information is collected until the real cause is determined.

The development phase.   This phase comprises the set of activities that lead to the generation of one or more solutions. Development is described in terms of two routines: search and design. *Search* is evoked to find ready-made solutions. The environment is scanned for solutions which have been used on previous occasions, or which have been prepared for situations similar to the one now encountered. The *design* routine is used either to generate custom-made solutions, or to modify ready-made alternatives identified by the search routine.

The selection phase.   The normative literature prescribes selection in terms of the determination of criteria for choice, the evaluation of the consequences of alternatives, and the making of a choice. Mintzberg's study suggests that selection is, typically, a multi-stage, iterative process. Three selection routines emerged from this study. *Screen* is evoked when search is expected to generate more ready-made alternatives than can be intensively evaluated and is more concerned with what is infeasible than appropriate. *Evaluation-choice* consists of alternatively judgment, analysis and bargaining. The normative literature emphasizes analysis (see Chapter 3). *Authorization* appears to be a typical binary process: accept or reject. Generally, the time for it is limited and it is a political process where power may be exercised to protect interests.

The Mintzberg model is general enough to describe any decision process. The general idea is that decisions are made within a process where:

- problems are not given, but are searched for or defined;
- solutions are not given or known, but are searched for or designed;
- the choice situation often comprises alternatives that cannot easily be compared, or where consequences are neither unique nor well known;
- it is not certain that the decided alternative can be implemented or executed as specified, or that consequences will be as anticipated.

Given these constraints, together with the limited cognitive capacity of human beings, the decision maker does not maximize (optimize) but chooses solutions that are satisficing. The model that describes decision making behavior under these constraints is also known as the 'administrative man' model.

4.1.5 A Framework for Understanding the Use of DSS in Problem Solving

The interplay of a *user* interacting with a *DSS application, a task* to be accomplished and the *technology*, can be explained using the concepts presented in Figure 4.2. As shown in this figure, a DSS application is a result of two forces: firstly, the demand of the decision maker to be better supported to perform the task more effectively, and secondly, the opportunities provided by the technology. In this chapter, we shall present the conceptual framework of DSS that supports effective decision making. This conceptual framework must include technologies available at the time of designing the system. For instance, a DSS to support the task of a sales person in a tour operator company will clearly be enhanced by the ability to present videos of vacation places. Therefore, in designing a DSS application it is not sufficient to concentrate on the task only, but also to take into consideration the opportunities offered by the technology.

This conceptual framework together with the available technology is synthesized in a development environment which will be used to support and speed up the process of application development.

The task the decision maker is expected to perform is usually broken down into a series of subtasks which have been identified above:

- problem recognition;
- problem diagnosis and structuring;
- decision problem modeling and alternative generation;
- choosing between alternatives;
- monitoring of the decision.

The functions the *DSS application* will provide to support the above subtasks are:

- information access and mining (drill-down);
- reporting (including exception reporting);
- decision situation structuring and modeling;
- computation of decision criteria;
- decision analysis;
- communication.

All or some of these functions should be provided in a DSS application. To implement the DSS application the user or designer (sometimes the same person) will use a software tool called a *DSS development environment* or *generator (DSSG)*. (Clearly it is possible to develop a DSS

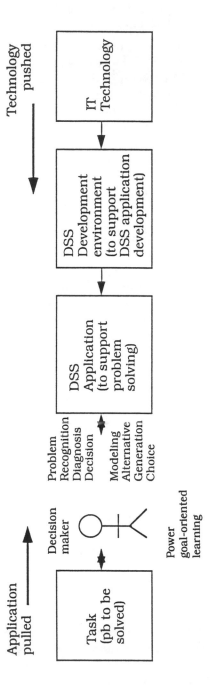

Figure 4.2 *DSS: a framework for understanding*

application with a general programming language but this situation will in most cases lead to such a costly and lengthy project that such a solution is infeasible or just less effective.) This generator will provide a formalism to:

- define and manage the collections of entities and their attributes represented as data structures in the problem;
- define the decision models needed to compute the decision criteria;
- define reports to present the various kinds of information used during the search for a solution in a way which is adapted to the problem and decision makers;
- define forms, i.e. display on the screen the structure of forms so that the users can enter information as if they were filling in a form;
- access specific algorithms used to process data, to help in the modeling of the problem (statistical explanatory methods, forecasting methods . . .);
- define decision situation (decision trees, influence diagrams . . .);
- define the interface between the user and the DSS application;
- send messages and data to other geographically dispersed users and define which of the resources of the DSS application should be shared among them when working in a distributed context.

The DSS development environment itself uses diverse information technologies. As would be expected the formalism used to define the entities and their attributes used in the problem and which manages the instanciation of these attributes will usually be a Database Management System.

The formalism used to define decision models will usually be a modeling language. The formalism used to define reports will have to provide a way to define presentation of information combining text, numerical variables, tables, graphics and images (i.e. it works in a multimedia mode).

During the task of data analysis or model building the user will need to use algorithms for identifying relations between variables (regression analysis . . .) or data analysis (hierarchical analysis, cluster analysis . . .).

In many cases the basic information used in the DSS application is coming from administrative forms. The FINSIM application which we present in (Klein, 1989) uses as basic information the data provided by the French fiscal forms defined by the central government to collect financial information on companies and compute the taxes they have to pay.

The development environment will be developed using object programming technology to provide a graphical interface.

One key concept of a DSS development environment is that it should provide the *same* formalism to achieve three fundamental goals:

- communication among users or between users and designers
- mathematical and logical treatment of decision models
- computer execution

In other words the application as it is defined using the formalism of the generator, should be directly executable by the computer.

This formalism should be directly understandable by users (managers or domain specialists), i.e. there should be no need of a human transformation by a specialist from the specification of the DSS application made by the user to the specification of the DSS application running on the computer. This means that the generator provides a certain number of tools such as *model solvers* and *query processors*. One of the important characteristics of a DSS applications is that they will evolve according to several forces:

- nature of the problem (importance, criticality . . .);
- dynamics of the environment;
- understanding of the problem by users (learning);
- resources (time, money . . .) available to improve the application;
- technological developments.

In other words a DSS application will usually be developed through an *adaptive* process of *learning* and *evolution*. As a consequence the DSS application is viewed as the result of the interaction between the DSS users, the DSS designer and the DSS generator. We would like to stress here the methodological importance of the DSS generator. The formal definition of a DSSG defines the class of DSS applications which can be described and as a consequence which can be generated.

4.1.6 Requirements for DSS Software

Given the above characteristics about the problem class that we wish to support, it is well accepted that certain requirements have to be fulfilled by DSS software. These requirements concern:

- end-user usage and interactivity;
- end-user definition;
- easy access to pertinent information;
- high interaction between users, the system and the learning situation;

- capacity to adapt to fast evolution of user needs;
- portability and peripheral support;
- realiability;
- performance.

We shall outline these requirements below.

End-user Usage and Interactivity

This requirement states that the end user should not have, during his exploration of the decision process, to use an intermediary (chauffeur) to request information from the system, or to explore some ideas or to compute criteria. This requirement is a direct consequence of the fact that:

- In the search for a solution the next step can be a function of intermediate results obtained. It would not be practical to call for an assistant at each such step. End users wish to test their ideas at once!
- The criteria of choice, the preferences of the user on these criteria and the risk aversion of the user cannot be always modeled (even if the theory exists!). Since this crucial information is specific to the decision maker it consequently cannot be inputted by a third party. Often the decision maker may not wish to communicate his or her preferences to others.
- Some information is highly confidential. The manager must be able to change inputs (questions, requests and so on) and obtain immediately the corresponding results. Only online systems enable such performance. The necessity of highly interactive systems for successful implementation of computer support was one of the first conclusions of researchers in the DSS field.

It is by studying a problem that a manager learns how to understand the problem better and to find a solution. The concept of a 'decision calculus' (Little, 1970) is related to this idea. As a consequence, the application interface providing the means of interaction between the user and the system has to be specifically designed for end users so that the conceptual distance between the user concepts and that of the interface is as small as possible. The support of a DSS application is related to the display of menus, to the syntax of the command language, to the dialog boxes, to the resources available in the DSS (data bases, data files, reports, interfaces) or the problem solving methodology itself: for example, the decision analysis methodology

(Chapter 3). *Hypertex* and *graphical interfaces* are now the technologies to fulfill this requirement as we shall show in Section 4.7.

End-user Definition

This requirement was introduced by Klein and Tixier (1971) under the name 'user–designer' principle. In many cases, the DSS is implemented by its user. This is the consequence of the fact that, often, a system for decision support is defined while the user works on his problem. In other words, the system which is given to the user does not solve his problem from the start, but is there to create the environment within which he or she will be able to solve it better than before (Girault and Klein, 1971).

In fact, if there is no discussion about the end-user of DSS, there is much debate about the end-user definition of a DSS. Even if the spread sheet software has shown that a very large class of DSS applications can be user defined there are several reasons why, frequently, a DSS cannot be implemented by the end-users. The most common reason is because the end-users are just too busy, not motivated enough or simply the system is too complex for them to develop by themselves.

Klein (1987 *et al.*, 1991, 1993c) gives some examples of such a situation. The DSS application he describes is a DSS for financial analysis and city planning which is used in many French towns (see Section 10.6). The final users of the system are, depending on the size of the city, the elected officials in charge of financial problems and/or the administrative staff (General Secretary, Administrative and Financial Manager and so on). The specification and definition of the first version of the system was carried out over a period of one year, during one day meetings held once every month, because the elected officials could not spend more time on the project. In this case, consultants have played the role of 'chauffeur' until the DSS constituted an environment attractive enough for the end-users so that they had sufficient interest to have it as a permanent assistant in their office. Starting from this point the user–designer principle has worked. Since then the system has been regularly improved by users and a user group was created.

The second reason which may prevent end-users from participating in the definition and design of the DSS is their number. The DSS for financial analysis and engineering, FINSIM (Klein, 1989), is a good example of such a system. FINSIM is a financial and credit evaluation system used in banks to prepare loan decisions related to companies. Such a system can be used by many people in a bank (in fact, all credit analysts). As a consequence, only a selection of potential users can take part in the definition and design.

One last, classical, reason for users not to participate in the design is that the organization in which they work wishes a certain category of employees to use a given methodology embedded in a DSS, for instance, to ensure homogeneity and consistency in the way the demands for loans is dealt with. As a consequence, the management does not wish to see each employee develop his own system.

Easy Access to Pertinent Information

A DSS application usually includes information about the problem domain and information about the support capabilities of the system:

- data useful in solving the problem;
- meaning of attributes of entities which are used in studying the problem;
- meaning of variables used in decision models;
- conditions of uses and underlying hypothesis of decision models;
- use of reports available;
- use of forms used to facilitate data capture and control;
- mathematical, statistical, probabilistic, forecasting, financial functions available in the application;
- syntax and semantics of command language and menu options.
- graphical user interface (GUI) structure

We shall briefly discuss below each of these kinds of information.

Data Access

In most problems the first step towards a solution is ready access to relevant data since it is through the study of these that, frequently, the problem is recognized and/or diagnosed.

In financial analysis, for instance, within a bank credit department, it is clear that to have an instantaneous and easy access to balance sheets and income statements of client companies requesting a loan is a necessary condition, and a first step to the support of the decisions of the credit analysts. In some banks, the volume of data is such (several thousands of balance sheets) that the data capture is done by specialized personnel and that the analysts only access the information and check it. Increasingly, the raw data is provided on tapes by specialized companies.

If the volume of data is important and the users numerous, data will have to be shared, and may be updated by users. The problem can be further complicated by the fact that the database can be evolving with varying time cycles for various sub-classes of data. For instance, in finance, balance sheets and income statements are annual, semi-annual or quarterly but stock prices can be weekly or daily.

Another difficulty in many DSS situations rises from the fact that information from different origins has to be taken into account and merged. For instance, in a DSS for management control, the support of diagnosis will imply access to accounting information (actual results) as well as budget information so as to compute variance. The accounting information will, most likely, come from the accounting system and the budgets from another system, or directly from the user.

Meaning of Attributes of Entities which are used in Studying the Problem

In many cases applications may use information related to collections of entities, such as persons, companies (in financial analysis), products, clients (in marketing). It is important to be able to have access not only to the values of the attributes of these entities but also the meaning of these attributes. For instance, an analyst is not only interested in the numerical value of a price index but also in the origin of the index (who is producing it and publishing it, when it is useful to use it and so on).

The meaning of a variable may have to be specified. The variable 'sales', for example: does it include the sales taxes or not?

As a consequence it is important for a DSS user to have access to texts giving or defining the meaning of the data available in the database of the DSS.

Conditions of Use and Underlying Hypothesis of Decision Models

As we have seen in Chapter 3, models to support decisions relate environmental, decision and goal variables. We shall call them *decision models*. In other words, a decision model is a formal representation of a *decision class* situation (see Section 11.3.5 for a discussion of this concept).

A DSS may contain several decision models. These models may have been defined and developed over a long period of time by different people. It is essential to have access to the catalogue of these models and to access information on the condition under which each model may be used. Such a situation is described in Klein and Villedieu (1987), Klein (1993c) for a DSS application to support financial analysis and planning, budgeting, project financial planning and debt management in French municipalities. In the case study at the end of this chapter (Exercise 4.14) we present a DSS application for management control in a decentralized company. The solution of this exercise implies the development of several decision models for its solution.

Use of Reports

Reports can be complex objects mixing text interspersed with numerical values, tables of numbers, graphics, images. A financial model such as FINSIM (Klein, 1989) is associated with several reports: balance sheet, income statements, ratios, etc. Such reports have been designed to facilitate the recognition of problems or to provide information to solve a problem. Access to the catalog of these reports and how to use them is important information which should be made available to users.

Statistical, Forecasting and Optimization Tools (Toolbox)

In many DSS both statistical routines or forecasting routines may be used to help in a given phase of the decision process to anticipate trends, seasonal factors, to measure causal relationships, to optimize and so on, such a need is presented in the case study for a management control DSS.

The possibility of accessing information using the methodology for short-term forecasting and its underlying hypotheses can be very helpful. Here, the DSS plays the role of a consultant specializing in statistical and/or forecasting techniques. Such a need is described in Gangneux and Rouxell (1988) and the technology for its implementations is described in Chapter 6.

Graphical User Interface, Command Language Syntax and Semantics, Menu Options etc.

All DSS applications mix different kinds of interfaces: windows, menus, command language, dialog boxes, icons, etc. It is essential to be able to use a graphical interface which will provide an assistance function of the context. The syntax of commands should be made available on line so that users do not have to type the syntactic units but only to select them as they progress in constructing their commands. Hypertex technology to support semantics of the commands is well adapted to this purpose.

Knowledge about the problem

The information about data, its meaning, and the decision models and displays that are readily available already constitute much knowledge about the problem. However, other forms of knowledge may be used as we have seen in Section 3.3.6, and this type of information plays a very important role in what is called expert systems and their associated knowledge bases. In particular, we shall propose, in Chapter 6, a new framework to integrate knowledge bases on decision methodologies, for instance decision analysis methods, statistical methods and so on.

High Interaction Between the Users, the System and the Learning Situation

The DSS user is in a heuristic search situation as described in Section 2.5.2 during his or her problem solving activity. Such a situation has been described in Girault and Klein (1971) for financial analysts working in investment departments. The analysts, for example, have, very often, to make compromises between deepening their search (studying a company in more detail) or widening it (studying other companies). Also, when using decision models for simulation purposes the analyst finds himself in a *learning situation*. This implies a high level of interaction so as to be able to see clearly the consequences of changes in hypotheses. This high interaction implies the existence of an interface and command language to let the user define what he or she wants the system to accomplish.

There is a definite *computer assisted instruction* aspect in the interaction of the user with the DSS.

The reason is that, while quantitative methods and normative models are developing rapidly in these fields, neverthelesss intuition, judgment and experience remain essential factors in the process of exploration of alternatives and the search for adequate tools. This implies that the key to success is not to develop better or more numerous quantitative numerical techniques but to continuously improve the search ability of the system user; to help him acquire better heuristics; and to improve his knowledge of the limits and applicability of the tools he has at his disposal (Klein and Tixier, 1971). This point will be developed in Section 4.5.4.

Capacity to Adapt to Fast Evolution of User Needs

If a DSS is providing good support it is very likely that users will perceive new problems and needs. As a consequence, the system will have to be able to respond to a fast evolution of user needs. This evolution can be in terms of extensions with respect to:

- new algorithms at the toolbox level;
- new solvers at the decision model level;
- new entities at the database level;
- new interface;
- new presentation of information.

This requirement has important consequences for the development method of a DSS application. As soon as the application is not trivial a team approach is needed. This is all the more important in order to insure perennity of the system and institutionalize it within the organization (several people must be able to work on its evolution). As a consequence the user-interface might be designed by a specialist consultant working with an experienced person in the domain, the reports and models may be defined by other users, etc.

Portability and peripheral support

Software applications in particular tend to have a longer life-cycle than operating systems and new hardware (platform). As a consequence it is important to be able to transfer these applications easily to run under new operating systems and hardware. This requirement has consequences for the DSS development environment itself. If the development environment can be transferred easily under new operating systems then the DSS applications will need no change. It is rather rare that no changes are required when the DSSG is made available under a new environment since the designers of the DSSG tend to take advantage of the specific capacities of the new environment and programming language.

For example the PC-OPTRANS development environment we describe in Section 4.5 was initially written in Pascal and was running under MS-DOS. The first version with a graphical interface; (OPTRANS Object) was written in the programming language C to improve portability. The different versions of the graphical library used made it available under DOS as well as OS/2 or UNIX. The second graphical version was written with C++ to take advantage of libraries of Objects available with the new C++ compilers for Windows. So it is important to check when selecting a DSS development environment that it is able to run under the most widespread operating system (DOS, Windows, OS/2, Unix, etc.) and is not specific to one operating system.

Reliability

This requirement is well known for online systems. Decision situations are usually situations for which users want to use their systems when they feel the need for it. They will not use for long a DSS application which is not reliable. The reliability problem exists at the level of the DSS application and at the level of the DSS development environment.

The reliability of an application is easier to obtain when it is developed with a DSSG since the definition of the application is understandable by the user and is structured. We shall develop this point further in Section 4.3. DSSG being large software their reliability relies on technologies which have proven efficient for large software. The use of object oriented technology for their programming is one example of such technology. We should also remember that advanced DSSG include their own DBMS component. This component should provide the standard procedures to restart in case of incident without losing more than the last transactions.

Performance

While this requirement is, as reliability, not specific to DSS applications, it is a very important requirement. DSS applications are interactive systems with graphical interface of a very different nature than transaction oriented systems where *simple* queries are made, and where all users are using the *same* application with the same interface (updating an inventory, making a reservation and so on) and sharing information. We should keep in mind that typical DSS applications integrate DBs, decision models, reports, forms and interfaces. A typical user may use any of these resources. A query from a financial analyst requesting a list of all companies in a financial data base which have had, during the last three years, an average annual growth rate of their profit superior to the industry to which they belong and a debt : equity ratio less than one is an example of a query which, even on a data base of a few hundred companies, may request a lot of resources in terms of computing and disk access.

Another example in the management control field is the case of a DSS used for financial control of subsidiaries or branches when the number of subsidiaries is large (several tens or hundreds) and when work on consolidated variables has to be done. Such a situation is described in the case study described at the end of the chapter.

DSS are systems with which users can create new objects: models, reports, data files or databases, such operations require powerful machines, which are available as PCs today.

4.2 FUNCTIONS OF A DSS APPLICATION

The functions that a DSS application should have can be derived from the main steps in the decision making process, described in Section 4.1.4.

4.2.1 Providing an Interface to Support the Man–Machine Interaction during the Problem Solving Task

The interface of a DSS application is a key element for its success because this is the user's view of the system. This multi-windowed interface is usually made of a *hierarchy of menus and icons* giving access to resources which are used to provide supporting functions. These menus and icons enable the user to select functions to:

- access and display information needed for problem solving;
- access statistical algorithms to study and describe in a more condensed manner the available information;
- display forms to input data needed to run decision models;
- display and print reports;
- solve decision models to obtain decision criteria;
- help him select between alternatives;
- store the decision and monitor it.
- transform objects into icons and the reverse.

The role of the interface is also to define the *structure* and *global logic* of the application. This logic defines the *order* in which the resources have to be used to obtain the result looked for or support the problem solving task. The above functions are the functions usually provided in an existing application. In fact, as we have seen, the system should also let the *authorized* user steer the evolution of the application (we shall see in Chapter 8 methods of development). This means that the user should be able to:

- access and modify the structure of the entities which are the sources of information, eventually create new ones;
- modify existing reports and define new ones;
- modify existing forms for data capture and define new ones;
- list the text of decision models, modify them and create new ones;
- list the interface and global logic of the application and change it if needed.

As we have said above the user interface of the application represents the *global logic* of the application: i.e. it defines how the resources are used given the way the user interacts with the application interface. A clear conceptual distinction must be made between the interface *description* of the DSS application and the interface of the application. The interface description of an application is a text; it is *static* as the text of a decision model. The interface of an application is what is displayed on the screen or what the user hears (in case of voice interaction) when he uses the application. The interface has a *dynamic* behavior when the application is used. This is the same distinction which is made between the text defining a model (static) and the execution of or interaction (dynamic) with a model. Figure 4.11 shows the interface of the Finplan application and Figure 4.16 the interface description defined with OPTRANS Object.

The interface of the application can give access to the interface of a resource provided by the generator. For instance, an option in the menu of the application may give access to the report generator so that the user can, not only use existing reports, but define new ones. The application interface is a layer between the user and the resources of the application. The general structure of a DSS application is presented in Figure 4.3.

Today the best interface technology is the object oriented *graphical interface* using multiple windows and mouse. In this kind of interface a window is associated to each resource and functions are associated to each window. For example a form will be displayed on the screen within a window to let the user type in the data requested. A report will be displayed on the screen within a window, etc.

When running the application the windows have a fixed position on the screen. But if the user selects the *development mode* of the application he will be able to modify each window. He will be able by direct action with the mouse to make it bigger or smaller, change its characteristics (colors, etc.), make it use the full screen or transform it into an icon etc. The user can scroll within a window if the content cannot fit in its present size, etc. Within a window can be present:

- text (such as the text defining a decision model);
- graphics (such as a curve, a histogram, a PERT chart, a decision tree, an influence diagram, etc.);
- an image;
- a mixture of text, tables, graphics and images (fixed or video).

It should be pointed out that DSS applications request a wide range of technics for user interaction. Selection of options in a menu or icons with a mouse is fine for calling (opening) a resource such as a data file, a decision model etc., but it is not adequate for more complex actions such as defining an equation or writing the text of a report. The

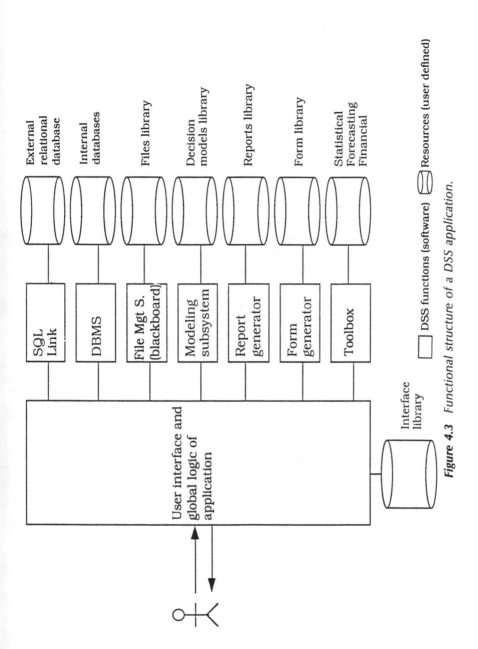

Figure 4.3 *Functional structure of a DSS application.*

ideal is to allow for alternative ways of interaction and let the user select what suits him the best. We have already pointed out that *hypertex* is a good technology to support the assistance function to help the user find information concerning which function of the DSS can help him perform his task. Voice interface is also gaining interest as this technology progresses. Hyper-information is the name given to various forms of linear and non-linear arrangements of information into dynamic electronic documents (Parsaye, 1993).

4.2.2 Supporting Access to the Information Needed for Problem Solving

Easy access to the information is the first support a decision maker requests from the DSS. In the JIIA-86 case study described at the end of this chapter, information is about products and branch results but should also be about all the resources of the DSS (data, decision models, statistical tools, displays available and so on). In the JIIA-86 case several users (branch managers) will need to interrogate and update the database at the same time, this will imply the capability of the DSS to provide database management subsystem functions (see Section 4.4.2).

With respect to the access of information in a database context (beyond the simple retrieval of information), two classical functions are the screening and sorting of information. We have pointed out above that a DSS should also provide information about the resources of the system in terms of:

- data useful in solving the problem;
- meaning of attributes of entities which are used in studying the problem;
- meaning of variables used in decision models;
- conditions of uses and underlying hypothesis of decision models;
- use of reports available;
- mathematical, statistical, probabilistic, forecasting, financial functions available in the application;
- syntax and semantics of command language and menu options.

The support the DSS application provides to its users is here an extension of their memory.

Computer assisted messaging for geographically dispersed users

When the decision process implies several dispersed users. Computer assisted messaging is a very efficient tool if the users are connected to the same network. The messaging system enables the decision maker to obtain information (data, opinions, etc.) useful for decision making. Computer message systems and computer assisted video-conferencing can play a very crucial role in the support of this phase of the process, in particular, when a decision has to be made under pressure of time, in crisis situation and also if the decision makers are not available at the same time. The importance of this function is well described in Hiltz and Turrof (1978) and Johansen *et al.* (1974).

The message communication function in DSS has, from our point of view, not received the attention it deserves. We believe that one of the main activities of managers is not only to make decisions but *to obtain commitment* from their colleagues and other employees of the organization. This point was stressed by Winograd and Flores (1986).

The existence of a good-quality computer-assisted messaging and PC based video-conferencing system such as PROSHARE from INTEL can expand the capacity of a manager to exchange information with others and obtain commitment to get certain tasks done.

4.2.3 Supporting Problem Recognition

Display of Information

Since the essence of problem recognition lies in the ability to detect discrepancies between present state and expected states, the display of information to highlight such discrepancies is essential.

The capacity to present information in different windows and to combine graphics, figures and color is a key element of good display for decision support. For example, in the JIIA-86 case study, the capacity to display trends in sales will help to pinpoint problems on product life cycles. Kahl *et al.* (1977) describe an interesting example of problem recognition through *variance analysis*. This case presents a multinational industrial company at the European headquarters of which the controllers use a DSS. The system enables them to display the global variance of any variable at different levels in the company.

In the database, a variable can be indexed by time, by the subsidiary marketing it, by the currency in which the variable is valued, and by the controller's point of view (is it an actual figure, a budgeted figure or a variance?). The controller can decide to display, for instance, the value of a variable (sales, operating margin and so on) for the company (as a whole or a subsidiary) at a given period in a given currency (see Figure 4.4). This value can be the actual value or the budgeted value or the variance (management control aspect). In the case described, the actual variables are entered in the system on a monthly basis in

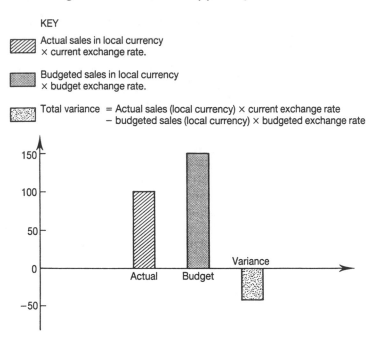

Figure 4.4 *The company global variance on sales for a given month*

local currency using the current exchange rate. The budgeted values are entered once a year during the budget period at the budget exchange rate which is decided as a forecast for the whole of the coming year.

So, the current exchange rate is the exchange rate observed on the money markets each month (in fact the exchange rate is different if the variable is an income statement item or a balance sheet item). The controller may then be interested to break down the global variance at the plant level by country (see Figure 4.5).

Let us imagine that the controller finds out that the negative variance is 80%, at the UK subsidiary. He or she may now be interested to know if this negative variance is due to an exchange rate problem (over which the plant manager has no control) or to an activity-level problem (over which he may have some control). For the French subsidiary, the negative variance can only be due to an activity-level problem since the consolidation currency is the French franc.

To solve this question the controller will ask for a breakdown of variance between the exchange rate variance and activity variance (Figure 4.6), and will see, clearly, that the problem is due to an exchange rate variance.

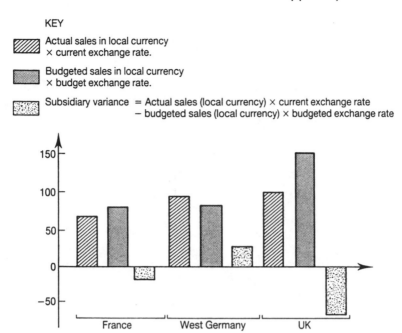

Figure 4.5 *Breakdown of sales variance by country, for a given month*

The controller has progressed considerably and very fast in the diagnosis of the causes of his initial observation. This type of support received from the DSS can be called the capacity to 'mine' or drill down a problem.

Given the importance of variance analysis in cost accounting much work has been done to develop systems able not only to point out whether a variance is worthy of investigation but also to diagnose the cause of the variance (quantitative or qualitative cause). We shall see that this can be done using knowledge bases (Chapter 6). The interested reader is refered to Hollander (1992).

Alerting

The alerting function of a DSS is a very important function with which to support problem recognition. The idea is that the user should be able to set conditions (predicates and rules) which, if they become true, will trigger the display of a report, or send a message, or, eventually, trigger some other action such as the computation of a model. This function is very useful when the decision maker is confronted with a large amount of data which is evolving very fast with time.

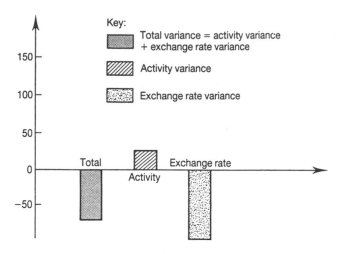

Figure 4.6   *Breakdown of variance between exchange rate variable and activity variance for the UK subsidiary*

This situation is found in trade rooms, where traders have to follow current information on several hundreds or thousands of securities. The trader using a DSS should be able to define conditions which, when fulfilled, will lead the system to flash a signal to him.

An 'intelligent' alerting system must be defined. We shall show (see Chapters 5 and 6) that an expert module is a good way to implement such a function.

As a conclusion to the support of the problem recognition phase we can say that the decision maker should be helped by the system during this phase to:

- determine what the questions (decision problems) to be answered are;
- define the hypotheses to be tested;
- define the effects to be estimated.

As can be seen, this kind of support is difficult to provide.

It is easy to display a message if a variable goes beyond a certain threshold, it is more difficult to diagnose what the real problem is. However, we have seen in Chapter 2 that since simulation of human reasoning is possible there is some hope that DSS will become more able to suggest diagnoses, we shall see how in Chapters 5 and 6.

4.2.4 Supporting Problem Structuring

Problem structuring is usually performed by breaking down the problem into subproblems and by identifying the relations between the subproblems in terms of input, output and control. The problem structuring usually leads to the definition of several models eventually to the definition of several DSS applications interacting with each other. Problem structuring will always be reflected in the user interface. Such a structuring process is described in Klein (1993c) in the domain of town financial planning. A DSS application is presented where a financial analysis and planning system is interacting with a debt management, a project management and a cash management system. For example, the problem of developing an acceptable financial plan for an industrial plant producing several products can lead to the definition of:

- a sales forecasting function and production model providing production level for the product as an input of the production model;
- a production planning model providing the level of orders and inventory for the raw materials and finished products;
- a financial planning model using the production planning model to produce the unit and period cost of production of the products;

Such a DSS application could be structured into:

- three models (sales forecast, production, finance);
- three reports (sales forecast, production plan, financial plan);
- an interface to interact with the application
  or to run the models in a batch mode;
- a data file;
- a data base containing the historical values of attributes of the products (sales level in quantity, etc.).

Such an application is described in Klein (1985) for a tannery, and Gangneux (1988) for industrial valve control systems.

4.2.5 Supporting Problem Formulation

The task will usually be to support the design and evaluation of alternatives and the evaluation of criteria. In such a task, as we shall see, models are efficient ways to design and test alternatives.

Importance of Model Formulation for Solution Finding

In financial and economic problems a decision maker is very often confronted with the necessity to make calculations. If a loan is made, a repayment schedule has to be computed, if an asset is acquired a depreciation schedule must also be computed according to a given method and so on. This need for computation would, by itself, be sufficient to justify the existence of an end-user language to define calculation.

The widespread use of spreadsheets has shown how large this need is. Its origin is found in the fact that after the information collection phase and problem definition or diagnosis of the decision process, the next step is the need to support transformation of basic information in order to produce more usable information, which will often constitute a criterion for choice. But there is another well-known fundamental reason for defining models. This reason is that the formulation of models is a crucial step in the scientific method applied to economics and social systems. And, since the scientific method has proved to be an efficient method to solve problems, we wish to take advantage of it. This method is based on a four-stage process:

(1) Observation of the system.
(2) Formulation of a logical, mathematical model that attempts to explain the observations of the system.
(3) Prediction of the behavior of the system on the basis of the model using mathematical or logical deduction.
(4) Performance of experiments to test the validity of the model.

It is clear that the information access function of the DSS will help in the first stage. Since the process of model building is made of two tasks:

(1) Finding out the variables to include in the model.
(2) Finding out structural (causal relations) among variables.

The capacity to decide if a variable should be in a model and to define what its relations are with other variables necessitates an *understanding* of the causal relationships in the *real system*, as well as the nature of the decision to be taken (as we have seen in Chapter 3).

Once a model has been formulated and validated we can use it to test alternative hypotheses. The hypotheses can be about:

● Environmental variables on which the decision maker has no control.

- Decision variables (for example, in a financial problem: investment, price, dividend policy and so on) on which the decision maker does have control.

A validated decision model provides us with a tool for tracing out the effect of alternative decision on the behavior of a system. In particular, these effects can be criteria to choose among alternatives. A specific characteristic of model formulation in decision problems is that the modeling function has to be performed on the economic system but also, in certain situations, on the user (preference modeling).

We have summarized the main steps of model formulation and validation in Figure 4.7.

Model Formulation

The next step in the decision process, after problem recognition, is usually the need to support transformation of basic data to produce more usable information. Such transformation can be done through models. The conceptualization can be done at the data definition level, as well as at the modeling level.

In this section we shall refer to the JIIA-86 case study. This case will be described in more detail at the end of this chapter.

In this case study the definition of the production cost at the branch level is presented, the definition of commercial cost at the product level and the definition of advertising at the product level are all typical examples of conceptualization at the data level. The computation of the market share is a more sophisticated example of such conceptualization, since market share is defined by a model with two recurring equations. Such a model can then be used to test market share evolution as a function of advertising budget as shown by Little (1970).

A user may be interested to compute forecasted income statement given an hypothesis on activity (sales) level. He or she might be interested to obtain a cumulative margin figure which he or she might consider to be an important criterion.

Choice of Model Formalism

One of the essential decisions when starting to model a system is the choice of the representation formalism.

- Is it an equation type modeling language, a decision tree, an influence diagram formalism, or a mixture of them?

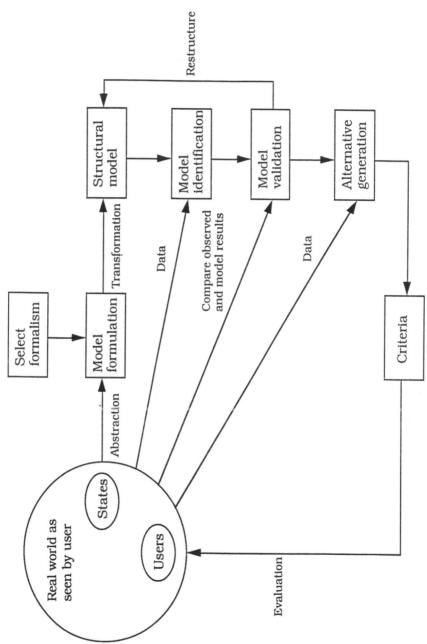

Figure 4.7 *The process of model formulation and validation in the study of real-world systems*

- How are uncertainty and time going to be represented in the formalism?
- Is the modeling system providing a way to model the user (preference, risk aversion and so on) as well as the economic and financial system?

Model Validation

Once a model has been formalized, the user is facing the problem of finding the values of the parameters of behavioral equations of the model. For example, in the FINSIM model described in Section 3.3.6 the user must provide the structural ratios relating a level of activity (sales variable) and a level of expenses (salary variable, for example). In the JIIA-86 case study the manager wants to use a short-term model for forecasting sales. This implies, for example, that he has to compute the equation of a trend plus a seasonal effect. To do this the user must use special statistical techniques (regression and so on). Many specialized methods have been developed for model identification and parameter computation. In this case, the DSS will attempt to provide the same support that a management scientist who specializes in short-term forecasting and statistics would do. We shall see in Chapter 6 that this function can be extended using artificial intelligence technology.

Access to Statistical or Optimization Routines

When studying information the analyst may be interested to use data analysis methods to structure information (cluster analysis and factor analysis are examples of such methods).

In certain cases an objective function can be defined and an optimization on decision variables can be performed. An interesting case is described in a financial and production planning situation by Jäger *et al.* (1988).

The statistical routines are useful in the process of model identification. The optimization routines are useful when an objective function is clearly expressed by the decision maker. In some well-formalized cases 'optimal' decisions can then be reached.

4.2.6 Supporting Decision Analysis

Model Manipulation for Solution Finding

Once a model has been defined it is important to be able to use it easily for solution finding. As we have seen in Chapter 3 when studying the normative point of view, it is very useful to distinguish in a model: decision variables (instruments), goal variables and exogenous variables. The usual assistance that a DSS will provide to support solution finding is the following:

- *Computation* of the system variables of the model.
- Assistance in *estimating* the value of certain variables (by using knowledge on the domain) or statistical methods.
- *Sensibility analysis* and *impact analysis* on criteria (goal variables) on environmental and decision variables following procedures introduced in the decision analysis cycle (see Chapter 3).

With a formalized model the user can generate alternatives (to which are associated criteria values) and choose among them. For instance, with the model FINSIM, described in Section 3.3.6, given a projection of financial needs, a financial manager will be able to define and simulate several financial strategies using debt, equity, leasing or a mixture of them.

Alternative Evaluation

In the domain of finance, a certain number of classical criteria for evaluating alternatives exist such as the net present value and the internal rate of return. If the decision maker wishes to follow the normative view of decision analysis we shall need functions to encode our knowledge on variables and preference for the outcome, as we have seen in Chapter 3. To decide among several alternatives the manager usually takes into account different criteria (goal variables). These criteria may be numerous and conflictive. Most of the time in real life the selection of one alternative is done intuitively. However, in finance, in particular, the modeling of the relation between risk and return for assets for which a market exists is known (Sharpe, 1963).

Multi-criteria Decision and Preference Modeling

As we have seen in Chapter 3, two rational decision makers using identical criteria can very well take two opposite decisions when facing the same alternatives. The reason is that their preferences for criteria are not the same.

Very often, decision makers do not wish to make their criteria or preferences explicit. They do not separate values and facts but, by judgment, they make a choice (see Section 4.1.4). However, in complex and non-repetitive situations with high risk they feel the need for support concerning their choice.

Much work has been done on assessment of multi-attribute utility functions as we have seen in Chapter 3, as well as on multi-criteria decision making.

If we wish to support the choice phase of the decision making process it is important to provide preference modeling and algorithms for multi-criteria decision making within the DSS. Even if these functions are not, at present, standard in DSS environments they have attracted more interest recently.

Group Decisions: Facilitating Negotiations

In many cases, the decision problem is faced by one person, in other cases many people are involved and negotiation is required. When many people are involved in a negotiation leading to a decision several types of problems are faced:

- Conflicting criteria and preferences.
- Different information available to each participant.
- Communication problems; in some cases due to the fact that they are geographically dispersed.

The problem of conflicting criteria and goals is a difficult problem. We have dealt with some of these aspects in Chapter 3.

Several technologies have been developed to support group decision making (see for instance, Kraemer, 1988). These technologies generally tend to provide a DSS kind of environment to members of the group.

When many persons are involved and geographically dispersed it is important that communication process be supported, not only to exchange basic data and share decision models, but also to help them in the negotiation process and to keep contact in-between face-to-face meetings. Electronic mail and computer-assisted tele or video-conferencing are very important functions of the DSS in such situations (Johansen *et al.*, 1974). The ability to support sharing of models, text, and display is a key characteristic of such environments. However, in contrast with most present electronic mail systems, the communication function must be integrated within the rest of the DSS. De Sanctis (1987) makes a classification of the kinds of support which can be provided to a group. The first level of support being communication, as emphasized above; the second level being decision analysis support; and the third level is providing knowledge bases and expert systems.

4.2.7 Supporting Decision Monitoring and Decision Quality Control

In many organizations once a decision is taken with the help of a DSS application one important step to success is to ensure that the decision is taken according to the rules of good behavior which have been developed within the organization.

For example in a bank hundreds of credit decisions may be made every week. It is important to be able to store the information and arguments on the basis of which the decision was taken to be able to have auditors study it later. It is also important to collect information on the file to confront the decision with later outcome. In the credit case it is useful to know if there was subsequent incident of payment with the client (delays, defaults, bankruptcy, etc.). This information is crucial to improve procedures.

4.2.8 Providing Information and Knowledge about the Problem Domain

To be of some value to a decision maker a DSS must include information and knowledge about the problem domain. The information and knowledge which is embedded in the DSS application includes typically:

- Information as *data* (numerical or not) describing the *attributes of entities* used in the problem and their possible occurrences. In the case of a DSS for financial analysis it will be the values of the financial accounts of the company being analyzed.
- Information under the form of *text* describing the *meaning of concepts* used in the problem formulation, the use of decision models and their validity conditions, the use of reports and their role in problem diagnosis, the origin of the information imbedded in the system.
- Information under the form of *variable names* used in decision models. These variable names may correspond to attributes of entities in the data base or have another origin.
- *Structure of decision models*. Much knowledge is involved in models. They provide:
  - a list of relevant variables to be used in solving a class of problems;
  - the causal relationship between these variables (numerical relation or direction of the variation).
- *Structure of reports*. Much knowledge is involved in the display of information to maximize decision support. A well designed report is a complex object mixing text, tables of figures well chosen graphical presentation of information and eventually images.

- *Rules, objects or other knowledge representation methods.* We shall see in Chapter 5, knowledge can be stored in different formalisms.

4.2.9 Providing Assistance during the Interaction with the System

Providing assistance to the user while he interacts with the DSS is of paramount importance in DSS usage. The system should provide different kinds of assistance:

- on its functions (how to retrieve information, how to diagnose problems, etc.);
- on the resources provided by the application (information in the DB, decision models with their goals, reports available, etc.);
- on the meaning of the vocabulary used in the system;
- on syntax of the command language;
- on the global logic of the application.

We shall see in Chapter 5 that the AI technology enable the DSS designer to much extend this capacity.

4.3 DSS GENERATOR OR DSS DEVELOPMENT ENVIRONMENT

Special software development environments also called generators or shells have had to be designed to implement DSS applications quickly, easily and reliably. Such generators integrate with synergy the computer technologies and solving methodologies (model solver, query processor, hypertex engine, report generator, etc.) required.

In the JIIA-86 case study, the solution to the problem implies the integration of database technology, modeling, display, statistical, client/server and telecommunication software. Such technology cannot be developed in a short time to solve the problem of a user; it must be readily available.

The manager who wishes to use a computer to support a decision rarely has the time to go through the standard steps of a software project of data processing type. These steps are usually known as the project life-cycle: requirements, specifications, design, unit programming, unit testing, integration, integration testing and maintenance. He works under time constraint and the implementation has to be done in a few months or weeks sometimes in a few days! If this constraint is not fulfilled the manager will solve his or her problem by other means and then deal with something else.

This does not mean that for a complex DSS application a user who is convinced of its usefulness will be unwilling to go through several steps to implement the DSS application (including a specification phase of a first version of the system, etc.). It means that a DSS application must as fast as possible improve the situation of its users and be ready to evolve according to their needs.

Clearly, a user plays a much more important role in the development of a DSS application than in a transaction processing application. In a transaction processing application the user expresses the specifications of what he or she wishes to a computer specialist, who will design a solution and implement it. In a DSS type of application the situation is different. We wish to supply a tool to support a given decision class, to a user, who will solve his or her particular problem. This tool constitutes an environment which must enable him or her to realize a certain number of functions. The problem is to create this environment in such a way that the tool assists the manager from the start, creating a better supporting environment for the devision class than in the preceding situation. (For example, by giving easier access to data, a better way to display information and the access to decision models to make computations and generate alternatives.) In other words, in certain situations, *the user is the designer* of his or her DSS. He or she may also find himself having to use a DSS which has been implemented for a specific decision class.

The characteristic of DSS situations is that the problem is in frequent evolution. Ill-structured problems usually evolve rapidly with time. Researchers and software companies have concentrated their efforts on developing software that is directly usable by end users after a period of education that is as short as possible.

4.4   FUNCTIONS OF A DSS GENERATOR OR A DSS DEVELOPMENT TOOL

Efficient implementation (fast and at low cost) of DSS implies the use of DSS development tools. We shall now present the conceptual structure of a DSS development tool, then discuss the main functions of such software.

4.4.1   The conceptual structure of DSS development tools

The conceptual structure of a DSS development environment is explained in Figure 4.8. This structure can be compared with the structure which was published in 1983 in Klein, Manteau. Some

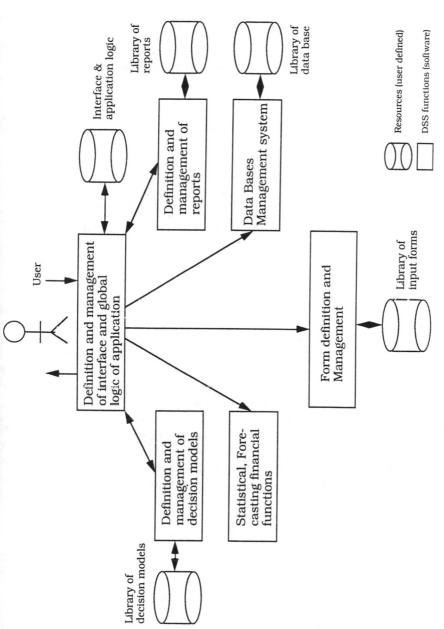

Figure 4.8 *Conceptual structure of a DSSG*

important progress was made in the field of DSS development environment from 1989 to 1994. This progress is related to the adoption of *graphical interface* and the *separation between the interface definition* and the other resources, in particular the modeling function. This separation was seen (Klein, 1993d) as an important problem to be solved. As can be seen from Figure 4.8 the user of a DSS generator is provided with an environment providing the following services to define his DSS application:

- a database management subsystem;
- a modeling subsystem;
- a report definition and management;
- a form definition and management subsystem;
- a set of functions (mathematics, statistics, data analysis, finance, short-term forecasting, etc.);
- a language to define the user interface and the global logic of the application.

A window will be associated to each of these services. These services will help the designer of the DSS application to define the functions of the DSS application: information collection, problem recognition problem structuring, problem modeling and decision analysis (see Section 4.2 above). The information collection function will be assisted using mainly the technology of data management and data base management systems. Other computing technologies useful here are E-mail or PC-based video-conferencing as soon as the decision process involves geographically dispersed persons.

The problem recognition function will be assisted by the report generator and data base management system. The problem structuring function will be assisted by the modeling language, the associated solver and the interface specification language. The decision analysis function will be assisted through the modeling function, the multi-attribute preference functions and/or algorithms for multi-criteria evaluation.

When using the DSSG the application designer will define five kinds of resources using the corresponding services:

- user interface and global logic of the application (using the interface definition language);
- decision models (using the modeling language);
- reports (using the report generator);
- forms (using the form management system);
- data files;
- data bases (using the DBMS).

We shall now describe briefly these functions starting with the data base resource.

4.4.2 DBMS

The importance of the DBMS in the DSSG is due to the fact that the DBMS technology solves two fundamental problems:

(1) Centralization, coordination, and diffusion of information in a community of users.
(2) Logical independence between data and the DSS application.

With respect to the first problem what has been true, historically, for data processing applications is also true for decision support applications. If the information required by several DSS users has to be shared, the functionality of a DBMS, as described below, is required. This DBMS will prevent the step-by-step creation of a large number of files as the DSS evolves, and keep data integrity.

With respect to the second problem we wish to point out that *data and model independence* is the key to smooth evolution of the system.

Since many DSS situations arise where managers have to make decisions relying on information taken out of a large pool of rapidly evolving data, a DBMS is required in these situations. However, if the DSS uses dedicated data files and performance is critical, then the DBMS is probably undesirable.

A DBMS *integrated* to the DSSG is necessary to achieve:

(1) the interface coherence of the development environment; and
(2) the integration of the DBMS component which we are looking for in the development of a DSS application where a large amount of data is needed.

The coherence should be achieved through a *common interface philosophy* and through the capacity of the designer to define an application where *exchange of information* between the data base and the other resources of the application (decisions models, reports, forms) are transparent to the user and where once information has been transfered from the data base to the application it can be used by decision models, reports, etc.

It is also often necessary to access information already stored *outside* the DSS application in widely available *multi-access relational DBMS* on main frame or on micro. The development of client-server architectures increases this need further. In this type of architecture the DSSG must provide a link to the leading relational DBMS through a SQL link. The DSSG should respect standards to access external relational data base. The Open Data Base Communication (ODBC) which has been developed by Microsoft Corporation is an attempt to define such a standard.

A DSS application will very often include:

- forms to update information associated with entities of the DB;
- reports using information coming from entities of the data base, etc.

It is classical to consider several levels of description of data:

- the user conceptual level;
- the logical level used by the DBMS;
- the physical level.

The conceptual level is the one of the user. The Entity Attribute Relationship (EAR) model is an example of a conceptual model. This model is independent from the DBMS used. The logical model (or schema) is the model used by the data description language of the DBMS. It is independent from the physical level but dependent from the DBMS used. The relational model and its associated tables is an example of a logical model. The physical level (also called internal level) describes how the data are stored in the memory of the machine. It has not to be known by the user. One of the important design problems of a DBMS integrated to a DSSG is that the logical model should be as close as possible to the users' conceptual model. In fact the users should be able to define its information using the conceptual model directly. This is what the multidimensional data models of most DSSGs integrating a DBMS module are doing. However the multidimensional models are not as powerful as classical relational models. The emergence of the Object Oriented Data Model which is close to the EAR conceptual model may be adopted in future DSSGs. However it is certain that for some time to come there will be a requirement for the DSSG to provide an easy SQL link to market standards for relational DBMS.

General Functions of the DBMS

A DBMS is the software that enables the user to organize data on peripheral drives and supply him or her with a query language to search and select that data. To obtain this result the user will describe, in abstract terms, what he or she wishes to do with the data, leaving the system to search as a function of the presentation and organization on physical support. In brief, a DBMS will provide the following functions.

Data definition

A language called the Data Definition Language (DDL) is provided to describe the data entities and their relationships which will be stored in the database. One of the problems of DBMS for DSS is that users have often to describe fairly complex numerical concepts at the database level. One of the first examples of DBMS design for supporting DSS was described in Klein and Tixier (1971) and Klein and Levy (1974).

Data manipulation

This function provides the user with a query language to interact with the database. This interaction takes the form of a dialog to search, select, sort and modify data.

In database terminology there are three classes of users: end users, application programmers and database administrators. Computer specialists will be able to use algorithmic procedures and end users will use a partially non-procedural command language. However, we have seen that end users, in management and in finance, in particular, wish to define complex models. These models will have to be fed by data coming from the database. A financial model such as FINSIM (Section 3.3.6) can be fed by data coming from a database of several hundreds or thousands of companies. In the JIIA-86 case study described at the end of this chapter a model will not only have to be fed by data in the database, but after a series of computations, will have to *update* the database with new data results from that computation. It is also fundamental that new attributes of an entity in the database can be defined using existing attributes.

Data integrity

The more abundant the information in a database the more risky it is to have a piece of data entered that is wrong with respect to the real world. To diminish this risk, the DBMS allow the user to describe rules to maintain the integrity of the database. These rules are called *integrity constraints*. They correspond to properties that should always be verified in the database whatever the data entered. For instance, in a financial database of annual reports the total assets should always be equal to the total liabilities in the balance sheet.

Control of access rights

If a database is shared among several users, certain subsets of data must only be used by authorized persons. A DBMS must provide procedures to control these access rights. For instance, in the JIIA-86 case study described at the end of this chapter a branch manager should not be allowed to *modify* other branches' data, but he may be allowed to *list* other branches' data.

The access rights are given by the database administrator who also has the responsibility for defining the logical structure of data, as well as the conceptual data model, and the integrity relations.

Concurrency control

Very often users of decision models or users of statistical routines access the same information in the database at the same time. The DBMS must provide procedures to detect cases when concurrency occurs and deal with it properly. For example, in the case of an inventory database, two users may request a certain quantity of the same item. These two requests have to be dealt with sequentially so as to find out if the first request can be satisfied, then if the second can.

Transaction recovery

In case of hardware failure the database ceases to operate. To make it possible for the system to restart when the incident has been corrected, the DBMS must keep information on transactions at certain control points to enable restarting of the database in a satisfactory state.

4.4.3 Modeling Subsystem

The modeling subsystem of a DSSG should provide several services:

- a modeling language, i.e. a formalism for modeling;
- a library of algorithms for solving decision models;
- an interface to manage the model base (menus, commands, etc.).

The modeling language is the tool needed to support the activities of *problem structuring* and *problem definition*. The task of problem structuring is also supported through the definition of the application interface. The capacity to define a set of decision models which exchange information is a key element when structuring a problem. For example a production model and a market model will produce outputs which in turn will serve as input to a financial model.

The library of solvers is needed since, as we shall see, many formalisms exist for modeling. A model without objective function may be solved by a simple recurring algorithm (substituting the name of a variable defined by an equation by this equation in the earlier equation . . .) on the contrary a model with an objective function which we try to maximize or minimize may need an optimization algorithm for its solution (the simplex method for example).

The language to manage the model base is needed since we have to: create models by giving them names, delete them when we do not need them any more, define them by expressing them as a text in a given formalism, etc. The language is also needed, as we shall see, in order to interact with a given model so as to support the decision analysis cycle.

The dominating modeling paradigm in domains such as finance, control, marketing, etc., is difference equation modeling. A model being a system of equations expressed by a given formalism. We have seen, in Chapter 3, the concept of decision tree and the more advanced concept of influence diagrams. We think that an ideal modeling subsystem should enable the user to combine decision trees or influence diagrams with a language to model the outcomes. Even in this restricted context it is not obvious what the main characteristics of a 'good' modeling language should be. To support the structuring of a problem by the means of a decision tree or an influence diagram requires graphical modeling tools to make them easier to use.

The support of the computation of the parameters of the decision tree or the influence diagram (outcome values and so on) requires an equation-oriented language. Several such languages have been developed. As a consequence, several kinds of modeling languages may be needed. A modeling language such as Dynamo is different from standard financial modeling languages in the sense that, for example, it distinguishes between several kinds of variables such as: levels, rates, auxiliaries and so on.

Also it should be recognized that the modeling language must support two kinds of modeling activities:

- decision model design;
- user preference modeling.

Decision modeling is the activity of designing models to represent subsystems or part of an organization (a financial model, a production model, a marketing model, etc.). In such models we have seen that it is important to structure the system variables in three classes: environmental, decision and final (or criteria).

User preference modeling is the activity of modeling user preference for criteria (attributes) associated with alternatives as we have seen in Chapter 3.

First of all we shall recall some important criteria in the classification of economic and financial models and derive some consequences for the modeling language itself. Then we shall study the integration needed between the modeling subsystem and the other subsystems of the DSS and the problem with using these models for decision support.

Types of Models

The classification of models is a complex subject. Several taxonomies of models have been suggested such as that by Forrester (1961), here, we shall only emphasize some important aspects of models which can be put in relation to the decision analysis methodology. These aspects are: deterministic versus stochastic, static versus dynamic, and linear versus non-linear (see Figure 4.9).

Deterministic

A deterministic model is a model in which no variable can take more than one value at the same time. Most of the traditional models in microeconomic theory are deterministic models as are most of the financial or corporate planning models described by Warren (1974), Carleton (1970a) and so on. The financial analysis and planning system FINSIM (Klein 1989) falls into this category. Analytical solutions are often the most efficient when using these models to compute variable values.

Stochastic

A stochastic model is a model with at least one variable which is uncertain and described by a probability function. Stochastic models are considerably more complex than deterministic. We have seen, when describing the decision methodology in Chapter 3, that when using models for decision analysis the transformation of a deterministic model into a stochastic one may be needed in order to support the decision analysis cycle. The adequacy of analytical techniques for obtaining solutions to these models is quite limited and simulation is often the only efficient solution.

Static

A static model is a model which does not take time explicitly into account. Most of the work carried out in the area of linear programming, non-linear programming and game theory deals with static models. Often, these models are deterministic and solutions can be obtained by analytical techniques such as optimality calculus and mathematical programming. The case of the portfolio problem as described by Markowitz (1959) and Sharpe (1963) falls in this class.

Dynamic

A dynamic model is a model which deals with time-lagging interactions between variables. Simulation has been rather widely used in the area of economic dynamics. Among the well-known applications of the simulation of dynamic systems are:

- Simulation of business cycles and macroeconomic growth models, Samuelson (1947).
- Simulation models of the firm such as Bonini (1968), Cyert and March (1963) and Forrester (1961).
- Financial planning models of the firm such as Warren (1974), Carleton (1970a), Alderberger (1976), and Klein and Levasseur (1971).

The modeling language

From what has been described above we can make conclusions about a certain number of criteria to evaluate a modeling language for decision support.

Naming system variables in a decision model

It is very important to be able to define names of variables in a clear and natural way. The user should not be too restricted in naming the model variables.

In fact it should be possible to keep a dictionary of the model variables with a short name and a long name, the short name being only used in decision models and the long name in input/output operations.

It should be possible to subscript model variables. The subscripting could be related to time, or any other entity (product, individual, etc.). An example is the following:

Cash $[t] = $ Cash $[t-1] + $ Cash flow $[t]$
SEM $[t] = \alpha^* $ Demand $[t] + (1-\alpha) \, ^* $ SEM $[t-1]$

It is better to use a different formalism for subscripting a variable and expressing a hierarchy of symbols in the evaluation of the expression. The parenthesis should be reserved to express operator hierarchy and the bracket to subscripting.

It is also very important to be able to associate a type (alphanumeric, integer, real number, Boolean, etc.) with a variable, its display characteristics (color, font, style, etc.), its limits (length for a chain, value limits for a figure, etc.), a unit measuring it (kilo, metres, second, etc.) and on which scale it is being measured. This can enable the system to perform dimension analysis on the model and automatically check the model for dimension errors with the variables. It may be important to be able to model the domain itself. This is easier in a DSS context since model variables are attributes of entities in the data base.

Relating values to model variable

This problem is related to our knowledge of the variables. If the variable is perfectly known we may be interested to define only a unique value for that variable. We may wish to designate a variable as an estimate and mark it as such (in which case any variable computed using it will also be market estimated). It should be possible to associate with a variable a probability distribution. This distribution can be observed (empirical) or theoretical. The statistical toolbox of the system (see Section 4.4.7) should provide algorithms to identify automatically parameters of standard distributions (binomial, poisson, normal, lognormal, etc.). It should be possible to build samples from the usual random process generators and as a consequence a uniformly distributed random number generator should be available.

Expressing relations between variables in a decision model

Most modeling systems in DSSG, provide the capacity to define quantitative relations between variables. For quantitative relations what is needed is to express parenthesized expressions using the standard mathematical symbols and mathematical functions. With respect to the functions the richness of the function library is an important criteria for the modeling language. What is available in the domains of statistics, probability theory, multi-attribute preference modeling, short-term forecasting, finance, marketing, production, may facilitate or make impossible the development of certain applications.

It should also be possible to express logical relation between variables using the logical connectives AND ($\wedge$), OR ($\vee$), NO ($\neg$) as well as conditional expression of the form:

If (condition) then expression 1 else expresion 2

ex:

If profit_before_tax > 0 then profit_after_tax = profit_before_tax $*0.40$
else 0

It should be possible to express *constraints* relating variables:

ex: production > 500
production < 3000 and production > 500

It should be possible to express objectives and if these objectives have to be minimized or maximized. It is clear that we should be able to define which variable (or function of variables) are to be optimized.

The resolution algorithm or solvers

Once a model has been expressed, the modeling system should provide a set of resolution algorithms to solve the model. This is where a modeling language differs from a programming language.

A programming language does not provide an algorithm for solving models, the algorithm would have to be defined using the programming language.

Figure 4.9 shows a typology of models and the name of some algorithms for solving them. For example, if we have the following models:

Model 1

$quantity_t = quantity_{t-1} * 1.15$	(1)
$price_t = price_{t-1} * 1.03$	(2)
$sales_t = quantity_t * price_t$	(3)
variable cost $t = quantity_t * unit\ cost_t$	(4)
total $cost_t = $ fixed cost + variable $cost_t$	(5)
$margin_t = sales_t - $ total $cost_t$	(6)

Model 2

$quantity_t = C_1 - C_2 * price_t$	(1)
$price_t = $ mark $up_t * $ total $cost_t / quantity_t$	(2)
$sales_t = quantity_t * price_t$	(3)
variable $cost_t = $ unit $cost_t * quantity_t$	(4)
total $cost_t = $ fixed cost + variable $cost_t$	(5)
$margin_t = sales_t - $ total $cost_t$	(6)

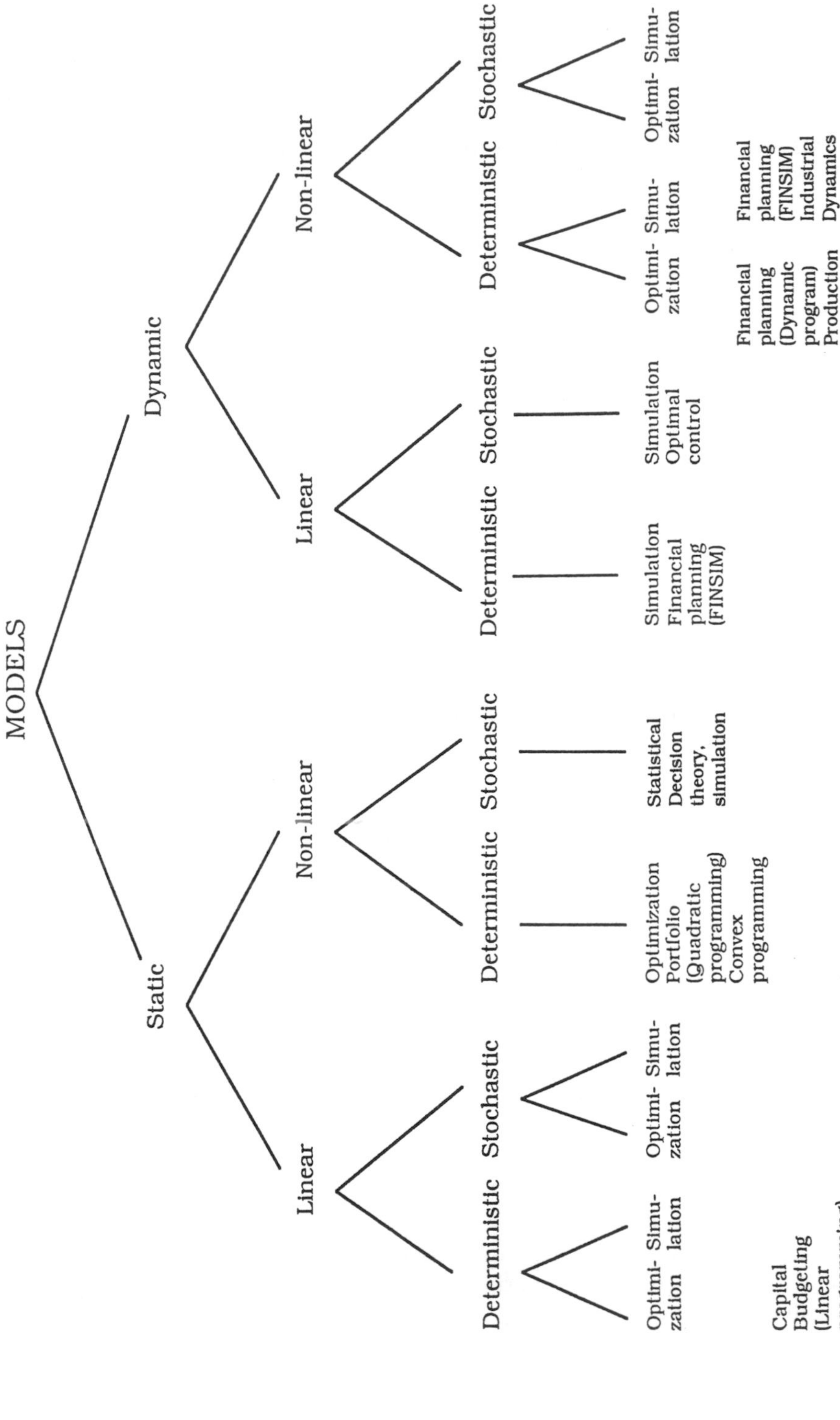

MODELS

Static

Dynamic

Linear

Non-linear

Linear

Non-linear

Deterministic   Stochastic

Deterministic   Stochastic

Deterministic   Stochastic

Deterministic   Stochastic

Optimi-   Simu-
zation   lation

Optimi-   Simu-
zation   lation

Optimi-   Simu-
zation   lation

Optimi-   Simu-
zation   lation

Capital
Budgeting
(Linear
programming)

Optimization
Portfolio
(Quadratic
programming)
Convex
programming

Statistical
Decision
theory,
simulation

Simulation
Financial
planning
(FINSIM)

Simulation
Optimal
control

Financial
planning
(Dynamic
program)
Production
planning

Financial
planning
(FINSIM)
Industrial
Dynamics

Figure 4.9 *A typology of models*

It is clear that in Model 1 the quantity sold and price are independent variables. The model can, in fact, be computed variable by variable for the first period, and then computed for the next periods. This type of model is easy to solve, recursively, to compute the value of the model variables at each period.

In Model 2, quantity and price are not independent any more: relation (1) shows that quantity is a linear function of price. The higher the price the smaller the quantity. Relation (2) shows that price is related to quantity. So it is easy to see that these two models may require different solution algorithms. Model 2 necessitates a simultaneous equation algorithm for a non-linear system.

The Gauss-Seidel method is an example of such a solving procedure for a model. But we have seen that some special solution algorithms may be required to solve model where objective functions can be defined.

User model interaction

User model interaction happens in any of the following cases:

- work on the text of the model to create or modify it;
- compile the model to obtain syntactic diagnosis;
- run it;
- interact with it for decision support.

The design of the decision model means that the user works in a text editing mode. Two modes are possible. The syntactic analysis is done while the user is editing the text of the model (line per line). The syntactic analysis is done as the first step of the compilation when the user is requesting it. A cut and paste function is here useful. With respect to the interaction with the model for decision support, the problem is to support the decision analysis cycle. It must be possible then to:

- make sensitivity analysis;
- make Monte-Carlo analysis.

The sensitivity analysis is needed to know if a variable should be present in a decision model or not. The Monte-Carlo analysis (or other method to deal with uncertainty) will be needed if the alternative selected in the decision situation changes when the variable under study changes its value on its possible interval of variation.

To support the cycle described by Howard and Matheson (1968) the user must be able to access special functions to:

- encode the prior knowledge about variables;
- encode the time preference of money;
- encode the risk aversion;
- make different kinds of sensitivity analysis.

4.4.4   Report Definition and Management (Report Generator)

The display of information is a key feature of DSS development environment. Significant progress has been made in report generators.

The first progress is to acknowledge that in the general case a report is an object mixing text (within which numerical values can appear), tables, graphics and images or maps.

As a consequence a report generator provides several services:

- a graphical interface to define reports;
- a language to manage the report base.

The language to manage the report base is there to let the user create, list and destroy reports. The interface to define reports is there to help the user type the text of his report using various fonts and character size, insert numerical values in the text as simple variables or as tables, insert images or maps. The interface of the report generator of the development environment is a mixture of menus, dialog boxes and direct action with the mouse. As a consequence the user must be provided with a publishing component and a way to improve the presentation of tables by direct action on their structure with the mouse. The progress made recently on report generators is clearly that reports are considered as complex objects made of other objects such as text, tables, graphics and so on.

4.4.5   Form Definition and Management (Form Generator)

This subsystem is needed in order to define sophisticated input screens.

In many applications basic information is contained in administrative forms. The role of the form generator is to define this form on the screen. The user just has to type in the data at the place reserved for it in the form. A form generator is similar to a report generator, but it is a more complex module. It must have the same possibility of designing a presentation of the screen, as the report generator but to this must be added the possibility of testing the inputted data (type, value taken in an interval, control of valid occurrences, etc.). In a similar way to the report generator this subsystem will provide:

- an interface to define forms;
- a language to manage the form base.

4.4.6 Graphics

The most usual graphics presentation are curves, barcharts and pie charts and various combinations of them in two or three dimensions. We have seen that graphics are objects which can be included in reports. The question is to know if it is desirable to be able to draw a curve without going through the report generator. A report can be made only of graphics. Given the large diversity of graphical presentation of information it is interesting to be able to access a tool to draw graphs. In some field of application special graphs are needed such as Gantt charts in production.

4.4.7 Library of Useful Algorithms

On certain occasions, a DSS application designer may need to access a library of statistical and/or management science models, in particular for statistical analysis, short-term forecasting, using OR methods, encoding knowledge and preference. For example a regression analysis can be used to identify the quantitative relation between variables. The result can then be used as a relation in a model. A segmentation analysis can be used to find out weight in a score function which will then be used in a model, etc.

4.4.8 Communication Between Users

The most standard way of exchanging information between geographically dispersed users connected to a computer network is through electronic mail (e-mail). However PC-based video-conferencing will be more and more integrated as a DSS function.

4.4.9 Exchange of Data in a Distributed Environment

We have seen in Chapter 2 that group decision processes are the most common in organizations. As a consequence DSS applications have often to be designed to support decision processes involving several persons working within an organization often in different places. We shall describe briefly two situations where distributed environments are needed.

An Application to Support Credit Analysis in a Bank

Credit analysts usually work in the branches of a bank and use a DSS application for financial statement analysis such as FINSIM, (Klein, 1989). The application is stored on the disk of the server of a LAN to which are connected the PCs used by the credit analysts.

The credit analysts use the FINSIM application to support their task. As a consequence they need to share accounting information concerning particular companies.

The accounting information on companies is stored in files on the disc of the server or in the database used by the application and also stored on the server. A request for a loan from a client or prospect in the French banking context may go through the following stages:

- preparation of the loan request by the customer account-manager;
- examination of the customer file by the branch manager who will add his or her comments to those already made by the customer account manager;
- transfer of the customer file to the group branch, where it is studied by a risk-analyst who will add his or her own comments;
- final examination by the 'credit committee'.

As a consequence the customer file must be transferred or accessed from headquarters or the head branch for analysis.

Also the client files at each branch must be used in order to compute statistics on all customers (such as a risk score, a discriminant analysis to compute parameters of a score function, or, as we shall see in Chapter 6, ratios for a knowledge base). This type of computation can be done, using the DBMS module, with the copy of the DSS application at headquarters. Then the result will have to be sent to each application in order to update part of it.

In fact the situation is more complex since, the study of a request for a loan usually implies using not only accounting information but also banking information (history of cash position on the company banking account, characteristics on loans, etc.). This information is usually already stored in a DBMS on a mainframe computer. When a credit analyst loads the accounting information concerning a client or a prospect (information stored in the local BD of his application), the application must also call for the banking information stored for example in the DB2 or Oracle DBMS on the mainframe. This is a client-server structure for the application.

As can be seen from this example the exchange of information is as follows:

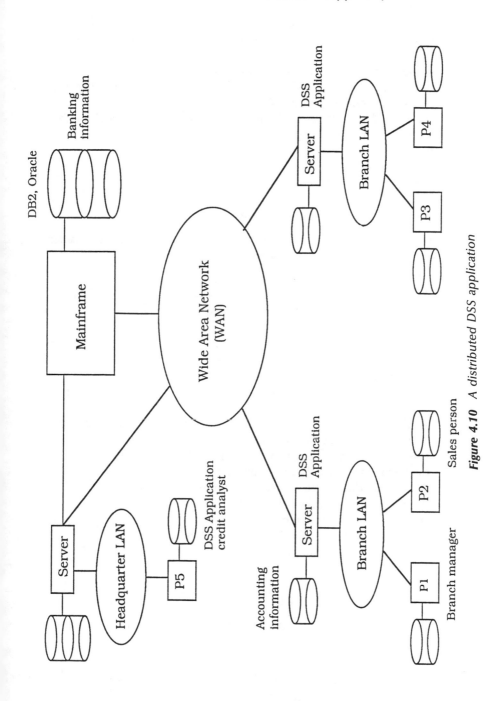

Figure 4.10 *A distributed DSS application*

- transfer of files from one server to another through the network;
- multi-access from stations connected to a LAN to the local database on the server;
- dispatching, from headquarters to the local workstations in the branches of files which are used in the application (updated statistics, updated knowledge base, etc.).
- transfer of data from the mainframe database to the local database for use in the DSS application;
- transfer of data from the local application to the DBMS on the local LAN of the headquarters.

4.4.10 Sharing of Resources

As can be seen from the above credit analysis example, the sharing of resources of the DSS application is needed:

(1) The application is stored on each station but then we have a problem since several users (group and headquarters) have to add information in the database.
(2) The application is stored on the server of the LAN to which are connected the stations. In that case the resources which must be shared among the users are:
   - the data in the database, since several users may work on the same company;
   - the models, since the same historical and forecast models may be used by several users.
   It is clear that the historical data will be the same, but the forecast data may differ from one user to another:
   - the standard reports are the same;
   - the ad hoc reports vary with each user;
   - the forms are the same;
   - the statistics files are the same;
   - the interface is the same.

4.4.11 Control of Access to the DSS Resources

Two types of access control are needed if we refer to the credit analysis case above:

- one is related to the sharing of resources problem;
- one is related to an authorization problem.

The authorization problem means that it will be possible for the DSS administrator to define a list of users with their access rights.

4.4.12 Assistance and Navigation

Assistance will be needed on the following topics:

- functions of the DSS application;
- syntax of commands;
- meaning of commands (semantic aspect);
- definition of concepts used in the DSS application;
- use of resources (data file, database, decision models, reports, forms, interface and global logic);
- methodological advice.

Assistance with the DSS Functions

This assistance can be implemented when designing the application user interface, by having a help option in the main menu.

Assistance with Syntax Errors and Debugging

When developing applications users will very probably mix commands, menus and icons if these three modes of interactions are available (which is necessary). The user should be able to obtain the syntax on request as he proceeds in expressing the commands so as to avoid any unnecessary typing. The problem of providing clear error messages at the application and decision model level is a complex one in DSS. The reason is that the DSS development environment which provides a syntax to describe the application (text defining the interface and global logic), the decision models, the database definition language and query language is very large. In the case we describe in Chapter 6 a language for knowledge base definition is added. Moreover the syntax is likely not to be of the LL(1) type. On the other hand the capacity to present clearly the text of a model in its totality is a great advantage compared with spread sheets. The existence of a debugger has proved very useful, such a tool should enable the user to trace the execution of the application as well as decision models.

Assistance for the Meaning of Commands

On request the user should be provided with the syntax of a command and explanation of the function of that command. In fact the user manual of the system should be on line in a *hypertex* mode. The table of contents should be displayed, and then by clicking on the section, the user should obtain the text of that section. The same process should be available for the commands and *index* of the user manual.

Assistance for the Meaning of Concepts

Concepts are used in several locations in the system; they can be used at the database level, when the user is defining entities and their attribute. It is very useful to be able to have a short and long name for concepts, also to associate a comment to an occurrence name. Concepts are also used at the decision model level.

For example a database may be made of entities which are companies, the attributes of these entities are their name, their industry code, the account and a date (fiscal year).

This is the case in the FINSIM application. The database is made of thousands of companies. To each company are associated attributes called accounts and a date (the fiscal year). The financial model is using the occurrence of the accounts as variable.

Description of a Concept when it is Defined from more Elementary Concepts

An attribute of an entity is a concept. Some attributes (known as variables or line labels in a decision model) are defined using other variables elementary or not. It is important that the system provides a command to obtain the definition of concepts from other concepts used in the definition until we obtain the elementary concepts.

Assistance for the Use of Resources

A DSS application provides numerous resources to the user (decision models, reports . . .). If these resources become numerous or their conditions of use complex it is useful to provide guidance to their use. We shall see in Chapter 6 that this can be done using an expert system component.

Methodological Advice

In many situations the user may need advice on the way to solve a problem. We shall see that this type of assistance can be provided through a methodological knowledge base.

4.4.13 Interface and Global Logic Definition and Management of a DSS Application

One of the important results of recent research on DSS has been the separation of the interface from the resources in a DSS application. The importance of this problem was pointed out during the II Ciocco conference in 1991 (Klein, 1993d), and the description of a solution was given in Klein and Traunmüller (1993a, 1993b) and Klein (1993e).

The main reasons why this point is essential are the following:

- the interface definition with a DSSG takes a large number of instructions and obscures the text of decision models;
- if we do not have a model made only of equations, then it is difficult to implement very useful algorithms such as equation reasoning;
- it must be possible to modify the interface without impact on the models and make changes in the models without impact on the interface;
- the interface is also the place to define the global logic of the application;
- it facilitates a clear definition of the functions of the application;
- it facilitates an orderly development of the application by a group.

The interface should in fact be a text defining menus with command window, their options, icons and the call to different resources (interaction between the user and the DSS application).

For example, let us define a simplified version of the interface of the FINSIM application as it is described in Chapter 3.

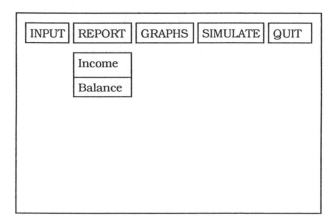

Figure 4.11 *FINPLAN main menu*

The application should support the task of financial analysis and planning and as a consequence the following functions should be provided:

- display a form to perform data entry (INPUT option):
- print reports (REPORT option);
- compute a historical model (HISTO);
- compute a forecast model: FINPLAN (SIMULATE option);
- quit the system (QUIT option).

4.4.14   Integration Needed between the Resources Provided by the Development Environment

The interaction between the resources creates a synergy between them. The most usual interactions are as follows:

Interaction between Model and Data base

The interface can be used to define a view of the database, and as a consequence retrieve data in the DB to provide the occurrences of variables associated with the DSS application. It can also load data in the DB to provide the occurrence of the attributes of the entities in the DB.

These instructions will provide the mechanism to update decision model variables with values from the DB and update attributes of an entity with values computed by a model.

Interaction between models

As we have seen in the preceding example a model is called up by the interface. A financial model may need a variable value (such as a share price, a cost of production . . .) which is computed by another model. Decision models have to exchange information. One way to do it is through the application file which then constitutes a blackboard type of architecture (see Section 6.3.2).

Interaction between model and report generator

The model is called up by the interface and executed, and as a consequence the variables' values are updated in the application file, then the interface calls up the report which will automatically use the variable value in the application file.

Interaction between model and toolbox of statistical algorithms

In fact the toolbox is used on several occasions during the modeling process:

- to describe data (descriptive statistical methods, classification algorithm);
- to test relations between variables (explicative methods such as a regression);
- to use short-term forecasting models.

The toolbox allows the user to apply these algorithms to the variable of the application and then use the result to build models.

For example a hierarchical classification can be used to define market segments in a marketing model. A regression analysis can be used to identify a relation between variables.

Interaction between Data Base and report generator

We define in the interface a view of the database. A view can be interactively defined by the user who is asked the value of the occurrence of an attribute. This value, such as an entity name, can be automatically transferred to the report. The report presenting the income statement is then called and the title of the report is automatically updated with the name of the company.

Interaction between Data Base and form generator

We define in the interface a view of the database. The view can be partially defined interactively by the user. An instruction of the interface displays a form taken out of the forms library. Once the data capture is performed by the user, the transfer of the inputted data to the database is automatically performed.

If we introduce the possibility at the interface level to loop on a view of the database it is easy to define an application which will:

(1) open a database containing data on companies;
(2) define a view of the database starting with a company;
(3) load the data in the file associated with the application;
(4) solve a model using these data;
(5) print a report using the data extracted from the DB and computed from a model;
(6) repeat the process for all companies or a subset of companies in the DB.

4.5 IMPROVEMENTS EXPECTED FROM DSS USAGE

The improvements due to DSS usage which have been claimed in the literature can be summarized as follows:

- greater effectiveness of decision making (quality of a decision);
- improved efficiency (reducing delay and cost for certain tasks leading to a decision or the solution of a problem);
- better communication among decision makers;
- improving the learning process of users.

4.5.1 Improving the Effectiveness of Decision Making

This is the most important claim of DSS literature. Two of the oldest examples are:

(1) The Laundry Equipment Case (Scott-Morton, 1971) where a DSS to support the work of the marketing planning manager is described.
(2) The evaluation work done in the SCARABEE project on financial analysis with the support of the SCARABEE DSS (Girault and Klein, 1971).

We shall recall some of these results starting with the Laundry Equipment Case. In this case, the task of the marketing planning manager is described and, also, which task combines the sales and production plans into specific production targets for the products for which he or she is responsible. The decision process that was made before the DSS was used was spread over 20 days each month. In his analysis of the situation, Scott-Morton points out that the inadequacies of the existing process were not caused by lack of competence but by 'technical constraints and cognitive limitations, particularly in terms of a lack of capacity to manage large computations and alternatives simultaneously'.

> 'It was decided to use exactly the same input data that the managers currently had available. In many respects the DSS was an improved methodology for handling the manual spreadsheets; it eliminated bottlenecks that prevented the following type of dialogue in the managers' meetings:
> '"Why don't we take a quick look at what the inventory will look like 7 months out?"
> '"I don't like that. Let's try it with 3 months' supply for July through to October."
> '"No, go back and adjust June and see if we increase production and get those inventories back in balance."

'Such dialogue was impossible before the DSS. More importantly, because of the bottlenecks, the managers' interactions were mutually defensive, even hostile. With the DSS, this changed to an atmosphere of joint exploration. The managers saw the graphical displays as a communication device. They explained ideas, pointed to supporting data, focused on details, looked ahead rather than concentrating on next month's plan, and made comparisons, and, of course, explored far, far more alternatives. Whereas, with the manual system, there was a large cost involved in considering even one more alternative, the DSS reduced the extra effort almost to zero. The result was that the six days of the manager's time spread over 20 days was reduced to half a day spread over two working days.' (Scott-Morton, 1971)

Analysis of these conclusions shows that a better decision was reached because:

- Problems or potential problems could be identified more easily (support for the problem recognition phase in Minzberg framework).
- Graphical output enables a more rapid assimilation of information (support of the problem recognition phase).
- It was possible to generate many more alternatives (support of the design of alternatives phase).
- It was possible to visualize and compare the consequences/outcomes of the alternatives more easily (support of criteria evaluation).
- An atmosphere of collaboration was created.

However it should be noted that we have since then learned that it is not sufficient to provide a DSS application in order to create such an efficient collaboration. The adoption of a DSS application is a social process and other conditions have to be met.

With respect to the SCARABEE experiment, conducted at the HEC Business School in France, from 1970 to 1974 the main ideas of the system were:

- To provide direct access to a financial database.
- To provide multi-access to this database through an interactive language, giving users the possibility to, not only retrieve and sort information under different conditions, but also to define new financial concepts with the language.
- To give access to a report generator to enable the user to define, very easily, any kind of simple or sophisticated report.
- To give access to a set of statistical tools integrated in the language to make their use extremely easy and comfortable.

Even if the main goal of the project was to develop a methodology of design of DSS software environments, rather than to provide a professional service to financial analysts, several experiments were conducted. The main results of these experiments were the following:

- Analysts could much more easily identify the companies requesting attention, due to the facility of filtering the database for companies that fulfill certain conditions.
- Graphical output was perceived as much more efficient in coming to conclusions, such as comparing the quarterly return of a porfolio with that of the market.
- It was possible to conduct useful statistical analyses which were impossible before (such as the relation between price and company fundamentals, or industry cross-section analysis to compare performance).
- Better heuristics were developed by professionals improving their problem-solving ability. In fact, the learning process of users was accelerated.
- The fundamental aspect of system interaction, to facilitate exploration of new ideas and the acceptance of the system (see Figure 4.12).

As a conclusion, we can say that the improved quality of decisions which is reported in the literature when using DSS is due to the following reasons:

(1) Easier access to information.
(2) Faster and more efficient problem recognition.
(3) Access to computing tools and proven models to compute criteria for choice.
(4) Ability to generate and evaluate a large number of alternatives.

It is interesting to note that if reasons (1) and (2) are directly related to the descriptive view of the decision process, as presented in Section 4.1.4, then reasons (3) and (4) are more related to the normative view and can be justified on a theoretical basis. We shall now give some hints about efficiency.

4.5.2 Improving Efficiency of Decision Making

This consequence is certainly the one which is the easiest to demonstrate and is so generally accepted that we shall not describe it here at length.

In the Laundry Equipment Case described by Scott-Morton, the length of the decision cycle was reduced by a factor of ten, since

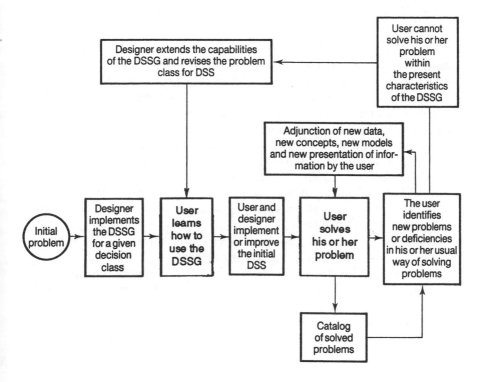

Figure 4.12 *Iterative evolution of a DSS and its development environment*

instead of using 20 days each month, the decision could be reached in two days.

In recent measures made with FINSIM (Chapter 3) used by credit analysts in banks, the difference was perceived to be mainly in the level of the quality of the decision, since studies are made in much more depth and with more detailed analysis. The task of financial analysis accomplished with the assistance of FINSIM is done much quicker (time usually divided by a factor of 3 or 4). The three main improvements concerning efficiency when using a DSS are:

(1) Reduction in the cost of the decision.
(2) Reduction of the delay to reach the decision for the same level of detail in the analysis.
(3) Better quality in the printed documents supplied to back the decision.

4.5.3   Improving Communication and Collaboration among Decision Makers

This consequence is certainly a very fundamental one. In many situations it can be considered one of the reasons for increased effectiveness. This consequence is very striking in the Laundry Equipment Case since, before the introduction of the DSS, two persons with conflicting goals were involved: the director of marketing and the director of production planning. In fact, a third person, the marketing planning manager, was introduced, whose task was to facilitate the discussion between the two others and help to come to an operational decision and solve conflicts. After the implementation of the DSS the atmosphere 'changed to an atmosphere of joint exploration'. This evolution can be explained easily in terms of decision analysis (see Chapter 3). By using a DSS the two managers had a model in common. We have however pointed out that effective collaboration is also relying on the organization dominant value system.

The different levels of knowledge about the problem then tend to disappear since variables and relations are made explicit and their value or nature can be discussed more easily and with precision. Divergences between decision makers can clearly stay, but then, there is precise knowledge on the nature of the difference of opinion, and the methodology of decision analysis can be used to solve it. Also, sharing a model will help separate differences between *facts* and *values* or preferences. As we have already seen the clarification provided by this separation is of fundamental support to the decision makers.

We recognize that certain people may not be willing to make things explicit in a decision and, as a consequence, are not likely to be pleased to see a DSS being used. But, such a situation is usually due to the fact that these people are not interested in the improvement of the decision or a discussion of their real motivations or preferences. The decision was already taken (maybe using the DSS); their goal is to have the alternative they have chosen adopted. This is then a different problem: how do you get your preferences adopted or shared by others?

4.5.4   Improving the Learning Process of Users

This consequence of using DSS is also clearly related to the effectiveness issue. In other words, it is because a DSS improves the learning process of users that the effectiveness of decisions is improved. This consequence has even been considered (Klein and Tixier, 1971) as a design criteria: 'a well-designed DSS is the one which speeds up the learning process of the user'. One of the founding ideas of the DSS school is a psychological one. Since, in many cases, the normative computer models were not successful, the recommended approach has been to provide the user with a computer environment within which he or she can accomplish the task more effectively (see Figure 4.12) and become conscious of inconsistency and deficiency in the decision processes:

- Easier access to pertinent information through the data management subsystem.
- Easier problem recognition through the display subsystem.
- Easier problem structuring through a modeling language (with emphasis on the clarity of representation of relations).
- Access to knowledge on the problem domain through existing decision models or the possibility to improve and make evolve the decision models.
- Easier and faster generation of alternatives through a model manipulation language.

In other words, this provides the user with a starting DSS environment which is better than the one available before.

The assumption is that if the ability to solve a problem relies on two major components: knowledge (in particular, methodological knowledge) and experience, then the environment will provide an easier way to use that knowledge (by making it easier to build models, for example), and, also, a way to speed up the process of building up experience, since it is much easier and faster to study cases. This process is presented in Figure 4.12 which is derived from an earlier version (Klein and Tixier, 1971). The implementation strategy of the DSS is worked out so as to initialize the learning process of the user and gear it to the evolution process of the DSS itself. We would like to stress that this learning process can start only in organizations where professional development is the dominant corporate culture.

Step 1 The designer designs and implements a DSS development environment (DSSG).

Step 2 The user learns how to use the DSS development environment.

Step 3 The user (or user + designer) implements the starting DSS application or improves the existing one.

Step 4 The user works with the DSS application to accomplish his tasks and solve problems, so adding to the catalog of solved problems.

Step 5 The user identifies new problems or deficiencies in his actual way of solving problems.

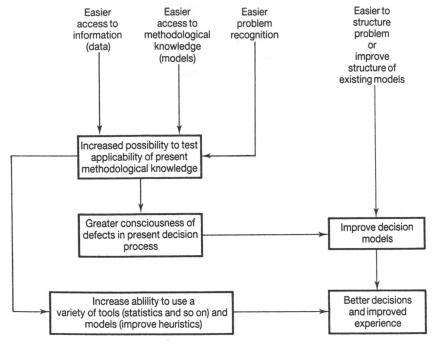

Figure 4.13 *Learning process with a DSS environment*

Step 6 If the user can extend the existing DSS application by adding new data, new concepts, new models and new presentation then go to Step 3, else go to Step 7.

Step 7 The designer extends the capabilities of the DSS development environment: adding a DBMS subsystem, extending the concepts of the modeling language, extending the possibilities of the report generator, adding new data types, adding new subsystems, go to Step 2.

Clearly this strategy is possible if the development environment can be extended easily. In other words, in the preceding example, the DBMS component must be readily available.

4.5.5   Possible Drawbacks of DSS Usage

We would like to emphasize here the fact that the availability of a well-designed DSS may also lead to some adverse effects. In our opinion, DSS are there to help managers to make decisions by providing them with a better understanding of their decisions, and how they relate to their preference. But, the main task of a manager is to act on his environment to help achieve the goals of his organization in supplying a service or goods to his environment (clients and users). The manager should always be very conscious not to forget to keep a good balance between studying the problem and acting to change the environment. Working with a DSS, as good as it may be, cannot change the environment. Environments are changed by human beings acting on them! This we can call the *problem of action*.

One of the pertinent criticisms of the DSS concept was made by Winograd and Flores (1986) in their book *Understanding computers and cognition*. The potential problems with DSS, as the authors see them, are the following:

- tendency to overemphasize decision making;
- assumption of relevance;
- unintended transfer of power;
- unanticipated effects;
- obscuring responsibility;
- false belief in objectivity.

Tendency to Overemphasize the Decision Making Aspect

The criticism is that

'The emphasis implicit in this approach serves to reinforce the decisionist perspective and to support a rigid status quo in organisations, denying the validity of more social, emotive, intuitive, and personalised approaches to the complex process of reaching resolution.' (Winograd and Flores, 1986)

We would like to emphasize here that we recognize that communication is a fundamental task of management; it is useless to try to tell if decision is more important than communication, since both are important and decisions rely on communication.

In some circumstances, the use of computers for communication will be considered as a much more important function than their modeling function. The development of electronic mail and computer-assisted video-conferencing is a good example of this evolution. Also the situation may be such that it is much more difficult to get the commitment of somebody to do a task than to decide that the task has to be done. As we have stated above any DSS application is designed to support a class of decisions. The consequence of this is, simply, that a new user of a DSS must be able, always, to use his or her (natural) intelligence to check that the decision he or she is studying belongs to the class that the DSS was built to support, partially or totally. This capacity of the user is not always easy to apply.

If it is not the case, the user must diagnose whether or not the DSS development environment enables him or her to extend the decision class for which it was built (within the time and budget constraint) to include the new decision. If this extension cannot be done then it is better not to use the system.

Assumption of Relevance

'Once a computer system has been installed it is difficult to avoid the assumption that the things it can deal with are the most relevant things for the manager's concern.' (Winograd and Flores, 1986)

As Winograd and Flores point out this behavior is characteristic of people who have not been educated to have 'a permanent attitude of openness to listening'. We could add: who have not understood that any computer application is built under a certain set of assumptions for its use by its designer. If the user is not able to recognize that the condition of use of the system does not fit these assumptions then the system can be harmful.

The problem is that the designer may not be conscious enough of these hypotheses.

Unintended Transfer of Power

The problem usually arises here if the design made by computer specialists tends to put more emphasis and value on efficiency and to devalue the 'need for human discretion and innovation'. The argument is certainly valid in the case of a full automatization of the decision process; it is much less valid for a DSS since the decision process is only assisted. This argument tends to disappear if the user plays a leading role in the evolution of the system.

Obscuring Responsibility

The proposition put forward by Winograd and Flores is that once a computer system is designed and in place, it tends to be treated as an independent entity. For them, the computer's role is not the one of a 'surrogate expert', but the one of an intermediary – a sophisticated medium of communication.

When a computer specialist or a domain expert builds a DSS application incorporating a formal representation of their knowledge or discourse (we shall see that this capacity is now much easier to accomplish with expert systems technology), the system will transmit the consequence of this knowledge to the users under the form of advice or statements.

According to Winograd and Flores we should be very careful to remember that the machine is an *intermediary*, the commitment inherent in the conclusion expressed is 'made by those who produce the system'.

We can, of course, only agree with the idea that the responsibility cannot be the one of the machine. We cannot however agree with the idea that the DSS is only a sophisticated means of communication. In most well designed DSS the system advice is the logical consequence of our data or hypotheses and preferences. However, it is essential to make sure, again, that the future users are properly educated to remember that any DSS or expert system is built within a background of assumptions about how the system will be used, and how its responses will be interpreted.

There is always a risk that a DSS is used in a way which does not fit the assumptions of the expert or designer. The only cure here is education.

4.6 SOFTWARE TOOLS FOR DSS APPLICATIONS DEVELOPMENTS

DSS applications have been developed using mainly:

- general programming languages;
- spreadsheets;
- specialized DSS development environments or generators.

We shall point out here some problems related with each of these tools.

General Programming Languages

The problem with programming languages is mainly that:

- They imply that the user will have the time and competence to learn and to use them if he wants to develop his application himself.
- They exclude the ability of the user to read the text of models if the application is developed by a professional. The text of models will be programmed in Basic, Fortran, Pascal, C or C++ and mixed with resolution algorithms and interface definition. As a consequence they usually require from the user a very careful initial definition of his needs and imply an implementation time which precludes them in many cases.
- They do not provide subsystems usually needed for DSS application development: data management, report generators, model solvers, etc.
- They make it more difficult for the application to evolve.

They may lead to a satisfactory solution if:

- the DSS application does not evolve too much;
- performance is crucial;
- there is no severe time constraint on implementation delay.

Spreadsheets

At the time of writing the problem with spreadsheets is that:

- they do not provide a clear understanding of an application global logic in using resources such as data, decision models, reports, forms, etc.;
- they do not provide a satisfactory readability of decision models;
- they do not provide a way to represent easily data structure more complex than two-dimensional tables;
- they prevent easy evolution of the application due to the non-separation between data management, models, form and report definition. All these tasks must be accomplished by the user within a grid of cells, a cell being able to contain a piece of data, a formula, and be used for presentation.

The consequence is that spreadsheets can be used for simple personal applications but are very risky to use for more complex or institutionalized applications.

The reason for the wide use of spreadsheets is that for simple applications users can and like to start by defining the presentation of the results they are looking for.

DSS Development Environments or Generators

What such systems provide to the user was described in Section 4.4.1. The most obvious advantages of such systems are that:

- they are designed for end-users or domain specialist (they follow on this point the same approach as spreadsheets);
- they provide the resources for application development (modeling language, report generator, user interface definition language . . .) and automate the integration between the resources;
- they allow the definition of much more complex applications than is possible with spreadsheets. These applications have a greater capacity to adapt to the evolution of user needs.

4.7 AN EXAMPLE OF DSSG: OPTRANS OBJECT

OPTRANS OBJECT is a DSS development environment, the goal of which is to provide support for all phases of the decision process and which follows the conceptual structure shown in Figure 4.3. OPTRANS object is the successor of PC-OPTRANS, the first version of which was described initially in the user manuals of version 2 (PC-OPTRANS, 1985).

The goal of the system is to explore solutions to some of the issues in DSSG research presented in Klein (1993d) and discussed during the NATO Advanced Studies Institute on DSS theory, held at II Ciocco in 1991 and the 2nd ISDSS conference held at FAW (Ulm Univ.) in 1992. Design considerations and descriptions of the system have been published in Klein (1993a, 1993b, 1993c). But for a detailed description of the system the reader is referred to the user manual (OPTRANS Object, 1994).

Some of the main issues were:

- separation of user interface definition and decision modeling;
- definition of graphical interface for DSS and KB-DSS;
- use of object-oriented concept in the design of DSSG.

We shall not discuss here the last topic but shall briefly describe some characteristics of the system.

4.7.1 Generator Structure

From the user point of view some design ideas of the system are as follows:

- The DSSG is viewed as a set of resources. To each resource is associated a window.
- The resources (or subsystems) are a DBMS, a report generator, a modeling language, a file management system, a toolbox of statistical algorithms, a language to define the application global logic and user interface.
- To the DSS application is associated an application file, a set of variables' names, heading names, parameters' names. Some of these variables are elementary; others are aggregates (i.e. computed from other elementary variables or aggregates). The application file plays the role of a blackboard structure for the resources which can be called for by the interface.
- The system provides a query processor for the database and a library of solvers for the models.

● The user interacts with the system through a command window, menus, local menus buttons associated with the windows, dialog boxes, text editors when defining decision models, application interface, etc.

The internal structure of the system (from the software engineering point of view) will not be discussed here. We shall just point out that OPTRANS Object is organized around a main loop which looks at the messages sent by the windows present on the screen. A pointer to the current active window is updated so that the system always knows which window has sent a message.

4.7.2 The Main Menu of the System and its Options

The aim of the main menu (Figure 4.14) is to allow the user to access the various resources available to him to define his application. The application menu will let him create a new application or open an existing one. A list of variable names, a list of heading names and a list of parameters' names is associated to each application. An application is made of the text of the interface, as many decision models as needed and as many reports as needed. The application can access files as well as databases.

The model menu allows the user to create or access as many decision models as needed by the application. The variables and headings of the decision models must be taken out of the list of variable names of the corresponding application. As a consequence the decision models' variable values are stored in the same application file which constitute a blackboard structure.

The report generator will allow the user to interactively create or access as many reports as needed.

4.7.3 The Definition of the Interface and Logic of the Application

Within the application window the user works in a text editing mode to define the application logic and the application user interface.

A simple example of the syntax to define the Finplan application interface (represented in Figure 4.11) and global logic is shown in Figure 4.16. Computation must also be possible at the interface level.

It is possible to parametrize occurrences values for attributes of entities in the database so as to communicate them automatically to the reports.

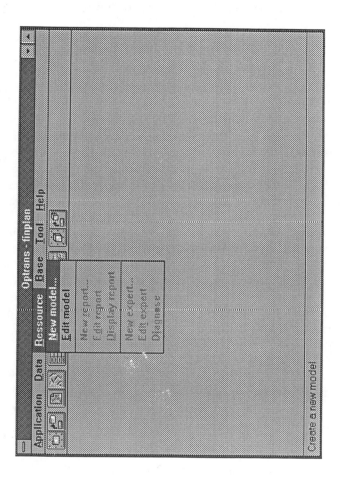

Figure 4.14 *Main menu of OPTRANS Object with application resources menu open*

When working with OPTRANS Object in a development mode and when evaluating an application the user can, by direct action of the mouse, act on menus and windows of the application. Output windows are automatically generated by the development environment. He can move them on the screen and change their characteristics so as to put the finishing touches to the application interface. The text of the user interface can be independently compiled and tested.

4.7.4   The Modeling Language

An example of a model written in OPTRANS Object is shown in Figure 4.15. Within the model window the user works in a text editing mode as for the text of the application. The user has all the relations of the model before his eyes which makes the model easy to analyze and work on. As can be seen from the example the decision model variables can be subscribed. (In the case presented the subscript is a time period.) The decision models can be independently compiled. The variable names must be taken out of the list of the application variables names. If a decision model is using variable names not in the application list, the new names must be first added to the application list. The same applies for the heading names. The relations may be followed by an expression indicating for how many periods they have to be computed. The generator is built in a way which makes it easy to use a library of solvers. The present generator uses two different solvers. The approach is different from a spreadsheet since the user has the full model before his or her eyes. The formulae are only written once and computed for a line and not a cell.

4.7.5   The Report Definition and Management

The concept of a report in OPTRANS Object is that of a white page on which the user writes with a text editor. The concept is more powerful than a standard full screen text editor because the user can insert in the text:

- data values coming from the application;
- tables coming from the application;
- graphics and images.

Tables made of lines, columns and figures can be modified directly at the screen with the mouse to constitute more sophisticated presentations.

The insertion of data values is made through dialog boxes. The user is given the possibility to move the tables, graphics and images

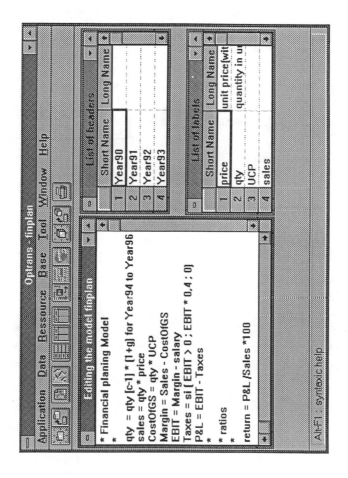

Figure 4.15 *The Finplan model and its associated window and the application labels and headers' names*

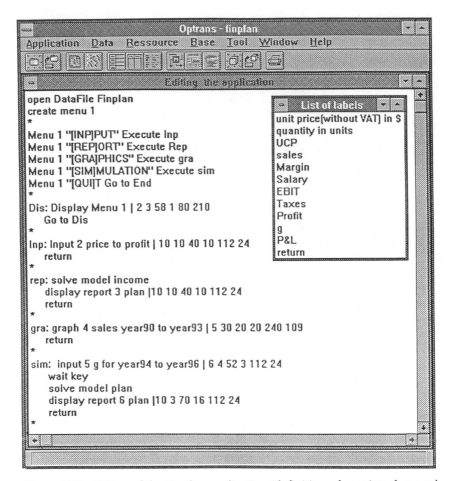

Figure 4.16 *Listing of the Finplan application (definition of user interface and scheduling of resources)*

where he wishes in the report by direct action of the mouse when he is working in the development mode. Reports can be automatically updated with information coming from models and/or databases. For example in the Finplan application the title of a report used by the application will be automatically updated with the name of the company selected in the database by the user when interacting with the application.

4.7.6 The Database Management System

The role of the DBMS of OPTRANS is to structure and manage large amounts of data which cannot be held in central memory. The database management system is of the multi-dimensional kind. Up to six dimensions are available. In such a system dimensions are equivalent to attributes in a table of a relational system. Occurrences of attributes are represented on the dimensions (Figure 4.19).

- It is also easy to implement using this method 'system' variables and 'private' variables. 'Private' variables are under user control. 'System variable' can only be created or deleted by the application administrator.

4.7.7 Integration between the Subsystems or Resources

The integration between the resources means that it is possible in an application to:

- control dynamically the order in which the resources are being used;
- transfer information from one resource to another and submit it to transformation within the resource it has been transferred to;
- share information coming from different resources using a blackboard architecture.

In OPTRANS Object it is the role of the interface to let the DSS application designer define the *logical* order and *scheduling* of resources usage including the interaction with the user himself. Values of attributes as well as their names can be transferred from the database to the application file. The application file plays a blackboard role in that sense that the application resources (decision models, statistical algorithms, etc.) can share information through this common structure. Values of model variables can be transferred to occurrences in the database. Attributes values in the data base can be transferred to reports as well as application variables names and values.

One important concept is that when information is transferred from one resource to another within the DSS application the information can be transformed in the resource where it has been transferred and not only displayed as an image. For example if we transfer attribute values from the DB to the application file they can be read and transformed by decision models of the application. If a map is used in a report as background to display pies representing market share of products by region the radius of pies must dynamically change as a function of the total sales within the region.

Exercises

4.1 Do you see similarities between decision problems for which the decision methodology (presented in Chapter 3) seems adequate and those problems which are considered to be 'ill-structured'?

What would be the point of view of a decision analyst on the concept of 'ill-structured problem'?

4.2 Can you describe situations where end-user definition of the DSS seems the appropriate solution? Describe situations where it is unlikely to be the best one.

4.3 Contact somebody in a company which is using a DSS Study:

(a) The decision that the system is expected to support.

(b) The functions in the decision process that the DSS is supporting.

(c) How the DSS was built (using standard programming language, using a DSS generator or coupling different existing software).

(d) Which persons were involved in the design and what the tasks of each one were.

4.4 Contact somebody who has been using a DSS generator to develop a DSS. Compare the subsystems (components) of the generator with the list given in Section 4.7.5.

4.5 (a) What are the consequences of not having a DBMS component in a DSS generator?

(b) What are the suitable characteristics for the DBMS component of a DSS generator?

4.6 (a) What are the modeling tools suitable in a DSS generator?

(b) What are the differences between a standard financial or marketing model and a 'decision model'?

4.7 What are the relations between a decision model and a decision tree or an influence diagram?

4.8 Obtain the documentation of several DSS generators, study and compare the modeling languages available. Is it possible to support user modeling?

4.9 What would you like to find in the toolbox of a DSS generator? Compare with the user manuals of existing DSS generators.

4.10 When is the communicatioan function of a DSS important?

4.11 What is the concept of synergetic integration?

4.12 Select a task involving a decision. Describe the functions a DSS should provide to improve effectiveness of decision making and to improve efficiency of decision making.

4.13 What do you think of the criticisms given by Winograd and Flores in Section 4.5.5?

4.14 A case study for a term project: the JIIA-86 case.

JIIA-86 CASE STUDY

In 1986, during the 'Journées Internationales de l'Informatique et de l'Automatique' (JIIA-86), a bench-mark for DSS development tools was worked out by two researchers. The idea was to ask the companies who were developing and marketing the leading DSS generators in the US and Europe to develop and present a DSS to support the decision processes and tasks which were described in a case called the JIIA-86 case. From an analysis of the solution developed with each system, it was then possible to make a comparative analysis of the main features of each DSS Generator.

We shall give here an adapted translation of the case. The solution which was developed using OPTRANS is available from the authors. On some points, we have extended the text of the case to make it more general and so that we are able to present more advanced features of the OPTRANS DSS. The first part of the case describes the company, its structure and the products sold. The second part describes the tasks to be supported and their associated decision processes. The third part deals with the structure of data in the company data files. The last part of the case lets each software company present the capabilities of their DSS solutions and environments which could not be demonstrated using the case as it is, and that they considered to be both specific and important to their development environment.

We propose this case study being used as a project in a single-semester course.

Description of the Company

The case was developed and inspired by the management control DSS needs of a French multinational company. For this test case the structure of the company was simplified.

The company does business in France and in Germany. The sales in Germany are carried out through a subsidiary. In France, the company has four branches: in Paris, Lyon, Nantes and Lille.

A production unit is located in Paris. The products manufactured and sold by the company can be broken down into three product lines: TV sets, hi-fi equipment and video equipment.

(1) The TV product line is made up of three kinds of products: black and white, color and portable.
(2) The hi-fi product line is made up of four kinds of products: tuners, amplifiers, record players and cassette players.
(3) The video product line is made up of two kinds of products: recorders and players.

The organizational and product structures are represented in Figure 4.17.

The German subsidiary only markets the hi-fi product line. The exchange rate used is 1 Deutsche Mark = 3 French Francs.

Description of Tasks to be Supported

The tasks to be supported can be broken down into three domains:

(1) management control,
(2) sales reporting and marketing,
(3) sales forecasting and financial simulation.

Each one of the tasks is now presented.

Management Control

One of the tasks to be supported by the DSS is the computation of monthly income statements. An income statement is defined by the following rules:

(1) For each month, each branch, and each product, a quantity sold (QTE) and a net sale is available (CA.NET).

Organizational structure

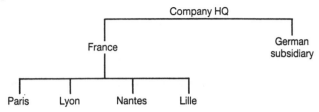

Product structure

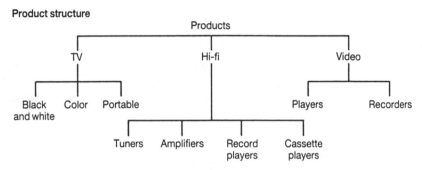

Figure 4.17 *The organizational and product structures of the firm in the JIIA-86 case*

(2) For each product and each country a unit price is available (PRIX).
(3) The gross sale (CA.BRUT) is computed using the quantity sold and unit price (CA.BRUT = QTE × PRIX).
(4) The percentage of discount (REMISE) is computed using the net and gross sale figures.

$$REMISE = (CA.BRUT - CA.NET)/CA.BRUT$$

(5) For each product and each month a cost of production is given (CT.FAB). The production costs are allocated over the branches in proportion to the CA.BRUT.
(6) For each branch and for each month a marketing cost is given (CT.COM). These costs are allocated over the products in proportion to the CA.NET (net sales).
(7) For each country and for the year an advertising cost is given (CT.PUB). This annual cost is divided by 12 and is allocated over the products in proportions to quantity sold (QTE).

(8) The margin (MARGE) is computed using the net sale and the costs.

$$(MARGE = CA.NET - (CT.FAB + CT.COM + CT.PUB)).$$

(9) The return (RENT) is computed using the margin and the net sale.

$$(RENT = 100 \times MARGIN/CA.NET).$$

Sales and Marketing

The French marketing department wants to perform a forecast of the sale of color TV sets for 1987. For that purpose, monthly data are available for the preceding 36 months, for each branch. These data give:

- the quantity sold,
- the unit price,
- the industry market in quantity,
- the industry average price,
- the advertising expense,
- the number of salesmen.

Sales Forecasting and Financial Simulation

The marketing department has computed quantities and sales forecasts for the year 1987. These quantities (NQTE) are given by month, by product and by branches. The pro forma income statement uses the same variables given before. The values of the variables are extrapolated using the following computation rules.

(1) The unit price (NPRIX) of products increases by 3% in January and by 2% in July for the French branches and by 4% in March for the German subsidiary (compared for 1986 unit price).
(2) The discount rate (NREMISE) will decrease by 1% compared to 1986.
(3) The gross sale (NCA.BRUT) is computed as before.
(4) The net sale (NCA.NET) is computed using the gross sale (NCA.BRUT) and the discount rate.

$$(NCA.NET = NCA.BRUT - (NCA.BRUT \times NREMISE)$$

(5) The cost of production (NCT.FAB) will be a function of the unit production cost of December 1986, the quantity and an inflation rate of 4%.

$$(NCT.FAB = NQTE \times CT.FAB \ Dec \ 86/QTE \ Dec \ 86 \times 4\%)$$

(6) The marketing cost (NCT.COM) will be a function of the total marketing cost for the year 1986 and an inflation rate of 3% (NCT.COM = CT.COM global 86/12 × 1.03%)
(7) Advertising costs (NCT.PUB) will be the same as the advertising costs of 1986.
(8) The margin (NMARGE) and the return (NRENT) will be computed the same way.

Assignment

1 Define, for the JIIA-86 case:

(a) The groups of users to be supported.
(b) The decision processes of each user group:
  – the controller and his or her assistants at headquarters,
  – the marketing manager and his or her assistants at headquarters;
  – the financial manager and his or her assistants at headquarters;
  – the production manager for each plant;
  – the branch managers and the manager of the German subsidiary.
(c) The possible architecture for the DSS. In particular, an architecture with centralized treatment and an architecture with distributed treatment.
(d) The required functions for the DSS (see Figure 4.18). The functions have to be described in the centralized solution and the decentralized solution with respect to:
(e) The database structure (see Figures 4.19 and 4.20), its definition and its retrieval functions.
(f) The decision models to implement:
  – margin, sort, max, forecast, income
(g) The display of information (reports and graphics).
(h) Which statistical tools should be available to support some of the required tasks.
(i) The global interface of the system.

The functions have also to be described from the point of view of: the headquarters, the branch, the German subsidiary and the plant manager.
  The distributed solution implies connections between the PCs at branch and plant level, and the HQ version.

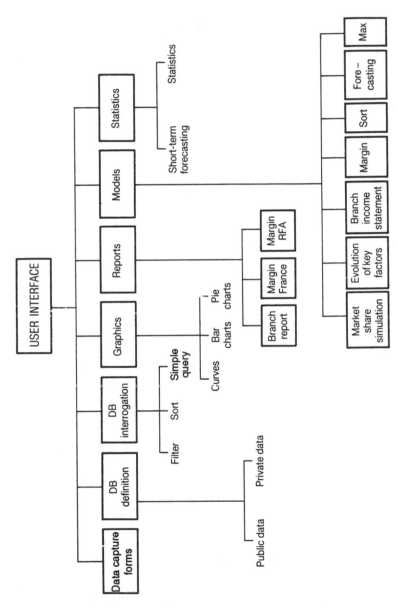

Figure 4.18 *Functions of the DSS implemented with OPTRANS to solve the JIIA-86 case (functions at HQ)*

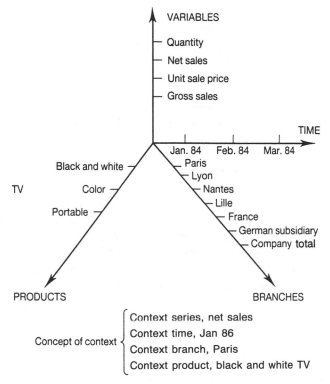

VARIABLES
– Quantity
– Net sales
– Unit sale price
– Gross sales

TIME

Jan. 84   Feb. 84   Mar. 84

Black and white

TV   Color

Portable

– Paris
– Lyon
– Nantes
– Lille
– France
– German subsidiary
– Company total

PRODUCTS

BRANCHES

Concept of context {
Context series, net sales
Context time, Jan 86
Context branch, Paris
Context product, black and white TV
}

Figure 4.19   *Conceptual structure of the database in the JIIA-86 case (HQ Version)*

VARIABLE: Quantity sold PRODUCT: Tuner		TIME: JAN 86 .... 5		BRANCH: LILLE .... 6 ....
JIIA–86	Quantity sold	Net sales	Gross sales	Discount
JANUARY 86	—	—	—	—
FEBRUARY 86	—	—	—	—
MARCH 86	—	—	—	—
APRIL 86	—	—	—	—
MAY 86	—	—	—	—
JUNE 86	—	—	—	—
JULY 86	—	—	—	—
AUGUST 86	—	—	—	—
SEPTEMBER 86	—	—	—	—
OCTOBER 86	—	—	—	—
NOVEMBER 86	—	—	—	—
DECEMBER 86	—	—	—	—
YEAR 86	—	—	—	—

Figure 4.20   *Data capture at the database level for a four-dimensional database*

2 Using a DSS development environment such as OPTRANS, implement a DSS to support the computation and display made by the user for any of the concepts described in the text of the case. The system should let the user plot any variable, for any branch and for any product:

(a) Compute for each month, at the branch level and at the product level, the margin and return. This can be done at the database or modeling subsystem level. Discuss the advantages of doing it at the database level.

(b) Plot the curve of the evolution of the gross sales (CA.BRUT) for the branch of Nantes and for the TV product line.

(c) Plot a pie chart showing, for the video recorder product line, the quantity sold at each branch from January to March 1986.

(d) Use the modeling subsystem and report generator to show a branch income statement with the best possible presentation.

(e) Define and print a report showing for any branch for each product and each month, from January to May its net sales (CA.NET) in increasing order, as well as its margin.

(f) Define and print a report showing for the German subsidiary and for the tuner product line the minimum and maximum net sales (CA.NET) and the corresponding month, as well as the average net sale and the cumulative net sales for the year.

(g) Show how the system can be used to report variance analysis at the product, branch or company level.

3 Using the toolbox subsystem of the DSS development environment show how to support the needs of the marketing management in term of:

(a) Statistics, and short-term forecasting (seasonality and trends . . .).

(b) Simulation of marketing decisions on sales.

(c) Graphics to support problem recognition and diagnosis.

4 Using the forecasted sales and the computation rules defined in the sales forecasting and financial simulation above:

(a) Define a model to compute, for 1987, the margin and the return by branch.

(b) Define and print an associated report showing, by branch, the change, in percentage, between 1986 and 1987 of the quantities sold, of the sales and of the sales margin.

(c) Use the DSS graphics capabilities to show the change in the sales margin in the following hypotheses:
- discounts are cancelled,
- catalog prices do not increase,
- inflation rate increase of 4% compared to the initial forecast.

(d) Show which command of the DSS you have to use to find out how many color TV sets have to be sold in Paris so that the sales margin is 55.

(e) Show the possibilities of the DSS concerning simulation (goal seeking, sensitivity analysis, impact analysis and risk analysis).

5 Evolution of the system. Define the likely evolution of user needs in terms of:

(a) database structure,
(b) model base,
(c) report base.

5
Expert Systems

5.1 INTRODUCTION TO EXPERT SYSTEMS

5.1.1 Knowledge-based Problem Solving

If one looks at any standard textbook in AI one will be amazed at the importance that games and game playing have in this field. In almost any book we find the same problems serving as expository tools: chess, tic-tac-toe, the 8-puzzle and so on. However, you never find games such as football, baseball and billiards. Why? Because chess, tic-tac-toe, and the 8-puzzle all are *formal systems*. Formal systems are characterized by three essential features; firstly, they are token manipulation games like moving a tile in the 8-puzzle; secondly, they are digital in the sense that a tile is either in a correct place or not; and thirdly, that, for any given position, there is a finite, and known number of legal moves that can be performed. Formal systems are self-contained, that is, they carry no references to the outside world which are of relevance to the game, and they cannot be interpreted to have any meaning outside themselves. Thus, formal systems can be studied without introducing the complex concepts of meaning and symbol structures. Formal systems are interesting in the sense that a state-space representation is the basis for problem solving, and that heuristic search is the major problem-solving method. Astonishing results have been achieved with computers that can play chess. Games, fascinating as they may be, are, however, fairly unlike most real-world problem solving. Although they may be interesting from a research point of view, due to large state spaces that require effective search algorithms (for example, chess playing), the problem itself is well structured and the domain knowledge limited and easily available. Research in AI on these problems led to the formalization of laws of reasoning, and general methods and strategies for problem solving. However, these general-purpose problem-solving strategies, successful as they may be in the world of games, failed in solving unstructured and uncertain real-world problems, problem areas, for instance, in which we develop expertise.

If you read carefully through the description of experts and expertise given in Chapter 2, you should observe one common thread through all of the features: the importance of domain knowledge in expert problem solving. If the problem-solving methods and strategies developed in the field of artificial intelligence should be applied to computerized expert problem solving, more emphasis had to be put on domain knowledge. The person to be given credit for this important observation is Professor E. Feigenbaum at Stanford University. In his work on computerized inferencing of plausible molecular structures of unknown chemical compounds, he experienced the severely limited power of general-purpose problem-solving methods and strategies. Human experts, however, rapidly eliminate implausible structures from the solution space by using domain knowledge. This observation led to one of the first computer systems to be labeled an expert system, the DENDRAL System (Buchanan *et al.*, 1969 and Feigenbaum *et al.*, 1971).

Later, at the International Joint Conference on Artificial Intelligence (IJCAI) in 1977, Feigenbaum formulated:

> 'the paradigm of expert system derives from the knowledge it possesses, and not from the particular formalisms and inference schemes it employs, and further, the expert's knowledge provides the key to expert performance, while the knowledge representation and inference schemes provide the mechanisms for its use.' (Hayes-Roth *et al.*, eds., 1983)

This new paradigm put emphasis on domain knowledge rather than on formal reasoning methods. Hayes-Roth *et al.*, 1983 elaborate further on this and give three reasons. Firstly, most of the difficult and interesting problems do not have tractable algorithmic solutions since many important tasks originate in complex social or physical environments. (This feature of problem solving is also the basis for decision support systems, as described in Chapter 4). Secondly, as we have already elaborated on, human experts achieve their high performance because they are knowledgeable in a specific domain. Thirdly, we have the need for knowledge in an ever-increasingly complex world. The complexity of our world is not created by the means with which we try to solve or reduce this complexity, but by the information technology itself. Using this technology large amounts of data are produced and by telecommunications these data are disseminated throughout organizations and society. We get easier access to more and more information. However, this information has no value unless we are able to utilize it. We need knowledge on *how* to use this information. Knowledgeable persons or experts are a scarce resource of the society. We have shown above that knowledge of a specific problem domain is the key component of expertise. Can we obtain this expertise from human experts and computerize it? If this is possible, then we may develop computer systems which can emulate expert problem solving. Such computer systems we shall call *expert systems*. An expert system is a computer program that uses models of the knowledge and inference procedures of an expert to solve problems. The knowledge consists of facts and heuristics. Heuristics are mostly private little-discussed rules of experience that characterize expert-level decision making in the field.

5.2 THE EXPERT SYSTEM ENVIRONMENT

At the beginning of this chapter, we defined an expert system to be a computer program that uses knowledge and procedures to solve difficult problems at the level of professionally-trained humans. We shall now look closer at the functional and structural properties of expert systems. Firstly, we shall introduce the key concepts defining the expert system environment. In subsequent paragraphs we shall develop some of these concepts in more detail. Figure 5.1 shows the main concepts associated with expert systems.

A computer program that employs knowledge and inferencing to solve problems is sometimes called a *knowledge-based system*. When knowledge and inference procedures are modeled after human experts, we call such a knowledge-based system an expert system. Thus, the knowledge and procedures represented in expert systems are descriptions of the heuristics and search employed by human experts in the field. Two characteristics are particularly important here:

(1) That the development of expert systems is based on a descriptive theory of human problem solving.
(2) That focus of development is a representation of expertise, that is, the knowledge acquired by humans through practice and learning.

An expert system is, therefore, built-in dialog with experts in the field. The task of eliciting and modeling this problem-solving knowledge and

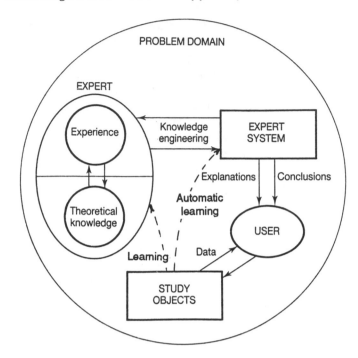

Figure 5.1 *The main concepts of an expert system*

building a computer system is called *knowledge engineering*. This task is carried out by a knowledge engineer; a system designer with some domain knowledge, skill in cognitive methods and techniques, and skill in computer programming. Knowledge engineering will be dealt with in more detail in Chapter 8.

Expertise is developed by training and experience. Sometimes, this knowledge is called *shallow* knowledge because it consists of all the peculiar heuristics and shortcuts that trained professionals have learned to use in order to perform better. However, experts in cognitive domains (which are the only experts we will be interested in) normally have a professional education. Their practice is anchored in a theory, in other words, in first principles, axioms, and laws. This knowledge is called *deep* knowledge and tends to be more general than shallow knowledge.

A true expert system must represent shallow knowledge. The advantage of computing this knowledge is that we obtain a computer program that behaves in similar way to an expert. The disadvantage is that shallow knowledge is about special-purpose methods. Therefore, expert systems are tailor-made for specific and narrowly-defined *problem domains*. A problem domain defines the entities, properties, tasks and events within which a particular kind of shallow knowledge works for problem solving. Typical financial problem domains for expert systems are credit evaluation, financial analysis, option trading, stock investments and so on. Also associated with the problem domain are the objects of study: patients, corporations and so on. By constraining the problem domain, high performance can be obtained. This performance, however, is purchased at a price: the resulting system tends to be a specialist that performs well at a few narrow tasks, but that is helplessly inapt at everything else. Therefore, a tendency in the development of expert systems is to now include more general, theoretical knowledge, on which the system can fall back when faced with problems that cannot be solved by shallow knowledge alone. The term *second-generation expert system* is used to denote systems which employ both experiental, shallow knowledge and theoretical, deep knowledge. It should be noted that the concept of knowledge-based decision support systems, which will be developed in the next chapter, are a kind of second-generation expert system since they employ the combinations of algorithmic knowledge usually represented as equational relationships, and inferential knowledge representing heuristics.

Haugeland (1986) has formulated several requirements that a problem domain must fulfill in order to make the development of an expert system practical. Firstly, the decisions must depend on a well-defined set of variables. Secondly, the values of these variables must be known. Thirdly, the exact way in which the decisions depend on the values of the variables must be known, and fourthly, the interrelations among the variables in determining the decision should be complex enough to make the expert system worth the effort to develop.

These stringent conditions may rule out a bulk of ordinary life, but as we have already seen and shall see, many specialized domains are suitable for expert systems developments.

The purpose of an expert system is to computerize the problem-solving skill of a highly recognized expert. Thus, this knowledge can be easily accessible and clerks, who have little ability to perform certain tasks can, by consulting an expert system, solve problems which otherwise would have to be handled by experts. Since human experts are scarce, but the need for their expertise high, expert systems can close the skill differentials between experts and problem solvers or decision makers in organizations. For instance, a bank, generally has a few, highly-skilled loan officers, often located at headquarters or large branch offices, but many tellers who serve the customers at all the branch offices. Credit evaluation skill, can by means of an expert system, be replicated to all who need this skill, thus decentralizing the decision responsibility without increasing risk. Furthermore, computerization of expertise is also a documentation of problem-solving knowledge and can be used for feedback to the expert and, thus, leads to improvements in expert skill.

In accordance with computer terminology we shall use the term *user* to denote the problem solver or the decision maker who is consulting an expert system for advice. In the literature about expert systems, much is said about the expert and knowledge acquisition, and little about the user and the user characteristics. Some recent work on user modeling focuses on these latter aspects. We believe that user characteristics impose severe constraints on the design of an expert system. One aspect which has recently been considered is the extent to which the knowledge gap between the expert and the user imposes constraints on the functionality of the system. A typical assumption in design is that the user is familiar with the vocabulary of the domain. Other aspects are rarely considered.

In Chapter 2, we have presented some of the recent work on unified theories of cognition. One of the important features of these theories is to present mechanisms for learning. If we want to reproduce this capacity in expert systems we must provide a learning mechanism in the development environment that can generate knowledge from facts (experience), (see for instance the description of the two systems SOAR and ACT* in Chapter 2). This chapter deals with the state of the art of commercial expert systems where learning is not yet available.

5.3 THE EXPERT SYSTEM FUNCTIONALITY

An expert system has two main functions:

(1) to draw conclusions, and;
(2) to explain its reasoning.

A conclusion can be a diagnosis of a disease or a recommendation for a particular financing scheme. It should be noted that the conclusion set always must be fully specified in advance. What the expert system can do is to find the appropriate element of that set, it being a diagnosis or a design. An expert system works in a consulting mode, that is, a user may consult the system for advice. During the consultation the user interacts with the system if the system requires information to perform the reasoning. During these interactions the system, however, is always in control, that is, the system poses the questions and the user provides the answers. The user cannot influence the reasoning process directly. Only the information entered during the consultation influences the reasoning. This is in contrast to a DSS where the user is, at any time, in control and can ask the system for data or calculations.

An important aspect of human problem solving is the capability of a human expert to explain how a particular conclusion has been reached, or to explain why certain questions are asked. We want an expert system to have similar capabilities.

We shall, however, return to consultation and explanation in more detail in the next section.

5.3.1 Consultation

A user may consult an expert system for assistance while performing a task like establishing a diagnosis or designing a plan, or for advice or recommendations in choosing alternatives in decision making. It is important to understand that the task of an expert system may be different from the ultimate task of the user. For instance, an expert system for credit decisions may be designed for alternative tasks such as:

(1) recommend an accept/reject conclusion;
(2) advise on creditworthiness;
(3) make a general financial diagnosis.

In the first task, the expert system almost makes the decision. In this case, decision authority can be transferred to people not particularly skilled in corporate finance and credit decisions. In the second task, the system supports a decision maker who may make the final decision on the basis of additional variables. In the third task, the financial analysis of the system is just one of several reports, on which, for instance, a credit committee may base its decisions.

In designing an expert system we have, therefore, to distinguish between the task of the domain and the task of the expert system.

Hayes-Roth *et al.* (1983) have made a typology of the kind of tasks that an expert system can deal with. Summarized and slightly modified, this typology of tasks is shown in Table 5.1.

An expert system can be designed to deal with one or more of these tasks. We have found, as we shall see in more detail later, that financial analysts deal with the interpretation of accounting data, prediction of key variables to estimate a company's future position, diagnoses of causes of potential problems, and prescriptions of actions to remedy for these problems.

Since diagnosis plays an important role in financial domains we shall look, in more detail, at a diagnostic reasoning framework and a particular problem-solving method for diagnosis known as classification.

Table 5.1 *A typology of tasks for an expert system. (After Hayes-Roth* et al. *(1983).)*

Task	Description
Interpretation	Inferring situation descriptions from sensor data.
Prediction	Inferring likely consequences of given situations.
Diagnosis	Inferring malfunctions from observation.
Prescription	Prescribing remedies for malfunctions.
Design	Configuring objects under constraints.
Planning	Designing actions.
Monitoring	Comparing observations to expected outcomes.
Control	Governing overall system behavior.
Instruction	Diagnosing, prescribing and guiding users' behavior.

Diagnosis

To make a diagnosis means to determine the cause of a problem on the basis of a set of symptoms or characteristics of the situation. In medical diagnosis, a disease may be determined from a set of symptoms of the patient. In fault diagnosis, malfunctions of equipments may be inferred from observations. In financial diagnosis, something can be said about profitability, liquidity and so on, on the basis of the financial data of the corporation.

Prior to expert systems, diagnostic computer programs were mainly based on statistical decision theory. More recently, however, diagnosis is more thought of as an inferential process with uncertain information, rather than statistical calculations with probabilities.

Diagnostic problems are solved through a process of hypothesis generation and verification. In a loan evaluation system, for instance, one may start with the hypothesis 'loan is rejected'. The diagnostic process works with the aim of verifying this hypothesis by comparing the conditions of this hypothesis with the data given of the applicant. If these data do not correspond, the hypothesis is rejected. The system will then take the next available hypothesis which is 'loan is granted'. Since we have only two hypotheses, and the first was rejected, the second must be true. In this case we have a very small conclusion set. For small conclusion (problem) sets, possible diagnoses can be tried in a systematic fashion. Each candidate is tried individually and proved to be true or false with some degree of uncertainty. Thus, at the end, a list of diagnoses may be produced ranking the problems in order of uncertainty. How do we handle domains where multiple problems may exist simultaneously? Obviously, we cannot just take the highest-ranking candidate, nor can we take all candidates over a certain threshold. Some diagnostic expert systems work with multiple diagnoses. For large problem sets it is inefficient to make an exhaustive search, that is, trying all candidates in the problem set. Hypotheses generation, then, becomes a required process. Here, symptoms may be used to generate plausible hypotheses which, in turn, are tried and verified. Information may be collected during the diagnosis process if necessary.

Classification

This is related to diagnosis and is the task of assigning to a particular object, the name of the class to which it belongs (the concept). The possible classes are predetermined. Each one is defined in terms of a set of typical characteristics. To classify a particular object implies finding a match between the characteristics of this particular object and one of the class-typical characteristics. For instance, medical diagnosis implies the assignment of a disease to a set of symptoms displayed by a person. Each disease has a set of class-typical characteristics which are matched against the observed characteristics (symptoms) of the person. When a match is found, the problem, in this case a disease, is classified.

There are many aspects of classification that complicate the inference procedure. There is the problem of necessary and sufficient conditions or typicality for a match. There is the problem of whether to find just one or all of the possible conclusions in a problem set, and in the case of multiple conclusions, how these conclusions should be interpreted. Are they to be considered conjunctive or disconjunctive sets?

In Chapter 2, when dealing with heuristic search, we saw that the search can be improved tremendously if we have information to successively exclude parts of the search space. A variation of this approach is called *successive refinements*. This, however, requires that the search space can be hierarchically structured into a class–subclass taxonomy. Furthermore, we need criteria (class-membership properties) to effectively discriminate among classes on the same level of the hierarchy. A classification algorithm is employed to successively zoom in on the ultimate solution.

5.3.2 Explanation

Generally, explanation means to justify a particular conclusion, that is, to explain the reasoning behavior. Experts can do this. Therefore, we want expert systems to have similar capabilities. And most expert systems have some sort of explanation facility.

The most common type of explanation is what is called *retrospective* explanation. *HOW* was a particular conclusion reached? Here the

```
Please enter the name of the fact to be explained ? >· FINAL_CREDIT_RATING
FINAL_CREDIT_RATING has been changed by Rule number 109
IF MANAGEMENT_COMPETENCE = C;AVERAGE AND OUTSIDE_CREDIT_RATING = A;NOT_BEEN_DONE
AND CREDIT_RATING = MARGINAL
THEN
FACTS_DEDUCED FINAL_CREDIT_RATING IS MARGINAL
CRITERIA_TO_EXAMINE LOAN
MESSAGE FINAL CREDIT RATING is marginal.
COMMENT New 6
FINISH_RULE
        The value of MANAGEMENT_COMPETENCE (C;AVERAGE) The level of this fact has
        already been put in from the keyboard
        The value of OUTSIDE_CREDIT_RATING (A;NOT_BEEN_DONE) The level of this
        fact has already been put in from the keyboard
        CREDIT_RATING has been changed by Rule number 90
        IF LIQUIDITY_OF_CURRENT_ASSETS = AVERAGE AND PROFITABILITY = MINUS_LOW
        THEN
        FACTS_DEDUCED CREDIT_RATING IS MARGINAL
        CRITERIA_TO_EXAMINE FINAL_CREDIT_RATING URGENT
        MESSAGE CREDIT RATING based on financial data is marginal.
        FINISH_RULE
                                                ·
                                                ·
                                                ·
                                                ·
```

Figure 5.2   *HOW example*

system will display the chain of rules that were executed in order to reach that conclusion (see Figure 5.2).

The second most common explanation facility is *WHY* the program asks the user a particular question during the consultation (see Figure 5.3).

```
Is the industry's rate of return (PRE TAX PROFIT TO TANGIBLE ASSETS) higher or
lower than the prime rate of interest
    A;LOWER
    .B;EQUAL_OR_HIGHER

Please put in the level :>
Now being looked at : Rule number 61
IF MEDIAN_PRE_TAX_PROF_RATIO_TO_PRIME_RATE = B;EQUAL_OR_HIGHER AND LOANTYPE = A;
SEASONAL
THEN
FACTS DEDUCED PROFITABILITY IS LOW
CRITERIA_TO_EXAMINE SEASONAL URGENT
MESSAGE PROFITABILITY is low.
FINISH_RULE
                                                            ─12:56─
```

F1Annul F2Trunc F3Recall F4Stop F5? F6Rule F7Why F8Restart F9Facts F10Zo

Figure 5.3   *WHY example*

Both HOW and WHY questions are facilities for the user. Sometimes, however, it may be useful to have a complete trace of the inference process. Here, all rules that are tried are displayed, not only those that were executed and shown in a HOW-explanation. A typical command executing this facility is *TRACE*. It is primarily to be used by the knowledge engineer during design and test phases, but also users can take advantage of this (see Figure 5.4).

The three facilities, WHY, HOW and TRACE are provided by most development tools. Explanation mechanisms may also handle hypothetical reasoning, WHAT-IF, where the system explains what will happen if a certain value-set or a rule-set is changed. A value-set change is well known in decision support systems where different scenarios can be built by the WHAT-IF mechanism. An expert system WHAT-IF explanation is different since here a rule set can be the object of hypothetical reasoning.

There are alternative implementations of explanation facilities, from simple list of the rule numbers that have been executed, through a display of rules as they are stored in the knowledge base, to a natural language translation. If one is using an expert system development tool, the explanation facility is normally part of that tool.

```
 1  treatment of the criterion RATIO_NET_WORTH_TO_DEBT
 2  Rule number 1 : RATIO_NET_WORTH_TO_DEBT IS UNKNOWN
 3  ........ the user enters YES
 4  Rule 2 verified
 5  the criterion is added to the pile CASH_ACCOUNT with priority URGENT
 6  End of the treatment of the group of rules
 7  treatment of the criterion CASH_ACCOUNT
 8  Rule 4 verified
 9  fact CASH_ACCOUNT <-- POSITIVE
10  the criterion is added to the pile FUNDS_REQUIRED with priority URGENT
11  End of the treatment of the group of rules
12  treatment of the criterion FUNDS_REQUIRED
13  Rule 6 verified
14  fact LAST_YEAR_INCOME_LESS_DEBT_PAYMENT <--POSITIVE
15  fact PROFORMA_INCOME_LESS_DEBT_PAYMENT <--POSITIVE
16  The system EXECUTES the model starting at line 6100
17  the criterion is added to the pile CURRENT with priority URGENT
18  End of the treatment of the group of rules
19  treatment of the criterion CURRENT
20  Rule number 13 : PERCENTILE_CURRENT_RATIO IS UNKNOWN
21  ........ the user enters B;BETWEEN_25%_AND_50%
22  Rule number 15 : MEDIAN  CURRENT  RATIO IS UNKNOWN
23  ........ the user enters B;BETWEEN  1.5  AND  2
24  Rule 16 verified
25  fact LEVEL_OF_CURRENT_ASSETS <--AVERAGE
26  The system EXECUTES the model starting at line 6300
```

Figure 5.4 *TRACE example*

Another explanation facility developed at the Intelligent System Laboratory at Carnegie-Mellon University by Kosy and Wise (1984), is an explanation of numeric values computed by a model. This explanation facility allows users to ask questions, in English, about observed results, for instance: 'Why did the current ratio go down in 1985?', and queries such as 'What is the formula for current liabilities?' The system responds with the variables that have significantly influenced the change of the value of current ratio, positively or negatively. This explanation facility, however, is more associated with DSS. A more detailed discussion on the explanation facility of expert systems is given in Wick and Slagle (1989).

5.4   PROBLEM SOLVING BY SEARCH

5.4.1   Search Space

In Chapter 2 we dealt with human problem solving. We saw that problem solving takes place in a problem space and that the process can be described as a search for a solution within this problem space. The most general method to apply is called generate-and-test in which new states are generated from previous states. Each new state generated is tested to see if it is a member of the goal state (see the generate-and-test method in Section 2.5.2). In this process, we have no information that states that one action is better than any of the other applicable actions. Only by systematically searching the state–space can we hope to find a solution. When we have no information about which action is better than others, or no information about the progress we are making in finding a solution to the given problem, then we are using a blind search or exhaustive search. Exhaustive search is very impractical when the number of states that must be examined is large.

At this point, we will introduce the standard terminology used in search. Problem solving by search is characterized by an *initial state*, that is, the initial situation given, and a *goal state*, a state satisfying the goal state description. The goal state may be reached by successively applying operators, a single operator transforms a state into another state, called an *intermediate state* if it is not the goal state.

We will use the term *successor* of i to mean a state j that is reachable from state i by a sequence of operator applications. The immediate successor of i is a state reached by applying one operator on i. The set of all states that can be reached by applying operators in sequence, starting at the initial state is called the *search space*. An exhaustive search proceeds, as we have seen, by each intermediate state generating the exhaustive set of successors. Thus, exhaustive search leads to a *combinatorial explosion*. Combinatorial explosion can be avoided, as we will see below, by having information at each state, about which of the immediate successors is most promising. The three terms: blind search, exhaustive search, and uninformed search have the same meaning and will be used interchangeably in this text depending on the context.

The objective of the search may be to find a goal state, for instance a diagnosis, or to find a sequence of operators (the path) to a goal state, as we have seen in the water jug example. In addition, the problem may be to find just any solution, or an *optimal* solution. To find an optimal solution requires an objective function. Most often we do not optimize a search problem but use heuristics to guide the search. Heuristic search is the principal problem-solving technique used in artificial intelligence.

A heuristic is a 'rule of thumb' that is used in problem solving. It constitutes the rules of expertise, the rules of good practice, the judgmental rules of the field, and the rules of plausible reasoning. Heuristics apply to specific situations – they constitute domain-specific knowledge. They point in interesting directions and almost always find a solution. But unlike algorithms, heuristics carry no guarantees of success. Heuristic search is different from exhaustive or blind search in the sense that it is informed. It uses heuristic information to select the most promising candidate (operator or immediate successor) at each intermediate state. Thus, at each state, all new states generated by the applicable-operators are sorted according to the heuristic information we use. This sort function is called the (heuristic) *evaluation function*. Evaluation functions will be dealt with in Section 5.4.3.

5.4.2 Search Trees

A simple way to implement any search technique is as a tree traversal. In computer science, a tree is a directed graph in which one node has no predecessor, this is the *root*, and some nodes have no successors, these are the *leaves*. The arcs (links) are called *branches*. No one node can have, as its successor, a node which also can be its predecessor. Each node in the tree can be assigned a level. The level number of a node is called its *depth*. The root of the tree has a depth of 0.

A *search tree* shows which paths in a state space have currently been explored. When the search begins the search tree consists of a single node, the initial state description. The search tree grows as the operators are applied to existing nodes. However, this process often leads to regenerating of nodes already in the tree, that is, that the search

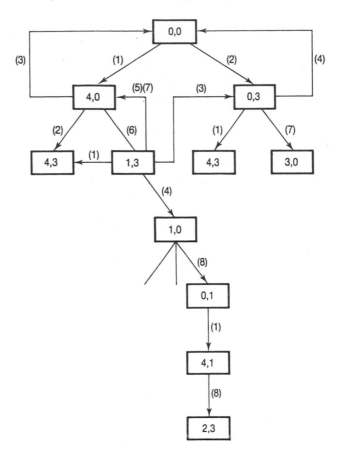

Figure 5.5 *Part of the search graph of the water jug problem. ((x) denotes the rule number executed)*

structure is more like a directed graph than a tree. In Figure 5.5 part of the search graph of the water jug problem discussed in Section 2.6.2 is shown. When the search process regenerates a node of the tree, it has found another, new path to this node. This path can either be ignored or old paths can be substituted, and the search tree is correspondingly changed.

It is helpful to classify the nodes of a search tree as either *open* or *closed*. An open node has not yet been examined for possible expansion. A closed node has already been examined. An open node is a leaf if it is the goal node or cannot be expanded otherwise. Usually it is not a leaf. All search techniques proceed by expanding open nodes. The particular search technique being used determines the order in which the open nodes will be expanded.

5.4.3 Search Strategies

The fundamental problem in controlling the search procedure is how to select, from the applicable set of operators at a specific node, the operator for execution. The selection criterion is known as the *search strategy*. An important characteristic of this strategy is how much domain knowledge it uses. At one extreme is the completely uninformed search, the blind search, where no information about the problem at hand is used. At the other extreme is a strategy employing enough domain knowledge to always select the 'correct' operator, that is, the optimal path to the goal state. We shall briefly describe three search strategies, two of the uninformed type: depth-first and breadth-first, and one informed search strategy.

Depth-first Search

A search which always proceeds in the parent-to-children direction until forced to backtrack is called a *depth-first* search. Backtracking is a general process which means that the search can stop in one direction, go back to a previous node and expand in a new direction. Intervening steps are disregarded. The depth-first strategy orders the open nodes in descending order of their depth in the search tree, that is, nodes on the deepest level are at the front of the list. Computationally, this can be accomplished by organizing open nodes as a *stack* data structure, that is, nodes are placed on, and removed from, the front of the queue (last in, first out).

Figure 5.6 illustrates a depth-first search carried out on the water jug problem. We start with the initial node (0, 0) which is placed on the stack called OPEN. We expand this node by executing all applicable rules, that is, R1 and R2. The expanded nodes are placed on top of the OPEN stack. At the same time, we create a list called CLOSED containing parent nodes. Using Figure 5.6 we can see how the search proceeds. Nodes already on the CLOSED list are not placed on the OPEN list to avoid recycling. There is a risk with the depth-first strategy that we may go on forever, deeper and deeper in the search tree. Therefore, we may want to set a bound on the depth in which we want to expand in one direction. This is called the *depth-bound* of the search tree. When this depth is reached, the process will backtrack and expand in a new direction.

Breadth-first Search

In the second type of uninformed search, the nodes are examined level by level. This is called a *breadth-first* search. This strategy orders the

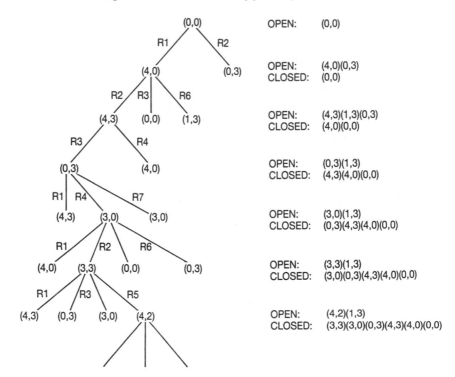

Figure 5.6   *Depth-first search*

open nodes in ascending order of their depth, that is, nodes on lowest level of depth are at the front of the list. Computationally, a data structure is established that organizes the open nodes as a queue: first in, first out. A breadth-first search starts with the initial node. When a node is expanded its successors are placed at the end of the queue. Figure 5.7 shows the search tree of the water jug problem using a breadth-first search.

Heuristic Search

In principle, the uninformed search methods always eventually find a solution to the problem. However, in searching large problem spaces these methods may not be feasible due to the problem of combinatorial explosion. This problem poses intractable problems to programs which attempt to play games like chess in this way. Since human beings are slower than computers in enumerating and keeping track of all possible alternatives, we can safely assume that chess champions do not work this way. Rather, they apply their experience to evaluate a few, but

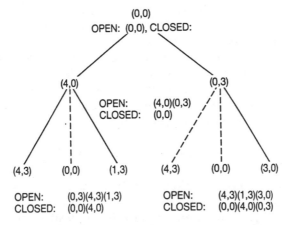

Figure 5.7 *Breadth-first search*

significant moves. How are these specific moves selected from all of the possible moves? A search which uses information about the current situation to traverse a search tree is called *heuristic search*. Heuristic information increases the efficiency of the search. Introducing the concept of efficiency requires a cost function to be associated with the paths searched. If we can obtain information about which of the open nodes are the most promising, we can order the nodes on the open list according to this. A function is required to estimate the cost from the current node to the goal node. Such a function is called a heuristic evaluation function.

In Figure 5.8 we have expanded a search tree. A node in the tree has an alphanumeric code which is the reference code for that node,

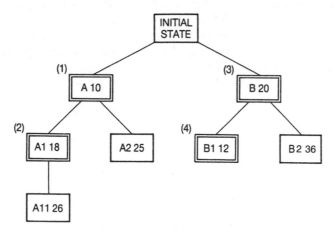

Figure 5.8 *An expanded search tree*

and a number which is the value returned by the evaluation function when applied to that node. This number represents an estimated distance to the nearest goal node. Nodes with doubled boxes are those that are expanded. The sequence of expansion is signified by the number outside the box. We can see from this example that search using an evaluation function is significantly different from the uninformed search techniques we have described above.

We can organize heuristic search in two ways:

(1) *Ordering of successors*, where we can use some heuristic information to estimate which successors look most promising. One very general evaluation function which is used in some expert systems is to expand on a node by applying the rule with the largest number of pre-conditions. One other typical search strategy is known as the A* algorithm. It orders successors according to a measure of their costs (distances) from the initial state, through the successor state and to the goal state. The A* algorithm is regarded as a basic search technique and is described in more detail below.

(2) *Constraining the generation of successors*, where the least promising children are disregarded from further search.

The A Algorithm*

The A* algorithm is a heuristic search technique that employs an evaluation function, called h, that measures the cost of going from the node to the goal node. Since this function is not known with complete accuracy, an approximation denoted h^* is used. For this algorithm to work correctly, $h^*(i) < h(i)$ for any node i. The A* algorithm chooses to expand on the node which minimizes the estimated cost function from the starting node to the goal node. Thus, we need to define a new function, f^*, which is the sum of costs from the start node to node i, denoted $g(i)$, and the estimate of the cost of the path from node i to the goal ($h^*(i)$). Thus:

$$f^*(i) = g(i) + h^*(i)$$

Furthermore, we define the cost of going from one node (i) to its immediate succesor (j) as $c(i,j)$. The procedure for the A* algorithm can be summarized as follows:

(1) Put the start node S on the OPEN list, set $g(S) = 0$.
(2) If the OPEN list is empty, the search terminates unsuccessfully.

(3) Select from OPEN list the node with the lowest f^*-value. Call it i. Test if the node is a goal node. If it is a goal node, then terminate the search. Otherwise, put node i on the CLOSED list.
(4) Expand node i by applying all applicable operators. If i has no successors, then go to 2.
(5) For all successors, j of i calculate:

$$f^* (j) = g(i) + c(i, j) + h^* (j)$$

Put all successors with their f^* values on the OPEN list. Go to step 2.

Notice that the A* algorithm not only uses, as its evaluation function, the cost of the remaining path from i to the goal, but takes into account how good the path to node i was. This is useful if we care about the path. However, if we are only interested in the solution we can define g to be 0, thus always choosing the node that seems closest to the goal. If we want to find the path involving the minimum number of steps, we can set g to 1.

5.4.4 Problem Reduction

In the search trees we have studied so far, the nodes of the trees have represented the alternative states in which the problem may be on its way towards the goal state. In a state–space situation, branches from a node to its successors represent alternative paths. Expanding a node this way is called OR expansion. Many problems can be solved this way.

However, we often solve a problem by decomposing it into two or more subproblems. Each subproblem can, in turn, be broken down into new subproblems. When a problem is solved this way, it is called *problem reduction*. Problem reduction can also be solved by search. In this case, each node in the tree represents a subproblem and branches from a node to its successors designate simultaneous requirements, that is, *all* branches must be searched before a solution is found. In terms of logic, this is called AND expansion. The given problem is the root of the search tree. All other nodes are subproblems. A leaf of the search tree can be:

(1) a primitive problem which can be solved;
(2) an unsolvable or a non-decomposable problem;
(3) a candidate node for further expansion (problem decomposition).

From mathematics we may remember that, in order to find the integral of a complicated expression, we could decompose the original expression into simpler expressions to which we could possibly find standard solutions to the integrals.

Perhaps a more typical example of a problem solved by problem reduction is the credit evaluation procedure employed in the expert system BANKER (see Section 5.10). Here, the credit evaluation problem is decomposed into a number of subproblems: (1) evaluation of management competence, (2) external credit rating, and (3) financial analysis. Some of these subproblems require further reduction: financial analysis can be broken down to a profitability and a solvency rating. Some can be solved in more than one way: for instance, profitability rating may be obtained by using company data only or by a comparison with industry ratios. We continue to break down the credit evaluation problem until a level is reached that can be handled by 'primitive' operations on known data. From this example, we have seen that the major expansion is an AND breakdown, but also that we may encounter alternative branches (OR expansion). The structure needed to represent problem reduction search is called an AND/OR tree. Notationally, the AND expansion is designated by a circular arc across the branches leading from a node to its successors. In an AND/OR tree for problem reduction an OR expansion requires only one of the OR-nodes to be satisfied for the search to proceed, while if one branch under an AND expansion fails, there is no need to explore further.

5.5 KNOWLEDGE REPRESENTATION

5.5.1 Knowledge Representation Methods: an Overview

To solve the water jug problem presented in Chapter 2 we needed to make a symbolic representation of the problem. A symbolic representation of the problem requires both a representation of the contents of the jugs (the states) and of the processes that act upon the states to transform them into new states (actions). Knowledge about states and knowledge about actions occurs as two kinds: declarative and procedural. In order to manipulate a symbol system it is necessary to have knowledge of both kinds. It is like playing a game where you need knowledge about the positions (states) and of the rules of the game (legal moves or actions). *Declarative knowledge* is a description of facts. It is information about real-world objects and their properties, and the relationships among objects. *Procedural knowledge* encompasses problem-solving strategies, arithmetical and inferential knowledge. Procedural knowledge manipulates declarative knowledge to arrive at new declarative knowledge. The distinction between declarative and procedural knowledge can be illustrated as follows:

(1) The contents of the two water jugs are x and y respectively and these are facts. We can use the ordered pair (x, y) to symbolize the facts represented in one state. This is declarative knowledge.
(2) An action which we may make is procedural knowledge, for instance:

IF $(x < 4)$ THEN FILL x to $x = 4$

It tells us what we can do.

Many of the objects we are concerned with in the real world are composed of elements which are themselves objects. For instance, take a car which is made of components, such as an engine and a gearbox, which again are made up of components. An object, in which we are not interested in finer details, is called a *simple* object. Otherwise, we call it a *structured* object. What is defined as a simple or a structured object is dependent on the context in which it is used. For the taxation authorities a car is a simple object. For a car repair mechanic, the car is a structured object. Facts about simple objects encompass properties of these objects, and facts about structured objects include knowledge about relationships among objects (the structure).

Knowledge representation means that knowledge is formalized in a symbolic form, that is, to find a symbolic expression that can be interpreted. In AI, we are interested in knowledge representation formalisms that can be manipulated by computer programs. In the following, we shall describe, in more detail, some formalisms developed in the AI area for representing knowledge and which are of particular interest to expert systems. It is required of a formalism that it can represent the knowledge of a domain adequately and efficiently. The representation formalisms we shall deal with are:

- property lists
- rules
- semantic nets
- frames
- logic

5.5.2 Property Lists

Simple facts can be described by propositions. A proposition is the smallest unit of knowledge that can stand as a separate assertion, that is, the smallest unit about which a judgment of true or false can be made (see Section 2.4.1). For instance,

'The company Alpha applies for a loan of $100 000.'

A simple fact has two basic elements: identification of an *object* and a *characterization* (a property) of this object. Objects may be physical entities such as a company, or conceptual entities such as a bank loan. In formal systems it is convenient to split the property element into two: a general characteristic, called an *attribute*, such as interest rate, and a *value*, such as 0.12. Thus the common way to represent a simple fact is as an:

<Object–Attribute–Value> triplet.

In the <O–A–V> triplet the term *object* means a unique reference to (an identification of) a real-world entity. In the proposition stated above, we use the name (Alpha) as a reference to the object of interest. An object belongs to a class, a category, which is usually determined by the context. For a bank dealing with loans (where the context is loan applications), company Alpha belongs to a category called 'company loan applicants'. In a <O–A–V> representation, the proposition above can be formally written as:

<Alpha, loan application, $100 000>

Some representation formalisms allow for the description of structural properties, where, in addition to the basic formalism of <O–A–V> triplets, a context type to which this triplet belongs can be defined.

Usually, an object has several properties. In the example above all of the accounting data such as sales, net profit, debt and so on are properties, that is (attribute-value) pairs, associated with the same object, namely, the company named Alpha. A property list represents this, as shown in Table 5.2.

If the object to which a property belongs is obvious from the context, then we may suppress the object reference term from the <O–A–V>

Table 5.2 *A property list*

Attributes	Values
Name	Alpha
Loan application	$100 000
Net profit	$25 000
Debts	$1 000 000

triplet, and we are left with (attribute–value) pairs. This representation form is more efficient, and in many cases sufficient. Take, for instance, a credit evaluation system dealing with one loan applicant at each consultation session. We do not have to make the object, that is, the loan applicant, consistently explicit during the processing of one single loan application. Therefore, it is not necessary to specify the company to which the data belong every time it is used. In PC-OPTRANS (see Chapter 4) facts are represented as (attribute–value) pairs, where the values are taken from a defined value set called *scale*. For instance,

Scale: status (unmarried, married, divorced)
Fact: civil status (attribute), status (value set).

For instance, we may have the following information on John Smith: civil status (married).

5.5.3 Rules

As shown in Section 2.6, production systems use rules to change the states of the problem space. Each rule consists of two parts: the operator that performs the state change, and the set of conditions that determines when an operator may be executed.

IF   conditions
THEN operation

If the conditions are logically evaluated to true, then the conclusion can be said to be logically true. The rule formalism can be used to encode:

(1) Inferential knowledge:
    IF   premises   IF   current ratio <1.5
    THEN   conclusion   THEN   liquidity is bad

(2) Procedural knowledge:
    IF   situation   IF   days sales outstanding >30
    THEN   action   THEN   check invoicing procedure

(3) Declarative knowledge:
    IF   antecedent   IF X is accounts payable
    THEN   consequent   THEN X belongs to current liabilities

Rules may be composed of a set of conditions and several conclusions, for example:

(1) IF current assets increase AND liquidity is good, THEN, apply for short-term loan
(2) IF land purchase OR building investment, THEN, apply for a mortgage loan.

Conditions and conclusions are propositions which can be evaluated to true or false. Rules (1) and (2) consist of antecedents of several propositions. In rule (1) both propositions must be true for the conclusion to be true. The antecedent of this rule represents a *conjunction* of propositions. In rule (2) it is sufficient that one of the propositions in the antecedent is true for the conclusion to be true. The antecedent represents here a *disjunction*.

If facts are represented as <O–A–V> triplets they can look like this:

IF   (company Alpha, loan size $4500)
THEN (company Alpha, loan reject)

This rule signifies that if the amount of loan applied for by the company is $4500 then it should be rejected (too small). We want to have more general knowledge encoded in the rules, say, for instance, that any company that applies for a loan of the amount less than $5000 should be rejected. We then have to introduce variables into the rules:

IF   (loan applicant, loan size <$5000)
THEN (loan applicant, loan rejected).

Here, the variables loan applicant and loan size have to be instantiated before the premise can be evaluated. Next, the two occurrences of the same variable in the premise and the conclusion must take the same value, namely, company Alpha.

Just as uncertainty can be attached to facts, this can also be done with rules, that is, even if the premises are definitely true, the conclusion may be less than definite. We can talk about uncertain facts and uncertain rules. Reasoning with uncertain facts and rules are dealt with in Section 5.6.3. Rules are used to represent relationships and are used together with some formalism for simple fact representation in the database, for instance, propositions or attribute–value pairs as shown above. In the production system architecture, inferential knowledge is represented as a set of rules. The state of the workspace determines which rules can be activated.

Rules are particularly suitable for representing inferential knowledge of the type that experts use (heuristics). They are simple to understand, and due to the inference methods used the reasoning can be comprehensively explained after a conclusion is drawn. The structure of the rules is uniform, thus permitting good readability of the knowledge. Also, each rule can be regarded as a separate chunk of knowledge. This offers *modularity* and flexible maintenance.

The rule representation formalism, however, has some disadvantages. As the number of rules increases, the processing efficiency decreases rapidly unless some structure is imposed on the rule base, for example, grouping of rules. Also, it is difficult to represent, explicitly, static knowledge about structured objects. For problem domains where it is important to represent this type of knowledge, production rules are used together with representation formalisms more appropriate for this (see below).

5.5.4 Semantic Nets

In Chapter 2 we showed that memory knowledge is represented as propositions, and that a collection of propositions makes up associative structures among concepts which we called propositional networks. These networks were originally called *semantic nets* because they were designed to represent general knowledge about the semantics of concepts, that is, the meaning of words for natural language understanding. They have later proved to be useful to represent facts about specific objects (knowledge representation).

A semantic net is an associative network of concepts. Concepts are represented as nodes and associations are represented as arcs. *Concepts* can be specific (instances) or more general (types). *Arcs* or links can represent any association between concepts. However, the most common structural relationships that we want to deal with, are:

(1) IS-A links used to define taxonomic relationships (class–subclass–instances), for example, 'A salmon IS-A fish', and 'A fish IS-A animal'. Taxonomic relationships are sometimes called *generalization hierarchies*.
(2) HAS-A (or IS-PART-OF) links which represent descriptions of objects (components), for example, 'Glass-IS-PART-OF a window', and 'A window IS-PART-OF a house'.

An example of a semantic network is shown in Figure 5.9.

An important property of taxonomic relationships is transitivity. This allows characteristics of higher level more general objects to be associated with lower level more specific objects by an inference mechanism. For example, from the two propositions:

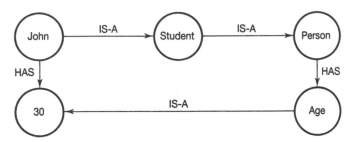

Figure 5.9   *A semantic network*

Jacques is a Parisien
A Parisien is a Frenchman

we can infer the property that:

Jacques is a Frenchman.

This procedure is called property inheritance, and is an important aspect of knowledge representation because it saves storing all implied relationships. Of course, this saving of storage space is traded with additional computation.

Several methods exist of reasoning with knowledge that is represented in the semantic net formalism. One of the earliest ones is called *intersection search*, where information is found by activating nodes and searching for the node where all the activation meets. For instance, the question 'What is the age of John?' will start in the Age and the John nodes, and meet in the node with the contents 30. Alternatively, reasoning is performed by *comparison of fragments* of the net. Here, the information required will be formulated as a net (a fragment) and compared to the stored net. For instance, the question posed above, is presented, diagramatically, in Figure 5.10. Semantic nets can also be traversed using rules of inference.

The advantage of semantic nets is the generality to represent any kind of structural knowledge. Also, it gives an integrated view of the knowledge. It is possible to add production rules to a semantic net, thus enabling the combination of the two representation formalisms. A

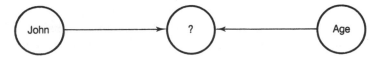

Figure 5.10   *A comparison of fragments in a semantic net*

disadvantage of semantic nets is processing efficiency. Also, maintenance can be a problem due to the integration of knowledge by pointers (links). Explanation of reasoning is difficult.

5.5.5 Object-oriented Knowledge Representation

Semantic nets are conceptually easy to understand and provide an appealing visual picture of a chunk of knowledge. However, as this chunk of knowledge becomes complex the number of nodes and links increases rapidly. There is a need to add more structure to the modeling language. One way to do this is to structure the world into distinct objects and map these objects into the data structures describing the real world. In this way the *object-oriented approach* to system development was established. The object-oriented approach is a result of developments in three different fields: programming languages, artificial intelligence, and databases.

The first object-oriented programming language is considered to be Simula-67 developed by researchers at the Norwegian Computing Center (Birtwistle *et al.*, 1973). Here, the first basic concepts such as objects, messages, and classes were introduced. After Simula followed two lines of development of object-oriented programming languages. First, completely new object-oriented languages were developed. The most prominent example here is Smalltalk-80 (see Goldberg and Robson, 1983). Second, extensions of more conventional languages to include object-oriented structuring facilities were established, for instance Objective C and C++ as extensions of the C language.

In the field of artifical intelligence the idea of frames as an object-oriented knowledge representation scheme was presented by Minsky in 1975. Frames will be dealt with in a separate section below. In the database area, the concepts of aggregation, generalization, and instance-of-relationships were introduced to capture more semantics (see for instance Smith and Smith, 1977).

Core Concepts in the Object-oriented Approach

Object

In the object-oriented approach, any entity in the domain, whether it is a thing, a situation, an event, or a concept, is uniformly modeled as an object. For example, an object can be a car, a stock, or an accounting item like cash. Each object is identified by an object identifier and is described by a state and a behavior.

Attribute

The state of an object is represented by its attributes, also called slots. An attribute has a name and a value. An attribute can be regarded as an object in itself with attributes such as data type, cardinality, allowable values, etc.

Method

The behavior of an object is defined by the methods (or procedures) that an object is capable to execute. A method can change, for instance, an attribute value of the object. Only methods contained within an object can change the attribute values of that object. This is known as *encapsulation*. No outside object or program should be able to access or modify the data enclosed within an object except via the object's own methods.

Message passing

In the object-oriented approach communication between objects is done by message passing. A message activates a method of an object. It may originate within an object, at another object, or from procedural code or rules external to the objects. A message is a request for information or a trigger for action. A message has the following form:

Receiver. Selector (Parameter)

The receiver specifies the object that will receive the message. The selector is simply the name of the method to be executed. If the method to be activated needs one or more parameters, the parameters are attached to the message and contained within parentheses. Message passing between two methods of the same object does not need to specify the receiver.

Class

Objects take two forms: classes (or types) and instances. Objects that share the same set of attributes and methods are organized into classes. Classes are abstractions. It is a means of grouping objects. An object must belong to only one class as an instance of that class. The relationship between an object and its class is the INSTANCE-OF relationship. An instance describes a specific occurrence in the real world.

A class has two roles to play. First, it defines the structure of the instances of that class by identifying the set of attributes and methods shared by all instances of that class. Second, the class is an object in its own right. It may have its own attributes (local attributes) that describe properties of the class as a whole.

Class hierarchy and inheritance

Classes that share common features can form a class hierarchy. Subclasses (also called child classes) in this hierarchy represent class *specialization*. For instance, cash is a subclass of current assets, or students is a subclass of persons. Objects linked together in a class hierarchy permit inheritance. The principle of inheritance makes it possible to define an attribute only once and let all subclasses inherit this value. If a lower level object explicitly contains a value in the attribute slot, then this value overwrites any inherited value. The inheritance principle also applies to methods. A subclass inherits methods and attributes from its superclass (also called parent class). It is also possible to specify attributes and methods for the subclass in addition to or as a modification of those inherited from the superclass. In a class hierarchy, the superclass is a general form of its subclasses. Therefore, class hierarchy captures the generalization (IS-A) relationship between one class and a set of classes specialized from it.

Figure 5.11 illustrates the use of an object-oriented representation of an accounting problem. The sales transaction passes a message to the finished goods inventory accounting system. When items are sold the stock volume has to be updated. Messages on stock values can be sent upwards in the class hierarchy to change the value of current assets. The advantage of the object-oriented approach is the object encapsulation. By this feature an object can be made sufficiently self-contained to be a module in several applications (reusability).

To see the object-oriented approach applied to the financial area, the reader is referred to Chu (1992) and to Yoon and Guimaraes (1992). We shall return to the object-oriented approach to expert systems when dealing with architectures in Section 5.7.

5.5.6   Frames

The frame schema was, as mentioned above, first proposed by Minsky (1975). He developed this concept from the semantic net formalism. A frame represents an object-oriented view in that it allows knowledge to be partitioned into discrete structures having individual properties.

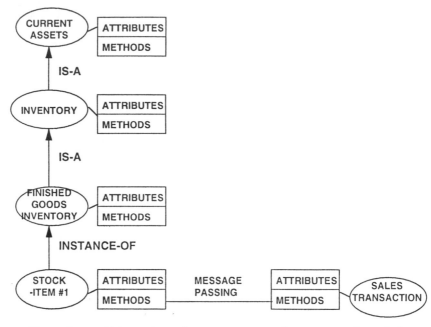

Figure 5.11   *Object-oriented representation of accounting knowledge*

'A frame is a data-structure for representing a stereotyped situation like being in a certain kind of living room or going to a child's birthday party. Attached to each frame are several kinds of information. Some of this information is about how to use the frame. Some is to do if these expectations are not confirmed.' (Minsky, 1975)

Minsky describes frames as a representation of *stereotyped* situations or objects that are typical (*prototypes*) of some category. We know that people organize their knowledge according to stereotypes, a standardized mental picture generally agreed upon, of objects and events. A stereotypical mental picture of a bird, for instance, will be a bird that can fly and not a bird like an emu which cannot fly. *Default value* is an important property of stereotyped situations. The bird stereotype, for instance, is likely to have a default value: 'flying'. When we describe a particular bird it will then inherit the value 'flying' from the class property of birds. However, when we describe an emu, the value 'flying' must be changed to 'non-flying'. In general, a default value is a value that we assume to be true unless we are told otherwise. Examples of situations of which we usually have a standardized mental picture, i.e. stereotypical situations, are:

- driving a car;
- eating in a restaurant.

Core Concepts of Frames

Frame

Each frame represents an object, its state and behavior. The state of an object is described by a set of attributes, in the frame terminology called *slots*. Each slot contains one or more *facets*. These facets describe data or procedures to be connected with the slot. Types of facets are: cardinality (single or multiple values), value type (numeric, text, Boolean, etc.) and allowable values. One particular feature of the frame system, mentioned above, is the *default value*. If the slot value is empty the default value is assigned to that slot value.

Demon

A particular type of facet is the demon, a procedure triggered whenever a slot is created, modified or accessed. Typical demons in a frame system are:

(1) *If changed*: a procedure attached to a slot which is executed whenever the value of the slot is changed.
(2) *If removed*: a procedure that is executed whenever a value is deleted from the slot.
(3) *If needed*: a procedure executed when a value is needed but not existent.

Frame hierarchy and inheritance

As for the object-oriented approach we have two types of frames: classes and instances. A frame can represent a class of objects or an instance (an individual object) of that class. As in the object-oriented approach, frames can be organized into hierarchies by two constructs: subclass links (IS-A) and membership links (INSTANCE-OF). Membership links is a classification mechanism, while subclass links is a taxonomy mechanism.

A frame representing a class can contain prototype characteristics, in other words, characteristics to be inherited down the frame hierarchy as well as characteristics of the class as a whole. To distinguish these two kinds of information from each other, two kinds of slots may be defined: *member slots* for attributes of each member of the class, and *own slots* for the attribute of the object represented by the frame.

Furthermore, a third type of slot is necessary, the *local slot*. Local slots take values for the object it is defined for only and can not be inherited.

Security system

Figure 5.12 depicts a partial structure of a frame representation of sequirities. Only frames representing bonds are shown disregarding

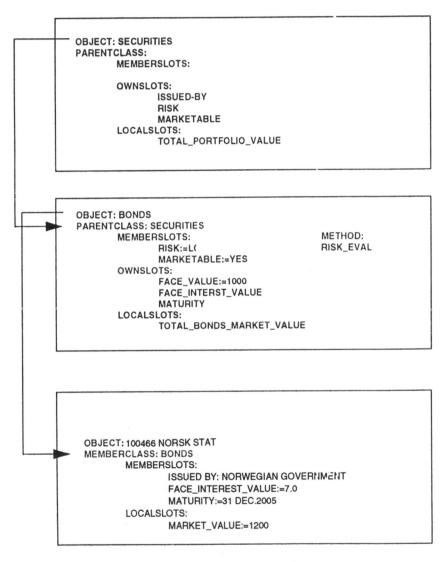

Figure 5.12 Frame hierarchy

other types of sequirities such as stocks etc. The slots representing attributes of the various classes are shown.

Slots inherited from parents are listed under PARENTCLASS and called MEMBERSLOTS. Thus for the frame representing the class BONDS, the slots, 'Risk' and 'Marketable' are inherited from the class security and are listed as MEMBERSLOTS under this PARENTCLASS. This means that all securities, whether bonds or stocks have these attributes. The slot 'Total Bond Market Value', the value of the bond portfolio, is a property of the class itself and defined as a LOCALSLOT. It is not inherited down the hierarchy. As can be seen, new slots can be defined on any level to be inherited downwards. These are listed under OWNSLOTS. New slots should be defined at the highest possible level. Adding new slots leads to specialization. For instance, bonds do have maturity dates which stocks do not have.

Slots are not only filled with values for their attributes. Often the information needed to fill a slot requires some conditional computation. In such cases it is appropriate to assign the name of the method that provides the required data. One set of standardized conditions that triggers these methods to be executed are the already mentioned demons: if-needed, if-added, if-changed. The concepts of specialization and inheritance also apply to methods.

An example of a method associated with the slot 'Risk' in the BONDS frame could be:

If changed: IF Risk $<$ C
          THEN Sell bond
          Compute: Total_Bondvalue = Total_Bondvalue-Bondvalue
          Send Message to Bank_Deposit(Bondvalue)
          Send Message to Security(Bondvalue)

If the credit risk of the bond changes to a grade lower than C, then an action to sell bonds with a risk value lower than C is triggered. The cash is deposited in a bank deposit account. A message is sent to the frame 'Bank_Deposit'. Also the values of securities are changed by a second message. The name of the method is 'Risk_Eval' and the method is triggered by the demon 'if changed'. Thus every time the value of the attribute 'Risk' is changed for any bond instance, the method is executed. This example shows that it is necessary to be able to communicate between frames in other ways than through the structural relationships such as inheritance and specialization defined by the frame hierarchy, i.e. by passing messages from one frame to another. This is done by message passing as shown in the example (see also the object-oriented approach above).

The behavior of a frame system is defined by the behavior of individual objects, and the patterns of communication between them.

5.6   REASONING WITH KNOWLEDGE

5.6.1   Hypothetical Deductive Reasoning

Deductive reasoning allows us to infer new facts from what is already known. For instance, given the two facts: company A has a current ratio of 2.4 and a quick ratio of 1.2; and also some general knowledge that if a company has a current ratio >2 and a quick ratio >1, then we can draw the conclusion that the liquidity of company A is satisfactory. In propositional logic we can express this as follows:

A1:   company A has a current ratio$=2.4$
A2:   company A has a quick ratio$=1.2$
A——▶B: IF company X has a current ratio >2
            AND company X has a quick ratio >1
            THEN company X has satisfactory liquidity.

- -

B: COMPANY A has satisfactory liquidity.

A deduction requires a set of premises, also called axioms. These premises can either be facts (A1 and A2 above) or implications (A→B). In addition, logic has some *rules of inference*. The most famous and the basic rule of deductive inferencing is *modus ponens*, which says that if A is true and (A→B) is true, then B is true. As shown in the simple example above, we also need to be able to instantiate general knowledge, that is, given that the implication is true for any company A. This rule of inference is called *universal instantiation*: if something is true for everything of a kind, then it is true for any particular instant of that kind.

Using these rules of inferences we can draw logically valid conclusions. Note that a formal logic system works with symbols. We cannot verify the symbolic value of a conclusion. What we know is that if we accept the premises to be true, then we accept the conclusion to be true.

A third rule of inference is *modus tollens*. This rule states that if we are given that the implication (A→B) is true, and that B is false, then we can conclude that A is false. This rule applies to the following situation:

(1) If the sun is shining tomorrow, then we will go swimming
(2) we will not be swimming

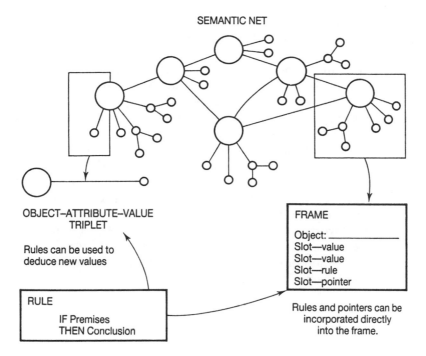

SEMANTIC NET

OBJECT–ATTRIBUTE–VALUE
TRIPLET

Rules can be used to
deduce new values

RULE

IF Premises
THEN Conclusion

FRAME

Object: _____
Slot—value
Slot—value
Slot—rule
Slot—pointer

Rules and pointers can be
incorporated directly
into the frame.

Figure 5.13 *Knowledge representation formalisms*

It follows from (1) and (2) according to *modus tollens* that: the sun is not shining tomorrow. This conclusion, as obvious as it may seem, cannot be reached by a *modus ponens* reasoning system on which most of the expert systems are built.

Chaining and Resolution

So far we have shown how the rules of logic, like *modus ponens* and *modus tollens*, can be used to draw conclusions from a simple set of premises. In larger reasoning systems, relationships between facts may be expressed indirectly through logical statements. We need procedures to draw valid conclusions from these larger sets of logical statements. Two procedures used in logical deduction are chaining and resolution.

Chaining is a simple method used in most expert systems based on production rules to form a line of reasoning. Here, the set of rules are organized recursively so that a fact concluded by one rule is used as a premise of another rule. Facts are propagated through the rule set until the desired facts are inferred. We shall return to chaining in Section 5.7.2 and show the procedure in more detail.

Outside the expert system field almost all computational logic programs use *resolution* (theorem proving and so on). Resolution proves conclusions by refutation, that is, to prove that a statement is true, resolution does this by showing that the negation of this statement is a logical contradiction. Many aspects of resolution are quite technical, and, hence, beyond the scope of this book. It requires using a logic formalism for representation, for example, predicate logic.

Hypothetical deduction means to start with a hypothesis (a conclusion) and then find the premises for that conclusion. If the premises are evaluated to true, then the conclusion is true. One problem with hypothetical deduction is to 'guess' the hypotheses to try and in which order they should be tried. The first version of BANKER (see Section 5.10) worked in a hypothetical deductive manner, where a list of hypotheses are pre-ordered, starting with the reject hypothesis. An alternative method of inferencing is called abduction. Abduction is a method of plausible hypothesis formation.

5.6.2 Plausible Reasoning

Unlike deduction, abduction is *not* a legal inference, that is, the conclusion drawn from a set of premises may not be true even if the premises are true. Abduction allows false conclusions. Logically, abduction can be expressed as follows:

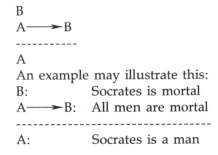

```
B
A ———➤ B
-----------
A
```
An example may illustrate this:
```
B:            Socrates is mortal
A ———➤ B:   All men are mortal
-----------------------------------
A:            Socrates is a man
```

Socrates could be a dog, in which case the premises are true but the conclusion is wrong. Nevertheless, abduction is a useful method of reasoning, very much used in human reasoning. Typically, in human problem solving, evidences are used to generate plausible solutions which are then verified. For instance, we may know the fact:

If company X has a sales problem, then the net cash flow will be scarce.

This does not mean that observing a reduced cash flow means a sales problem. However, it may be a plausible explanation. We would say that we have *explained* the symptom 'scarce net cash flow' by assuming that there is a problem with sales. Thus, reasoning of this form is a well-controlled form of explanations. A set of symptoms can be used to delimit the search space and to set up an ordered list of hypotheses which can be tried. When one hypothesis is chosen, this hypothesis is used to define the evidence set to be looked for. In certain problem domains, for instance, medical diagnosis, where the solution space (the diseases) is very large, abduction can be used to make good guesses of which disease to hypothesize about first. For further details about abduction, the reader is referred to Charniak and McDermott (1985).

As we have seen, abduction can lead to wrong conclusions. Put in another way, abduction can give more than one answer. Socrates could be a man or a dog and so on. Abduction introduces uncertainty to the reasoning process. We can look for more and more evidence until we find one hypothesis which is more likely or probable than others.

5.6.3 Reasoning with Uncertain Information

Deductive reasoning is based on true/false values, so-called two-valued logic, as we have seen above. However, real-world situations are not always such that things are either true or false. On the contrary, nothing in life is certain. Things may be likely, uncertain due to the stochastic nature of the world, or uncertain due to deficient information. Information is deficient because it may be incomplete, inconsistent or not fully reliable. How can we deal with decision making and problem solving in this uncertain world?

To be able to reason with uncertain information we need to *represent* uncertainty, to *combine* uncertain information, and to draw *inferences* from this uncertain information. Various methods or approaches exist; some are numeric and some are non-numeric.

As we have seen in the preceding chapter, the Bayesian approach is the classical method in normative decision theories dealing with uncertainty. The basic element in the Bayesian approach is *probability* – a number that we can use to represent uncertainty. More recently, Schafer (1976) introduced the evidence theory – an extension to the probability theory using the concept of *belief function* to measure uncertainty. Combining evidences based on belief functions is known as the Dempster–Shafer theory of evidence (see, for example, Zadeh, 1981). During the past years, the Dempster–Shafer theory has attracted considerable attention as a promising method of dealing with problems of uncertainty in expert systems. However, problems remain before it can be employed in efficient problem-solving procedures. A third measure of uncertainty – *possibility* – has been proposed by Zadeh (1981). The possibility theory is a development of the Fuzzy Set Theory (Zadeh, 1965) for representing vagueness inherent in linguistic variables.

For instance, the variable AGE takes the values OLD, AVERAGE and YOUNG. Corresponding to each word of this value set is a fuzzy set of values from the universe of discourse of this variable, and there is a mapping function between the two. For instance, if I am 40, how true is it that I am OLD?

$$p((\text{OLD})\ (x=40))=0.5$$

This proposition states that if x is 40 the possibility (likelihood) of being classified as old is 0.5. We see that in fuzzy logic we deal with non-integer logic and we can deal with logical combinations of propositions. Also we can define fuzzy rules.

These three methods to deal with uncertainty are examined in more detail in Bhatnagar and Kamal (1986). The strong feature of these methods is their theoretical foundation. Their weakness is, however, the computational inefficiency in drawing inferences with uncertain information. Therefore, several other schemes have been developed under the label of *inexact reasoning*. Their common feature is that they work well but have only a weak theoretical basis. One such scheme is based on what are called certainty factors.

Certainty Factors

Let us see how one of the early expert systems, the medical diagnostic system MYCIN, deals with uncertainties. In MYCIN, the numbers attached to facts and rules are called *Certainty Factors* (CF). A certainty factor takes values in the range $(-1, 1)$. If the value is positive one believes that the fact is true; if it is negative one believes that the fact is not true, with complete knowledge at each extreme $(-1$ and $+1)$. Certainty factors can be calculated for concluded facts using the following:

(1) The CF of a conjunction of facts is equal to the minimum CF value of the individual facts.
(2) The CF of a disjunction of facts is equal to the maximum CF value of the individual facts.
(3) The CF of the conclusion produced by a rule is the CF of the premise multiplied by the CF of the rule.
(4) The CF for a concluded fact produced by one or more rules is the maximum of the CFs produced by the individual rules.

An example may clarify these aspects. Consider the two rules:

R1: IF A AND B THEN E (CF=0.5)
R2: IF C OR D THEN E (CF=0.7)

and the observed (given) facts:

A(CF=0.3), B (CF=0.7), C(CF=0.5), D(CF=0.6)

With what certainty factor can we conclude E? A premise consisting of a conjunction of facts is evaluated to:

min (CF_A, CF_B) = min (0.3, 0.7) = 0.3

A premise consisting of disjunction facts is:

max (CF_C, CF_D) = max (0.5, 0.6) = 0.6

Applying R1 we conclude E with the following certainty factor:

$CF_E = 0.3 \times 0.5 = 0.15$

Applying rule 2 we get:

$CF_E = 0.6 \times 0.7 = 0.42$

According to (4) above, we conclude E with:

max (CF_E, CF_E) = max (0.15, 0.42) = 0.42

There are other methods with which we can combine the same concluded fact from several rules. It seems likely that if one arrives at the same conclusion from different reasoning chains, that is, that more positive information emerges, the confidence in the conclusion increases beyond that of the conclusion from any single rule. One way of dealing with this is to define an increment factor which is added for each new rule concluding with the same fact. The increment factor is defined as the remainder to certainty multiplied by the certainty factor for the new fact. The new certainty factor then becomes:

$CF = CF_1 + (CF_2(1 - CF_1))$

In our example above this will give:

$$CF = 0.15 + (0.42(1 - 0.15))$$
$$\underline{CF = 0.51}$$

The order in which certainty factors are combined does not matter.

In MYCIN, uncertainties are propagated through the rules of an inference chain. A rule succeeds to draw a conclusion if the certainty factor of the concluded fact is greater than 0.2.

5.7   HOW AN EXPERT SYSTEM WORKS

5.7.1   Basic Architecture

One of the basic characteristics of expert systems is the separation of knowledge from the problem-solving algorithm. Knowledge is specific to a particular problem domain and the tasks to be performed. Problem-solving algorithms, on the other hand, can be employed across several domains and tasks.

Expert systems originate, as we have seen, from the production systems. The main difference is the emphasis put on knowledge and that the real 'intelligence' of a system lies in the knowledge it possesses. The basic architecture of an expert system is much the same as that for production systems. The two central components of this architecture is the knowledge base and the inference engine (see Figure 5.14).

The *knowledge base* contains the domain specific problem-solving knowledge. The problem-solving knowledge consists of all kinds of knowledge that is used by a domain expert: descriptions of objects and relationships, description of problem-solving behavior, heuristics, constraints, uncertainties, etc. We can organize our knowledge into two types: facts and hypotheses. Facts represent what we know at any time about the problem we are working at (declarative knowledge). Facts are either given by the user or deduced by the expert system during the problem-solving process. In the production system terminology this is the workspace (see Chapter 2). Hypotheses represent IF-THEN relationships (rules) between the facts.

The *inference engine* is a general program that activates the knowledge in the knowledge base. It performs inferencing to reach a solution on the problem worked at. The inference engine represents a control strategy: forward or backward chaining (see 5.7.2 below). It determines which rules to apply on the facts. In determining which rule to apply the inference engine may have to choose among several executable rules. Therefore, it needs a conflict resolution strategy. Generally speaking, we have two such: depth-first and breadth-first (see Section 5.4.3).

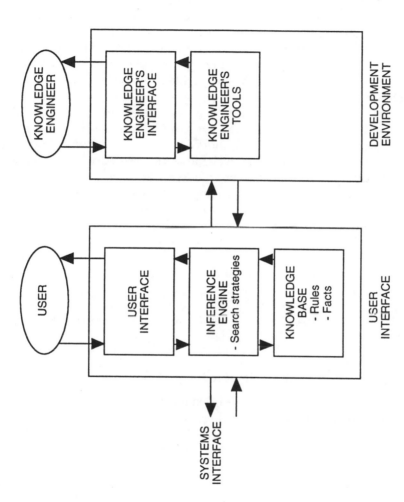

Figure 5.14 *Basic architecture of an expert system*

In addition to the knowledge base and the inference engine we need an *interface* between the user and the computer. This interface enables the user to communicate with the expert system application. In this part we have not included the development environment interface such as a rule editor etc. used by the knowledge engineer.

From this basic architecture of expert systems several lines of development have evolved. First, we can distinguish between the problem-solving approach and the object-oriented approach. The choice of which approach to employ is a matter of the complexity of the domain. The problem-solving approach puts, as the name indicates, emphasis on how the problem is solved: the heuristics and search strategies that are employed to perform the inferences on the facts given. This approach is a direct inheritance of the production systems. It is dealt with under the label of *rule-based expert systems* below. However, there are two kinds of knowledge that go into the knowledge base: declarative and procedural knowledge. Declarative knowledge can be modeled as a set of objects and relationships. An object-oriented approach means to focus on objects and organize domain knowledge around these objects and relationships as already dealt with above. Frame-based expert systems are common in complex domains where we need to put more structure to the declarative knowledge. We shall deal with these systems under the label *hybrid expert systems*. Other architectures have been developed to take into consideration other aspects of the domain knowledge. We shall briefly describe the following architectures: *model-based expert systems, case-based expert systems* and the *blackboard architecture*.

5.7.2 Rule-based Expert Systems

The architecture of rule-based expert systems is based on the production system concept. The main component here is a set of rules representing the knowledge of the system. We have seen from Chapter 2 and the description of the SOAR system that all knowledge, declarative as well as procedural knowledge, is represented as rules. Thus the declarative knowledge that 'Country code of Norway is 47' is written in the rule representation formalism as 'IF Country_Code is 47 THEN Country_Name is Norway'. However, in most rule-based systems the knowledge base consists of two parts: a *rule base* and *facts*.

Each rule in the rule base represents a piece of knowledge, a chunk of know-how. Rules are particularly useful for representing heuristic knowledge as shown in the following example:

```
IF      (1) Management competence is good
and     (2) External credit rating is fair
and     (3) Bank's credit rating is marginal
THEN  Loan is rejected
```

Here we have represented the heuristic relationship between a set of input variables (conditions) and an output variable (conclusion). The domain knowledge is comprised of such rules. In addition we may have rules representing structural relationships of the domain, as shown in the following example:

```
IF      Cash
THEN  Current assets
```

The other part of the knowledge base consists of the facts. A fact is a description of an entity, like:

Management competence is good

Facts represent assertions about properties or relations. Facts can be entered into the system by the user or it can be deduced from a rule like 'Loan is rejected' in the example above.

Facts are represented as attribute–value propositions as above, as property lists, or as object–attribute–value triples (see Section 5.5.2).

Facts are declared to the knowledge base. In PC_OPTRANS facts are declared by giving them names, and allocating a value scale, that is, a set of legal values that the fact can take, and giving it an initial value. The initial value is set to UNKNOWN if the value is not known.

<Fact name> <Value set> <Initial value>

Each fact can be associated with a text, a message or a prompt, which will be displayed by the system when the user is required to input the value. An example is:

```
CHILD    NUMBER    UNKNOWN
'How many children do you have?'
```

The conclusion of an IF-THEN statement can include more than just inferred facts. The conclusion may contain actions that should be executed if the rule is fired, for instance, direct the search to other parts of the knowledge base (this will be dealt with below), calling a particular model, executing a procedure or displaying a report.

Structured Rule Bases

Rule-based systems can broadly be classified into simple and structured rule-based systems. In a simple system, all rules in the knowledge base are kept on the same level and available for search at every search cycle. For larger rule bases, the search efficiency can be improved considerably by structuring the rule base so that search can be limited to segments of the rule base. This also helps in comprehending and maintaining the rule base. A segment is called a *rule set*. A rule set is a named collection of individual rules pertaining to a distinct aspect of a problem. As we have already seen above, we often solve a problem by decomposing it into subproblems, each subproblem eligible for further decomposition. We have called this problem reduction (see Section 5.4.4). For example, financial statements analysis is performed by breaking the problem into subproblems such as liquidity, profitability, etc. as shown in Figure 5.15. This logical structure of the problem can be mapped into the knowledge base if we have structuring facilities for the rule base available. Here, we will have one rule set for each subproblem. When we reason about liquidity, search is only performed within the liquidity rule set. The structure that we impose on the knowledge base is a kind of meta-knowledge (i.e. rules about rules).

A rule set has a name. The four rule sets of Figure 5.15 are:

- overall conclusions;
- liquidity;
- financial structure;
- operating profitability.

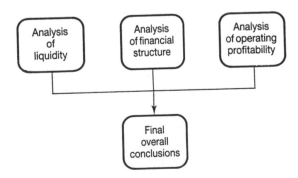

Figure 5.15   *Decomposition in financial statement analysis*

In Figure 5.16, we have shown how the knowledge base is set up in PC-OPTRANS. We have to declare the rule sets, known as CRITERIA in PC-OPTRANS. Then follows the SCALES, that is, the legal value sets of the facts, and the value of the facts themselves. Finally, we have the rules ordered according to the rule sets (CRITERIA) they belong to. In Figure 5.16 only one rule is shown. As can be seen, the concluding part consists of more than just a FACTS_ DEDUCED.

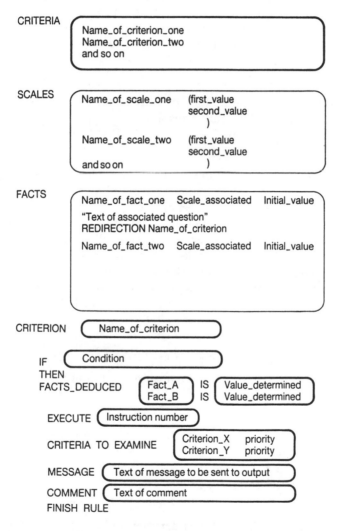

Figure 5.16 *Elements of the knowledge base in PC-OPTRANS*

Inference Procedures in Rule-based Systems

A rule-based expert system works as a production system (see Chapter 2). The mechanism that performs the search and reasoning in rule-based systems is in the expert system terminology called the *inference engine*. The inference engine puts the knowledge of the knowledge base into work to produce solutions. It is activated when the user initiates a consultation session with the system. The inference engine performs the control cycle of production system, that is, finds the rules whose conditions *match* with the given facts, *selects* which rule to be executed, and *executes* the rule by adding the deduced fact to the working memory. To recall the control cycle of production systems:

(1) Selection of rule candidates: pattern matching.
(2) Choice of one rule: conflict resolution.
(3) Execution: deduction.

Deduction by formal reasoning requires formal logic, also called rules of inference. Most inference engines are based on the rule of inference known as *modus ponens* (see Section 5.6.1).

A rule-based system reaches its final conclusion by a series of elementary conclusions. When a rule is applied and a new fact is concluded and added to the workspace, a new pattern of data is created that may match with new rules. This sequence of steps of linking rules with premises and conclusions is known as *chaining*. Inference engines work in two basic modes: forward and backward chaining.

Stylized example

Let us see how the two modes of reasoning work in principle. Consider the following knowledge base:

Rule base	Workspace
R1: IF A AND B THEN D	A,B
R2: IF B THEN C	
R3: IF C AND D THEN E	

Forward chaining implies that the inference engine works from the initial content of the workspace towards a final conclusion through a series of *match–choose–execute* cycles. During each cycle, the rule-based inference engine will search through the knowledge base for a rule whose premises (antecedents) match with the current content of the workspace (true facts). This leads to a set of rules whose antecedents conditions are satisfied such as rules R1 and R2. Next, the inference engine executes one or all of these rules. Which ones or in which order is determined by the search strategy applied (see Section 5.4.3 above). If it is a depth-first search only one rule will be executed, for instance the first found rule. If R1 is chosen, the fact D is deduced and added to the workspace. The next cycle of rule matching gives only one candidate, R2, assuming that we do not recycle into already visited states of the search space. Executing R2 adds C to the workspace. Finally, rule R3 can be executed and we arrive at the fact E which is now concluded as true. The reasoning can be illustrated by an inference tree as shown in Figure 5.17.

This way of reasoning is also called *data driven* since the procedure involves a movement from data towards the goals. When we are presented with new facts, we react to these facts.

Backward chaining makes the inference engine work backwards from a hypothesized conclusion (a goal to be proven) to determine if there are data in the workspace to prove the truth of the goal.

For example, considering the knowledge base above, one can start with the goal proposition E, and try to determine whether the known facts in the knowledge base allow us to prove that this goal proposition is true. The inference engine finds rule R3 which concludes with E. It will replace E with the two subgoals C and D which are the premises of the rule R3. It proceeds with each one in turn, looking first for a

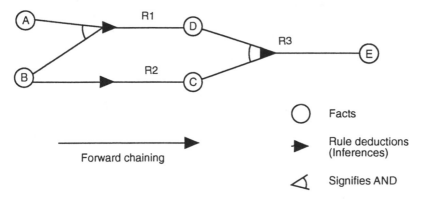

Figure 5.17 *Forward chaining decision tree*

rule that concludes with C, and next a rule that concludes with D. By the rule R1 it determines that for D to be true, A and B must be true. Since A and B are true facts stored in the workspace, D has been verified as true as well as C (by R2), which again leads to the conclusion that E is true. The inference procedure in this case can be seen as a sequence of backward goal proving cycles. During each cycle, the inference engine maintains a list of goals and subgoals which have yet to be proven to be true, for the ultimate goal to be proven true. The inference tree is shown in Figure 5.18.

Backward chaining is also called *goal directed* because we start with the final goal and from there create subgoals which in a sequence of rule-matching cycles are going to be verified or falsified against the true facts of the workspace. It is also related to goal directed human behavior. When we have a certain goal to solve, we start by breaking the goal into subgoals, and then trying to solve each subgoal separately.

To give a more comprehensive view of the backward chaining process we shall use a more elaborate knowledge base where neither the rule base nor the initial workspace is sufficient for the final goal to be proven. In this case, true facts may be added to the workspace by an external agent (the user) by request from the inference engine as this proceeds through the reasoning process. The input data needed is determined by the path that the reasoning takes through the search space.

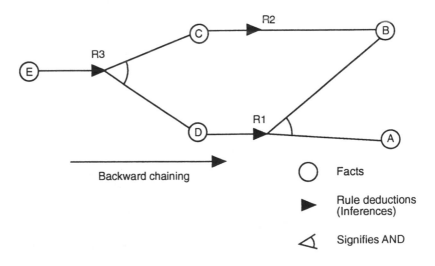

Figure 5.18 *Backward chaining decision tree*

Banker rule subset

Rule 1:
IF	(1) Management competence is good
and	(2) External credit rating is fair
and	(3) Bank's credit rating is marginal
THEN	Loan is rejected

Rule 10:
IF	(1) Loan type is seasonal
and	(2) Profitability rating is high
and	(3) Solvency rating is low
THEN	Bank's credit rating is marginal

Rule 20:
IF	(1) Cash/current liabilities >0.1
and	(2) Tentative solvency rating is low
THEN	Solvency rating is low

Facts:
Bank's credit rating	UNKNOWN
Cash/current liabilities	0.18
External credit rating	FAIR
Loan	UNKNOWN
Loan type	SEASONAL
Management competence	UNKNOWN
Profitability rating	HIGH
Solvency rating	UNKNOWN
Tentative solvency rating	LOW

In backward chaining reasoning, the inference engine is directed to one of the defined goal rules, here rule 1. It will start the processing by looking at the antecedent conditions of the rule. In this case, we have an antecedent representing a conjunction of three propositions, i.e. all three must be true for the conclusion to be true. If one of them fails, the rule is rejected and the inference engine will look for another goal rule. The first proposition to be verified is 'Management competence is good'. The inference engine will first go to the *facts* and try to find a value for this variable. In our case there is no value assigned to this variable yet (designated by the term UNKNOWN). Therefore, the inference engine proceeds to the *rule base* to see if there is a rule that concludes with the 'Managerial competence is good'. In our case, there is no such rule. The inference engine then addresses the *user* to ask for the value of managerial competence. If the user inputs the value 'good' then the inference engine proceeds with the next proposition of the antecedent. Otherwise, the rule is rejected. It now proceeds to proposition (2) of rule 1. It performs the same procedure by looking up the facts. This time it succeeds in finding a value, the value 'fair', thus this proposition is also true, and it proceeds to the third proposition 'Bank's credit rating is marginal'. It looks through the facts, but the value of this variable is UNKNOWN. It looks for a rule to deduce the value and finds rule 10.

Now, it starts to work on rule 10 by adding the three conditions of the antecedent of this rule to the list of goals to be proven. Loan type and Profitability rating are both found in the *facts* memory, and a new rule to deduce the value of proposition (3) is found in the *rule base*, i.e. rule 20.

The inference engine now adds the conditions of the antecedent of rule 20 to the list of goals to be proven. Both propositions of this rule antecedent can be verified since both values that make the goal to be true are in the facts memory.

The inference engine has reached a true conclusion on solvency rating which by rule 10 makes the conclusion that bank's credit rating is marginal is true. Thus we have arrived at true antecedent conditions of rule 1 and we have proven that the conclusion 'Loan is rejected' is true.

Backward and Forward Chaining

Backward and forward chaining are two basic modes of reasoning with rules. The decision of which to choose depends on the characteristics of the problem, and sometimes of the software tool that is used for the implementation.

The choice between backward and forward chaining is decided primarily by two factors: expert reasoning mode and efficiency. *Expert reasoning mode* refers to the way the expert reasons in the particular domain. If the expert uses problem reduction as a search method, then backward chaining is more appropriate than forward chaining. *Efficiency* refers to the search for a solution. If there are a large number of goals compared to input data, then forward chaining is the most efficient search technique and vice versa. This can be illustrated diagramatically as shown in Figure 5.19.

It is possible to use a combination of backward and forward chaining. In describing diagnosis and classification above (see Section 5.3.1) we have seen that it sometimes is inefficient to use an exhaustive search in a backward reasoning process. Here, symptoms (input data) may

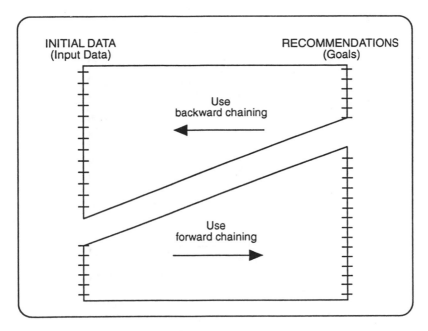

Figure 5.19 *Choosing between backward and forward chaining (from Harmon Associates)*

be used to find plausible solutions, which then in turn are tried verified in a backward chaining process.

5.7.3 Hybrid Expert System Architecture

A hybrid expert system is a combination of rule inferencing and frame or object stored knowledge (see Figure 5.20). In this case we divide the domain knowledge into a domain model and a problem model. The domain model describes the facts and relationships making up the domain either by the frame schema or by the object-oriented approach. The problem model describes modules of inferencing. The two models communicate with each other through the facts that enter into the conditions of the rules.

In the hybrid architecture the usual characteristics of the two techniques are present. Thus, the frame schema will carry with it the structural relationships such as inheritance and specialization as well as the methods, such as demons, and message passing. The rule system, on the other hand, carries with it the inference mechanism with search strategies and pattern matching.

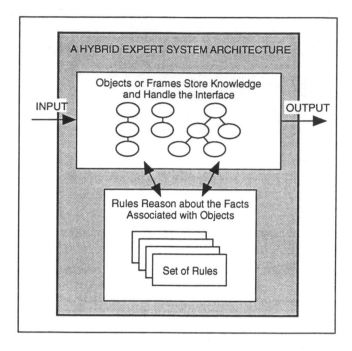

Figure 5.20 Hybrid system architecture (from Harmon Associates)

5.7.4 Other Architectures

1. Model-based Reasoning

Model-based reasoning is based on fundamental knowledge of the problem domain, so-called deep knowledge, as opposed to the shallow, experiential knowledge (heuristics) used in rule-based systems. The relationships modeled could be either structural or behavioral. Structural relationships are used frequently in diagnosing equipment problems. Here, the system consists of a model of the device to be diagnosed, its components and assembly. By using these, basic knowledge conclusions about causes of a failure can be identified. An example of a model-based expert system for equipment failure diagnosis can be found in Fulton and Pepe (1990).

A behavioral model will consist of causal relationships. These causal relationships can be quantitative or qualitative. In DSS we are used to quantitative models where relationships are expressed as equations. By means of such models we can do scenario analysis of various kinds, such as what-if analysis with, for instance, an income statement model.

Bauwman (1983) has presented a causal model with qualitative relationships for financial diagnostic reasoning. Financial diagnostic

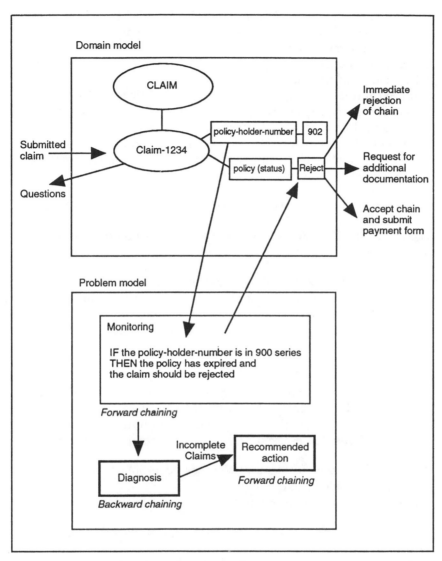

Figure 5.21 *Example of a hybrid system for insurance claim processing (from Harmon Associates)*

reasoning requires knowledge about dynamic relationships within the firm. These relationships represent causal structures that describe the functioning of a typical firm. It describes how the various states and variables that characterize the operations of the firm, such as demand, sales, and production capacity influence each other. This model allows two kinds of inferences. Given a certain finding, it contains (1) the consequences of this finding for other states and variables of the firm, and (2) the possible causes of this finding. This model is defined as a series of qualitative expressions. Figure 5.22 visualizes some relationships of the model.

A typical rule-based system represents heuristic knowledge. Here, experience is coded into rules representing short-cuts in reasoning procedure. In model-based reasoning, the reasoning follows the fundamental relationships, that is, the cause-and-effect paths.

An expert analyzing the financial situation of a company may draw the following conclusion:

'Demand is down because of excess production sales price is too high'

Using our causal model, the model will reason along the causal paths as follows:

'The demand is down because market share is down. Market share is down because relative prices is too high. Relative price is the difference between sales price and industry average sales price. Market share can be increased by reducing this difference, i.e. reducing sales price.'

2. Case-based Reasoning

The idea of case-based reasoning is to adapt solutions of similar problems to the current problem. Case-based reasoning is a kind of analogical reasoning which is very popular in human cognition and problem solving. Case-based reasoning consists of two major steps:

(1) find those cases in memory that solved problems similar to the current problem; and
(2) adapt previous solutions to fit the current problem.

An important component of a case-based reasoning system is the *case library*.

The *inference cycle* of case-based reasoning consists of the following major steps (Figure 5.23):

● retrieve;
● adapt;
● test solution.

A critical step in the process is to find and retrieve a relevant case from the library. Cases are stored and retrieved by indexes. The retrieved

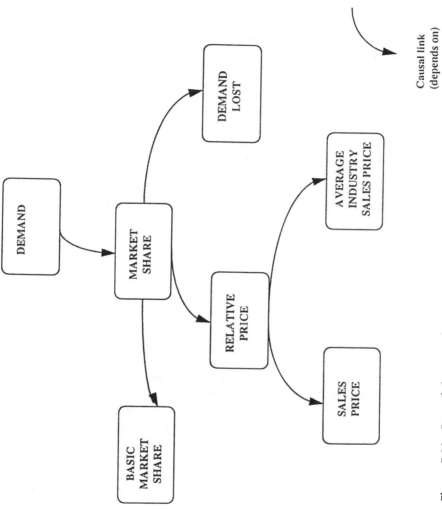

Figure 5.22 *Part of the causal structure of the model of the firm (from Bauwman, 1983)*

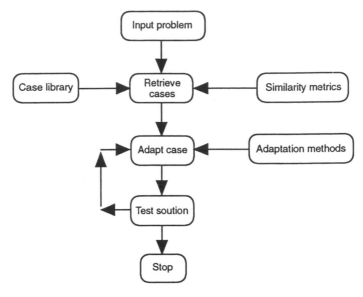

Figure 5.23   *The solution structure in case-based reasoning*

case contains a solution. This solution is then adapted to the new situation resulting in a proposed solution. The adaption process consists of modifying parameters of the old problem to fit to the new one. Finally, the solution is tested. If the test is successful then we have a working solution and the case can be added to the case library. If the test fails, then we have to change the adaption parameters or the retrieval indexes in order to retrieve a new case.

We see from the figure that we need similarity metrics, i.e. measurements and criteria for similarity. Furthermore we need adaption rules, that is, knowledge about what can be changed and how it can be changed.

A more detailed process of case-based reasoning is shown in Slade (1991). Compared to rule-based reasoning, knowledge acquisition is easier in case-based reasoning due to the granularity of knowledge. In rule-based systems rules and logic are generated from historic cases, while in case-based systems knowledge is represented in precedent cases.

Case-based reasoning can be used where the domain is precedent-based, for instance in medical diagnosis, auditing, and claims settlement. It is also useful in domains which lack a causal structure, thus making it difficult to generate detailed rules.

The basic justification of case-based reasoning according to Riesbeck and Schank (1989) is that human thinking does not use logic (or reasoning from first principle).

3. Blackboard Architecture

The blackboard architecture is an architecture that enables independent knowledge sources to communicate through a central device – the blackboard. The main components of a blackboard system is shown in Figure 5.24.

The *blackboard* holds the problem-solving data in a global data store or database.

The *knowledge sources* contain the knowledge required to solve the problem. Each knowledge source can be considered as a specialist in a specific type of knowledge. Knowledge sources are rules with condition and action parts. The condition part specifies the situation under which a particular knowledge source could contribute to an activity. Thus the knowledge sources act opportunistically to determine when it can contribute to the solution of the problem under consideration. All knowledge sources are independent, but cooperate to solve the problem.

The *scheduler* determines which knowledge source can contribute to the solution in the blackboard next.

Blackboard architectures have the advantage of easily integrating different types of knowledge in a single problem-solving system. Because each knowledge source is independent, the resulting system is modular. This facilitates system modification and evolution. The application of this architecture is shown in Section 6.3 when dealing with KB-DSS development environment.

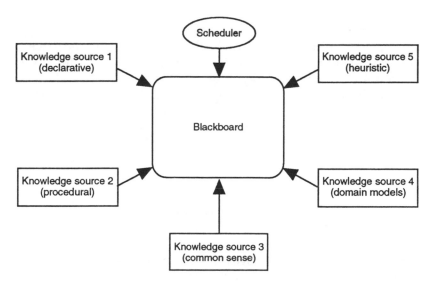

Figure 5.24 *Architecture of a blackboard system*

Blackboard systems were first successfully used for speech understanding (see for instance in Englemore and Morgan (1989) on Hearsay-III). Also in other application areas the blackboard architecture has been applied with success such as tax planning with ExperTax (Shipilberg *et al.* (1986)) and also in the most recent version of FINSIM (Chapter 9).

5.8   TOOLS FOR BUILDING EXPERT SYSTEMS

5.8.1   Introduction

To have an expert system performing problem solving within a domain implies having encoded knowledge and reasoning in a form that can be programmed into a computer. This programming is done using a language which can be translated into elementary computer instructions. Over the years, languages have been developed containing constructs that make it easy to write programs for symbolic processing.

However, a more recent development in software programming, is not to have only a language, but to have a package of utilities including editors, window management and so on. Two generic names often used for these packages are 'programming environment' or 'development tool'. They can be found under different labels depending on the application area, for instance, DSS generators, 4 generation languages, application generators, or expert systems shells.

A programming environment provides flexibility in software development which is needed where the problem may change or where the understanding of the problem domain is part of the system development process (prototyping).

There is a need for a variety of support functions during the life cycle of an expert system. For cost-effective use of the expert system technology, expert systems development tools are required.

Primarily, there are three categories of tools for implementing expert systems on computers:

(1) general programming languages;
(2) special production systems programming languages;
(3) expert systems shells.

Moving from general languages to shells implies sacrificing generality and flexibility in choice of solutions. On the other hand, development time is shortened and the programming skill needed is less specialized.

General Programming Languages

These range from algorithmic languages such as Pascal and C, a functional programming language such as LISP or a logic programming language such as PROLOG. As we have already said, LISP is the dominant computer language in the field of artificial intelligence, at least in the United States, but PROLOG is gaining ground. LISP and PROLOG provide concepts and procedures to deal with representation and control in search-based problem solving. Any control strategy or search procedure can be programmed in LISP. Also, the recursion control structure in LISP allows for easy representation of structural knowledge as well as simple facts. However, the more general the concepts, the more freedom is left to the system designer. It expands the space of problems that the system may be appropriately used for, but it puts more demand on the skill of the designer.

Special Production Systems Programming Languages

These are another class of tools that come closer to the programming needs of production systems. Examples of this class of languages are OPS5 and ROSIE. The special characteristic of these languages is their powerful pattern-matching capability. This permits quite complex patterns to be represented and processed and the expert system to be tailored to the characteristics of its problem domain. The generality is restricted compared to LISP, but general enough to deal with most production systems.

Expert System Shells

These are highly specialized tools for building expert systems in special domains, for instance, for diagnosis. One of the first shells developed was EMYCIN; basically, it is a domain (knowledge)-independent version of the medical diagnostic system MYCIN. One of the major advantages of an expert system shell is the speed by which an expert system can be built. Utilizing all the general functions of the tool, only the domain knowledge has to be provided. By using EMYCIN, the loan evaluation system BANKER was programmed in a couple of days. The functions of an expert system shell are illustrated in Figure 5.25.

With built-in representation formalisms for knowledge and facts, and an inference engine to perform reasoning, then time and cost-efficient development must be traded with generality and flexibility. Therefore, expert system shells are developed for more specific problem domains. For instance, EMYCIN is developed for diagnostic problems where it

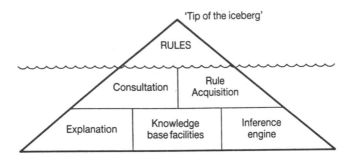

Figure 5.25 *Functions of an expert system shell. (Reproduced from Rich, C. and Buchanan, B. (1985) Expert Systems–Part 1, Tutorial No. 5 IJCAI, 9)*

is appropriate to employ a backward chaining, goal-directed search technique.

Since the days of EMYCIN and other pioneering programming tools for expert systems development, the number of shells in existence has increased greatly. From mini-computers and LISP workstations these tools have expanded into the PC environment. Also, they now exist more and more in two versions, one development and one run-time version. In the early days one could distinguish shells from each other by the knowledge representation formalism they used. However, today, many systems use multiple formalisms, for instance, both frames and rules. Such systems are called *hybrid systems*.

Today we can distinguish better among shells according to the computer environment they reside on. Gilmore and Howard (1986) categorize shells into *small*-scale and *large*-scale expert system tools.

5.8.2 Functions of Expert System Tools

The tool used in building an expert system offers a specific perspective on the problem domain. Each tool has a conceptual model or framework for its knowledge representation and reasoning mechanism. On the one hand, these concepts help the designer in representing a problem domain. On the other hand, they constrain the aspects of the knowledge to be modeled.

In discussing the major functions of expert system tools, we shall do this under the following headings (see Figure 5.26):

- knowledge representation languages;
- methods of reasoning;
- development environment;
- user environment;

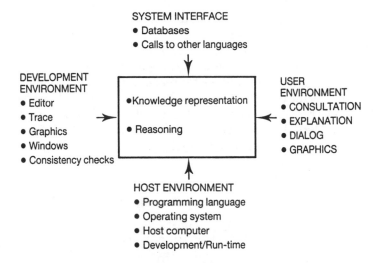

SYSTEM INTERFACE
- Databases
- Calls to other languages

DEVELOPMENT
ENVIRONMENT
- Editor
- Trace
- Graphics
- Windows
- Consistency checks

- Knowledge representation
- Reasoning

USER
ENVIRONMENT
- CONSULTATION
- EXPLANATION
- DIALOG
- GRAPHICS

HOST ENVIRONMENT
- Programming language
- Operating system
- Host computer
- Development/Run-time

Figure 5.26   *Tools for building export systems*

- host environment;
- system interface.

Knowledge Representation Languages

A knowledge representation language is, on the one hand, a conceptual framework, and, on the other hand, a coding scheme for knowledge. At the moment, no generally-accepted standard or terminology exists for knowledge representation languages. They must accommodate declarative and procedural knowledge of the types that we have already discussed in Chapter 4. We shall not repeat all aspects of knowledge representation here, only point to some aspects:

- All tools have primitives for representing simple objects and their attributes (facts) either in the form of <object–attribute–value> triplets or attribute–value propositions.
- All tools have primitives for handling inferential knowledge. Most common are rule-based tools that utilize IF-THEN rules and employ the *modus ponens* general logic inferencing rule for deduction.
- Some tools can handle procedural knowledge as procedural attachments to declarative knowledge.
- Some tools can handle structural relationships between objects explicitly and treat complex objects as entities of their own. These tools usually have knowledge, both declarative and procedural, associated with the individual objects (simple and complex).

Inheritance mechanisms are found in these tools. Most common are frame-based representations.

- Some tools may handle structural knowledge by subdividing the knowledge base into a hierarchy of partitions.
- Most tools provide primitives for reasoning with uncertainty. Most common is the certainty factor method, first employed by EMYCIN.
- Few tools provide mechanisms for handling algorithmic knowledge or do analytical modeling inside the reasoning system. Some tools allow calls to other languages, such as, Pascal or FORTRAN, where this can be done.

Methods of Reasoning

Existing expert systems tools usually use either forward or backward chaining, or both, to control the search for rules in the knowledge base. Some tools do not have a built-in forward or backward chaining procedure. It is merely the ordering of the rules in the rule set that determines the sequence of the search.

Another aspect of the reasoning mechanism is the conflict resolution strategy employed, that is, how to choose the order of rules to be executed when more than one rule has conditions that match the workspace. The most commonly used conflict resolution strategy is the *first found* strategy. Here, the first applicable rule is taken from the applicable rule set.

Development Environment

Beyond the knowledge representation language the system designer, or knowledge engineer, needs further aids. To be able to apply the primitives of the representation language effectively, tools can be developed to provide services such as:

- Knowledge base editing. Tools may have their own editor or use external editors (for example, a text editor). External editors may create several problems: they are not adjusted to the specific knowledge representation language of the tool, on-line consistency checking and knowledge base updating cannot be done, thus, the state of the system is lost if a modification has to be done.
- Effective interfaces, for instance, by the use of graphics. Graphics are particularly useful to edit structural relationships.
- Analytical tools to easily find represented knowledge, for instance, which rules are updated by, or related to attributes; consistency checks and so on.

- Inference tracing to help in error findings during execution of a knowledge base. Also, the capability to set interrupts in the reasoning process at critical points is useful in the testing of an expert system. The ability to ask for explanations (HOW and WHY questions) is helpful in the development phase as well as in the usage phase.
- Screen format utilities to design the end-user interface. Most expert systems work in a dialog mode with the end-user, who provides the necessary input data. Window management, screen titles and so on, are facilities that will reduce the design efforts.

User Environment

The environment in which the end-user interacts with the system can be of several types:

- line edited question–answer interfaces with natural language parsers;
- menu-driven dialogs with single or multiple answers to prompts;
- graphics.

Also, a help facility is an important part of the end-user environment. Help can be needed for several purposes:

- to use the system facilities;
- to explain the format of the input;
- to explain concepts used;
- to explain protocols used in solving the problem.

Furthermore, end-user access to the knowledge base and the database is provide by some tools. Tools without a special run-time version will have the same facilities available for the developer as well as the user.

Host Environment

The host environment includes the computer hardware, the operating system, the programming language, and the version in which systems can be developed and run. The host computer can be of four types:

(1) PCs,
(2) work stations (multi-tasking and large screens),
(3) LISP work stations,
(4) time-sharing on mainframes or minis.

Programming languages will be LISP or PROLOG, the typical AI languages, or algorithmic languages such as Pascal, FORTRAN or C.

Systems may run in a compiled run-time version or in interpreted development versions.

System Interface

The system interface may include data extraction from external databases, procedures to connect to other language or packages (modeling languages, spreadsheet programs and so on).

5.9 EXPERT SYSTEMS OPPORTUNITIES

The expert system technology has proved its applicability in many different areas. The technology – also called knowledge technology, establishes an opportunity to computerize knowledge, the ultimate property for better skill, better competence, and better performance. In order to evaluate these opportunities we shall look at this in three steps:

(1) the feasibility of the technology;
(2) how to share computerized knowledge;
(3) what this means in business terms.

5.9.1 Technical Feasibility

We have, in our previous description of expert systems, touched upon several of the factors that must be present for an expert systems approach to be feasible. Both the information processing paradigm of human problem solving developed by Newell and Simon, and the knowledge paradigm of expert systems presented by Feigenbaum are important fundamental issues in evaluating tasks and problem domains feasible for expert systems development.

In general, expert systems can be developed where:

- the task requires symbolic reasoning more than numeric calculations;
- heuristic search is used more than algorithmic procedures;
- domain-specific knowledge is more dominant than common sense;
- the task must have well-defined solutions, that can be specified in advance;
- the inference logic is predetermined;
- the task must be of manageable size, but complex enough to benefit from an expert system.

Furthermore, one or more experts available for knowledge acquisition must exist, that is:

- the expert must be willing to participate;
- the expert must be able to articulate his or her problem solving;
- there exist cases which can be used for knowledge acquisition and validation.

5.9.2 Knowledge Sharing

Replications of expertise is the major driving force for expert systems applications. It affects business in many ways, which we shall look closer at in a moment.

Because of the replication opportunity of expert systems, developments of expertise in new areas can be made cost effective. For instance, the knowledge base on XCON, Digital Equipment's expert system for VAX configurations, was developed by pooling together several knowledgeable persons, such as product designers and sales consultants, to produce the integrated knowledge required to help in this complex task.

Another important factor of computerized knowledge is well-documented know-how in a domain. Knowledge used by experts is rarely available for inspection, evaluation or control. Experts are usually evaluated on their results, not on how they arrive at these results. With a computer system one obtains a detailed documentation of this knowledge. A corollary of this is a better understanding of the task. For example, the application of expert systems to the interpretation of the UK social welfare benefits rules has helped to identify anomalies in the statutes and in the detailed interpretation of the rules (Butler Cox and Partners Ltd, 1987).

One last point about knowledge utilization to be mentioned here is the opportunity to capture and store knowledge. Expert systems have been used in situations where expertise is in danger of being lost, for instance, due to retirement or due to product obsolescence.

We can summarize the advantages of knowledge sharing by the following:

- replication and enhancement of expertise;
- relieve experts of trivial tasks;
- cost-effective expertise development;
- documentation and better understanding of performance knowledge;
- capturing and storing.

Table 5.3   *Contrast between human and artificial expertise*

Human expertise	Artificial expertise
Perishable	Stable
Difficult to transfer	Multiplicative
Difficult to describe	Documented
Unpredictable	Consistent
Expensive	Cheap
Creative	Monotonic

Some of these factors are related to a comparison between human experts and artificial expertise. These two types of knowledge are contrasted in Table 5.3.

5.9.3   Business Opportunities

The benefits of the expert system technology are to be found in the applications. What are the benefits to be achieved, and how can we express them in business terms? In this section we shall treat this subject more generally, but the reader is referred to Chapter 12 for more examples and cases of the expert system technology applied to financial problems.

Cost Reductions

Replicating expertise from the few who have it to the many who need it has cost savings aspects. Experts are expensive, and become more so as they specialize within narrow domains. Therefore, transferring knowledge to lower-skilled personnel also implies that cheaper personnel can perform the tasks. An example of this is found in Coopers & Lybrand, an international audit and accounting firm. This firm decided to develop Expertax, an expert system that would enable less-qualified personnel to handle the simpler tax problems, freeing the experts to concentrate on the difficult problems where their specialist knowledge is of most value. The non-expert can now advise on the simpler tax problems, which form the majority of the cases anyway, without having to refer them to the tax expert. The benefits: *reduced time* and *costs*.

Another important cost factor is increased productivity among clerks or professionals by using support tools such as an expert system. One example is PlanPower, and expert system developed by Applied Expert Systems (APEX) Inc., in the United States. This expert system is developed to produce personal financial plans. The process of

Table 5.4 *Opportunities provided by PlanPower*

Change type	Benefit	Valued outcome
Business process change	Eliminate steps in a business process, thereby eliminating key cost element(s)	Financial analysis costs reduced by 50%
	Eliminate steps in a business process, thereby compressing process time	Financial analysis time reduced from weeks to days
Product change	Create barriers to competitive entry	Financial product/service sales no longer limited by analysis talent
	Raise customer or supplier switching costs	Locks customer and representatives to the company
Work content change	Change work to use less-skilled personnel	Reduction in training costs
	Change work to use fewer skilled personnel	Ability to integrate subspecialities
	Change work to improve results of process	More consistency, diligence applied to customer service

(Reproduced from the Manual of PlanPower, courtesy of APEX Inc.)

providing comprehensive advice to one person, which previously took several days to produce, can now be made in less than one day. In addition, more alternatives are analyzed and solutions are more customized to the clients' preferences and needs. Table 5.4 shows the opportunities provided by PlanPower.

One cost reduction factor, as we have just seen, is to use lower-skilled, lower-cost personnel to perform tasks. Another cost reduction factor is the increased automation of services that can be achieved with expert systems. New generations of automatic tellers and telebanking systems will, to a greater extent, incorporate knowledge bases for such tasks as credit granting, stock investments and so on. With expert systems and knowledge bases integrated, more and more, with other computer applications of an organization, one can imagine many places where reasoning can add values to these systems. One example is the recognition and handling of bad debts in a credit institution. American Express has developed an expert system called 'Authoriser's Assistant' running on a Symbolics LISP machine but fully integrated with a mainframe system with databases and statistical models.

Loan or credit management has two cost components. One is related to the cost of processing a loan application. The other is related to the risk of losses due to bad payments. Many financial institutions have experienced, with serious consequences, what insufficient credit evaluation can lead to. Now the situation is changing, and most credit-granting institutions are putting more emphasis on credit evaluation again and are looking for better aids to perform this task. Risk analysis is not only important in granting credit, but can be applied to almost any task in the financial domain.

Added Values

It is often said that the expert systems technology is not a typical efficiency technology, that is, applications are not justified primarily on the basis of cost reduction. Improved effectiveness, that is, added values, are more in focus. Since this technology is also called a front-office technology these added values are primarily found in changes in products and services.

Many expert systems are advisory systems. They can provide advice directly to customers, thus creating a new type of product, or they can produce advice in new ways, thus improving customer services.

Let us look at some added value effects of better customer services. Better customer services can be achieved by:

- more consistent services;
- more comprehensive services;
- more decentralized services;
- more customized services.

Multiple expert systems behave consistently. The same conclusion for a given case will be reached in any location using an identical knowledge base. This is particularly important for organizations having a widespread geographical operation dealing with the same tasks everywhere, for example, banks, insurance companies, and auditing firms. People, on the other hand, are less predictable, which means that a loan application, having been rejected in one branch office, may be accepted in another.

More comprehensive services can be accomplished by integrating expertise of different sub-specialities into one system. For instance, until recently, banks had separate departments for bonds, stocks, saving deposits and so on. Advice on bond investments was given by the bonds department, and advice about stocks, from the stocks department. With an expert system, knowledge about different investment alternatives can be integrated into one knowledge base and one system.

More decentralized services follow from replicating and integrating expertise. For instance, decision responsibility for higher credit limits can be granted to branch offices. More customized services are an important benefit of expert systems. Brochures and manuals give general information. For instance, most countries require that their inhabitants must fill in a declaration form of income and wealth for taxation purposes. To help people do this, general instructions are available. However, many people have difficulties in finding the specific rules and statutes that apply for them personally. An expert system can guide in finding these specific rules by intelligent questioning.

The increasing level of complexity in society puts more demand on expertise. This is true in all sectors and at all levels, corporations as well as individuals. The information technology puts information systems in the market-place with easy access to all kinds of information. The bottlenecks are no longer due to the lack of information, but due to lack of know-how about how to use this information effectively. Information about stock exchange values, foreign currency exchange rates, and so on, has no value unless it can be used in decision making. Directives, instructions, rules, regulations and laws play a greater and greater role in our society. We need help in applying all this correctly. Human expertise is expensive, but expert systems are affordable.

With respect to new products, two aspects are relevant. Expert systems can make customer advice cost-effective in new market areas. For instance, banks can now offer advice to lower-scale customers. Another aspect is that new products can be spin-offs of expert systems developed for other applications. One bank, using an expert system for credit evaluation, found opportunities for marketing the financial analysis necessary for this evaluation as a separate product.

Adding values by expert systems is one way of gaining *competitive advantage*.

Training

Another category of benefits is that of more efficient and effective training by means of expert systems. By using an expert system one can create a complete learning environment in which novices can be trained in expert problem solving, thus transferring knowledge about heuristics as well as theories. A complete learning environment must enable the student to pass smoothly through the different stages of learning:

(1) the cognitive stage,
(2) learning methods and,
(3) practicing.

Training with expert systems is superior to other media such as 'on-the-job' training or classroom teaching, in many respects; it is quick and accurate, there is rapid feedback, uniformity, and there is coherence and so on. Also, the knowledge technology allows us to move from individual learning and expertise to organizational learning and expertise.

Summary of Benefits

The following summarizes the major benefits of expert systems that have been described above:

(1) Cost reduction
    (a) distribution of expertise to lower-paid personnel;
    (b) improved productivity of knowledge workers;
    (c) reduced risks and losses.
(2) Added values
    (a) better customer services:
        (i) more consistent
        (ii) more comprehensive
        (iii) more decentralized
        (iv) more customized
    (b) New products
        (i) cost-effective advice in new market areas
        (ii) new products
    (c) Competitive advantage
(3) Training

5.10　BANKER – AN EXPERT SYSTEM FOR CREDIT EVALUATION

BANKER is an expert system that makes a credit evaluation of bank loan applicants. It is an expert system because it employs knowledge and inferences to draw conclusions. The set of conclusions consists of ratings of the creditworthiness of a company according to the following scale:

(1) High
(2) Average
(3) Marginal
(4) Low – loan not to be granted

Also, BANKER is an expert system because the knowledge and inference procedures are modeled after human experts, bank loan officers, and they represent heuristics and search strategies employed by these people. Furthermore, BANKER is implemented in a development tool that enables us to separate knowledge from the problem-solving program.

BANKER was first developed using EMYCIN (Van Melle and Bennett, 1981) and run on DEC 2060. It was later converted to a PC environment using PC-OPTRANS as the development tool. The PC version of BANKER will be described in this section.

5.10.1 The Domain Knowledge of BANKER

To determine creditworthiness of a business loan implies making an evaluation of the loan applicant's capability to service the debts over the time horizon of the loan. With respect to the present and near future (less than one year) this is very much dependent on the current financial situation of the company. With respect to the future, it is dependent on the company's ability to generate earnings, that is, the profitability. The current situation can very much be determined by the data of the balance sheet. However, in the long run, more judgmental factors such as market demand, management and so on, should be included. Since debt management concerns the future, with either a short or a long time-horizon, there are many uncertain factors to be considered. Therefore, the risk of credit granting must be evaluated. The heuristics that experts use take all of these factors into consideration.

Cohen *et al.* (1966) have studied how bankers make decisions. They have presented a decision model of the procedures that commercial banks use in evaluating applications for business loans. Here, we shall focus on the heuristics that they found bankers were using in performing credit analysis. Many of these heuristics are used for interpretation and qualifications of calculated numeric variables and ratios. The bankers do not specify liquidity, for instance, in terms of a number. They do this in qualitative terms such as high, average, low and so on. But how can they? In Cohen *et al.*'s model, qualifications are done by comparing figures of the company with industry. Thus, the heuristics consist of selecting appropriate variables, choosing the right combinations, and making interpretations and comparisons that enable the decision makers to qualify key concepts such as solvency and profitability. There are five parts to this credit evaluation model:

(1) Is the bank's share of risk clearly unreasonable?
(2) Does the firm have enough current assets?
(3) Are the firm's current assets sufficiently liquid?
(4) Is the firm sufficiently profitable?
(5) What is the final credit rating of the applicant?

Each of these parts represents a problem to be solved and the conclusion of one subproblem influences the solution of the next. The knowledge base and the conclusion set for each of these parts are shown in Table 5.5.

5.10.2 The Computer Program

Since BANKER operates in the financial domain we may expect the need for numeric calculations as well as reasoning. Numeric calculations are performed to compute aggregated financial ratios and to generate present and future cashflows. Using a particular programming tool, PC-OPTRANS, requires knowledge and reasoning to be formulated in the syntax of the tool. PC-OPTRANS was described in Chapter 4 and will, therefore, not be dealt with here. We shall just note that it is a rule-based expert systems development tool. The knowledge base can be segmented. Reasoning can be forward (data) driven or backward (goal) driven.

We have to define our problem space in such a way that PC-OPTRANS's inference engine can work. This definition is done by specifying a problem-solving graph (see Section 5.3) for the problem space, that is, we define the relationships between the final conclusions and the input data. As we have seen, Cohen *et al.*'s model describes a structure of the problem space. In Figure 5.27 the problem-solving graph, also called inference structure, of BANKER is shown. It is divided into four parts:

(1) input data
(2) calculations
(3) reasoning
(4) final conclusions

Part of the knowledge base of BANKER is shown in Figure 5.28.

Table 5.5 *Contents of the knowledge base and the conclusions for different parts of BANKER*

PART	KNOWLEDGE BASE	CONCLUSIONS

(1) Is the bank's share of risk clearly unreasonable ?	(1) Net worth/total debts < minimally acceptable
	    If yes then reduce loan
	
	(2) Cash account < 0
	    If yes then reject loan application
	
	(3) Cashflow to debt service coverage < 1
	    If yes then reject loan application
	
	(4) Cashflow declining
		(1) Loan application is processed
		
		(2) Loan amount is reduced and processed
		
		(3) Loan is rejected. Risk is too high.

(2) Does the firm have enough current assets ?	Heuristics about interpretations of the following variables:
	
	(1) Level of net working capital
	(2) Trend in net working capital
	(3) Current ratio
	    • Firm
	    • Industry
		Tentative solvency rating:
		
		• High
		• Average
		• Low
		• Low minus
		• Reject

(3) Are the firm's current assets sufficiently liquid ?	Heuristics about the interpretation of the following variables: (1) Cash to current liabilities (2) Cash + receivables to current liabilities (percentile value) (3) Trend in inventories (4) Inventories to current assets (percentile value) (5) Tentative solvency rating.	Final solvency rating • High • Average • Low • Low minus • Reject

(4) Is the firm sufficiently profitable ?	Heuristics about the interpretations of the following variables:
	
	(1) Net profits (historic and trends)
	    • Level
	    • Trend
	    (percentile value)
	(2) Debit to assets
	(3) Debit to assets > prime rate of interest
	    • Firm
	    • Percentile value
	(4) Type of loan (seasonal or long-term).
		Profitability rating:
		
		• High
		• Average
		• Low
		• Low minus
		• Reject

(5) What is the final credit rating of the applicant ?	(1) Credit rating based on financial analysis:
	
	    • Loan type
	    • Solvency rating
	    • Profitability rating
	(2) Management competence
	(3) Outside credit rating
		Final credit rating:
		
		• High
		• Average
		• Marginal
		• Reject

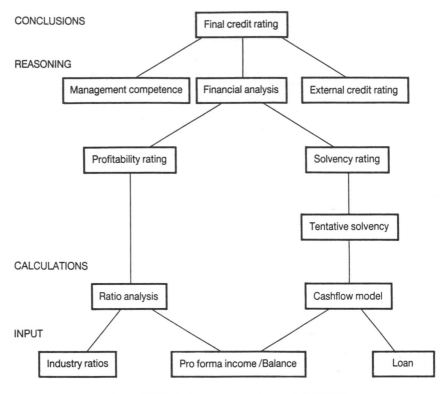

CONCLUSIONS

REASONING

CALCULATIONS

INPUT

Figure 5.27 Inference structure of BANKER

5.10.3 Consultation with BANKER

A consultation with BANKER can be divided into four parts:

(1) preparing the input data
(2) reasoning
(3) explanation
(4) reporting

Preparing the input data consists of entering or editing data from financial statements – three years of income and balance sheets – and entering budget data (Figure 5.29).

When the input data have been entered, a display of some aggregated financial variables are shown in order to check the validity of the data. Next, the computation and reasoning through the parts (1) to (5) of the credit evaluation model can start. Here, the window facilities of PC-OPTRANS are used to make the interaction with the user

```
CRITERIA
        RATIO_NET_WORTH_TO_DEBT
        CASH_ACCOUNT
        FUNDS_REQUIRED
            •
            •
            •
        LOAN

SCALES

AVERAGE (A;LOWER
            B;EQUAL_OR_HIGHER)
BOOLEAN (YES
            NO)
CREDIT (TOO_LOW
            MARGINAL
            AVERAGE
            HIGH)
CURR_RATIO (A;AMONG_: THE LOWEST_25%
            B;BETWEEN_25%_AND_50%
            C;BETWEEN_50%_AND_75%
            D;AMONG_THE_HIGHEST_75%)
RULES

Rule number 2
IF RATIO_NET_WORTH_TO_DEBT = YES
THEN
CRITERIA_TO_EXAMINE CASH_ACCOUNT  URGENT
FINISH_RULE

CRITERION CASH_ACCOUNT

Rule number 3
IF CASH<= 0
THEN
FACTS_DEDUCED CASH_ACCOUNT IS NEGATIVE
CRITERIA_TO_EXAMINE LOAN URGENT
FINISH_RULE

Rule number 4
IF CASH > 0
THEN
FACTS_DEDUCED CASH_ACCOUNT IS POSITIVE
CRITERIA_TO_EXAMINE FUNDS_REQUIRED URGENT
FINISH_RULE
```

Figure 5.28 *An excerpt from BANKER's knowledge base*

convenient. A layout of the screen is shown in Figure 5.30. The three windows have the following purposes:

Window 1 is used to communicate results from the analytical models to the user. Here, calculations performed, that are needed by the user in order to answer questions posed by the expert system, are displayed.

HISTORIC DATA			BUDGET DATA	
L1 C1	YEAR 1		L16 C4	PRO FORMA
TURNOVER	29754		PRIME RATE OF INTEREST	0.16
COST OF GOODS	13489		AMOUNT OF LOAN	1000
OTHER VARIABLE COSTS	1766		CURRENT MATURITIES	1000
FIXED COSTS	12541		LIMIT OVERDRAFT	4500
DEPRECIATION	751		CHANGE IN TURNOVER	0.1
INTEREST PAYMENT	453		RATIO OF CONTRIBUTION MAR	0.48
TAXES	366		INVESTMENTS	1000
CASH	4907		BUDGETED FIXED COSTS	15000
RECEIVABLES	6430		BUDGETED DEPRECIATION	1100
INVENTORIES	3136		CHANGE IN CURRENT ASSETS	0.1
INTANGIBLE ASSETS	650		CHANGE IN SHORT TERM CRED	0.1
FIXED ASSETS	14720			
OVERDRAFT	1949			
SHORT-TERM CREDIT	5275			
LONG-TERM DEBT	1512		12:29	

F3Recall   F4Quit   F5Same value   DATA_FILE FIN_DAT   70 lines 5 columns

Figure 5.29   *Input screen*

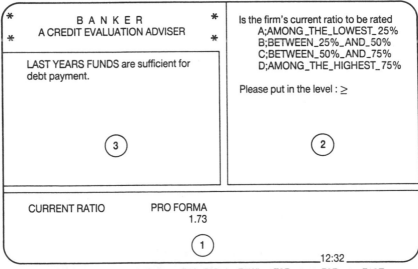

F1Annul F2Trunc F3Recall F4Stop F5? F6Rule F7Why F8Restart F9Facts F10Zone

Figure 5.30   *User interface and screen layout*

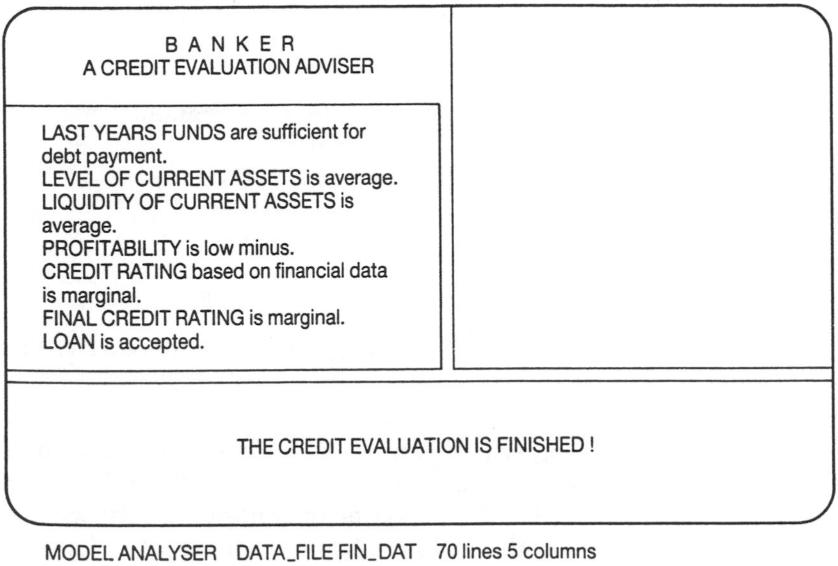

```
┌─────────────────────────────────────────────────────────────┐
│                                                              │
│          B A N K E R                                         │
│       A CREDIT EVALUATION ADVISER                            │
│                                                              │
│   ┌──────────────────────────────┐                          │
│   │ LAST YEARS FUNDS are sufficient for                      │
│   │ debt payment.                                            │
│   │ LEVEL OF CURRENT ASSETS is average.                      │
│   │ LIQUIDITY OF CURRENT ASSETS is                           │
│   │ average.                                                 │
│   │ PROFITABILITY is low minus.                              │
│   │ CREDIT RATING based on financial data                    │
│   │ is marginal.                                             │
│   │ FINAL CREDIT RATING is marginal.                         │
│   │ LOAN is accepted.                                        │
│   └──────────────────────────────┘                          │
│──────────────────────────────────────────────────────────── │
│                                                              │
│            THE CREDIT EVALUATION IS FINISHED !               │
│                                                              │
└─────────────────────────────────────────────────────────────┘
```

MODEL ANALYSER   DATA_FILE FIN_DAT   70 lines 5 columns

Figure 5.31   *An example of BANKER's conclusions*

Window 2 is the communication medium between the user and the expert system. As shown in the figure, a menu-driven dialog is used. *Window 3* displays the intermediate conclusions that the system reaches. The system will show conclusions on each of the steps (1) to (5), as shown in Figure 5.31.

BANKER also uses the explanation facilities of PC-OPTRANS as already shown in Figures 5.2 and 5.3.

Exercises

5.1   Show a search tree for the problem of acquiring a new car. Use a problem reduction solution method and illustrate it by using an AND/OR tree.

5.2   John Smith, who is a financial analyst at Stockbroker Ltd, has just bought a new house in Westend for $250 000. He has financed this property by a mortgage loan of $125 000 by ABC bank, and by a loan from his employer of $60 000. John is 40 years old and is married to Susan. They have three children who are five, eight, and fourteen years old.

The house has a beautiful garden, four bedrooms and garage.

Make a formal representation of this description using the knowledge representation formalisms:

- property lists
- frames
- semantic nets

5.3 How do object-oriented knowledge representations relate to frames?

5.4 A problem-solving search can proceed either forward (from a known start state to a desired goal state) or backward (from a goal state to a start state). Describe the difference between the two chaining procedures, and discuss what factors determine the choice for a particular problem.

5.5 What do expert systems and DSS have in common? What are the primary differences between the two?

5.6 What is required of the problem domain in order to make the development of expert systems practical? How will these requirements constrain the application of the technology?

5.7 Expert systems are formal systems. Explain. Use BANKER to illustrate the criteria of formal systems.

5.8 What are the primary components of expert systems?

5.9 What is the function of the inference engine?

5.10 What are the main features of an expert system shell? What are the advantages and disadvantages compared to general programming languages such as LISP and PROLOG?

5.11 What can be achieved by knowledge sharing?

5.12 Diagnosis is a general task which is found appropriate for the expert systems technology.

(a) Give three examples of diagnostic problems in different domains.

(b) When is hypothetical deductive reasoning appropriate for diagnosis? Explain.

(c) When is it not? Explain.

5.13 Expert systems have been created to assist in tax declaration. Give examples of three facts and three rules that might be part of the knowledge base of an expert system for personal tax declarations.

5.14 The following rule is part of an expert system's knowledge base:

If product category is automobile, then advertising media is newspaper.

This expert system is designed to help people choose an advertising medium for a particular type of product. Give examples of a rule to which the inference logic would chain forward from the foregoing rule and backward from the foregoing rule.

5.15 Do you see any danger or disadvantages of the expert systems technology?

5.16 Case Study: loan evaluation.

XYZ Bank is a small savings and loan bank with 24 branches. Its customer basis consists largely of medium-income individuals. The bank grants credits for a large range of purposes: real estate, car purchase, various consumer products and so on. The branches employ 52 full-time employees and 24 part-time employees at the teller desks. The policy of the bank has been to authorize the head of the branch to deal with loans without collateral to the amount of $25 000 and secured loans (for example, mortgage loans) to the amount of $85 000.

The bank is currently changing its policy. They want to turn the branch into a more customer-friendly environment where personnel are delegated more functions and are given more customer responsibility. The problem is, however, that the current personnel has rather low skill in dealing with new functions such as credit evaluation. Furthermore, the turnover rate of the employees, especially the part-time employees, is rather high.

To prepare for the change of strategy, you are called upon to develop an expert system for evaluating individual loans. The objective is to make the branch personnel capable of dealing with credits within the limits the head of the branch was only authorised.

You have been assigned to one of the credit specialists at headquarters, Dave King. During an interview with Mr King, he told you how to deal with loan applications of this kind. He asks the loan applicant a series of questions. On the basis of the responses to these questions, he evaluates the effects of these factors on risk and repayment capability. On this basis he makes a final conclusion.

Dave King asks the client about the following aspects:

(1) Size and purpose of the loan.
(2) Age and education.
(3) Family status: married, number of children, age.
(4) Employment: current employer, number of years employed.
(5) Repayment capability: income, special commitments.
(6) Risk: wealth and debts.
(7) Customer relationships: number and types of accounts, payment history.
(8) Collateral: security, guarantee.

In the interview with Mr King, you agree to use the following scales on all of these factors: 'strong', 'weak', and 'poor'. In dealing with repayment capability, Mr King is using a rule-of-thumb which says that total debts should not exceed three times the annual income.

Assignments

1 Define the conclusions you want the system to give.

2 Define the inference structure and draw an AND/OR search tree for the reasoning (hint: employ a problem reduction method).

3 Write the rules (for instance, by using the PC-OPTRANS syntax described in this chapter) that make the reasoning possible. Write at least one rule for each concept of the inference structure. Make your own assumptions if necessary.

4 Show explicitly the rules that lead to questions to the user (leaves of the search tree).

5 Suggest numerical calculation (analytical models) that may be included in the system.

How would you determine the benefits of the system?

6
Knowledge-based Decision Support Systems

6.1 THE NEED FOR A NEW FRAMEWORK

We have seen, in Chapters 4 and 5 respectively, the conceptual frameworks of DSS and of Expert Systems (ES) which we can call classical. One of the main conclusions of Chapter 5 is that the technology of expert systems provides us with two new possibilities:

(1) The ability to build systems which can simulate reasoning.
(2) The ability to build systems which can explain their reasoning and conclusions.

It is clear that this capacity can be very helpful in a DSS. Zannetos, as far back as 1968, had already foreseen some of the properties of future MIS using AI technology. However, his paper deals mainly with MIS and not DSS and no applications were presented. A conference was held in October 1984 on Expert Database Systems (EDBS). A study of the proceedings shows that the main issue addressed during the conference was the coupling of expert systems and database systems which is, clearly, a key issue in the integration of DSS and ES. EDBS are defined by John Smith (1986) in his keynote paper as 'systems for developing applications requiring knowledge-directed processing of shared information'. To our knowledge, work on the integration of ES technology within the DSS framework began appearing in the literature in June 1985 with the Maratea NATO Advanced Study Institute's conference proceedings on DSS Theory and Applications (Holsapple and Whinston, eds 1987). We shall study first the enhancement of DSS through expert system technology and then the new KB-DSS paradigm.

6.1.1   Enhancement of DSS through Expert System Technology

If we take the classical framework of DSS which was presented in Chapter 4, we can extend this framework in six different directions, which we now describe.

Expert Advice on a Specific Problem Domain

This level is very straightforward, expert advice means going beyond the usual capacity of a DSS to ask for an *expert opinion*. This capability requires a KB of *domain* knowlege, for example, financial analysis KB for a DSS to support company credit decisions.

One fundamental aspect to be noted here is that expert advice very often requires a significant amount of symbolic reasoning, this adds a new dimension to the functions of a DSS. We have presented the possibility of expert advice in Section 5.10, in the case of financial analysis.

The idea is simply that, even if present DSS help the user to define concepts, to compute procedures, to run decision models, to present reports as sophisticated as desired and so on, DSS will not give expert advice as a human being would. Clearly, it is possible with traditional programming to print messages giving conclusions if a series of conditions are fulfilled, but it is not possible to do so with the flexibility derived from the separation of the knowledge and reasoning mechanisms of ES as we have seen in Chapter 5. This expert function adds an expert assistant to the DSS, the conclusions of which may or may not be followed by the user.

Integrating the ES component in the DSS conceptual framework will considerably increase the expertise embedded in the DSS and will improve the capacity for the users to enhance this expertise. In fact, the expert system component will increase the learning process of the user and reinforce the user–system feedback loop as described in Section 5.5.

Explanation of the Conclusion of the Expert

As we have seen, an additional value of the ES technology lies in the capacity of the system to provide an *explanation* of the reasoning process (see Section 5.3.2).

This capacity is very important because it reinforces the idea which has often been promoted by researchers in the DSS field: that a good

DSS should improve the learning process of the user (see Section 4.5.4). It is clear that the explanation function is essential because:

- Users tend to have more faith in the result and more confidence in the system.
- Assumptions underlying the system are made explicit rather than staying implicit.
- System development is faster because the system is easier to debug.

Intelligent Assistance to Support the Decision Analysis Methodology

We consider intelligent assistance to support the decision analysis methodology as one of the most essential consequences of the integration of the DSS and ES technology. As we have seen, decision analysis is a powerful aid in helping individuals to face difficult decisions.

It is now possible to put, in a knowledge base, the methodological knowledge we have described in Chapter 3 to analyze a class of decisions. Such a knowledge base can be used, for example, to help the decision maker to:

- define a decision model or an influence diagram;
- assess a probability distribution;
- assess value functions.

Explanation of a Model Result and/or Model Behavior (Qualitative Reasoning Based on Influence Networks or Causal Graph)

Two main reasons exist for considering this improvement. The first reason is related to the limits of first generation expert systems. The second reason is related to the existence of decision models as a standard essential knowledge representation method in many domains of application.

It is well known that the representation of knowledge as rules (which is still the most widespread) may lead to a complex knowledge base even for a simple problem. For example, if we take three values to qualify the evolution of a variable (increase, stable, decrease) and we wish to describe the situation with respect to both margin and sales taken together in a company we may need up to $3+3+9=15$ rules. The same reasoning would apply to qualify the evolution of a ratio. To facilitate the coding of knowledge it would be necessary to use a model of the domain, but then (it would) be necessary to reason using the quantitative equations of the model which leads us out of the first generation expert system framework. Two other classical limits of first generation expert systems are the updating of a knowledge base which may lead to coherence and completeness problems (see Section 9.2), and rigidity in the sense that the knowledge base may progressively represent a specific reasoning scheme. The solution is to represent explicitly deep knowledge under the form of models.

The second reason is that since we have decision models in a DSS it is important to be able to obtain explanation by using the logical structure of the models themselves and the causal relationships among variables. This means using the logical structure of the model itself and the causal relationships among variables. Work in that direction has been published by Kosy and Wise (1984), Chidan *et al.* (1988), Page (1990). Two conferences were organized on this subject by Singh (Ed) in 1991 and 1993 and Trave-Massures.

This technology was implemented in the 'IFPS Plus' DSS generator as reported by King (1986), in two simple experimental financial models by Page (1990) and in the most notable way by the CROSBY DSS used by Price Waterhouse (Haamscher 1994).

These systems are able to perform *comparative evaluation* of situations using a model of the application domain. A comparative evaluation is the capacity to point out and explain the difference between several situations (for example two scenarios). The model may be quantitative or qualitative.

In such an environment the modeling system should provide in addition to the solver a comparative evaluation algorithm which will be able to give explanations of:

- up/down evolution of a variable;
- no change in the evolution of a variable;
- differential magnitude of peaks/dips;
- trends;
- comparisons of 'what if' cases, etc.

The first step to a good understanding of a model is to be able to read the text of the model (usually a set of equations) and understand easily its logical structure (structural relationships between variables).

Already it is clear that the advantage of a modeling language of a DSS generator over spreadsheets is the capability of the modeling language to express more clearly the relations of the decision models. But the second condition for an efficient implementation of equation reasoning algorithms is the separation of the text of the model and the text defining the DSS application interface as pointed out by Klein (1993d). This is one of the reasons why we believe that the possibility of the development environment to separate the interface definition and the decision model definition is a fundamental characteristic.

Assistance when using Statistical, Optimizing or other Operations Research Techniques

It is well known that many managers do not use such techniques properly because they do not have the expertise to master them. For example, many managers do not know or remember the underlying assumptions for appropriate applications of a multiple regression model. The usefulness of an expert assistant is obvious but in many cases the cost or the non-availability of such an assistant will prevent the use of these methods.

Embedding an expert component in the statistical module of a DSS which uses a specialized methodology knowledge base (in statistics or short-term forecasting or some operation research technique) should improve the situation considerably. In fact, such an intelligent assistance can have three main goals:

- guide a novice user in using the tools properly;
- help the user learn good strategies for using the tools (improve heuristics);
- discover domain knowledge from large database.

The first goal, guiding a novice user was considered by Chambers *et al.* (1981) and attempts have been made to include intelligent interface systems in existing packages expert software for regression analysis and software which helps users identify an appropriate analysis for the type of data at hand (Hajek 1982).

The second objective is to teach good strategies for using of the tools. In the statistical domain, data analysis strategies are the result of training and experience. This knowledge can be formalized into rules which constitute specialized KB (Hajek and Ivanek, 1982).

The third goal, discovering domain knowledge from a large database, can be achieved by using, for example, lagged correlations to generate a set of hypotheses which can then be tested. The statistical expert systems cited above incorporate many elements of automatic model building. In general, decision analysts share the same decision process as data analysts except that decision making problems are more complicated and often include the data collection phase. A first step (in this direction) is to provide an intelligent user interface for using the KB-DSS resources.

An example of such a knowledge base which has been developed to constitute an 'intelligent assistant' in the field of short-term forecasting is presented in the work of Milanese *et al.* (1991).

Guidance in Using the DSS Resources: Developing Intelligent User Interfaces

Very often, as DSS applications evolve, users increase the number of decision models they use, or develop slightly different versions of a model. This is the case with the FINSIM financial model (Section 3.3.6). The financial analysts, according to the situation or the decision to be studied make different calculations and as a consequence will use slightly different versions of FINSIM. This change in the calculations is a classical one for dealing with accounts such as leasing expenses, subcontracting, provisions and so on. The number of such recalculations the user should decide on may be around ten. To assist such users, a simple KB can be defined that will ask the user questions concerning his (or her) problem so as to help him (or her) in selecting the right calculation options.

A similar situation is described in Klein (1993c) who describes a set of integrated DSS for financial planning in French municipalities. The model base of the application contains three different decision models which support different phases of the decision process of city managers in their planning and budgeting work. To assist such users a simple KB can be defined that will ask the user questions to help him select the right model.

When a DSS becomes institutionalized in a company or organization, the number of databases, decision models and reports can increase considerably. We have observed this in a large French company (where the controllers began using OPTRANS in the main division to generate DSS for budgeting, simulations and forecasts). After two years of usage, the number of models increased from zero to one hundred and the number of reports from zero to two hundred.

When time or money constraints make it difficult for users to attend training seminars on the use of DSS, it is clear that some kind of expert assistance to select the appropriate resources is useful. This expert assistance should take the form of an intelligent user interface which helps the user select and use the resources of the system properly.

Assistance in Formulating Certain Questions

When confronted by a large database with complex relationships, the formulation of certain questions can be difficult. An ES could help the user to formulate his or her request.

Intelligent Support During the Model Building Process for a Specific Class of Decisions

It was stressed by Klein (1977) that it should be possible to use AI technology to automatically define a financial analysis model such as FINSIM from the definition of the list of variables used in the balance sheet and income statement. This basic list of variables is available to the analyst when he starts his study of a company and needs to define a financial model to generate a pro forma balance sheet and income statement.

The idea of intelligent support for model building is that domain knowledge can be used to support the process of constructing analytical models.

Use of intelligent support in model building has been dealt with by several researchers and most notably by Mike Uschold (1993). The new possible services we can expect from an intelligent component in the modeling subsystems are:

- acts as an expert modeling consultant;
- acquisition of simulation model specifications;
- automatic documentation of models in the domain terms;
- automatically writes, compiles and solve models.

Use of intelligent support in model management has also been dealt with by several researchers. Elam and Konsynski (1987) provides a review of the main concepts of model management (see Chapter 11) and Blanning (1991) provides a review of the use of expert systems technology in model base management.

6.1.2 Contributing Disciplines and their Roles in the KB-DSS Paradigm

As we have seen from the above examples, the goal of KB-DSS is to integrate, with the capabilities of traditional DSS: data management, modeling language, decision methodology, display of numerical data and so on, the new advances of ES with its symbolic reasoning and explanation capabilities.

However, we want to stay within the paradigm of DSS, that is, to *support* decision making. Now, as we have seen, we may, as we perform the decision making task, have to solve very specialized problems requiring expertise for their solutions. We want to be able to provide this expertise in the form of knowledge bases along with reasoning capabilities.

The integration of DSS and ES leads to a new conceptual organization, which we shall call the KB-DSS framework. The basic disciplines, which are the basis of this new framework, are: linguistics, formal logic, cognitive psychology, computer sciences, mathematics, statistics and economics. These basic disciplines have given birth to theories, methods and techniques which are: artificial intelligence, management information systems, behavioral decision making, decision analysis and operations research.

When these methods and techniques have been used in the domain of management decision making they have led to the evolution of two kinds of systems for decision support: DSS and expert systems.

Until recently, the DSS technology relied essentially on the disciplines of management information systems (in particular, for data management subsystems), management (for the domain knowledge) and modeling (from the descriptive, as well as normative point of view), statistics, and other OR techniques.

Integrating expert system technology into DSS technology adds, to this list of disciplines, a reliance upon formal logic, computer science, linguistics and cognitive psychology.

We believe that, in the future, most decision support systems will provide some form of expert system technology to achieve the capabilities listed above and, as a consequence, the DSS development environment will have to supply the ES function in an integrated fashion. The ambition of the new KB-DSS framework is to achieve synergies, as we shall see in this chapter, by integrating the ES technology into the DSS framework.

6.2 THE NEW CONCEPTUAL FRAMEWORK

The conceptual framework of a KB-DSS application is different in regards to the one of a DSS application because as we have seen new capabilities are possible based on intelligent assistants.

6.2.1 The Functions of a KB-DSS Application

The functions of KB-DSS applications are the same as the one described in Section 4.2:

- providing an interface to support man-machine cooperation during the problem-solving task;
- supporting access to relevant information during problem solving;
- supporting problem recognition;

- supporting problem structuring;
- supporting problem formulation and analysis, etc.

But this time the functions of the KB-DSS application will be enhanced to provide 'intelligent assistance' to the user during its problem-solving task. This enhancement will be obtained by the use of two new components:

- an inference engine and a knowledge-based management system to provide 'expert assistant' to the user;
- an equation reasoning algorithm included in the modeling subsystem.

The new functional structure is presented in Figure 6.1 and can be compared with Figure 4.3.

It is now possible to use the knowledge-based management system to formalize knowledge in different domains related to the task to be supported by the application.

- A knowledge base can be defined to help the user of the application select the right resources in terms of decision models, reports, databases and knowledge bases.
  The FINSIM KB-DSS (Klein, 1989) application uses several knowledge bases for financial diagnosis, more than 12 different kinds of reports, various recalculation options in the financial model and can access three large commercial financial databases. A good way to assist the user to select the right options is to define the knowledge about these possibilities under the form (of several tens) of rules. By requesting assistance, the application will run the inference engine which will automatically ask questions to decide which option should be selected.
- A knowledge base can be defined to help the user in selecting the right statistical method in analyzing his data.
- Several knowledge bases can be selected to make a diagnosis or define plans to reach a goal: a synthetic KB or a detailed KB. A KB could be designed to build a financial plan for a given scenario. In an application similar to FINSIM called SEXTAN (SEXTAN, 1988) the system calculates levels of credit for long and short term loans as well as overdraft.
- A methodological knowledge base can be defined to support the decision analysis methodology presented in Chapter 3.
- A methodological knowledge base can be defined to support the model building process.

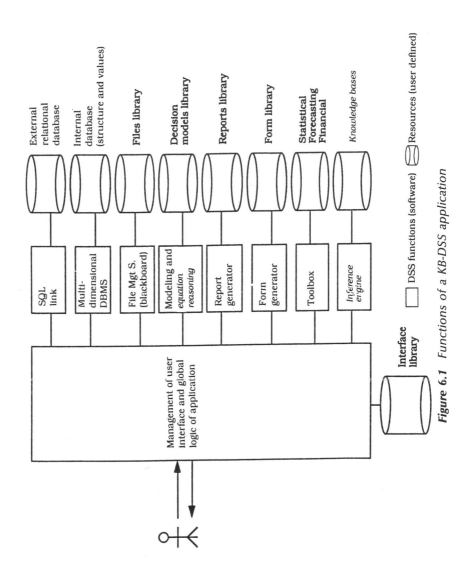

Figure 6.1 *Functions of a KB-DSS application*

The equation reasoning option could be used to make automatically comparative analysis of the behavior of financial models' variables in different scenarios.

Figure 6.1 shows the new possibilities of the application. If knowledge has been formalized under the form of rules, for example, to constitute knowledge bases, it is now possible to request the reasoning mechanism (for example an inference engine) to conclude what can be logically derived (what is true) from the knowledge stored under the form of rules and the observed facts. The observed facts can come from the outside databases, the internal databases, the decision models through the application file.

The KB-DSS application now appears as:

- a system to collect and store facts on the outside world and to infer from these facts what can be concluded as true (diagnosis);
- a system to express goals and to infer from known facts how they can be reached if certain hypotheses are true (through a reasoning mechanism using causal relationship in models or using knowledge bases);
- a system to design alternatives and their associated consequences and provide methodological assistance to select between them (decision analysis).

Clearly these properties are possible if there is communication of information between the resources of the KB-DSS application. The rules of a KB must be able to use facts stored in the application file and these facts can come from the databases, the decision models, the user himself or other knowledge bases.

6.2.2 Example of the Integration Needed between the Components in a KB-DSS

Integration is one of the principal problems facing designers of KB-DSS development tools. There is a fundamental difference between compatibility between two programs (systems or subsystems) and integration between two programs (systems or subsystems).

Several attempts have been made to make existing DBMS or modeling systems and ES compatible through a common file. Many such links have been tried between a spreadsheet and an ES shell, for example, to develop KB-DSS in financial analysis. Usually, these attempts have been doomed to failure since such a file interface can only be useful if the information needed by the expert system is known in advance, which is rarely the case.

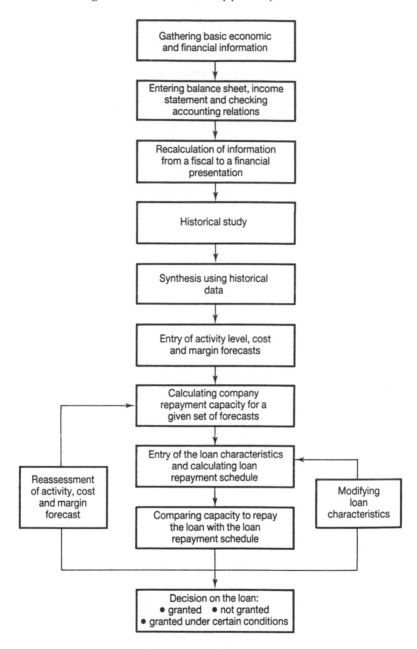

Figure 6.2 *The decision process used by a credit analyst when deciding whether or not to grant a loan to a company. (Reproduced from Klein (1988). FINSIM EXPERT: a KB-DSS for financial analysis. In* Proceedings Eurinfo 1988, *Bellinger, H. J. et al. eds)*

The information needed by the ES is changing, according to the initial data available and to the interaction with the user. The KB itself is evolving and, as a consequence, will need information from the DB and the models which are also evolving.

What is really needed is a KB-DSS development environment (or generator) which is built (designed) from the start to communicate between the expert module and the traditional modules of the DSS development tool. As we shall see later, this raises unusual performance problems.

We shall give a simple example of the kind of interaction which is needed in a KB-DSS generator by using the case of financial analysis, which will then be used to present a real application of the KB-DSS framework. This example, taken from Klein, 1988 will emphasize the main steps of the decision process of a credit analyst as presented in Figure 6.2.

(1) *Gathering information*. The credit analyst must first obtain the basic economic and financial information needed to make the analysis. This information is usually found in the annual reports of the company and other sources (industry studies, professional magazines and so on). This step is supported in the traditional DSS framework by the data management module and, eventually, by the data communication function which enables access to a financial data bank. During this stage, the user needs to access the database of financial and general information on a company over time. This information is mainly numerical (value of the accounts of the balance sheet and income statement), but is also alphanumeric (nature of activity, main contacts and name of shareholders). With a DSS generator, the user can design the interface to facilitate the input of data.

(2) *Checking the data*. The credit analyst uses a spreadsheet (paper or computerized) to standardize the data and check basic accounting relations. The data is spread in an homogenous way. Accounting relations should be used to check errors, which can be done easily with the modeling part of the KB-DSS generator. However, some transformations of the data are complex and imply considerable financial, accounting and fiscal knowledge. These checks are usually supported by the model component; however, if the problem is more complex it could also be supported by an expert module. In this case, an inference engine that reasons on a KB containing accounting knowledge is used to check accounting consistency.

(3) *Aggregation of information*. Basic information, which is usually fiscal information, is compiled and transformed by the analyst into

reports suitable for financial analyzer. This step can be supported by the data modeling and report components of the KB-DSS generator.

(4) *Historical study.* During this phase the analyst studies the evolution of the company from several points of view, usually: financial structure, return, liquidity and growth potential. To do this, he or she computes diverse financial aggregates (cashflow, ratios, working capital and working capital requirements) and displays them in different forms (reports and graphics).

This step can be supported by the report generation and graphics subsystem of the KB-DSS generator. Several reports must be available in the report directory. The analyst will, typically, want to display these various reports, such as income statements and balance sheets recalculated for financial analysis and fund flow analysis, as well as financial aggregates, such as ratios. The graphics subsystem is essential at this stage for the display of the various graphics that the user may wish to generate.

(5) *Synthesis and first diagnosis* using historical data. Using the preceding information the analyst makes a tentative conclusion about the credit rating of the company, he or she may include in his or her reasoning, outside credit ratings and information which would be available if the company is already a client (such as information derived from the history of the cash position of the company).

A synthesis is made by the analyst in order to reach a first conclusion on the basis of criteria such as short-term risk, return and structure, as obtained in step (4).

For this step an *expert module* is needed to infer the conclusions using information calculated in steps (3) and (4).

(6) *Repayment capacity forecast.* When a loan implies a certain risk (given the loan's size relative to the size of the company, or given a long repayment period) the decision cannot be made using only historical data and must consider what is the expected capacity of the company to repay the loan in the future. Therefore, the analyst must make assumptions about the company's activity level, costs and margins in the future, to compute future cashflows.

This step can be supported using a model, window management, and the graphics functions of the KB-DSS generator.

Note that the control is passed *back* from the inference engine to the model, since calculation must now be done on the forecast part of the model.

(7) *Loan characteristics definition and calculations* of the repayment schedule. Given the loan characteristics (amount, duration, interest rate and start of repayment period) the repayment schedule is calculated. The consequences of the loan have to be taken into

account: added interest, modification of financial structure, changes in funds flow statement and so on.

(8) *Comparing capacity to repay* (cashflow available for repayment) with the loan repayment schedule. The company must have a future cashflow sufficient to make repayment possible. However, because we are in an uncertain world, this cashflow (capacity to repay the loan) is not certain and the analyst may be inclined to:

(a) take a safety margin (use of break-even analysis)
(b) use other information to assess the risk

(9) *Reassessment of assumptions* to take into account uncertainty. The analyst is usually given an assumption of future sales levels by the client company. He or she will try to assess the risk by changing some of the assumptions (sales growth rate, costs, margins and so on) to make a sensitivity analysis. He or she will eventually loop on this step as many times as he or she feels are needed.

Steps (7), (8) and (9) can be supported by the modeling subsystem of the KB-DSS generator. We would like to stress the point that the modeling language should provide a certain number of financial functions such as loan repayment schedule and net present value as well as commands to perform impact and sensitivity analyses.

(10) *Final decision* on the loan. The analyst will then use the information and the conclusions obtained by the analysis of past data, together with the information obtained from the forecast study, to conclude his or her decision about the loan.

The support of this step implies the use of the expert module of the KB-DSS. However, it should be noted that the rules of the knowledge base will have to use the forecasted value of the variable and not the historical value as in step (5).

6.2.3 Communication and Control Needed between the Application and the Expert System Resources

We can see from the above example that in order to reach a conclusion, the expert part of the system must use:

- observed elementary data (such as elementary accounts from the balance sheet and income statement).
- data that is calculated from the observed elementary data. This calculated data (also called an aggregate), is defined and computed at the database level or in a model.

A possible sequence of interactions between the user, the Finplan application and the resources used to support the task is described below. A partial description of the application interface is described in Figure 6.4 which can be compared with 4.16.

Step (1) Gathering information. The application (or interface) opens the Finplan Database and the Finplan application file. The user interacts with the menu of the application to indicate with which company he wishes to work. The name of the company is used to indicate the view of the DB. The data of the company is transferred to the application file.

Step (2) checking the data. The application (or interface) calls the inference engine and uses the knowledge base 'test' to check the accounting consistency of the data.

Steps (3) and (4). Aggregation and display of information. The application calls the model solver in order to compute the variables values of the historical model, then print a report.

Step (5). The user select the diagnosis option. The application calls the inference engine and uses the knowledge base 'anafi' to provide the user with a financial diagnosis.

Steps (6), (7) and (8). Repayment capacity forecast and repayment schedule and comparison. The user interacts with the application to input the sale growth rate and loan characteristics. Then the application solves the model 'plan' by calling the model solver and then prints the report income. During this phase the user may request access to statistical routines (mainly if working with quarterly data). Then, the application passes the control to the report generator so as to display the reports selected by the user.

If the analysis leads the user to simulate different financial policies, the application may pass the control to some other specialized model (evaluation of the price of a share).

Step (9). Final decision on the loan. The application passes the control to the inference engine to use a knowledge base containing financial analysis knowledge. (The knowledge base used: 'anafi' is the same as the one used for historical analysis, to enforce consistency in the evaluation.) The inference engine provides its advice and passes back control to the application.

We can see from the above example that, in order to reach a conclusion, the expert system must use observed data which is in the company data file (or database according to the version of the DSSG used). This data is elementary or aggregate.

The aggregates are computed in one or several modes. Therefore, rules of the KB will require information (values of variables) from the models and *full communication* is required between models and the KB. For example, in the rule concerning liquidity shown in Figure 6.3, we

```
┌─────────────────────Knowledge Base──────────────────────┐
│                                                          │
│  IF liquidity ratio < 1 THEN liquidity ratio = bad       │
│                                                          │
└──────────────────────────────────────────────────────────┘
```

```
┌──────────────────────────Model──────────────────────────┐
│                                                          │
│  Liquidity ratio = short-term assets/short-term liabilities │
│  Short-term assets = cash + accounts receivable + clients │
│  Short-term liabilities = bank + accounts payable + suppliers │
│                                                          │
└──────────────────────────────────────────────────────────┘
```

```
┌────────────────────────Database─────────────────────────┐
│                                                          │
│  Cash                                                    │
│  Accounts receivable                                     │
│  Clients                                                 │
│  Bank                                                    │
│  Accounts payable                                        │
│  Suppliers                                               │
│                                                          │
└──────────────────────────────────────────────────────────┘
```

Figure 6.3 *Communication: knowledge base↔model↔database in a KB-DSS application*

have indicated the location of each variable, both in the model and the database.

The ratio of current assets/current liabilities can be calculated in a model but the elementary variables will often be stored in a file or the database (this is particularly likely where data on large number of companies is stored). Some early technical implementation of such a communication link is described in Klein *et al.* (1987). The integration which must be achieved is represented in Figure 6.3.

6.2.4 New Capabilities

The availability of a KB-DSS development environment, leads to the definition of new capabilities (which previously untractable, can now be easily implemented). Some of these capabilities are the following:

- Coupling 'deep knowledge' provided by causal models with 'shallow knowledge' provided by symbolic techniques.
- Developing intelligent user interfaces to select resources available in the system or to interact with a numerical model.
- Designing a more powerful learning environment.
- Supporting the use of the toolbox with intelligent methodological assistance.
- Supporting the decision analysis cycle.
- Providing a modeling assistant.

Coupling 'Deep Knowledge' and 'Shallow Knowledge'

The development environment corresponding to the KB-DSS framework makes it possible to couple equational or causal models (numeric programs) with symbolic reasoning. The FINSIM system (Klein, 1989) is an example of the coupling of a financial simulation model with reasoning, to create a much more powerful decision support tool.

The equation model usually contains causal knowledge of a *theoretical* nature while the rules of the knowledge base contain more experiential knowledge.

As we have seen in the preceding section, during this reasoning we need to use the model to compute criteria and then use it to go on with the reasoning. This is done easily within the KB-DSS framework. Another interesting approach is to integrate knowledge representation facilities into numerical modeling language in order to enhance its expressive power (Page *et al.*, 1993, Boudis, 1994).

Developing an Intelligent User Interface

As we have pointed out in Section 4.2 decision support problems in management may lead to the development of several decision models integrating numeric algorithms and techniques. It is possible, with the new KB-DSS technology, to define intelligent front ends which will guide the user in selecting and using decision models.

A similar idea is found in Abernathy *et al.* (1985) who describe a system which, in a domain other than business, provides an intelligent interface for numeric simulation.

Designing a More Powerful Learning Environment

It is already clear that the explanatory facilities of the expert component of a KB-DSS provide a means to reinforce learning by users. But the learning can also take place at the machine level. Several publications (Cooper and Kornell, 1986 and Brigg, 1986) have shown that it is possible to extract new knowledge from numeric processes and data. Typical applications are extracting classification and relational rules from test and model data.

A similar problem is faced when the system includes a toolbox (statistics and so on) subsystem. The concept of supporting the use of the toolbox with intelligent methodological interface was described more fully in Section 6.1.1.

Supporting Intelligent Processing

The goal of such applications is to reduce the computing resources and time associated with expensive numeric processes by substituting simplified algorithms where appropriate.

Supporting the Decision Analysis Cycle

It has already been pointed out (Klein and Pezier, 1975) that one way to reduce the cost and increase the speed of implementing decision analysis has been to build a DSS which would include, not only decision situation structuring aids, but also advice on using the methodology. This was done with the ARBRE software (Klein and Pezier, 1975) but the technology of ES was not widely available then. Recently, this idea was developed markedly by Holtzman (1989) in the medical field.

> 'A rule-based system is an excellent way of implementing the analysis of a class of decisions. The goal of this particular system is to constructively prove the existence of a formal decision model that represents the decision being analyzed.' (Holtzman, 1989)

A KB/DSS is, clearly, a tool to support individual decision within a given decision class. For Holtzman, analyzing a class of decisions 'consists of developing a domain-specific knowledge base for a rule-based system that contains a set of assertions designed to guide the analysis of *specific* decisions in a way that reflects the decision maker's unique situation'.

The KB/DSS framework is particularly well suited to implement such a specific KB on decision analysis coupled with influence diagrams or other decision models. This idea will be developed in Section 11.3.5.

Providing a Modeling Assistant

It is possible to implement a KB to help the user define which are pertinent variables and relations in a given domain of application.

6.2.5 Is there a Need for a Definition of a KB-DSS?

We can ask ourselves at this point if a new definition of a KB-DSS is needed or if our previous definition of a DSS (Section 4.1.2) is still sufficient. We think an improvement on the previous definition is made if we make the definition more precise by stating:

A KB-DSS can be defined as a computer information system that provides information and methodological knowledge (domain knowledge and decision methodology knowledge) by means of analytical decision models (systems and users), and access to data bases and knowledge bases to support a decision maker in making decisions effectively in complex and ill-structured tasks.

The difference is that the new definition now clearly states that methodological knowledge is one of the resources that the system should provide. This methodological knowledge can be provided using the standard (modeling) technology or the expert system technology, or even better, by coupling the two.

The designer's choice is a pure technical choice. Both technologies are available and he or she should have the competence to decide when one is more appropriate than the other.

The methodological knowledge should be domain knowledge as well as decision methodology knowledge. In other words, a KB-DSS has the clear ambition to improve on the present state of things by providing (on request by the user) domain knowledge as well as decision methodology knowledge. The definition also stresses the point that, in many circumstances, the analytical decision models will include both types: economic marketing, financial, . . . models and user preference function models.

6.3 THE KB-DSS DEVELOPMENT ENVIRONMENTS OR GENERATORS

6.3.1 Functional Requirements for a First-generation KB-DSS Development Environment for Business

We have seen some of the main ideas of the KB-DSS framework in Section 6.2. The goal is to create a development environment which will enable the designer to define KB-DSS which will integrate with *synergy* the DSS capabilities and the ES capabilities. In other words, to define systems that combine the modeling and data management capabilities of DSS with the symbolic processing capabilities needed in complex and ill-structured situations. The environment will have to provide, for the DSS part, the DSS functions we have described in Chapter 4:

- data management or database management functions;
- access to outside database (ex. SQL link);

- modeling (system and user) and model management;
- report generator and report management;
- form generator and form management;
- toolbox of statistical, forecasting and financial algorithms;
- interface design and global logic of the application.

For the expert part, the functions have been described in Chapter 5:

- equation reasoner;
- knowledge base management;
- inference engine;
- explanation algorithms.

As well as the standard support functions of a development environment such as:

- trace (at the modeling level as well as at the expert system level);
- coherence testing for the knowledge-base;
- editors (application, model, knowledge base);
- debuggers, etc.

With the above functions it will be possible to build KB-DSS which will provide many new functions such as:

- giving advice on specific problems;
- assisting the user with methodology on decision analysis;
- intelligent user interface;
- explaining conclusions or plans.

In domains such as finance, marketing and management in general, a high level of integration between data access, computation, modeling and symbolic reasoning must be achieved. In a KB-DSS, the situation is more complex than in what has been called Expert Data Base Systems (EDBS).

In expert database systems, the main problem is the coupling of database management and expert systems. The integration of DBMS and ES is, clearly, a fundamental problem of the KB-DSS architecture. However, the KB-DSS problem is more complex since it requires the integration with synergy of two other main subsystems: the modeling (system and user) and the toolbox subsystems.

Another fundamental constraint of the KB-DSS environment is that we are working with *end users* and we cannot expect end users to use an environment which requires them to express their ideas in a logic programming language such as PROLOG. Exactly as with DSS, we must keep the user/designer concept in the KB-DSS (see Section 4.1.6). The overall integration needed between the components (or subsystems) is represented in Figure 6.4. The integration of the components of a DSS application has been described in Section 4.4.14. Some of the main communication and control links in a KB-DSS framework are the following:

- application interface/inference engine;
- modeling/equation reasoner;
- KBMS/DBMS;
- KBMS/modeling.

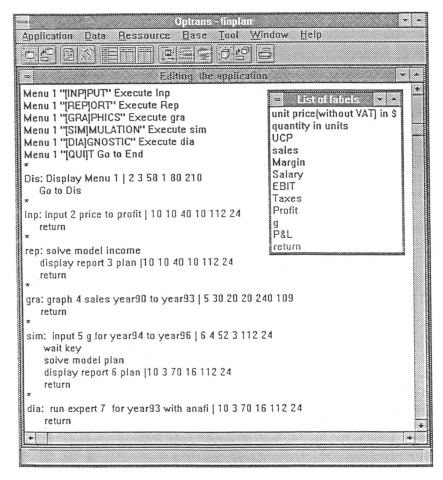

Figure 6.4   *Listing of the Finplan application, showing the 'Diagnosis option' and the call to the expert*

The *application interface/inference engine* link means that the user must be able to call the inference engine from the interface of the application. This is required any time we need to access an expert function (to make a diagnosis, build a plan, etc.). This capacity as it is implemented in OPTRANS Object is shown in Figure 6.4 which shows the text of the application with the interface definition and global logic.

The text of the application is similar to the one of Figure 4.16. One new option has been added to the application menu: 'diagnosis'. This option lets the user request an expert diagnosis. The expert diagnosis is activated by the instruction *run expert with* anafi which uses the knowledge base 'anafi' to produce a financial diagnosis of the company once the historical model has been solved.

Another knowledge base called 'test' is being used to automatically check the validity of accounting data. The instruction *run expert with* 'test' calls up a knowledge base 'test' to check the accounting relations which have to be verified.

The *equation reasoning module* uses the model text to build the causal graph between the model variables. This causal graph will be used to explain the evolution of variables in terms of other variables.

The *kbms/dbms communication* implies that a rule can use facts values which are stored in a DB as attributes of entities. This type of link is mainly useful when reasoning uses attributes from several entities, in that case an inference engine using variables in rules (order one logic instead of order zero+) will be more efficient.

The *kbms/modeling communication* implies that a rule can use facts the value of which comes from model variables. Symmetrically a fact concluded from a rule can be passed to a model.

6.3.2 Methods Concerning Communication between the Resources within the Application

A fundamental point of the KB-DSS architecture is the way communication is made possible between the different functions. The methods used to provide the communication link between the functions can be of different types.

Loose Coupling

This can be achieved using a global memory to share variable values and a clear separation between symbolic and numeric functions (model calculation). This type of coupling is sufficient to implement intelligent user interface, interpretation of computed results from models and overall control of the problem-solving process. In many circumstances, loose coupling is preferable. This is the case in data interpretation problems.

In other words in a closely coupled system, between database and expert system, there is no dynamic link between the expert system and the DBMS. Data is down-loaded to the expert system from the database prior to the execution of the expert system. When the data has been processed the expert system asks the database for new data. This approach corresponds to the repeated execution of two steps: first a computation on the part of the expert system to generate a query for the DBMS, second the DBMS executes the query and delivers the result to the expert system.

One possible problem with this approach is related with the problem of inconsistency if the data retrieve from the DBMS is used while the original version of the data is updated.

A loose coupling may be used to access a relational database external to the application. This coupling may imply the generation of a query which is transmitted to the query processor of the RDBMS. It is executed and the result of the query transmitted to the application file where it is accessible by all the functions of the application.

Tight Coupling

In a tightly coupled system, data is retrieved from the database as and when required during the execution of the expert system. The DBMS however still acts as a slave to the expert system. One of the drawbacks of this architecture is a slowing down of the expert system performance.

In the case of the communication between the inference component and the database component, the communication component has direct access to the inner low-level mechanisms of the DBMS, such as the access functions.

Integration through an Independent Control Component

We would like to point out here that we have proposed another integration strategy (see Figure 6.4) to allow the components (ES, Report Generator DBMS, modeling system) to operate either as entirely separated subsystems or as cooperative subsystems. The scheduling and control strategy should reside in an independent subsystem which manages the interaction between the components or subsystems. This is the strategy implemented in OPTRANS Object.

Blackboard Architecture

When developing KB-DSS applications it is very useful to be able to use a blackboard architecture to pool together the results (facts) provided by the different sources of knowledge of the application.

In a blackboard architecture, a common data structure (the blackboard) is kept through which the different knowledge sources interact.

Figure 6.5 shows an example of the transfer of information which is made possible by such a structure in a KB-DSS framework. This figure can be compared with Figure 4.3. The advantage of the blackboard architecture at the KB-DSS *application* level is to decompose the problem-solving process's knowledge and to allow all problem solving and other meta-level information to be uniformly represented in the blackboard, independently of the processes. Individual symbolic and numerical processes can be incorporated as separated multi-level knowledge sources.

Our purpose, here, is not to deal with the more complex problem of communication between functions at the development environment level. We shall just point out that the object-oriented programming technology helps to improve the quality of the development environment software in terms of extensibility and reliability.

6.3.3 Example of a KB-DSS Development Environment: OPTRANS Object

The OPTRANS Object development environment which we started to describe for its DSS part in Section 4.7 is an attempt to provide the environment which will give the user the capabilities listed in the present chapter.

The Expert Component

The expert component of the development environment is an inference engine of order $0+$. The knowledge representation technique used is rules. The engine is able to make forward, backward as well as mixed chaining. The syntax of rules is described in Chapter 5 (see in particular Figure 5.16). Rules can be regrouped in rule sets. A very important feature of the system is that rule sets can be called by a rule with different levels of priorities. This mechanism was described initially in Klein *et al.* (1987). It enables the designer who has knowledge on knowledge decomposition to use this meta-knowledge to speed up the search process during inferencing.

Some form of non-monotonic reasoning is also possible through forced re-examination of a rule-set on the observation of new facts which lead one to question the preceding conclusion. Uncertainty at the knowledge base level is dealt with using the technique of uncertainty factors described in Section 5.6.3. The call to the inference engine is done from the application by the instruction *run expert with* <knowledge base name> as shown in Figure 6.4. The system provides an explanation function described in Section 5.3.2.

Concluded fact values will be stored in the application file. Rules can use any variable name of the application the values of which are stored in the application file. 'Experts' can share information through this common file (see below blackboard architecture).

A rule can set in motion an action such as printing a report, running a statistical routine of the toolbox etc.

The Blackboard Structure

The designer of a KB-DSS application with OPTRANS will be provided automatically with a blackboard architecture. The application file is in fact as described in Figure 6.5, a structure common to the sources of knowledge which originate from:

- the decision models (deep knowledge);
- the databases;
- the knowledge bases;
- the statistical algorithms of the toolbox.

The purpose of the blackboard is to hold computation and solution state data needed by and produced by the knowledge sources.

The scheduling and the use of these sources of knowledge we have called resources is done at the application level (see Figures 4.16 and 6.4).

So this architecture supports:

- diverse sources of knowledge (facts stored in the database, decision models, statistical results, knowledge bases, . . .)
- use of problem-solving algorithms clearly separated from knowledge (model solver, inference engine, equation reasoner, . . .)
- multiple representation of data and knowledge

Implementation

The first version of OPTRANS Object was available for computers under DOS. This version is programmed in Watcom C and requests a minimum of 4 Mo of central memory. A more recent version is written in C++ for Microsoft Windows. The system can be transferred to other OS by mainly recompiling the graphical library.

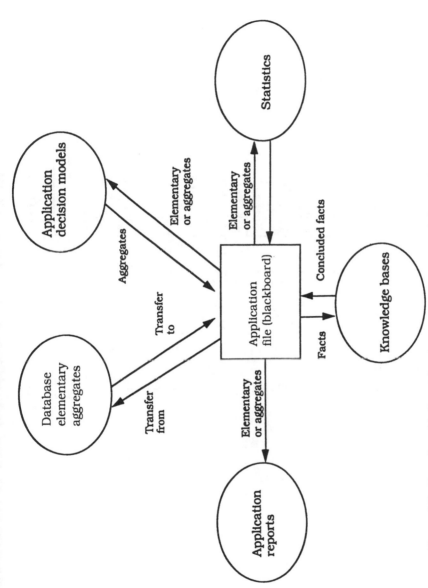

Figure 6.5 *Transfer of information between resources and the application file (blackboard)*

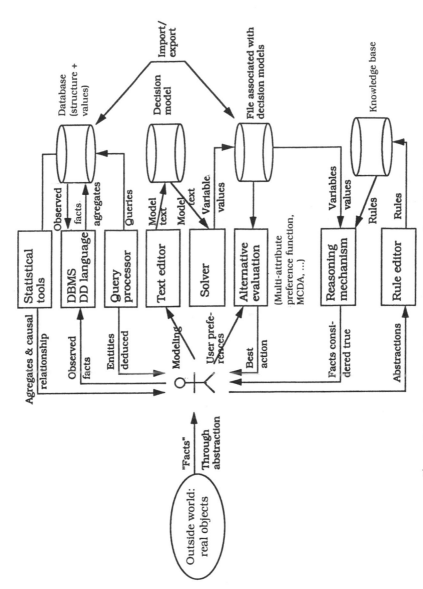

Figure 6.6 *Interaction between the user and the KB-DSS resources*

6.4 THE EPISTEMOLOGICAL SITUATION OF KB-DSS

One interesting question is related to the type of inquiry a KB-DSS designer is involved with; another is related more precisely to the type of knowledge he develops.

6.4.1 Types of Inquiry Involved in KB-DSS Application Development

The goal of the first OR work was clearly empirical: to give a scientific explanation of the facts and make successful predictions of the effectiveness of new weapons.

The goal of a DSS is more prescriptive since it is to assist the decision maker in choosing among alternative courses of action.

Anybody who has been working as a professional in the field of DSS knows that the technology he or she is promoting is used as a vehicle for persuasion and argumentation.

It is well known that in mature disciplines like physics or mathematics, the continuity, what Toulmin (1972) calls a 'genealogy of issues' and related concepts and tools, is maintained by a real process of innovation and selection. This process is performed through a professional 'forum of competition' within which new ideas can be criticized and eliminated to maintain the coherence of the discipline.

In the case of KB-DSS we are facing the case of a clearly composite discipline comprising a stock of theories, conceptual frameworks and techniques for dealing with theoretical and practical problems. We can also view it as a profession comprising a set of institutions, roles and people whose business it is to apply and improve these methods and techniques. For example, the International Federation of Information Processing (IFIP) and its specialized working group on DSS, the International Society for DSS, the DSS International Journal, etc . . .

When a designer is implementing a KB-DSS, for example for marketing analysis, he or she is looking for facts, he or she usually elaborates a theory to explain the facts (how the market works) and finally he or she uses the facts and theories to make predictions about future operations. This part of the job is, clearly, of a scientific nature. However, as we have seen, the KB-DSS will not only be used for prediction (simulation), it will also be used to provide a normative methodology to compare alternatives be it through decision analysis or a knowledge base.

Here, the designer has translated his or her analysis of a class of decision into a decision analysis methodology which, combined with the knowledge of the user (domain expert) and the specific situation knowledge, should help the user to come to the conclusion concerning what is the 'best' or, at least, a satisfactory decision for him or her. In other words to build a KB-DSS application requires both a descriptive and a normative approach. The reader is referred to Kyburg (1991) for areas of inquiry which need the two points of view, to Bagozzi (1984), Hunt (1994) and Leong (1985) for methodological aspects of theory construction.

6.4.2 Types of Knowledge which are used in KB-DSS Application Development

It is useful to look at the work of a KB-DSS designer in terms of the knowledge he creates as he defines the KB-DSS application and the knowledge which is provided by the generator.

Knowledge related to Modeling Entities of the Real World

As a designer is analyzing his problem he will be led to define the data which are needed to solve it. For many situations a first step to a solution is ready access to relevant data. As a consequence the designer may start by defining the facts that are *relevant* to its problem. It may be the list of variables which are useful when making a financial analysis of a company and the list of companies to consider. This situation is common when the user needs, to solve his problem, to work with vast amounts of data. This is typically the case in financial analysis, in portfolio management or product management in a supermarket.

The concepts which are used by the user may be objects (or entities), their attributes, relationship between objects, the objects constituting classes. On the other hand the system will provide a *formal language* to define these objects (data definition language) and manage them (data manipulation language). The data manipulation language will usually provide a *command processor* to create new facts from existing ones (see Chapter 4). In this way the user will be able to define and extract (using the *query processor*) new knowledge from a given database.

Knowledge Concerning Relations between Variables (Modeling) and Criteria for Evaluation of Alternatives

Once basic facts (data) which are relevant to a problem have been defined we have seen that the application designer is led to model economic system and users' preferences.

The reason for modeling economic systems in decision support are numerous and have been presented in Section 4.2.5. The modeling phase leads the designer to make explicit his knowledge of relations between variables. The variables being attributes of entities which are relevant to the problem.

Among the model variables some play a special role: criteria.

The model is used to simulate possible scenarios which correspond to different values for decisions variables. These scenarios are evaluated using the criteria by the user.

In this task the user develops models which represent his knowledge of causal relationship between variables, as well as criteria he considers pertinent to evaluate alternatives. The system will provide methodological knowledge to solve the models (model solver), a formalism to perform modeling and in certain cases an algorithm to perform model- based reasoning.

Knowledge Concerning the Way to Present Information for Problem Analysis

This type of knowledge is related to the way information should be presented to users to improve understanding, problem diagnosis and scenario evaluation. This knowledge is becoming more important as the diversity of types of presentation is increasing (mixing of text, tables, graphics, maps, images, etc.). The knowledge provided by the system is concentrated in the report generator which is able to combine these types of information.

Knowledge Concerning Preference Modeling

This knowledge is related to the way of handling the modeling of multi-attribute preferences. The system provides standard functions the parameters of which have to be identified.

Knowledge used in Reasoning about the Problem

This knowledge is expert knowledge, used when making a diagnosis or building a plan. The task of the user will be to make explicit the knowledge under the form of a rule base as seen in Chapter 5. The system is providing the knowledge for:

- the automatic inferencing mechanism to conclude what is true from the knowledge base;
- automatic explanation of the concluded fact;

- coherence control of the knowledge base as it will be shown in Chapter 9. Interactions between the user and the DSS resources are shown in Figure 6.6.

6.4.2 KB-DSS Application as Theories

We have shown (see Section 6.1.1) that applications which are developed using the KB-DSS framework can have new interesting properties to improve decision support.

A good way to define precisely these properties is to study the formalism of the development environment and its associated semantics. The development environment is a formal system. The great advantage of having a development environment (runnable on a machine) is that it makes the KB-DSS theory testable. As Paul Thagard (1988) has pointed out, implementing the theory on a computer implies that the theory has been completed and has been formulated unambiguously and precisely.

In developing KB-DSS we try to implement systems which use information and produce conclusions which are reasonable. Clearly this forces us to understand what rationality is. We have proposed in this book a framework for coupling KBs and DSS (including decision theory). A framework cannot be evaluated in the usual scientific way, it is evaluated in terms of the fruitfulness of the applications (theories) it generates. If the KB-DSS applications lead to many accurate accounts of interesting phenomena and if it improves support for decision classes, the framework will be regarded as fruitful.

Exercises

6.1 What is the basic idea underlying the KB-DSS framework?

6.2 What are the basic components (subsystems) of a KB-DSS development environment?

6.3 What are the main communication requirements between the components (subsystems) of a KB/DSS.

6.4 What are the new possibilities offered by KB-DSS over DSS and classical expert system shells

6.5 (a) Select a spreadsheet and compare its functions in the light of the KB-DSS framework, do the same with an expert system shell.

 (b) Take the user manual of OPTRANS Expert and study its functions in the light of the KB-DSS framework. Are all kinds of integration between subsystems provided? Do you see reasons why some of them are not provided?

6.6 Make a critical evaluation of FINSIM (Klein, 1989) or BANKER. In particular consider the functions given to the analyst to support his or her decision. Which KB could be added to the system to improve the support?

6.7 This is a study project for a term's work on a KB-DSS to assist in the completion of private individuals' income tax returns. This project has been used with success in the context of French tax regulations. It can be adapted to suit the tax laws applicable in any given country. A KB/DSS must be developed which:

- asks the user for information about his or her family situation and income;
- assists the user in calculating, precisely, the income from property and financial assets to be taken into account;
- assists the user in evaluating the various deductions which he or she is entitled to make from his or her income;
- calculates the number of allowances resulting from the user's family situation;
- calculates the tax payable before deductions;
- assists the user in evaluating the various deductions he or she can make from the tax payable;
- calculates the tax due and payment dates.

For the reductions and allowances, the system must, therefore, look at:

- family situation (married, widowed, divorced, number and age of children);
- income of spouse and children;
- family situation of children and other dependents;
- special conditions: handicaps, war pensions and so on.

The system must be able to deal with incomes from the following situations:

- salaries;

- salaries and other income from companies of which the user is director or shareholder;

- pensions;

- rent of property;

- interest;

- profit from the sale of property or financial assets.

6.8   A case study for a term project: A KB-DSS for personal loan evaluation.
This assignment for a term project is inspired by the loan case in the OPTRANS user manual.

The system to be implemented is made of a model and a knowledge base of 35 to 50 rules.

The application to be designed is intended to help a banker decide whether or not to grant a personal loan to a customer. The application is made up of a model called LOAN which is used to compute a certain number of variables, and a KB containing the rules which represent the knowledge the banker is using to decide on the loan.

The loan model

Before considering the loan, the banker needs to know a number of facts about the customer and about the loan being asked for:

- the customer's annual income;

- the amount of the loan being asked for;

- the duration of the loan, in months;

- the annual interest rate applicable.

From this information, he or she will calculate, before going any
   further:

- the amount of the monthly repayments on the loan (constant payments);

- the total amount to be repaid (capital plus accumulated interest).

The formula used to compute the monthly repayment is the following:

monthly repayment = amount of the loan*(annual interest rate/12)/ (1 − (1/coeff))

with coeff = (1 + (annual interest rate / 12*loan duration)

In a second step, add a routine to compute another schedule for LOAN repayment (non-constant schedule), and ask the user to choose the one that he or she wishes. This is not to be done in the first simplified version.

The input of this information, the calculations and the display of the figures in a window on the screen are carried out by the model LOAN.

One window is used to enter numerical data about the loan and the customer's annual income, and a second window to display calculated data. In our case, the banker is willing to display the monthly repayment and 1/3 of the customer's monthly income, in the same window.

The first group of instructions sets up and names the numerical variables used by the model and by the rules of the KB. A second group of instructions activates one of the windows and asks the user to input values for the numerical variables. A third group of instructions uses the numerical values entered by the user to calculate a number of aggregate variables. One of these aggregates is the maximum repayment. This variable measures what experience has shown the banker to be the maximum amount of his or her monthly income a person should allocate to pay back a loan. In other words, repayments above this amount sharply increase the risk for the banker, from a statistical point of view. A fourth group of instructions display, in another window, the entered and calculated values. Finally, a last block of instructions activates the windows used by the expert and set the expert in motion (specifying the reference column by its header).

The knowledge base LOANEX

We shall outline the structure of the knowledge base used in this very simple example using PC-OPTRANS notation.

The analysis of the problem can be broken down into six subproblems, each dealing with a particular aspect. These are represented in the knowledge base by six rule subsets (or criteria), which are the following:

(1) LOAN

(2) INCOME

(3) ABOVE FIFTY

(4) BELOW FIFTY

(5) FAMILY

(6) GUARANTEE

The value of a certain number of variables will be assigned by the inference engine. These variables are: CHILD, FAMILY, GUARANTEE, MARRIED, PROFESSION, WEALTH, LOAN. At the beginning of the reasoning process these variables are set as *undefined*.

At the end of the reasoning process the variable LOAN should take the value either 'granted' or 'rejected'.

ASSIGNMENT

1 In this loan example we wished to improve the KB by introducing several improvements: we wanted to define wealth in terms of assets held by the prospect. The types of assets to be considered are real estate, financial and cash. We also wish to use the profession of the prospect to deduce the stability of his or her job. We shall consider, for example, the following categories: unemployed, manual worker, farmer, employee, middle-management, top management and lawyer.

Define the new rules using OPTRANS syntax, modify the KB, recompile the KB and test the new system. You can also integrate information on the outlook of the industry.

2 In this loan example which knowledge would you like to take into account to make your decision?
Example of such knowledge:

● Is the prospect already a client of the bank? If yes use the information available on his or her bank account (mean level of the account, maximum debit and so on). If not, add a rule stating that his or her salary should be paid into an account at the bank to obtain the loan.

- Take into account the type of asset which is financed. If it is of a real estate kind, then the risk can be reduced through mortgage. The mortgage is compulsory above a given amount.

Define the new rules using OPTRANS syntax, modify the KB, recompile the KB and test the new system.

The rules

In each rule subset or criterion we shall find a set of rules dealing with the knowledge used to solve this subproblem.

Rules of the criterion LOAN
These rules are the first to be examined since the criterion (rule subset) LOAN is the first one declared in the above list. The first criterion LOAN deals with the rules which conclude if the loan is accepted or rejected, or if the first administrative constraint to be accepted is fulfilled.

The rules of the criterion INCOME
These rules cause a second process to be performed:

- Rule 5 expresses the idea that if the monthly repayment is less that 1/10 of the maximum repayment (given by the 1/3 rule) then the loan is granted.

- Rule 6 states that if the monthly repayment is greater than the maximum repayment (given by the 1/3 rule) then the loan is rejected. In other words, the banker does not wish to make the loan if the client will have to spend more than 1/3 of his or her monthly income to pay back the loan.

- Rule 7 states that if the monthly repayment is greater than half of the maximum repayment then the banker wishes to study what kind of guarantee he or she could have.

- Rule 8 states that if the monthly repayment is smaller than half of the maximum repayment then the banker wishes to study the family situation of the client.

According to this analysis, the system will examine either the rules of the criterion ABOVE FIFTY or those of the criterion BELOW FIFTY.

Rules of the criterion ABOVE FIFTY
With these rules the banker attempts to take into account the guarantee he or she can obtain, as well as the family situation when the premise of rule 7 is true.

Rules of the criterion BELOW FIFTY
The rules of this criterion state that the banker will not grant the loan if he or she has no guarantee when the premise of rule 8 is true.

Rules of the criterion FAMILY
In this set of rules, the expert takes into account the family situation of the client (number of children, marital status and so on)

Rules of the criterion GUARANTEE
The rules of this criterion attempt to combine the wealth and profession variables into a judgment on the quality of the guarantee which can be expected.

7
Knowledge Modeling

7.1 INTRODUCTION

When Feigenbaum and his colleagues at Stanford University were developing the first expert system they coined the term *knowledge engineering* to describe the process that created an expert system and the term *knowledge engineer* to describe someone who develops an expert system:

> 'The knowledge engineer practices the art of bringing the principles and tools of AI research to bear on difficult application problems requiring experts' knowledge for their solution. The technical issues of acquiring this knowledge, representing it, and using it appropriately to construct and explain lines-of-reasoning, are important problems in the design of knowledge-based systems. . . . The art of constructing intelligent agents is both part of and an extension of the programming art. It is the art of building complex computer programs that represent and reason with knowledge of the world.' Feigenbaum (1977)

Knowledge engineering is a special kind of systems analysis. The purposes of both are the same: to make a specification of an information processing system that can be implemented and run on a computer. The general processes involved are the same: analyzing a task in order to specify a problem solving process, designing a computer program, programming and implementation. However, to build a knowledge-based system is different from building conventional information processing systems in several respects. Firstly, the characteristics of typical problem domains are different. An expert system imitates and emulates human expert problem solving. Thus, the problem solving process is very much hidden in the mind of an expert. Secondly, the target computer system, the knowledge-based system, has a different architecture from conventional information processing systems. A knowledge-based system has a knowledge base and a reasoning system. The focus of the systems analysis process must, therefore, be on knowledge, and in particular, heuristic knowledge.

The task of systems has changed over time as new information technologies and better development tools have been created. These developments have led to new applications and less basic computer skills in the building of such systems. Integration of the computer technology into organizations requires more complex analysis of the application areas, skill in organizational, social and cognitive disciplines, and conceptually richer methodologies for systems analysis. A shift from a dominating technical skill toward contextual skill (organizational, social, business, cognitive and so on) has taken place. Knowledge engineering is a system analysis methodology which requires much contextual skill.

Feigenbaum calls knowledge engineering an *art*. It is true that most expert systems development, until now, has focused on computer representations and program design. By means of very powerful development tools, so-called expert system shells, rapid prototyping has been the dominating approach. Tool skill has been more emphasized than methodological competence in performing problem analysis. As a result, the development of a knowledge engineering methodology has been lagging behind the practice of building expert systems. Lack of concrete methods and techniques of knowledge engineering has led to the common apprehension that the performance of this task is more of an art than a science (see the citation from Feigenbaum above). The practice of building expert systems is very similar to what is found in other areas where computers are applied to ill-structured problems, for instance, in developing decision support systems for complex decision making processes.

In areas where we have highly developed and functionally integrated development tools, like DSS generators or expert system shells, the system development process has been very much driven by the technology.

In a technology-driven process the functionality of the application system grows incrementally. In the context of prototype systems, new ideas are generated and new opportunities are seen in a dialog between the system builder and the user or expert. Thus, application complexity is reduced by successive redefinitions, and the lack of contextual skill is overcome by rapid prototyping.

In a problem-driven approach *analysis* is at the forefront. The problem domain is thoroughly analyzed, structured and specified. A conceptual model of problem solving (with knowledge and reasoning) is specified and implemented as a *base version*, from which prototyping can take over for testing, validation and growth of the knowledge base.

A strong critique of rapid prototyping can be found in Laske (1986). He claims that expert systems built by rapid prototyping are built on two 'particularly unhelpful, if not entirely wrong, assumptions'. The first assumption is that the knowledge engineer is a neutral arbiter between the expert and the development tool. The second assumption is that human experts can be tapped directly by verbal retrieval cues (for example, questions) that force the expert to make performance-unrelated observations and comments to his solution process.

Paul Johnson (1983) observed a medical professor in two different situations: (1) actually performing medical diagnosis in clinics, and (2) teaching students how to do the same thing. He discovered that the professor did not teach what he seemed to do clinically. When confronted with this conclusion, the professor explained that he did not know how he actually performed his diagnoses. At the same time, he needed to teach the students and, therefore, created plausible means for doing the task.

The second assumption violates the methodological preconditions for achieving valid verbal reports, that is, reports that really verbalize true performance of the expert. The latter argument is founded on the theory of human problem solving described in Chapter 2. According to Laske (1986) knowledge elicitation based on some form of dialog between the expert and the knowledge engineer (questions, retrospection, rapid prototyping and so on) can only give knowledge about the task environment. He calls these systems *competence systems*. By using concurrent verbal protocols performance knowledge can be elicited. He calls these systems *performance models of expertise*.

It is said that knowledge engineering is the bottleneck of expert systems development. More recently, therefore, we have seen attempts in the literature to present descriptions and models of this process that are theoretically founded and that can be taught.

The influence of cognitive psychology on knowledge engineering methods and techniques seems to be much less than the influence of this field on the architecture of expert systems. The latter is directly derived from the production systems which, as we have seen in Chapters 2 and 5, were an outcome of research on human problem solving.

However, there are some early examples of cognitive approaches, for instance, INTERNIST (Pople, 1982). Also, there is a growth in the area of building, knowledge engineering methodologies more closely on cognitive psychology models, methods and techniques (for example, Breuker and Wielinga (1984), Boose (1984), and Laske (1986)). However, despite the upsurge of interest, cognitive approaches in knowledge engineering are, according to Slatter (1987), more exceptions rather than the rule. He claims that most of the best-known systems, such as MYCIN, PROSPECTOR, DENDRAL and R1/XCON were constructed with little or no explicit aim of modeling expert thinking. In commercial applications of today's expert systems technology the emphasis is firmly on achieving expert-level performance by using formal problem solving methods.

Yet despite a lack of formal tradition, principles of knowledge engineering have started to emerge recently founded on theories of cognition. An important contribution was Newell's (1982) description of the *knowledge level*. In the late 1980s knowledge acquisition methods and tools built on the concept of knowledge level have emerged. Knowledge level analysis is the term used when a system is specified on the knowledge level. This is, however, still very much on a research stage and we shall give a brief introduction to this in Chapter 11.

In this chapter, we shall present a cognitive approach to knowledge modeling. It is the process of transferring transcripts of verbalized knowledge into a formalized form that can be processed by a computer. Thus, modeling knowledge is the process of formalizing (and inducing) general task knowledge from individual performance knowledge.

We shall start by giving a brief overview of some approaches to knowledge acquisition, followed by an overview of the knowledge modeling process taken as the basis for our approach. This process description builds on the two basic concepts from Newell and Simon's theory on human problem solving: task environment and problem space (Newell and Simon, 1972). Task analysis gives knowledge about the task environment. Performance modeling is concerned with eliciting, analyzing, and formalizing the knowledge in the problem space of an expert. Most of this chapter will be devoted to performance modeling and the analysis of verbal reports. A methodology is presented which put more emphasis on *conceptual* analysis of such reports than is typically found in other studies of performance using protocol analysis (see for instance, Biggs and Mock (1983) or Bouwman *et al.* (1987)). They are more focused on processes.

Finally, we demonstrate this methodology using a case from financial analysis, and the development of an expert system for financial counseling called SAFIR.

7.2 KNOWLEDGE MODELING – AN OVERVIEW OF THE PROCESS

7.2.1 Traditional Views of the Process

One of the first more systematic attempts to structure the process of knowledge engineering was described by Hayes-Roth *et al.* (1983). Here, the term *knowledge acquisition* is used for the process of transferring and transforming knowledge about expert problem solving from the knowledge source to a computer program. Thus, the term knowledge acquisition is used synonymously with knowledge engineering. The process is defined in terms of the following stages:

(1) *Identification* of problem characteristics, that is, what is the problem domain, and who are the experts and the users.
(2) *Conceptualization* of knowledge, that is, the concepts used to describe objects and relations in the problem domain.
(3) *Formalization* which is to put a structure to the knowledge, that is, to map the knowledge into an adequate task framework, for example, a diagnostic framework.
(4) *Implementation* is the mapping of knowledge in a formalized task framework into the knowledge representation formalism of the chosen implementation language, for example, rules or frames.
(5) *Testing* the validation of knowledge and reasoning.

Another attempt to compile our knowledge on knowledge acquisition was done by Welbank (1983). She confirms the opinion given above of this task, that the focus is more on building systems than on knowledge acquisition. Furthermore, it is difficult to find descriptions of actual methods that the knowledge engineers can use and the exact problems that they have encountered. Welbank also describes a staged process of knowledge acquisition. She divides the process into the following three stages:

(1) obtaining the basic structure of the problem domain;
(2) producing the first working system;
(3) testing and debugging.

A more comprehensive text on knowledge acquisition is found in Hart (1986). However, she admits herself that the text is more a collection of ideas. Methods found in other disciplines are brought together with the purpose of being applied to the development of expert systems.

More research-oriented reports on knowledge acquisition are found in Clancey (1984) and Breuker and Wielinga (1984). References to more recent literature is found in Chapter 11.

7.2.2   A Cognitive Approach

The methodology for knowledge modeling described in this chapter presumes that the knowledge-based system to be developed is designed to emulate expert problem solving. To adequately understand and represent expertise in a conceptual model, two kinds of knowledge must be present: task and performance knowledge.

A knowledge modeling methodology must provide a way for both kinds of knowledge to be modeled. We shall suggest a two-stage knowledge elicitation process starting with task analysis, followed by a performance study as shown in Figure 7.1.

Task Analysis

'What is of interest here is the task demands, their interrelationships, the goals or criteria for task completion, and a set of rules that can accomplish the goals given some set of initial conditions.' (P. E. Johnson, 1984, p. 369)

The first stage is to develop a model of the task for which we want to build an expert system. The purpose of a task model is as follows:

- to prepare the setting for performance studies of expert problem solving;
- to function as an interpretative framework for protocol analysis;
- to establish user characteristics;
- to establish the criteria for choosing an expert;
- to specify performance criteria for the system.

To prepare the setting for further data collection on performance requires that:

- the task is well defined, which means that the problem is clearly stated, and the conclusion set is well defined;
- a set of relevant cases are available, containing enough information for problem solving.

To develop an interpretative framework for performance analysis, requires a model of the task. A task model is a general, competence model of how a typical expert might perform the task in question. It is a

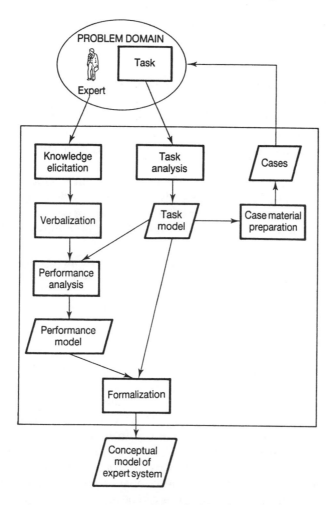

Figure 7.1 *A two-stage knowledge elicitation process*

first-order model which will be developed further as more empirical data is available. It is the basic structure of the problem solving process involved and a general model of the reasoning steps. Thus, this task model is a decomposition of the task into subtasks and a specification of the flow of control between the subtasks.

In addition to the task model an interpretative framework must consist of a general *domain description*, usually as found in text-books, or other reference documents. The domain description consists of:

- a vocabulary of the domain, that is, what are the task-relevant terms that are specific for the domain?
- theories and methods.

To establish the characteristics of a user involve determining:

- the competence level of the users, that is, who are the users and with what methods are they familiar?
- the role of the user in problem solving and decision making.

The final purpose of task analysis is to make an evaluation of the potential costs and benefits of a knowledge-based system for the task. Waterman (1986) has formulated some guidelines for considering expert systems development. He summarizes these guidelines as follows:

'Consider expert systems only if expert systems development is possible, justified, and appropriate.' (Waterman, 1986, p. 327)

He develops a set of task attributes for this evaluation.

Performance Modeling

Performance modeling is an approach to knowledge engineering which utilizes models, hypotheses, methods and techniques from cognitive psychology in the building process of expert systems. Performance modeling refers to a strategy in expert system design which seeks to elicit real problem solving knowledge from human experts. This knowledge, which is in the mind of the expert, is made explicit through verbalization. Slatter (1987) calls this approach cognitive emulation which, according to him, is both a descriptive concept and a prescriptive principle. As a descriptive concept, it can be argued that expert systems incorporate many features characteristic of human information processing. As a prescriptive principle, it refers to system work in which an explicit strategy of emulating human cognitive processes is followed.

Performance modeling deals with knowledge in the problem space, that is, knowledge about problem representation and problem solving in the mind of the expert. The modeling is executed in two major steps:

(1) knowledge elicitation;
(2) performance analysis;

Using verbalization as our main method for knowledge elicitation, performance analysis starts with verbal reports (protocols) and ends with a performance model of the expert's problem solving process for each case solved. The protocols collected present detailed step-by-step traces of the expert's problem solving behavior. We shall develop a protocol analysis methodology which is particularly suited for knowledge-based system development. Performance analysis is divided into the following tasks:

- concepts identification and classification;
- conceptual structuring;
- qualifications of comparative and evaluative concepts;
- problem solving strategies.

These tasks will be further dealt with in Section 7.4.

7.3 KNOWLEDGE ACQUISITION

7.3.1 Modes of Knowledge Acquisition

According to Kim and Courtney (1988), knowledge acquisition approaches can be classified in terms of two dimensions: strategic and tactical. The *strategic* dimension is concerned with the way the knowledge acquisition processes are driven: knowledge engineer-driven, expert-driven, or machine-driven. The *tactical* dimension is concerned with the techniques that are used for each strategic category. Specific techniques include interviews, protocol analysis, the repertory grid method, visual modeling and so on.

Knowledge engineer-driven knowledge acquisition is the classical approach. Here, the knowledge engineer interacts directly with the expert to model domain knowledge of two kinds: task knowledge and performance knowledge. Necessary skills and requirements for a successful knowledge engineer include good communication skills, empathy and patience, persistence, and intelligence (Hart, 1986). Techniques used in this approach are interviews, protocol analysis, repertory grids, and others.

Expert-driven knowledge acquisition is an approach where the expert encodes his or her own expertise and enters this knowledge directly into the computer. The key assumptions behind this approach are that (Moore and Agongino, 1987):

(1) The expert can learn and use the encoding interface.
(2) The expert can identify variables and relationships among them.
(3) The expert can structure a refinable model by using a structured approach to one's domain.

(4) The inevitable loss of clarity in encoded knowledge is acceptable if the expert can assure the performance of the model.

Visual modeling techniques are used to construct domain models. The objective of this approach is to give the user the ability to visualize real-world problems, and to manipulate elements of it naturally through the use of graphical entities. Further information on visual modeling is found in (Pracht, 1987).

Machine-driven approaches to knowledge acquisition are associated with a more general field within artificial intelligence, known as *machine learning*. The most widely-used technique in machine learning is learning by examples based on inductive inference. The basic idea here is to present, to the machine, a set of example cases consisting of solutions, along with the attributes which were considered in solving those problems. A computerized algorithm is then used to infer rules from these examples. The research on computer inductive inference is still at an early stage of development. For more details the reader is referred to Delgrande (1987) and Michalski *et al.* (1986).

In the rest of this chapter we shall consider the knowledge engineer-driven approach to knowledge acquisition.

7.3.2 Creating the Environment for Knowledge Acquisition

In the knowledge engineer-driven approach, the knowledge engineer works with the expert in the context of solving problems. Welbank (1983) develops a number of problems that one should be aware of in establishing the task environment for knowledge acquisition.

(1) The expert is inaccessible due to time constraints, and location constraints.
(2) The expert is unenthusiastic. This is often due to a lack of understanding of what the purpose of knowledge elicitation is.
(3) Generating enthusiasm can be done by giving information about the task prior to performance, and give the expert feedback on performance as fast as possible, for instance, by prototyping. In this way the expert can get an idea of what the end result looks like.
(4) Lack of communication between the knowledge engineer and the expert. Our experience is that the knowledge engineer should have a good knowledge of the domain. This will ensure a common frame of reference in terms of the vocabulary and theories between the two. However, the knowledge engineer should be careful not to take over as the expert. This follows from the theory of tacit knowledge dealt with above. Another problem with a knowledge

engineer who is very knowledgeable in the domain, is that analysis and interpretation can be biased in the direction of the knowledge engineer's own understanding of the task.

(5) Lack of domain knowledge. In order to establish a minimum level of frame of reference for adequate communication and feedback for motivation the knowledge engineer should have some domain knowledge.

(6) The inarticulate expert. This aspect has already been dealt with. It is the paradox of expertise, rephrased, which says that the more of an expert you are, the less able you are to describe your own problem solving, or as Ericsson and Simon (1984) put it: 'as reasoning becomes more practised and faster, it sinks out of consciousness'.

(7) No awareness at all. There are situations where knowledge is entirely inaccessible to awareness. This seems to be true of learned skills, such as playing a piano. Welbank (1983) reports of this unawareness in computer programming.

(8) Misleading models. This is phrased in another way by Waterman (1986): 'Don't believe everything experts say!' Therefore, reports by experts must be validated and the problem solving process carefully observed to see that the experts solve the problem according to the task analysis done, that is, that the information given to solve the case is really used.

(9) The expert becomes a moving target. The expert may not have a consistent way of solving similar problems. Also, the expert may be influenced by feedback from the knowledge engineer in subsequent problem solving.

7.3.3 Knowledge Acquisition Techniques

In this section, we shall analyze some knowledge acquisition techniques used by the knowledge engineer to elicit human cognition and problem solving behavior. Several techniques exist – each one having both strong and weak properties. Therefore, the techniques described are not mutually exclusive, but should be used complementarily. Furthermore, we shall only give some examples here. The presentation is not meant to be comprehensive.

Interviews

Interviewing experts is the most familiar knowledge acquisition technique used for building knowledge-based systems, together with rapid prototyping. Interviewing is widely used, probably because it is simple and easy to perform. However, care in the preparation phase is a prerequisite for obtaining useful results. We may distinguish between two types of interviews: unstructured and structured.

Unstructured interviews

These are most akin to normal conversation. The knowledge engineer asks questions and the expert answers. The preparation involved before an unstructured interview is to set up a list of topics one wants to know more about.

The basic structure of unstructured interviews is: addressing and probing. Topics are addressed in a breadth-first or depth-first manner, and probes are used to encourage the expert to talk, to dig deeper into a topic, to specify directions one wants to pursue, or to provide a change in view of a particular topic.

Structured interviews

These are more like an interrogation and are based upon a predefined set and sequence of questions. The knowledge engineer asks for clarifications, explanations, justifications, consequences and so on. The purpose of a structured interview is to obtain a detailed insight into the domain. It may uncover concepts and conceptual structures of the domain, qualifications of variables, justifications and explanations.

According to Welbank (1983), knowledge engineers have mainly used interviews in building expert systems. Interview data tends to be at the level of rules and general principles. It does not elicit performance behavior. On the other hand, interviews produce background knowledge.

Advantages

Knowledge which is explicit to the expert or can be easily probed, can be elicited quickly by interviewing. This technique is useful in early phases to inquire into the basic structure of the domain (task analysis) and in refining a knowledge base.

Disadvantages

Firstly, it is difficult to acquire relevant and correct knowledge. Knowledge elicited is general, inconsistent, incomprehensive, and imprecise. Secondly, it is unsuitable for acquiring performance knowledge. Thirdly, the interviewing process lacks overall structure.

This lack of structure makes analysis of interviews difficult (Kim and Courtney, 1988). Fourthly, interviewing is time consuming and tedious.

Verbal Protocols

Verbal protocols are used to obtain information about the cognitive processes of a subject dealing with a problem. They are literal transcripts of the expert's verbalization, as recorded on audio tape. There are several techniques for obtaining protocols: retrospective, introspective, interpretative, and concurrent 'thinking aloud' verbalization. Concurrent verbalization causes minimum interference with the problem solving process and will be discussed in more detail below.

In order to collect a concurrent verbal protocol the subject is asked to verbalize his or her thoughts during task performance.

Concurrent verbal protocols directly tap the successive states of heeded information in the mind of the expert. According to Ericsson and Simon (1984) this method comes closest to the reflection of the cognitive processes:

> 'We claim that cognitive processes are not modified by these verbal reports, and that task-directed cognitive processes determine what information is heeded and verbalized.'

Most people cannot verbalize as fast as they can think. People also forget to verbalize, and some repetitive cognitive processes may be automated and thus unavailable for tapping. However, for verbal reasoning tasks such as problem solving and decision making, Ericsson and Simon (1984) conclude that:

> 'the performance may be slowed down, and the verbalization may be incomplete, but . . . the course and structure of the task-performance will remain largely unchanged.'

Although verbal protocols provide a dense trace of cognitive behavior, and the information present is valid, some information is still unavailable, thus leaving out some details of the subject's behavior.

It is important that the setting for concurrent verbal protocols sessions comes as close to the natural task environment as possible. Several preconditions have to be satisfied for a successful session with the expert to be accomplished:

(1) The sample of cases chosen is crucial and the cases must be representative for the task.

(2) The task must have a clearly defined conclusion, that is, it must be possible to determine when the task is completed.
(3) The task must contain sufficient data for completion in one session.
(4) The data must be presented to the expert in a familiar form.
(5) The expert should be given a test case in order to become familiar with this experimental technique and to obtain feedback from the knowledge engineer about the verbalization performance.

During a session, as few interruptions as possible should be made by the knowledge engineer. Only when the expert stops verbalizing should the knowledge engineer interfere.

The resulting protocols consist of a continuous string of words expressions of facts and affects, which may, at first glance, look rather disorganized. Protocol analysis is the task of formalizing these chaotic verbalizations into structures and knowledge about problem solving behavior – knowledge that is an accessible representation. We shall deal further with protocol analysis in Section 7.4.

Advantages

It provides a natural setting for problem solving where performance knowledge can be elicited through verbalization of thought processes. The result is a richness of detail and a high temporal density of oral responses. It is particularly useful in obtaining behavioral evidence in complex tasks (Biggs and Mock, 1983).

Disadvantages

Giving protocols can interfere with task performance. Protocol analysis is a skilled and difficult task and is time consuming. Transcripts can be highly ambiguous, requiring much interpretation when analyzed (Slatter, 1987). It does not provide assistance to the knowledge engineer in identifying and acquiring deep knowledge of the domain.

Prototyping

The importance of feedback and context has already been mentioned. One means of using feedback is to build a prototype system, once enough knowledge has been collected. This prototype can be used to further elicitate knowledge of two kinds:

(1) To test already implemented knowledge, and identify missing knowledge.

(2) To reveal missing patterns in the rules and fill these.

Advantages

Puts the expert in the context of using the system, thus, he or she has a greater realization of the purpose of the knowledge engineering activities.

Disadvantages

No performance knowledge is elicited.

The Repertory Grid Technique

Another well-known technique for knowledge acquisition, which is taken from the field of cognitive psychology, is the repertory grid technique developed by Kelly (1955). Kelly viewed a human as a 'personal scientist' with his or her own personal model of the world. This scientist seeks to predict and control events by forming theories and testing hypotheses. Based on this perspective, Kelly developed a 'personal construct theory'. The model of the world is made up of individual personal constructs. The repertory grid technique is a way to elicit these personal constructs.

A personal model consists of elements and constructs. *Elements* are objects of the domain: cases or examples, that the expert will select. For instance, when studying credit evaluation the expert may be asked to select five cases (loan applications) that are important. These are the elements. Then the expert is asked to compare successive sets of these elements, listing distinguishing characteristics. A *construct* is a bipolar characteristic which each element has to some degree. An example of a construct is management competence: good or bad. A numeric scale is assigned to each construct for subsequent analyses. There are several ways to elicit these constructs from experts, see, for instance, Hart (1986). Having elicited the important constructs, the expert rates each element according to these constructs. A table of constructs and elements with the ratings is referred to as the repertory grid. This grid now represents the expert's view of the world (domain).

Once the grid has been elicited it can be analyzed to help the expert identify structures and patterns in the grid. One method of analysis is *cluster analysis* which helps to identify differences and similarities among elements. For more details, the reader is referred to Hart (1986).

Recently, elicitation and analysis of repertory grids have been made available through interactive computer programs (for example Boose, 1985).

Advantages

Grid techniques are best suited for well-structured problems, like diagnosis and classification, where the elements of the solution space can be enumerated prior to the time of problem solving. They are well suited for elicitation of traits and for building relationships.

Disadvantages

Grid techniques are not well suited for problems of design and planning where unique solutions are derived from components of the problem. No deep knowledge and no performance knowledge can be elicited.

7.4 PERFORMANCE MODELING: THE PROTOCOL ANALYSIS

We shall adhere to the assumption that performance studies of expert problem solving can best be done by verbal protocols (see Laske (1986) and the above discussion on methodology). The major task in knowledge modeling is, therefore, an analysis of verbal protocols. However, as we shall see in the next section, protocols may be complemented with interviews or other techniques, to acquire as much knowledge as possible.

7.4.1 The Protocol Methodology

The aim of the protocol methodology is to obtain access to the subject's problem space – that is, the internal or cognitive representation of a task. This problem space provides evidence of information processing and choice behavior of the subject. Such evidence can help to explain problem solving behavior and to explain differences among several individuals.

Protocol analysis is not a uniform technique. How the analysis is done depends upon the focus of the study.

In studying individual problem solving behavior, Newell and Simon's (1972) theory of human problem solving has provided the theoretical foundation for many protocol analysis studies (see, for instance, Biggs and Mock (1983) and Bouwman *et al.* (1987)). The essential task of these studies has been to search for goals, operators and states of knowledge in the subject's problem space. Since the operators represent a subject's processes or actions, they have been of primary concern in many of these studies. In Biggs and Mock's study

(1983) 14 operators were defined and classified into four general categories: task structuring, information acquisition, analysis, and action. Similarly, in the study by Bouwman *et al.* (1987) activities were defined (and coded) into 21 types and classified into the following five categories: reading and examination, reasoning, goals, memory access, and comments.

The purpose of our study is to produce the knowledge required to emulate expert behavior. We shall put emphasis on *conceptual analysis*, that is, which concepts are used by the expert, and in which relationships do they enter. After having identified the conceptual relationships we will use interviews and prototyping to qualify these relationships in terms of logical inferences, plausible inferences, numerical relationships and so on.

Our first attempt to produce a rule-based expert system (a production system) for credit evaluation by protocol analysis failed. This analysis was carried out to the level of detail of the Problem Behavior Graphs (PBG), described in Newell and Simon (1972) and to the activity levels as described in Bauwman *et al.* (1987). These findings may seem contradictory to Newell and Simon's results, who claim that a production system can be induced from the PBG.

The contradiction between our experience and the findings of Newell and Simon may be explained by differences in task complexity. In crypt-arithmetic, the kind of problems studied by Newell and Simon, the task is difficult but structured, and the goal state is distinct and definite. In credit evaluation, task complexity is great, there is not one single, definite answer and no normative solution. The process involves evaluation and judgment. Therefore, there is not one distinct path from the initial state to the goal state.

7.4.2 The Set-up for Data Collection

Følstad (1984) has given some practical hints about the collection of verbal protocols. Before the protocols are collected the subject (expert) should be given an explanation of what the experiment is about, what the purpose is, and what is to be expected as the outcome of the experiment. The purpose here is to motivate the subject. Next, the subject is given *instructions* which explain, more specifically, how the experiment is to be accomplished. The first part of these instructions tells the subject what the problem is, for instance, 'based on the given case material make a credit evaluation of this company'. Next, the subject is told how to perform the task, that is, to think aloud, for example, 'think, reason in a loud voice, verbalize everything that passes through your mind as you solve the problem. I am not primarily interested in your final conclusion – but in your thinking behavior, in all your attempts to find a solution, in whatever comes to your mind, no matter whether it is a good or a bad idea, or a question. Don't plan what to say, or think before you speak, but rather let your thoughts speak, as though you were really thinking out loud. Don't let my presence disturb you'.

If the subject does pause, it is necessary to intervene and remind the subject to continue to talk.

The session must be carried out in an environment that is free from external disturbances and with the tape-recording equipment as unobtrusive as possible for the subject. It is important to give the subject a task environment that is as natural as possible. A task analysis must be done prior to the protocol collection where the problems presented to the subject represent relevant cases, have sufficient information for problem solving, and have a clear problem statement.

7.4.3 Conceptual Analysis

According to Sowa (1984) the purpose of conceptual analysis is to produce a catalog of concepts, relations, facts, and principles that make up a domain – the *ontology* of a domain. The theoretical foundation of concept definitions is found in Chapter 2.

We shall now describe a protocol analysis method with focus on conceptual analysis, and with the purpose of producing a knowledge base in a computable form. According to what we have said above this means that we must be able to express concepts and concept relations in a precise way, which, for natural concepts, may lead to problems. However, we shall only deal with domains where concepts, to a large extent, are technically defined and expressed in precise terms. For instance, in financial analysis, the vocabulary is given by accounting terminology concerning financial statements and ratio analysis.

We shall divide the task into four subtasks:

(1) concepts identification and classification;
(2) conceptual structuring;
(3) qualifications of comparative and evaluative concepts;
(4) problem solving strategies.

Subsequently, we shall describe the conceptual framework of each subtask. In Section 7.5 we shall illustrate the practical use of the methodology.

Concept Identification and Classification

Protocols contain information that reveal many aspects of the subject's concern about the task. They not only contain information about cognitive behavior, but also reveal information about the subject's familiarity with the task, uncertainty about how to approach the task, emotions and so on.

We shall only concern ourself with task-specific knowledge, knowledge which describes the subject's *cognitive* behavior.

We shall perform this task in three steps:

(1) identification of natural concepts of the domain;
(2) segmentation;
(3) classification.

Identification of natural concepts of the domain is done by matching terms of the protocol with theoretical concepts of the domain. In financial analysis this is done by matching terms of the protocols with accounting terminology.

For instance, the subject says: 'Let us use as a rule of thumb that if return on investment is between 10 and 15, then it is slightly less than satisfactory'. The object of interest here (the domain concept) is 'return on investment', a term well known in the vocabulary of financial analysis. At this stage of analysis we also have to look for synonyms. Terms that are identified as meaning the same thing may be replaced by synonyms. Some care has to be exercised here in order not to lose semantic content.

Segmentation of a protocol means to split it into parts. The segmentation criterion is an identified object and everything that is said about this object in one sequence. For example:

> 'Let us use as a rule of thumb that if return on investment is between 10 and 15, then it is slightly below satisfactory. If it is below 10, then it is clearly less than satisfactory. I don't think it is necessary to make any steps below that. But when I see that it moves towards 1–12%, then I say, well, well, this starts to become fair.'

A segment is a paragraph of the protocol concerning *one* object. This object is called the *focus object*. It is described by relations to other objects, verbs, prepositions, and adjectives. A paragraph can be split into *topics*, each one being a description element or argument about the focus object.

Classification of arguments can now be done on the level of a topic of each focus object. The following classifications are used: A focused object is described in terms of evaluative and comparative concepts, or in terms of explanatory concepts and type hierarchies. All these descriptive concepts we call *attributes* of the focused object.

(1) *Evaluative* attributes are associated with absolute values and explicit norms, for instance, profitability is good. We denote evaluative attributes by the term 'level'.

(2) *Comparative* attributes are associated with relative values and explicit differentials, for instance, profitability is improving. We shall denote comparative attributes by the term 'trend'.

(3) *Explanatory* attributes and type hierarchies define concept relations. We shall not, at this stage, define the kind of relation (causal, definitional and so on), but only denote the relation by the name of the object which occurs in a descriptive role. For instance, we may note from the protocol: Return on investment (ROI) has improved due to faster turnover of assets. Here, we shall identify the objects of the relationship, that is, ROI and 'asset turnover', and save the expert's description of this relationship in what we call a *topic line*. A subsequent task, qualification, will formalize and qualify this relationship.

A classified protocol, as shown in Table 7.1, can now be used to compile everything that is said about one object (the focus object) and all relational objects to this focused object.

Conceptual Structuring

By compiling the set of classified protocols, we have a collection of all that is said about each object and its relations upwards (its role as an explanatory object), and downwards (its role as a focus object). Thus, we can produce a conceptual structure of the domain. This conceptual structure describes *which* objects are related. From this structure

Table 7.1   A classified protocol

Focus object	Attribute	Topic line	Protocol reference
ROI	Trend	A sizeable dip in 1985	Loan officer 1
ROI	Level	Clearly less satisfactory	●
●	●	●	●
●	●	●	●
ROI	Asset turnover	Improved due to faster turnover	●

Table 7.2 *A classified protocol with explanatory attributes*

Focus object	Attribute
Profitability	Productivity
Profitability	Cost structure
Productivity	Sales per employee
Productivity	Contribution margin per employee
Cost structure	Sales growth
Cost structure	Contribution margin
Cost structure	Growth in fixed costs
Contribution margin	Sales
Contribution margin	Contribution
Contribution margin	Fixed costs

knowledge about *how* objects are related can be specified. We shall particularly be concerned with inferential and algorithmic knowledge.

A classified protocol with explanatory attributes is shown Table 7.2. From Table 7.2, we can draw the conceptual structure shown in Figure 7.2.

Qualifications

Evaluative and comparative attributes, on the other hand, must be assigned values. Since we are dealing with human reasoning, these attributes will take qualitative values: good, bad, marginal and so on. This process of assigning qualitative values to an attribute is called *qualification*. For example:

Return on investment   level   very good above 20%

Qualification implies defining a value set, also called a *scale*, and defining equivalence among separate scales, for instance, the equivalence between a numeric scale and a qualitative scale.

Return on investment   very good   >20%
                         satisfactory 15–20%
                         marginal   10–15%
                         very low   <10%

Relationships lead to aggregated variables, for instance liquidity, and the relationships are formalized using production rules. The topic lines are the basis for qualification of the relationships. Qualified descriptive objects are entered in the conditional part of the rule, and a qualification of the aggregated variable is made in the conclusion part.

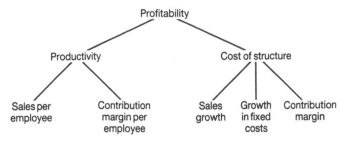

Figure 7.2   *A conceptual structure*

Problem Solving Strategies

How does the subject approach the problem? We can describe this on two levels, the task level and the performance level. On the task level we arrive at a general model of problem solving. The processes we identify are assumed to be common across several subjects in a domain. This model we have called a task model. For financial analysis we have defined a task model consisting of the following subtasks: financial statements validation and adjustment, ratio analysis, interpretation, diagnosis, and recommendations for change.

On the performance level, individual behavior is identified with respect to information search and reasoning.

In this study we have taken the task model as the basis for the overall design of the expert system. However, within each subtask performance knowledge has been modeled and implemented. No particular problem solving strategies have been defined on this level.

7.4.4   A Conceptual Model of a KBS

Above, we have considered the process of task analysis and performance analysis. At the end of these processes we arrive at a model of the knowledge and the reasoning process. We shall refer to this model as the *conceptual model* of a knowledge-based system. It represents the knowledge used to solve a particular class of problems in a domain. This knowledge should be organized in such a way that it can be implemented as a knowledge-based system on a computer. This requires that:

(1) the conclusions or results of the reasoning process are explicitly specified;
(2) subproblems are identified and further decomposed;
(3) the input level of observations or findings is determined;
(4) the relationships between observations and conclusions (the inference structure) are established.

The conceptual model should be free from any tool-specific terminology or computer representation formalisms. Furthermore, the knowledge must be general enough to solve most of the problems in the domain in which the system is going to work. The performance knowledge arrived at by protocol analysis must, therefore, be generalized.

We can now work out a more detailed specification of what this conceptual model should contain:

Task:	conclusions
Facts:	input data (findings/observations)
Algorithmic knowledge	models, equations
Inferential knowledge:	heuristics, logic, rules
Problem solving strategies:	chaining, conflict resolution

7.5 SAFIR – AN EXAMPLE OF THE KNOWLEDGE MODELING PROCESS

We shall now use the methodology described above in the development of SAFIR, a corporate financial adviser in domains dealing with credit evaluation, corporate acquisition, financing of investments, and restructuring of the financing of corporations. SAFIR was developed by extensive task analysis and performance studies of a domain expert. Methods used for knowledge acquisition were interviews, verbal protocols and prototyping.

We shall look at performance modeling of an expert dealing with financial problems. This section is based on a thesis by Lyngstad (1987).

7.5.1 Knowledge Elicitation

The first session that was held with the expert was partly an interview and partly a protocol collection. The purpose of this session was for the knowledge engineer to become acquainted with the task and for the expert to gain some experience about concurrent verbal protocols. Methodological aspects about protocol collection were evaluated and the first proposal of a task model was presented.

Altogether, six sessions were performed with the expert. Protocols of eight cases were collected and three unstructured interviews were conducted. Everything said was tape recorded, resulting in 150 pages of type-written reports.

Session (1) Interview: task analysis
Session (2) Protocols of companies 1, 2 and 3

Session (3) Protocol of company 4
  (a) interview about model specification
  (b) interview about model qualitative variables and
  (c) their scales.
Session (4) Interviews
  (a) about financial actions
  (b) about formalization.
Session (5) Protocols and prototyping
  (a) companies 5, 6 and 7.
Session (6) Protocols, prototyping and interview
  (a) protocol of company 8
  (b) review of prototype.

Each of the sessions had two main objectives:

(1) to test and review knowledge representations
(2) to identify new knowledge.

7.5.2   Concepts Identification and Classification

We shall now perform a conceptual analysis of the following sample protocol from the SAFIR project (translated from Norwegian):

> 'I notice that financing costs have fluctuated somewhat. The reason for this is not easy to say. I guess that they have gone up in 1985 due to the dramatic increase in the overdraft. They have gone up by 4.3 million (Norwegian kroner). Long-term debts, I see, have increased sharply in 1985, and dropped strongly in 1984. Why this is so I cannot see immediately from the figures here. It does not look like that the drop in long-term debts is financed by an increase in short-term debts. So, most probably it is a realization of assets.'

This verbalization is a direct transcript of the tape recording of the expert's thinking-aloud protocol (apart from the English translation). This protocol is now analyzed for task-relevant knowledge. By using the vocabulary from accounting and financial statements we can identify task relevant objects, like financing costs, overdrafts and so on. Then, we divide the protocol into parts, each part saying something about one particular object. In our case the whole sample protocol says something about financial costs. This part can be further divided into topic lines: statements saying something about the object in focus (properties or relations to other objects).

The protocol now looks like this:

SEGMENT (Focus Object): FINANCING COSTS

Topic 1: – fluctuating

Topic 2: – guess . . . gone up in 1985 due to dramatic increase in OVERDRAFT . . . gone up by 4.3 million (Norwegian kroner)

Topic 3: – LONG-TERM DEBTS . . . sharp increase in 1985 . . . strong drop in 1984. Why . . . I cannot see immediately

Topic 4: – It does not look likely that the decrease in LONG-TERM DEBTS is financed by increase in SHORT-TERM DEBTS

Topic 5: – Probably a REALIZATION.

We have denoted objects of the domain (accounting concepts) by upper-case letters.

Editing a protocol in this way is helpful in order to obtain a better view of the task relevant knowledge in the protocol.

Classification of objects and object relations can now be done on the level of topic lines. Several protocols can now be compiled into one set, the classified set of protocols, containing everything that is said about an object.

The classification of SAFIR protocols resulted in 440 classified statements. Table 7.3 shows all of the classified statements on return on investment (ROI).

7.5.3 Conceptual Structuring

Conceptual structuring is based on the compiled set of classified protocols. Implicitly, there is a conceptual structure of the domain in the statements. However, to make this structure explicit is not a simple task. Furthermore, taking all the relationships defined by the classified

Table 7.3 *A classified protocol for SAFIR*

Focus object	Relationship	Topic line	Protocol
Return on investment	General	Calculated	1
Return on investment	General	Needs decomposition	2
Return on investment	Level	13.2% improvement	3
Return on investment	Level	Rather hopeless	4
Return on investment	Level	Between 14 and 16, Satisfactory	1
Return on investment	Trend	16.2, definitely better	5
Return on investment	Assets	Kept growth down	5
Return on investment	Assets T–O	Reduced by 50%	2
Return on investment	Profit margin	Not quite satisfactory	6
Times interest earnt	ROI	Too high financial costs	7
Return on equity	ROI	Reasonable relations	1

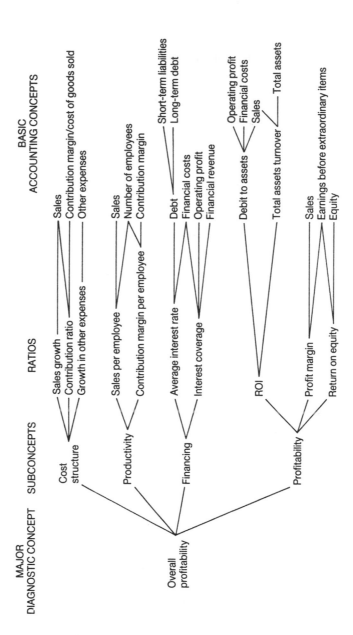

Figure 7.3   *Profitability inference structure*

statements probably results in a complex network. To turn this structure into a hierarchy which can form the basis for calculations, logical deductions or plausible inferencing, requires interpretations.

In structuring the domain, the task model is helpful, in addition to the classified protocols. Also, it is helpful to let the expert specify the specific goal states of the diagnosis. The goal states of the financial diagnosis were defined, by our expert, to fall into two categories: (1) operational issues which are primarily related to profitability measures, and (2) status issues which are primarily related to financing measures.

The classified protocols are now turned into the two inference structures shown in Figures 7.3 and 7.4, for profitability and financing respectively.

7.5.4   Qualifications

An important task in financial analysis is ratio calculations and ratio analysis. For a ratio to have any meaning it must be interpreted. Here, interpretation means to qualify numeric ratios, that is, what does it mean that return on investment is 14.9%? Our expert interpreted this figure to be 'fairly good'. But what is the equivalent qualitative scale on a numeric scale?

By interviewing the expert it was possible to find one qualitative scale that could be used for level variables and one scale for trends. The two scales are shown below:

Scales

Level	Trend
● very good	● strong growth
● good	● moderate growth
● satisfactory	● stable
● less satisfactory	● moderate decline
● not satisfactory	● strong decline
● bad	

If desirable, a unique scale can be built for one particular ratio. Usually, this scale is a slight modification of one of the scales above. Also, for a ratio it is possible to use only part of the scale.

Having created the scales, the next step is to assign numerical values (thresholds) to each qualification. For the ratio 'return on investment' it looks like the following:

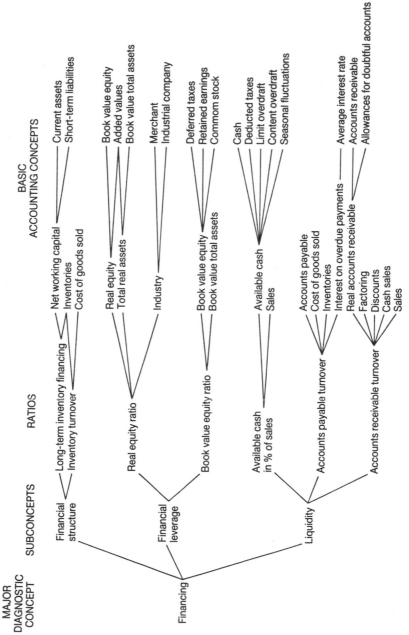

Figure 7.4 *Financing inference structure*

Scales

Qualitative	Numeric
• very good	>20%
• good	15–20%
• satisfactory	12–15%
• slightly less than satisfactory	10–12%
• not satisfactory	<10%

7.5.5 Problem Solving Strategies

The very first concurrent thinking-aloud protocol gave a good indication of the expert's problem solving process. The expert starts by familiarizing him or herself with the information sources he or she has, that is the income statements and balance sheets. He or she interprets figures and starts to identify problems. Next he or she proceeds to an evaluation of ratios, followed by the other subtasks specified in the task model.

7.5.6 The Conceptual Model of SAFIR

At this point we can assemble the results of the task analysis and the performance studies under a coherent framework, called the conceptual model of the expert system.

The task is financial diagnosis of a corporation. The components of the diagnosis are:

• profitability
• financial structure
• leverage
• liquidity

The values of the diagnosis 'level' are:

• very bad
• bad
• satisfactory
• good
• very good

The values of the diagnosis 'trend' are:

• strong decline
• moderate decline
• stable
• moderate growth
• strong growth.

PROFITABILITY

	1984	1985
Return on investment (%)	8.3	14.9
Profit margin (%)	0.7	1.5
Interest coverage (%)	1.1	1.3
Average interest rate (%)	9.1	13.7

Return on investment is satisfactory.
Profit margin is too low.
Interest coverage is less than satisfactory.
Average interest rate is high.
The company has satisfactory operational profitability, but the financing of
capital is expensive. Therefore, the overall profitability is low.

FINANCIAL STRUCTURE

	1984	1985
Long-term inventory financing (%)	31.5	79.5
Inventory turnover (days)	182.9	52.4

Long term financing of inventories is good.
Inventory turnover is average.
The company has a satisfactory relationship between long-term debts and short-term liabilities.
Long-term financing of inventories is increasing sharply.
Inventory turnover is decreasing sharply.
Relationship between short-term liabilities and long-term debt has improved.

FINANCIAL LEVERAGE

	1984	1985
Real equity ratio (%)	18.5	16.9
Accounted equity ratio (%)	1.8	3.4

Real equity ratio is satisfactory.
Financial leverage is satisfactory, but accounted equity is rather low.
Real equity ratio is declining somewhat.
Financial leverage is weakening.

LIQUIDITY

	1984	1985
Available cash (% of sales)	4	14.5
Accounts receivable turnover (days)	53.5	33.5
Accounts payable turnover (days)	121	101

Liquidity is good.
Accounts receivable turnover is normal.
Accounts payable turnover is very high.
Available cash is satisfactory, but accounts payable should be decreased in
order to avoid interest on overdue payments.

Figure 7.5 *Financial diagnoses from SAFIR*

Factual Knowledge

- Input data (findings/observations) which are found in financial statements and notes. These data are mainly time-series of data for the accounting periods provided.
- Derived data from the input data, either by inferencing or numeric computations.

Analytical models can be formulated where causal relationships and definitional relationships can be expressed in terms of algorithms or equations. From the task model and the performance studies we have identified the need for two models:

- ratio calculations;
- fund flow statement generation.

Inferential knowledge is particularly present in tasks dealing with interpretation and diagnosis. Using the rule formalism, but not constrained by any computer tool syntax, we could formulate the inferential knowledge as shown in the following rule:

IF   the level of return on investment is very good;
AND   the level of net profit margin is at least good;
THEN profitability is very good.

Problem Solving Strategy

The task analysis indicated that the process starts in diagnosis, but moves rather quickly to search for problems in the input data. The search strategy formulated for SAFIR is backward chaining but with a metarule that controls reasoning within all the subcomponents of the diagnosis.

SAFIR has been built using the development tool PC-OPTRANS. A print out of the diagnoses is shown in Figure 7.5.

Exercises

7.1   What is knowledge engineering? Describe knowledge engineering as a systems analysis task. What distinguishes knowledge engineering from conventional systems analysis?

7.2   Three different modes of knowledge acquisition have been described. Give a short description of these.

7.3   Interviews are used for knowledge acquisition. We distinguished between two types of interviews. Which? Discuss when each type can be appropriate for knowledge acquisition. What are the general advantages and disadvantages of interviews as a knowledge acquisition technique?

7.4 Some people have argued strongly against rapid prototyping. They claim that this technique does not produce a cognitive model of the problem solving process. Why? What are the advantages of prototyping?

7.5 You have been called in as a knowledge engineer to develop a stock investment system. You will start the process by performing a task analysis. Present an analysis of this task, including a task model.

7.6 Describe the set up for concurrent (think-aloud) verbalization.

7.7 The analysis used for protocol analysis puts emphasis on conceptual analysis. Describe the tasks performed to analyze a protocol.

7.8 Describe the components of a conceptual model of a knowledge-based decision support system.

7.9 Discuss how verbal protocols can be used to study:

(a) performance differences between experts and novices in problem solving;

(b) categories of behavior displayed by several experts;

(c) information acquisition used by experts;

(d) decision processes.

7.10 Discuss the pros and cons of using multiple experts in developing an expert system.

7.11 Group work: one knowledge engineer and one domain expert.

(a) Provide a city map and select a departure point and a destination point on the map.

(b) Assign the roles of knowledge engineer and domain expert.

(c) The knowledge engineer should describe the task environment, for instance, which transportation facilities are available, at what time of the day the travel takes place and so on.

(d) Carry out performance study on the domain expert who is planning the route from the departure point to the destination point.

(e) Perform a conceptual study of the verbal protocol.

Material required: road map of a city and recording equipment.

8
Building and Implementing Knowledge-based Decision Support Systems Applications

8.1 HISTORY

One of the first papers on the design of DSS was Gerrity's thesis (1970) from the Sloan School of Management, followed by a series of papers (1971) by the same author. At the same time, Segal (1970) was working along the same lines at the Moore School. Some of John Little's papers (1970) were important from the design point of view. Some people working on management information systems had ideas relevant to the use of artificial intelligence in such systems but they were not working specifically on information systems to support decision processes. This was the case for Caroll and Zannetos (1967). Other people working in the field of artificial intelligence saw, clearly, the deep relationship between AI and problem solving. This was the case of Newell (1979) and before this the well-known research of Simon on GPS and the less known work of Teitelman.

Klein (1977) expressed a number of ideas about the introduction of AI technology in DSS, but did not present design methodology and realization. Bonczek *et al.* (1981) explore the language system for a DSS based on formal logic. Lee (1983) first defined the concept of KB-DSS.

In fact, until 1985, the AI research community and the DSS research community were working separately. To our knowledge, the topic of integration of AI technology into the DSS framework and the precise concept of the KB-DSS and working prototypes first appeared in the proceedings of the Maratea Conference on DSS Theories and Applications (1985).

As a short introduction we shall give a brief description of three approaches in the DSS literature before we propose our methodology for building and implementing a KB-DSS system.

Gerrity's approach. In a paper Gerrity (1970) points out that the key problems in the design of successful Man–Machine Decision Systems (MMDS) are not technological but rather methodological in nature. Gerrity presents an approach which is close to that of Ackoff (1967) in the sense that it also argues strongly for replacing a *data-centered* or machine-centered view of MIS design with a *decision-centered approach*. Gerrity emphasizes the fact that he adopts a view of design as a process of problem finding and problem solving, as introduced by Pounds (1969). The methodology proposed by Gerrity follows this problem finding/problem solving pattern with 'normative and descriptive model comparison yielding gaps or problems which are reduced by application of operators designed into the MMDS'. The key feature of Gerrity's approach is the emphasis on doing both a descriptive model and a normative model of the decision process, then trying to close the gap (see Figure 8.1).

The SCARABEE approach. This was developed by researchers at the Business School Hautes Etudes Commerciales (HEC) (see Klein and Tixier, 1971; Girault and Klein, 1971; and Klein *et al.*, 1974). The contribution of the SCARABEE project was, mainly, to show the importance of two points which had been ignored in the early literature on DSS design: *the language* and *the evolution* which have important implications on the design. The SCARABEE approach advocates an evolutionary development of a DSS where requirements identified during the study of the task and the decision process are implemented successively. Also, the SCARABEE project provided a set of design principles, methodologies and techniques for DSS development environments.

Keen–Scott Morton normative view. Scott Morton (1971) has given a description of the design process which is based on Gerrity's approach. A more refined view of this process was later presented by Keen and Scott Morton (1978). Their idea is that a pre-design

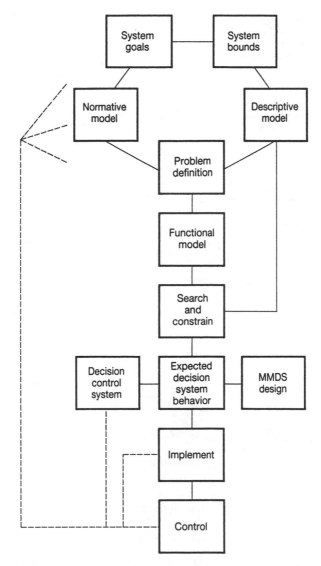

Figure 8.1 *MMDS design methodology. (Reprinted from the design of man–machine design systems: an application to portfolio management by Ferrity, T. P. Jr, Sloan Management Review, **12**, 1971, pp. 59–75, by permission of the publisher. ©1971 by the Sloan Management Review Associaton. All rights reserved.)*

phase is needed to build the socio-political climate for change and commitment, a kind of contract for action among the participants. Also in this approach a normative model is developed as a reference for change (see Figure 8.2).

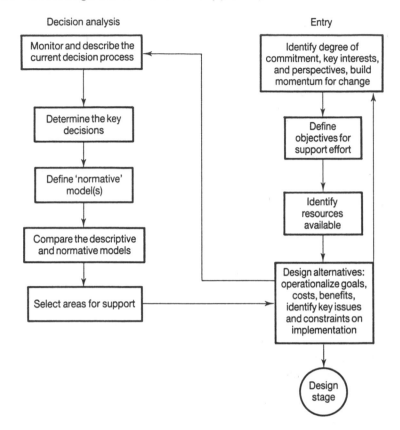

Figure 8.2   *The pre-design cycle. (Reproduced from Keen, P. G. and Scott Morton, M. S.* Decision Support Systems, An Organizational Perspective. *Addison-Wesley.)*

8.2   BUILDING THE KB-DSS

8.2.1   The KB-DSS Design Process

Many of the ideas which have been expressed above are important and useful, most of them have the advantage of being independent of the technology. However, technology has also given birth to new possibilities within the concept of KB-DSS. We need to reassess the design problem given the KB-DSS technology and the existence of new development environments. The 12 steps that we propose are presented in Figure 8.3.

We shall now study each one of these steps. We wish to point out that we have put ourselves in the most general situation. We consider

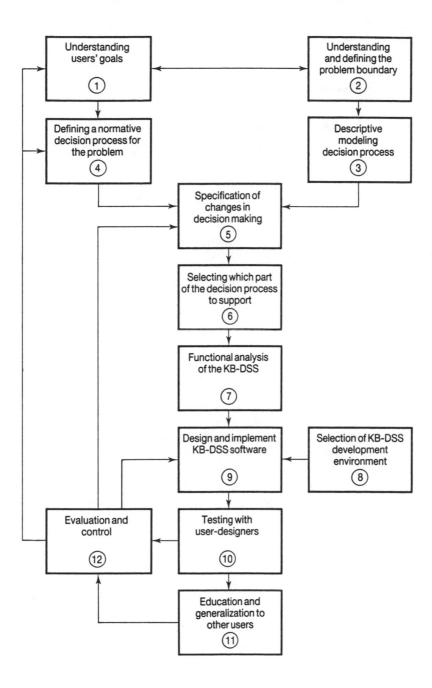

Figure 8.3 *Proposed methodology for the KB-DSS implementation process*

this situation as being the one we are in, when we have to build a KB-DSS for a large community of users. The situation where the designer and the user of the KB-DSS is one and the same person is an easier case to solve.

This design process was discussed by Ganzendam (Ganzendam, 1993).

8.2.2 Understanding Users' Goals

When we build a system for ourselves this step is usually not too difficult. Since we wish to build a KB-DSS it usually means that we have an idea of what to expect from such a tool. The usual goals are to be able to:

- recognize a problem situation;
- diagnose a problem;
- generate alternatives;
- compute criteria;
- evaluate alternatives;
- select one alternative.

easily and quickly, but the goals can also, more generally, be to improve the way that a problem is presently solved, or facilitate communication between individuals to ease the reaching of a solution.

If we are in charge of, or involved in the design of a KB-DSS for several potential users and, chiefly, if the number of potential users is large, the task of finding out user goals or principal objectives is more difficult, and conflicts of objectives are possible. We may also be in a situation where users have no goals, except the one of doing their tasks as usual (which implies making a decision or proposing a decision for approbation), then the will of their management to change the way this task is being performed may be and is usually felt as a threat.

In such a situation, the task of the KB-DSS designer is to understand the motivation of future users and to find out how the introduction of the new system can be felt as an opportunity to achieve their own goals and not to oppose them. It is clear that the motivation of users may be very different from one to another.

This raises the problem of goal coherence between users and between users and management in the design.

Since this section is on design and not implementation we shall not go deeper into this question here. We shall study the typology of situations found in implementing KB-DSS and present implementing strategies in Section 8.3.2.

8.2.3 Understanding and Defining Problem Boundaries (Problem Structuring)

This step is here to acknowledge the well-known fact that a decision maker may not have a clear picture of the problem that he or she is facing. We may have a problem, but no real decision maker has been identified yet. This step will include identification of:

- the decision maker(s);
- the relationship of the decision maker (client) with the decision structure of the organization;
- the decision boundaries that the decision maker must accept as fixed, as well as those that he or she feels he or she can challenge or has control over;
- the problem that will be solved if an alternative other than the status quo is chosen;
- the willingness and ability of other decision makers and experts in the organization to cooperate and provide inputs to the analysis;
- the dominant corporate culture in the organization.

For example, in the case of the design of a KB-DSS for credit analysis, such as FINSIM (Klein, 1989), the design of the system is not going to be the same if the problem is to provide the tool to a limited number of specialised credit analysts (say from one to five) of a regional bank or if the problem is to provide a tool for the credit analysts of a large national bank. In large banks, loan decisions can be made in several hundred main branches. Another constraint may be the wish of management to compile a centralized financial data bank of balance sheets and income statements of clients and prospects.

The financial analysis process to be supported may be performed with different perspectives. For example, it can be performed with the goal of supporting a decision to:

- grant a loan;
- invest in a company;
- approach a company to offer banking services (marketing point of view).

It is very important to know if all of these decisions situations have to be supported or only one of them, since the people involved are not going to be the same and the information and criteria used are very likely to be different even if much of the basic information is going to be common to all.

Another example can be to find out if the loan decision to be supported will involve an organization decision process with several people working at different locations, such as branches and headquarters.

The persons involved in the decision process may be the customer account representative, located at the branch and in charge of the customer application, a secretary to prepare the file, a credit analyst located in a main branch whose task is to evaluate the risk and a loan committee at headquarters which will take the final decision. In such a situation it is clear that the system should support a series of different tasks all of them contributing to support the organizational process of decision making.

- a task of collecting the accounting and banking information on the prospect and analyzing the financing problem in order to find a solution (customer account representative);
- a task of establishing the application file for the credit committee (secretary);
- a task of analyzing the risk involved in the proposal of the customer account representative (loan officer);
- a task of providing printed documents for the credit committee.

The support of such a decision process clearly implies that the same KB-DSS is used at several locations (branch, main branch, headquarters), that the file can be updated and transmitted to each location and that functions of the KB-DSS exist to support each of these sub-tasks.

The benefit should be measured in terms of efficiency (saving of time in processing the file) and effectiveness (absence of errors in computation, more detailed analysis, better evaluation of risk, better quality documents for discussion, etc.).

The KB-DSS designer should be in a position, after learning the above information, to suggest and describe, to the decision makers, the benefit that a KB-DSS will have.

However, this last task is not always easy to perform since prediction (for example, the percentage decrease in loans giving rise to repayment problems) is not easy to identify if no experimental measure has been made already somewhere on a similar problem.

A certain number of problem structuring aids have been proposed in the literature. The reader is referred to Kepner and Tregoe (1981). As a conclusion, we can say that the problem structuring and definition or redefinition should lead to the creation of alternatives.

8.2.4 Understanding and Defining Actual Decision Processes

If the decision which is studied is repetitive then an understanding of the actual decision process is essential. This is a descriptive step. It is very important to come to a clear understanding of the present decision procedure since this knowledge will be needed to evaluate what is feasible in terms of improvements if the KB-DSS is implemented. If we have to implement a KB-DSS for a large population of users, they are very unlikely to use exactly the same decision process. This is the case of a situation where we wish to support decision for a large group of credit analysts.

The sub-steps for the identification of the decision process are the following:

(1) Describe the general task within which the decision process occurs.
(2) Describe persons involved in the decision process and the sub-tasks they accomplish:

- domain knowledge used for studying the problem;
- problem diagnosis methodology and task knowledge;
- alternative generation;
- facts and documents used to obtain criteria;
- computation method of criteria;
- presentation of criteria;
- constraints to be taken into account.

In fact, each one of these steps defines information and knowledge which is being used, and ways of checking the validity of the used information.

The KB-DSS designer can use Mintzberg *et al.*'s framework described in Section 4.1.4 to help him or herself in the description of the decision process.

Once the major phases of the decision process have been described, the designer will often have to start defining variables (facts) used to compute criteria and decision models. A formalism for model description such as the one described in Section 4.4.3 will be useful.

It must be acknowledged that according to the problem the description may be: data intensive, computation intensive, knowledge intensive, etc. Three useful tools to structure decision situations are decision tree, influence diagrams and cognitive mapping we have described them in Chapter 3.

The decision trees and influence diagrams help, in particular, in assessing which are the alternatives, and the type of relations between variables.

The equation models have to be defined to describe how criteria are computed.

8.2.5 Defining a Normative Decision Process for the Problem

The task of the KB-DSS designer is then to analyze the decision process, make a diagnosis and define an improved process.

The normative point of view of decision making that we have seen in Chapter 3 is useful here. However, we should not consider that the normative point of view always implies the use of decision analysis methodology (a theoretical norm).

As we have seen in Chapter 5 (on expert systems) the normative point of view can be defined by extracting the knowledge from one or more experts and structuring it into a knowledge base (an empirical norm). This knowledge base may not use explicit preference functions and probability and yet will still be acceptable as a good normative process (or empirical norm).

Clearly, if the KB-DSS is designed to support the rational decision analysis point of view we shall need a simulation language supporting certain and uncertain variables but also, in the toolbox of the system, algorithms to help the user elicit knowledge and preferences.

As we have seen in Chapter 6 a key new possibility offered by the KB-DSS framework and corresponding development environment is the capacity to couple symbolic and numeric computational processes. In the definition of the normative decision process the designer should define with great care how numeric algorithms or models can be used in the steps of a reasoning process to reach a solution.

A very important step in the definition of the normative decision process is the scheduling of the use of the different resources.

The decision makers are making use of data, models and knowledge in a certain order which may be a function of the problem. The ideal interaction between the user and the resources during the problem solving task is a key factor for an efficient solution.

8.2.6 Defining Changes in the Decision Process

Once the normative decision process, indicating how things should ideally be done, has been defined, changes to the actual decision process can be designed.

However, certain other elements must be taken into consideration: for example, the fact that the KB-DSS is going to be used by many decision makers, so we should evaluate to what extent improvement in the decision process can be assimilated by all of them.

We should always remember that the adoption of a DSS is a social process. This implementation problem will be addressed in Section 8.3.

We know that a decision maker, properly supported and in an organization where the management has created a value system favorable to learning, will see his or her decision process evolve and is very likely to request new capabilities from the system. The designer should anticipate what is the probable evolution and define a system which will be able to support this evolution in the decision process. For instance, in the loan analysis case, for which FINSIM was implemented, it is possible that the user is not using any kind of formal or explicit evaluation function to combine criteria. The choice is made by judgment.

It may happen that the analyst would like to have a systematic way to evaluate the multiple criteria as we have seen in Section 3.3.4 (such as a score function or other such normative method). Another situation is found when the analyst is using historical data only to make a conclusion and is not using any forecast or hypothesis, or that he or she is not using any fund flow analysis to study the evolution of the cash position of the company when theory can demonstrate that it should be done to improve the decision.

8.2.7 Selecting Which Part of the Decision Process to Support

The designer will have to define the starting environment of the user. This definition is a skill and is difficult. As pointed out already in the SCARABEE project the starting environment has to be good enough for the user to feel comfortable in it, yet it should not be too sophisticated (so as not to frighten the analyst) and it must be sufficiently powerful (or the analyst will not see the interest of the DSS).

In an early version of FINSIM, for example, it was decided not to support a multi-criteria evaluation function neither to support an industry analysis (cross section) but only company analysis (time series). On the other hand it was decided to support the part of the normative decision process using forecasted data (likely evaluations).

In other words once the differences between the descriptive model and the normative model have been clearly identified the task of the designer is to evaluate which part of the descriptive model will be combined with which part of the normative model to constitute the starting environment.

8.2.8 Functional Analysis of the KB-DSS

The purpose of this step is to define the main functions and the overall architecture of the system (the conceptual model). An example of such an analysis was given in the exercise 4.14 for a management control DSS. A second example is given in Section 7.5 with emphasis on knowledge modeling. A third example is given in Section 11. At this point it is decided which part(s) of the decision process to support.

For instance, make a diagnosis on historical data based on the computation of a certain number of criteria, generate alternatives using a simulation model or use an expert system to simulate a reasoning process, etc., constraints of the overall design are also defined at this point. Is the system going to be a distributed system, with several KB-DSS components exchanging information through a network or not?

Usually a first list of reports, decision models, data structures, input forms, knowledge bases are needed at this point. A first sketch of the application user interface should be used to define the way these resources are going to be used by the user during the problem solving process.

The designer should at this point be able to decide which components of the KB-DSS should be needed: database management system, knowledge based management system, toolbox or just the modeling language, the report generator and user interface definition system.

The main task of the functional analysis are shown in Figure 8.6. The designer should provide a first list of the resources used by the future KB-DSS application in terms of:

- user interface and global logic of the application;
- a first list of variables needed with a distinction between elementary variables and aggregates;
- models;
- reports;
- input forms;
- knowledge bases (inferential knowledge);
- algorithms to be found in the tool box (statistics, forecast, preference and risk modeling).

Once this analysis is completed, it will be possible to select, properly a development environment.

8.2.9 Selection of a KB-DSS Development Environment

At the time of writing five main development environments are available for designing DSS, KBS or KB-DSS applications.

(1) Standard programming languages such as BASIC, PASCAL and C.
(2) Symbol manipulation or AI languages such as LISP or PROLOG, or object-oriented programming languages.
(3) Expert system shells.
(4) DSS development environments.
(5) KB-DSS development environments.

We have already introduced the differences between expert systems, DSS and KB-DSS in Chapter 6.

We have listed expert system shells and DSS development environments (generators) since they are important tools to be used in developing classical expert systems or classical DSS, respectively, but we shall not consider them here since we are concentrating on the development of KB-DSS and, also, since we have explained, why this new framework should replace the two others as soon as we need to integrate the DSS and expert system functions.

This, clearly, does not mean that the designer should not select a DSS development environment when no expert function is needed – be it for purely economic reasons – software licences for KB-DSS development tools being, naturally, usually more expensive than licences for DSS development tools.

In the context of this book, we shall, therefore, only consider alternatives (1), (2) and (5), that is, the choice between a third-generation language, a symbol manipulation language or AI language and a KB-DSS development environment.

The first criterion for a decision is going to be related to the choice of the designer of the KB-DSS. If the designer is the future user then the important point is to evaluate the capacity of the user to master the development tool and/or to assimilate the concepts used in the tool.

It is clear that most managers do not have the time, competence or motivation to master a third-generation language or a symbol manipulation language such as LISP, PROLOG or Smalltalk.

On the other hand, there is considerable evidence that hundreds of thousands of managers or knowledge workers are able to use spreadsheets, several thousands are able to use DSS or KB-DSS development environments. The reason for this is, simply, that in standard third-generation procedural languages and in symbol manipulation languages the formalism which is used is not coherent with the usual managers' conceptual view of the world.

Even with the classical case where the programming language is provided with a graphical library to define the user interface the time needed to master such a language usually by far exceeds the time a manager or domain specialist can afford to allocate to such a task.

Clearly, in some special cases where the user is familiar with languages such as BASIC or PROLOG this argument does not hold, but these cases are unlikely to be very numerous in management circles for some time!

We now consider the other criteria for choosing the KB-DSS development environment, the designer being a domain specialist or a professional in KB-DSS design.

The most important of the other criteria is the availability of standard KB-DSS *components* (subsystems, as we have seen in Chapter 6).

If a third-generation programming language is used the designer will be facing the task of interfacing or developing the major subsystems usually found in KB-DSS: the database management subsystem, modeling language, graphics, report generation, inference engine and knowledge base management.

If the modeling language for example is not available it means that a programmer will have to be involved everytime the decision model must evolve. This is usually not acceptable.

Host language of DBMS are not adequate for decision modeling.

The most obvious cases where the use of third-generation language is useful are cases where special characteristics are needed which are not yet provided by standard development environments, or where the development environment is not available under the required operating system. For example, a trade room or a production management KB-DSS may require real-time capabilities which are not provided by the available generators. With respect to an example that deals with the first case, we know of a bank which decided in the 80's to write its KB-DSS application in COBOL, since there was no KB-DSS tool available under this real-time monitor at the time of the decision. Here, the operating system was considered to be the constraining factor.

If a symbol manipulation language is used then the most important problem will be the necessity, in a KB-DSS application, to execute a minimum of procedural code as the consequence of a fired rule or slot of an accepted object. Access to external procedures, written in FORTRAN, BASIC, PASCAL or C are important for reasons of efficiency and expediency. Computationally intensive procedures will gain from being written in a language which compiles efficient native code on the host machine, and existing subroutine libraries (in statistics, OR, and forecasting) may provide proven code which it is more expedient to use than to rewrite.

Another problem of symbol manipulation languages and PROLOG, in particular, is their inability to represent uncertainty.

Finally, the same argument holds for this class of language with respect to the components, all of the standard KB-DSS components will have to be rewritten!

As we can see, in most cases, the use of a KB-DSS development environment will be the right solution. The problem facing the designer will then be to select the right tool within this category.

We shall recall the main criteria for such a development environment.

Criteria related with functionalities of the development environment

- Graphical user interface definition system.
  This system should be object oriented and should allow the designer to use icons, define hierarchies of menus as well as the global logic of the interaction between the application user and the application resources (decision models, reports, . . .).
- Report generator.
  This system should allow the user to define reports interactively. The report should be able to integrate objects such as texts, tables, graphics, maps, images and video.
- Modeling language.
  The important point here is the matching of the modeling formalism of the environment and the modeling which is needed, and also the variety of solvers which may be needed. We have in Section 4.4.3 presented some key criteria for a modeling system.
- Form definition.
  The definition of forms for input and the corresponding controls is essential. It is very important to be able to reproduce administrative forms which are often complex and to check that the environment is sophisticated enough to reproduce on the screen what is needed.
- Database management system.
  We have pointed out in Section 4.4.2 that the most widely used formalism in DSS environment development has been the multi-dimensional one. The object-oriented formalism is certainly more adequate as soon as complex entities have to be dealt with for problem resolution. We have, however, pointed out that the ability to access widely used relational DBMS is an important criteria if the functional analysis indicated that access to information found in other transaction oriented Information Systems is critical.
- Knowledge-based management system
  The key issue here is the matching of the knowledge representation method and the knowledge to be represented. Certain hybrid

systems allow the use of several knowledge representation methods.

- Toolbox.
  The designer should check that he will find the algorithms which are useful for the planned application. Standard libraries of algorithms are found in finance, statistics, and forecasting.
- Communication interface, LAN version and client/server architecture. The designer should check what are the facilities offered for designing distributed applications. Is a LAN version of the development available? Which server can be used in a client/server architecture?

Criteria related with the platforms (hardware + operating system) for which the environment is available.

Is the environment available on the platforms used in the organization or should the acquisition of new platforms be considered?

Other criteria

The other classical criteria are the reliability of the supplier, the price of the environment, the quality of the documentation and of the supplier training and support. More and more environments include the user manual in a hyper-text mode. The quality of documentation is not directly related to its size.

8.2.10   Design and Implementation of the Initial KB-DSS

The tasks to be performed at this step are outlined in Figure 8.7. They are:

(1) data analysis and modeling;
(2) form definition and input verification;
(3) decision model design and testing;
(4) report definition;
(5) knowledge base modeling and testing;
(6) overall user interface design and global application logic definition.

The study of the data to be used in problem solving should lead to the list of variables used in the application. It is important at this step to define the list of elementary variables and the list of aggregates (non-elementary variables) which will be used in decision models. These variables may be attributes of entities constituting a database. The elementary attributes are usually facts describing the real world.

The form definition means using the form generator of the environment (this can be an independent function or included in the application interface definition function). It should be remembered that often an input form will be of a composite kind mixing for example: text in one window, a graphic in a second window, computation or model results in a third window, input and control in a fourth window.

Decision model definition will use the list of variables identified at this stage. Only aggregates variables will be defined in models. Parameters of relations of the models may need identification using statistical or artificial intelligence techniques found in the toolbox.

Knowledge base modeling was described in Chapter 7. The order in which these design tasks are performed is highly dependent on the decision process that is to be supported.

In some cases, where the first task is to support the problem detection phase of a user working with a large number of entities (products, companies and so on) a database must be defined, with aggregates that compute variance between actual and budgeted data and some reports, including graphics.

In a situation such as the credit analysis case described in BANKER or FINSIM, the first task to support is the computation of alternatives with the corresponding evaluation criteria. As a consequence, a decision model may be the first thing to define and implement.

In other situations, where much knowledge is being used in symbolic reasoning, but where not much computation is performed (in law for example), the design of the expert system component may be the starting point in the design of the KB-DSS.

A good method with which to start the design is often to imagine the ideal user interface of the application. This user interface will help the future users to react and to indicate their needs. This user interface can also be of help to define the user manual of the future system, this user manual being updated when the final version is finished.

We shall now study each one of these steps. We wish to recall that we put ourselves in the most general situation. We consider this situation as being the one we are in when we have to build a KB-DSS for a large community of users.

The situation where we build the KB-DSS for ourselves is a particular case that is easier to solve.

Data Analysis and Modeling

Design

The user/designer uses the description of the information used in the decision process to model the data used.

The problem here is to use a modeling formalism which is as close as possible to the conceptual constructs of the users. The data models available for this purpose are mainly the relational model. But as is well known the passage from a conceptual model to the tables of the relational model used in a relational DBMS is not an easy step for most users. This is why for simple or medium complexity problems the multidimensional model, which is a simple way to represent relationships between attributes of entities (or data as functions of attributes of entities), is easier to use for most managers. We believe that we shall see in the future the development of entity attribute relationship data models used in the DBMS of the development environment since they are usually the closest to the end user's conceptual framework. The other possible solution being object oriented DBMS.

Data loading

The goal of this operation is to enter and store the data in the database, that is, the entities and the values of their attributes. Four main ways of loading the database can be used:

(1) by reading outside static files; (on disk or CD-Rom)
(2) by direct entry through a form at the screen;
(3) by a real-time data feeder;
(4) by using an SQL link to a relational DBMS.

In the first case, the data reader function of the development environment will be used. In the second case, it will be necessary to define form to enter the data. The third case is found in real-time applications (trade rooms).

The data reader will be used to define the structure of the outside file and access methods and read it. Very often it will be necessary to use the capability of the KB-DSS to pass control to an outside procedure since complex testing, aggregation and sorting may be needed to generate a file which can be read directly by the data reader.

The model can be used to check relationships in data and avoid data errors. The form is used to guide the user when typing data.

The loading of the database can be a complex and delicate task when the number of entities is large and when it is necessary to update the database from files having a different structure and access methods.

Decision Model Design

The analysis of the decision process has pointed out the information that is used by the decision maker as he or she studies a problem in order to reach a decision, in particular, the criteria which are used to evaluate alternatives.

The user-designer must define the variables and relations which are used in the computation of these criteria.

In the FINSIM example, the user computes ratios (variable or financial aggregates), in order to measure short-term risk, the return on assets and the leverage of the company. The user will have to define the relations needed to compute these ratios from more elementary system variables for which it is easier to give estimates.

To compute the criteria (variables) the decision model must, usually, be fed with data stored in the application file coming from two sources:

(1) the database (or data file);
(2) the user.

The system variables used in the model will be classified, as we have seen in Chapter 3, between environmental variables, decision variables and goals. The environmental variable may come from the database or be introduced directly by the user during his or her interaction with the system. The same applies for the decision variables.

The designer will, as a consequence, have to define:

● The user/decision model interaction to provide decision variable values and environmental variable hypotheses.
● The database/decision model interaction to provide the model with the data needed to solve it and the database with model results.
● The expert system/decision model interaction to provide the user with the analysis of model results.
● The expert system/database interaction to provide the expert component with facts stored in the database.

As we have proposed (see Section 6.3.2) an efficient way to describe these interactions is through an independent component using a blackboard structure. It may be necessary to define an expert which will move into action when several other sources of knowledge have been used. This expert will observe the results (facts) provided by each knowledge source and will conclude new facts using these previously obtained results.

These interactions will be defined through the interface definition language and will take the form of: questions and answers between the application and the user, choice in dialog boxes, or choice of options in menus. All these interactions should be defined in a non-procedural way and should be transparent for the user which should only work at the logical level. The user interface of the Finplan example (Figure 4.16 and Figure 6.4) gives a very simple but straightforward example of such interface-model interaction. As for Finplan the FINSIM application described in Chapter 3 requests a minimum of two models: a model for the computation of criteria based on historical facts (variables) and a model for the computation of criteria based on forecasted facts (variables).

Report Design

This task is crucial to support the decision process since information:

- stored in databases and/or application file;
- computed by models;
- capture from input forms;
- generated by the reasoning mechanism, etc.

have to be displayed in order to let the user:

- assimilate the information;
- analyze the information;
- decide on further action.

In the general case a report will be defined as a text interspersed with variable values, tables, graphics, maps used as background and images.

Use of color reports

The use of color can improve, considerably, the speed of assimilation of information by the decision maker. In a bar chart such as the one used to demonstrate the diagnosis support of a KB-DSS for management control (Figures 4.4, 4.5 and 4.6), red could be used to illustrate negative variance, and black could be used to illustrate positive variance.

Certain physiological laws have to be respected. For example in presenting the penetration of a product or density of population on a map, the high density area should not be represented by light color and low density with dark color.

Form design

This task is crucial to facilitate data capture by users. The form generator let the user define interactively the input zones on the form as well as the label of the windows corresponding to each input zone and the associated controls.

Knowledge Base Design

The methodology required to perform this task was developed in Chapter 7. The designer will have to select one knowledge representation method if the expert component of the KB-DSS development tool provides more than one (in certain cases, he or she may mix several of these).

The application may require several knowledge bases. For example, in FINSIM different kinds of knowledge bases have been defined to support the different kinds of diagnosis needed, according to the type of financial analysis requested.

Here, we would just like to stress the point that, in our experience, it is very important to have the possibility of demonstrating simplified knowledge bases to the expert in order to help him or her structure his or her knowledge.

Running such a simplified knowledge base helps very much the expert to define his or her ideas.

Application Interface Design

The application interface is defined using the interface definition language. This language allows the designer to define:

- hierarchies of menus;
- the scheduling of resources usage;
- questions/answers;
- composite displays;
- import/export data from the database;
- computation.

An example of a very simple application menu was given in Figures 4.16 and 6.4. According to the option of the menu which is selected the designer defines in the interface text the instructions to call the needed resources (solve a model, print a report, set in motion the inference engine and so on). As a consequence it is at the interface level that the scheduling of resources is defined. This scheduling being controlled by the action of the user selecting options of the menus or clicking on buttons or icons.

It is also at the interface level that the values of parameters can be fixed. This is done through input/output instructions.

If the information does not justify the use of the form generator the data capture should be done at the interface level. This implies the ability to define windows and use input/output instructions at the interface level. In other words the interface should be able to call the window manager to define composite display. A composite display will mix in several windows of the same screen: data or results of computations, graphics, text coming from the expert, menus, icons, images, etc. For example the introduction of hypotheses for the forecast model of FINSIM is made of six windows as shown on Figure 10.8.

One interesting new possibility that is available with a KB-DSS development environment is to build an 'intelligent' overall user interface which will guide the user in selecting the application adapted to support his or her task.

8.2.11 Testing with Designers

Once a KB-DSS has been implemented it is essential to test it thoroughly. The decision models and knowledge bases have to be tested after completion, as well as the overall system when it is finished. This testing phase should be done, firstly, with the users who took part in the design.

In the case where the KB-DSS is being implemented by the user for his or her own use the testing period can be reduced, for obvious reasons. The methodology for knowledge base verification and validation is presented in Chapter 7.

During the testing and evaluation phase, it is good practice to write a user manual for the system.

In the case where the KB-DSS is implemented for a larger group of users, the education of these users must be carried out.

8.2.12 Education of Users and Generalization

The education to be provided to users is largely dependent on their implication in the design, their level of expertise and the goal that the organization is trying to achieve in making the KB-DSS available to them.

The introduction of the KB-DSS to help perform the users' tasks has to be carefully planned. We recommend the organization of a seminar for this purpose. The seminar should cover the following points:

- explain the overall goal of the system;
- discuss the decision process being used by the present decision makers and collect remarks;
- discuss the decision process as management would like to have it performed and collect remarks;
- discuss the function of the KB-DSS and present it for a typical case;
- have the participants analyze a set of carefully-chosen cases and solve them using the system;

- explain how improvements will be integrated in the system, through, for instance, regular meetings to evaluate the support that the system is bringing, and which changes should be integrated into it.

The existence of a user manual is not necessary for the standard use of the system, but it is always very useful in such a seminar, and as a reference document. A user manual should contain not only a commented run of the system but, also, the equations of decision models and an explanation of their workings.

We shall discuss this point, in more detail, in Section 8.3.3, where we discuss implementation problems.

The seminar should be directed by one of the best experts of the organization on the topic of the application, so that there are no questions about competence. Management should be present to, at least, introduce the seminar and to show their commitment to seeing the system in use.

The experts teaching the seminar should be the ones who were leading the design of the KB-DSS.

One important idea that the seminar should get across is that KB-DSS are there to help people *improve themselves from a professional point of view and not replace them*. We shall discuss this further in Section 8.3.3.

Management should remember that the adoption of any system is a social process. If the dominant value system or corporate culture within the organization is not the search for professional improvement there is a little chance to see the system being used if it does not provide some clear advantage to users. A necessary condition for success is a good design but it is not a sufficient condition. A well designed system may fail if there is no motivation on the user side to improve tasks and decisions. To create this motivation is an essential management task.

The role of users in the evolution of the system should be stressed, in particular, how to monitor its performance, evaluate it and make it evolve. A second seminar, at least, should be planned after a few months of system usage, to evaluate the system and monitor its evolution.

8.2.13 Monitoring and Evaluation

Results of evaluation of DSS, ES, or, KB-DSS have not been widely reported in the literature. A framework for results of evaluation is given in Section 9.2.

An example is given by Klein (1977). In the case reported, the evaluation attempted to measure *perception* of improvement on a credit analysis task on two points:

(1) Capacity of the DSS to deal properly with a variety of examples.
(2) Perception by the users of the capacity of the DSS to improve the decision.

The experimental design was worked out with two sets of users, some working with the DSS and others with pencils and calculator. The users were given information on companies (including balance sheets and income statements) and had to provide a financial analysis of them and a recommendation for granting a given loan or not. Information on perception was collected using questionnaires. Information on hard data, such as correctness of computation of the capacity to repay a loan over a given horizon using information provided in the case, was also used.

8.2.14 Evolutionary Design Strategy

Figure 8.3 contains a certain number of loops which convey the idea that the design is not linear but iterative. Most of the time it is useful to implement a first version of the system which can be considered as the minimum nucleus.

This nucleus (or starting version) may include only simple interface, a simple decision model, a first data file or database, or a first simple presentation of the results in a report, and a knowledge base containing only a few rules. The role of this minimum version is to help users define their needs in terms of:

● entities and attributes needed (data);
● user interface;
● decision models variables and relationships;
● reports;
● input forms;
● type of assistance requested from the expert module.

The availability of a KB-DSS development environment makes it possible to have an evolutionary design of the application, in the sense that the initial version is progressively improved to fulfill the needs of users, needs which become more precise as the users interact with the application.

This design method is related to the learning process of users. The method was described in Section 4.5.4 for DSS with the shade that the availability, now, of KB-DSS development environments makes it less likely that the environment (generator) itself has to be modified during the design.

In this type of design methodology the application is *continuously evolving* from the minimum starting environment to the presently-used version. However, it happens that after an initial version was implemented, experience with users leads to a design that is very different and sometimes incompatible with the initial one. In that case, the designer throws away the initial version, which can be called a prototype and a new one is designed taking into account what was learned.

The term continuous evolution has to be understood as the release of regular updates. In the case where we have a large number of users, for obvious management reasons it may not be desirable to have continuous changes in the application.

Problems raised by the design and implementation of the various knowledge bases of a KB-DSS have been dealt with in Chapter 7 (we refer here, mainly, to the domain-specific knowledge base, and not to the methodological base).

A KB-DSS development environment presents the essential characteristics to allow the designer to use and combine a variety of design strategies.

It is possible to start the design of the application as with a spreadsheet by defining *the display of results (reports)* which are looked for. For this it suffices to create the application with its associate list of variables names and headings names and use the report generator to define the reports without having inputted any data or define any computation or model. The models and data will be added in a second step to compute the values which will be displayed by the reports. The interface is added last to guide the user when interacting with the application for problem solving.

It is possible to start with the *models*. It suffices to create the application with its associated list of variables names and headings names and then to define the models. The reports will be added in a second step to present the results. The interface is added last.

It is possible to start with the *database*. This approach is natural if the user is working with a large number of entities and his first problem is to structure his data and interrogate the database to point out problems and learn by querying the database. The designer can then start defining his application interface which will import and export information from the database to be used for reporting or computation by models.

It is possible to start with the *knowledge base*. This approach is valid if the domain of application is characterized by a large amount of expert knowledge and the designer wishes to simulate reasoning to obtain diagnosis or build plans. The user creates the application and the associated list of facts used in the reasoning and then defines the knowledge base. If computation is needed during the reasoning models are defined. The interface is improved in a second step.

It is possible and much better to start with the *user interface* and the *global logic* of the application and its associated variable and heading name list. The other resources are added, as the designer wishes, as a function of the nature of the application, the availabilities of competences, etc.

We believe that one of the key advantages of the KB-DSS development environments is their aptitude to support flexible design strategies.

8.3 IMPLEMENTING THE KB-DSS

The preceding section on building KB-DSS dealt with the design problem independently from real-life constraints. Implementation can be defined as the process of converting an initial conception of a system into a tool that is used effectively.

We shall, in this section, recall the main problems which are found in implementing KB-DSS. As we shall see, the problem of implementing KB-DSS is very intricately related to the introduction of change in organizations, in particular, the introduction of changes related to technological innovation. We shall then recall some theories about how to introduce change and how we can use some of these ideas in introducing KB-DSS.

Section 8.3.3 will deal with the recommendations that have been found useful in order to create the necessary conditions for successful implementation.

8.3.1 Standard Problems in Implementing KB-DSS

Following Alter (1980) we have classified the problems of implementation into four categories.

Technical Problems

The technical problems can be, themselves, broken down into hardware problems, software problems and technical design problems. Also, as pointed out by Alter, we should distinguish a technical *constraint* from a technical *problem*.

Hardware Problems

Classical hardware problems are characterized by insufficient processor power, insufficient response time, limited core memory, limited disk space available and physical compatibility between components of the configuration.

One of the classical problems is to decide on the appropriate hardware configuration on which to run a KB-DSS application.

A PC with a INTEL 486 processor, which was a very good choice for running a financial analysis KB-DSS may be a hardware-limited machine for running a KB-DSS with a graphical interface and a database components as soon as the user wishes to make an industry analysis involving the manipulation of thousands of companies data, since the database component requires a machine with a more powerful processor.

The same database component may require much more disk space than the KB-DSS without the database component in order to store the same amount of data. The ability to deal easily with more complex data structures has to be paid by more complex software using more disk space and more CPU resources.

Software Problems

Most KB-DSS software development environments are available under several operating systems. However, they are not usually available under all operating systems. A graphical library or an object library may be compatible with a given operating system and not another. Large or complex software are often not fully reliable.

Data Problems

Most data problems seem to be of two types: problems due to the nature of the data itself, and problems associated with the data feeder.

Problems due to the nature of the data

A non-exhaustive list is the following:

- data is not correct,
- data is not timely,
- data is not measured or structured properly,
- too much data is needed,
- data does not exist.

In the case of non-correct data, the solution can be found, from time to time, in standard techniques of data checking. One classical method is to use redundancy and relations between pieces of data in order to check their validity.

If the data is derived from other sources, a monitoring procedure should be worked out to check the data values. But we should always remember that people are very reluctant to compute data which are the result of a complicated process and, also, are not very good at it.

In the case of non-timely data, it seems that the only way to solve the problem is to modify and simplify the system for generating the data. A system can fail just because it is not updated with timely data. A portfolio management system which is not updated with an acceptable frequency for the portfolio manager will undoubtedly fail.

The inadequacy between the structure of the data obtained from transactions processing applications and KB-DSS applications is a classical problem. This shows the importance of the data reader function of the DSS.

A KB-DSS for financial planning in a bank may request, every month, a given list of data from the accounting file of the bank and the values of the balance of the accounts. The accounting system may be able to produce, easily, the balance of the accounts, but not an unchanged list of accounts, since this list is modified nearly every month. As a consequence, an intermediate procedure is required which will aggregate the changing list into a fixed list.

A classical problem related with data structure is due to the incompatibility of the measurement assumptions and periodicity between outside data (such as industry market data) and the data used in the proprietary databases of the KB-DSS.

Some such problems can be solved by using very flexible and simple to use data management components of KB-DSS that develop a procedure to rescale or recombine the improperly indexed data. Some problems cannot be solved, except by regenerating the coherent data at a cost which may be considered prohibitive.

In the case where too much data is being needed then this can be due to a bad model design. The designer has forgotten that variables should be included in the model only as long as they are useful in making appropriate decisions (see Chapter 3 for the decision analysis cycle). Then, the solution is to design simpler or more aggregated decision models. If the model design was done properly, then the solution is to develop efficient ways of extracting and combining data, usually from large-scale data processing systems.

If the required data does not exist then this may be due to the fact that the data was never stored in a machine-readable form, or in a data management system.

Before starting the implementation effort the designer should check that the cost of storing and maintaining data will not be too high.

In a more serious situation, the data never existed. In this case, the cost of generating or estimating the data can be studied but it is better to check this once the models are defined, before implementation!

Problems associated with the feeder role

This problem is associated with the fact that, many times, the necessity to generate data was considered a threat by people in a feeder role. The problem to solve here is how to motivate people in supplying data for a model, the interest of which they do not see, or which they see as a tool for overseeing the quality of their work.

Conceptual Problems

These problems are related, on one side, to assumptions concerning people and, on the other side, to software and modeling.

Assumptions about people

Usually, designers are over optimistic with regard to users' willingness and/or the ability to figure out how to use systems or to spend time feeding the system with data. One of the consequences of this observation is that it is not sufficient to give the users a good user manual or to design a friendly interface, it is necessary to train users in solving real problems with the system and check they have the time and motivation to use it.

One of the interesting new possibilities of the expert component of KB-DSS is that it should allow us to design systems which guide the user from the methodological point of view, however, this is still at the research stage in most cases. We have already emphasized the importance of the dominant organizational value system for the adoption of a DSS within an organization.

Conceptual design problems related to modeling

The common errors here are to attack the wrong problem, or to try to use an existing model which does not fit the case.

Little (1970) has made a well-known analysis of such difficulties. Stabell (1974) reports on a portfolio management DSS which was designed to support a portfolio-oriented process that determined purchases and sales taking, as a starting point of each, the requirements of an individual's portfolio.

In fact, the real process started with attractive purchases or sales of securities and then searched for a match with portfolios.

The under-utilization of the system was due to the fact that it was not oriented toward the decision process that actually existed, or else that the gap between the existing process was too wide.

The idea here is that you have to be very careful in your design not to implement changes in the decision process that go beyond what will be accepted by users. Another design error is to attack the 'easy problem'. In particular, many financial planning systems do not contain formal methods for modeling the market outside the firm. The problem is that the modeling of this market mechanism is a difficult problem. Little (1970) gives examples of such models for consumer goods.

People problems

Alter classifies, under this title, what he calls syndromes and manifestations, syndromes being the things people complain about and the emotions that they feel. In this category are syndromes such as 'the analysts are scared that the computer would replace them' or 'there is a new person in charge of the system and he is not interested in the system'.

The problem here is to discover if the difficulty is coming from the people, or from real technical problems, as the observer (a consultant of a member of the organization) is always biased by his or her own viewpoint and by knowledge concerning people and technology.

The manifestation of people problems can be revealed by disuse or misuse of the system. As we have seen above, they do not use the KB-DSS because they do not see how to use the system to solve or simplify their everyday tasks or they are not willing to make an effort to try to use it, or they do not see any advantage in changing their habits, or they oppose the values implied in the use of KB-DSS.

Fundamental limitations

Another classical problem is found with users who expect too much from KB-DSS. We have seen this problem becoming more acute with the introduction of the AI technology. Some people believe that, with the AI technology, no limitations will remain to the possibilities of DSS. It is clear that if learning is a key aspect of intelligence, knowledge-based DSS have still their future ahead of them! Also the characteristic of being conscious of what one knows remains a human privilege. The reader is referred to Penrose for an account of the present debate on AI and consciousness.

8.3.2 Introducing Change in Organizations

It has long been recognized that the process of introducing change is a key determinant of the ultimate success or acceptance of that change. An important literature is devoted to the implementation of computer-based systems and/or management science techniques. Kolb and Frohman (1970), Zand and Sorensen (1975) and Ginzberg (1975) are examples.

Since the implementation of a KB-DSS always constitutes some kind of change in a work environment, it is worthwhile studying what sociologists write about the implementation of such systems.

We have described a normative process by which KB-DSS systems projects should take place. This normative description is useful in appreciating the impact on project success of two key variables: the degree to which the user initiated the project, and the degree to which the user participated in the development effort.

The Lewin–Schein Theory

According to this theory change consists of three steps:

(1) *Unfreezing*: creating an awareness of the need for change and a climate of receptivity to change.
(2) *Moving*: developing new methods and/or learning new attitudes and behaviors.
(3) *Refreezing*: reinforcing the changes that have occurred, thereby maintaining and stabilizing a new equilibrium situation.

Zand and Sorensen (1975) applied this change theory and list some key issues at each step, these are presented in Figure 8.4.

The Kolb–Frohman Model

Kolb and Frohman (1970) propose a seven-step process between the user and the designer of a system (see Figure 8.5).

Typology of Situations Found in Implementing KB-DSS

It is common experience that:

(1) the degree to which the user *initiated* the system development effort, and;
(2) the degree to which the user *participated* in the system development effort are key variables explaining successful implementation.

	Favorable	Unfavorable
Unfreezing	1. Top and unit managers felt the problem was important to company. 2. Top managers became involved. 3. Unit managers recognized a need for change. 4. Top managers initiated the study. 5. Top and unit managers were open, candid. 6. Unit managers revised some of their assumptions.	1. Unit managers could not state their problems clearly 2. Top managers felt the problem was too big. 3. Unit managers did not recognize need for change. 4. Unit managers felt threatened by the project. 5. Unit managers resented the study. 6. Unit managers lacked confidence in the management scientists. 7. Unit managers felt they could do the study alone.
Moving	1. Unit managers and management scientists gathered data jointly. 2. Relevant data were accessible, available. 3. New alternatives were devised. 4. Unit managers reviewed and evaluated alternatives. 5. Top managers were advised of options 6. Top managers helped develop a solution. 7. Proposals were improved sequentially.	1. Management scientists could not educate the unit managers. 2. Needed data were not made available. 3. Unit managers did not help develop a solution. 4. Unit managers did not understand the solution of the management scientists. 5. Management scientists felt the study was concluded too quickly.
Refreezing	1. Unit managers tried the solution. 2. Utilization showed the superiority of the new solution. 3. Management scientists initiated positive feedback after early use. 4. Solution was widely accepted after initial success. 5. Unit managers were satisfied. 6. Solution was used in other areas. 7. The change improved the performance of the unit.	1. Management scientists did not try to support new managerial behaviour after the solution was used. 2. Management scientists did not try to re-establish stability after the solution was used. 3. Results were difficult to measure. 4. Standards for evaluating results were lacking. 5. Top managers ignored the solution recommended by the management scientists. 6. Solution was incompatible with the needs and resources of the unit. 7. Top managers did not encourage other units to use the solution.

This was considered to be so important that much of the work on DSS and KB-DSS development environments was made with the assumption that, in many cases, the only way to achieve a successful implementation was to have the user work in an environment where he or she could define and implement his or her system. The Lewin–Schlein theory and Kolb–Frohman models also imply that these variables are associated with successful implementation.

Alter (1980) has formalized the classical implementation patterns. The initial push to develop a DSS is, according to Alter, of three types: user stimulus, managerial stimulus and entrepreneurial stimulus.

Systems initiated through user stimulus are those in which user perceived the need and pushed for the initial implementation effort. Systems initiated through managerial stimulus are those in which the user's organizational superiors perceived a need for a DSS for the user. Initiation through entrepreneurial stimulus means that a person inside or outside the organization made an effort to sell to people, in the organization, the idea that a DSS or a KB-DSS development environment should be implemented.

Managerial and entrepreneurial stimulus are often intertwined since, in many cases, the DSS or KB-DSS concept is sold to a manager, who will then 'convince' a subordinate as to its merits. This is why, in Alter's presentation, managerial and entrepreneurial stimulus are lumped into one category. From this analysis, Alter defines six implementation situations:

Situation 1 is the ideal situation, the client/user is ready to buy and get involved in a cooperative problem definition and problem solving effort, in addition to buying a product such as KB-DSS development environment.

Situation 2, the client/user is buying a product (solution) rather than a service. The main issue is to complete the system to specifications within the time and budget constraints.

Situation 3, the user was not involved in initiation, but it is possible to convince the client/user that the system is needed and to obtain his or her involvement in its development.

Situation 4, a consultant or salesman attempts to sell the DSS or KB-DSS idea to the user. This is a very common situation, and a situation that any consultant interested in implementing DSS or KB-DSS should master.

Figure 8.4 *(opposite)* *Key issues in the Lewin–Schein theory of organizational change. (Reprinted from 'Theory of change and the effective use of management' by Zand, D. E. and Sorendson, R. E. published in* Administrative Science Quarterly, **20***(4) by permission of* Administrative Science Quarterly

1.	*Scouting*: User and designer assess each other's needs and abilities to see if there is a match. An appropriate organizational starting point for the project is selected.
2.	*Entry*: User and designer develop an initial statement of project goals and objectives. Commitment to the project is developed. User and designer develop a trusting relationship and a 'contract' for conducting the project.
3.	*Diagnosis*: User and designer gather data to refine and sharpen the definition of the problem and goals for the solution. User and designer assess available resources (including commitment) to determine whether continued effort is feasible.
4.	*Planning*: User and designer define specific operational objectives and examine alternative ways to meet these objectives. Impacts of proposed solutions on all parts of the organization are examined. User and designer develop an action plan that takes account of solution impacts on the organization.
5.	*Action*: User and designer put the 'best' alternative into practice. Training necessary for effective use of the system is undertaken in all affected parts of the organization.
6.	*Evaluation*: User and designer assess how well the goals and objectives (specified during the Diagnosis and Planning stages) were met. User and designer decide whether to work further on the system (evolve) or to cease active work (terminate).
7.	*Termination*: User and designer ensure that 'ownership' of and effective control over the new system rest in the hands of those who must use and maintain it. User and designer ensure that necessary new patterns of behaviour have become a stable part of the user's routine.

Figure 8.5 *A normative model of the consulting process in system development activities. (Reprinted from an organization development approach to consulting by Kolb, D. A. and Frohman, A. L.,* Sloan Management Review, **12***(4), 1970 pp. 51–65, by permission of the publisher. ©1970 by the Sloan Management Review Association. All rights reserved.)*

This situation is, clearly, a more difficult one to start with, however, many successful innovations have been introduced into an organization in this way, since most new ideas often originate outside the settings in which they are applied.

Situation 5 is also a very common situation. The user is obliged to use the system because management wants it. We shall discuss such an implementation pattern in Section 8.5.

Situation 6. In this situation, an OR department or the R&D unit of the computer department develops a prototype to anticipate user needs. This situation is slightly similar to the situation where an outside software or consulting company is attempting to sell the idea of a new system to support a task.

In fact, the situation we are facing is slightly more complex than the one described by Alter. This is due to the fact that between turnkey systems and systems which are fully implemented by users is a wide range of situations where there is a partial implementation by users.

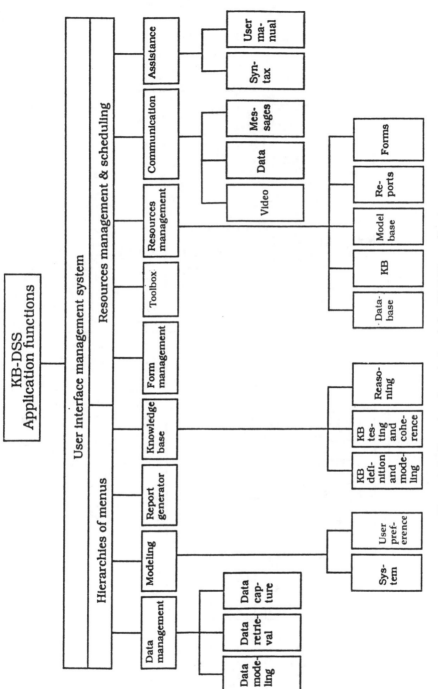

Figure 8.6 Functional analysis of the KB-DSS application

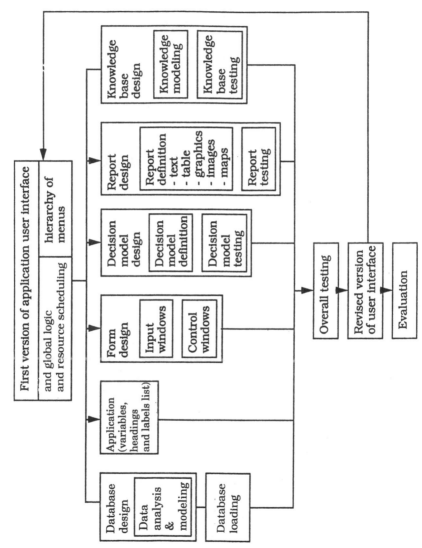

Figure 8.7   *Design steps of the initial KB-DSS application*

In a KB-DSS, it is easy to involve the user in model, display or knowledge base modification or in implementing new models; we shall see such a situation in Section 8.5.

Decision Process Required in Order to Start a KB-DSS Project

Experience has shown that, usually, three groups of people are involved in the decision to implement a KB-DSS in an organization. These people are: users, management and computer department representatives.

By users, we mean the people who will use the system, or else someone who is the head of the user department. By computer department representatives, we mean the people whose tasks it is to keep as coherent as possible the software and hardware equipment of the organization. By management, we mean the group of people that has the responsibility for deciding on a resource allocation which may go beyond the user's authorization.

Clearly, in many organizations, the computer department is not involved in the KB-DSS project if the project has no link (such as data transfer) with the other computer applications under its responsibility.

However, in the most general case, the computer department is involved, in particular, when the head of the computer department has understood that the KB-DSS will play an important role in the organization. Then, it is his or her task to advise users on available applications and/or development environments and to provide consultants to help users implement their applications.

As shown in Figure 8.8, the user will have to move through a series of stages, starting from ignorance of the concept through to project participation.

Management will have to move from ignorance of the concept of the decision through to allocating resources to a KB-DSS project and monitoring it.

The computer department will also have to start from ignorance of the concept right through to the task of surveying KB-DSS development environments, advising users on such environment and eventually supporting users through advice, consulting or direct participation.

8.3.3 Creating the Conditions for Success (Key Success Factors)

As we have seen above, many reasons may make implementation difficult or impossible. As can be expected, ideal situations are very rare in real life. Alter (1977) defines eight main reasons that can reduce the success of the implementation process:

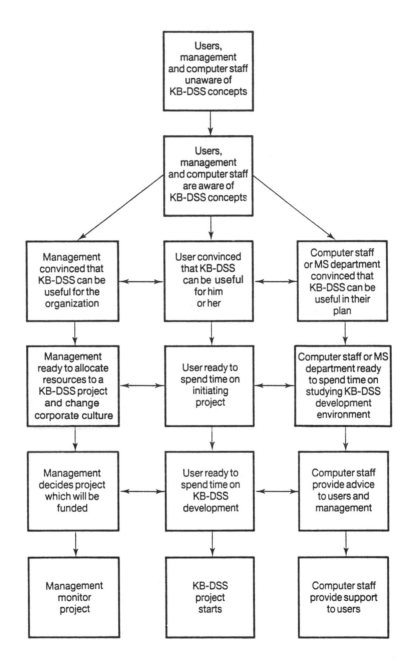

Figure 8.8   *Steps made by users, management and the computer department when implementing a KB-DSS project*

(1) non-existent or unwilling users;
(2) multiple users or implementors;
(3) disappearing users, implementors, or maintainers;
(4) inability to specify purposes or usage patterns in advance;
(5) inability to predict and cushion impact on all parties;
(6) lack or loss of support;
(7) lack of prior experience with similar systems;
(8) technical problems and cost-effectiveness issues.

These factors are called 'implementation risk factors' by Alter.

Alter was working with the DSS conceptual framework in mind, but the situation is not changed drastically within the KB-DSS framework, however, some risk factors are greater. For example, a KB-DSS, due to its expert component, may be perceived, by a user, a greater threat than a classical DSS.

We give below some advice to help decrease these risks.

Select High Pay-off Applications

Whenever possible, it is important to select a domain of application for the KB-DSS where pay-off can be measured (in terms of efficiency and/or effectiveness), demonstrated and is significant.

It will be very difficult to obtain management support for an application, which may be very exciting from the intellectual point of view, but does not lead to some clearly defined potential improvement for the organization. Criteria for evaluation are described in Section 9.2.

In some domains (such as financial analysis, option pricing . . .), software or other specialized companies have developed and marketed prototypes or products. It is possible to acquire (or develop) these prototypes which can be used to experiment and define the pay-off and the conditions of success.

Select a Competent Designer

No good system can be developed without good people to design it. The person in charge of the development should have experience of KB-DSS design. If this is not the case, an experienced consultant can be a major reason for success. The mastery of the development environment by the designer is a key success factor.

If the designer is not used to the development tool selected, he or she should follow a training seminar on the tool and, if possible, start the design with a consultant who is used to the tool.

Select a Good User or Expert

It is not possible to design a good KB-DSS if the design team does not include an expert. At the very least, it must include a competent user. If there is no expertise there will be no expert system or KB-DSS.

Obtain User Motivation and Commitment

It is essential to have not only competent but also motivated users.

The user must be willing to involve him or herself in what can be serious, important and tiring work. The user can see the project as an opportunity to improve his or her knowledge and professional competence or increase his or her power in the organization. This kind of motivation is particularly suitable because it is very likely to happen and the user will usually be very satisfied. The increase in professional competence usually means promotion and a higher market value of the person. The task may be new and challenging and lead to publication of articles in professional magazines which is another way of improving user image.

The user should commit him or herself to work on the project until it is achieved and, eventually, take part into the maintenance of models and knowledge bases.

One of the classical difficulties is that, if many potential users exist, they cannot all be involved in the design. One solution is to involve them in the evaluation of the system. This will give them the opportunity to improve the system. We have also stressed the point that user-commitment is also a function of the dominant organizational value system, which is a management responsibility. If users are overworked it is not easy to get them involved in a new system.

Do not Start with the Most Complex Application

The reason for this is that a very important learning process occurs during the definition and design of a KB-DSS. As a consequence, it is better to start with a simple but useful application in order to improve the expertise of the organization in mastering this technology.

Once a simple application has been successfully implemented, much has been learned and it will be easier to deal with a more complex one.

Obtain Management Support

Management support is needed to obtain the funds for the project and the collaboration of users and the computer services. In particular, it is essential that management decides to enable some of their best experts to spend time on defining the KB-DSS. As we know that most experts are very busy this is one of the most difficult decisions, since management will have to accept that, in the short run, the kind of competence they need the most will be less available, since time will have to be devoted to the definition and design of the application.

It is not sufficient to have management support for the decision to design and implement a KB-DSS, management support will be needed to institutionalize the system.

If the management's attitude ranges from indifference to tolerance once the system is implemented, this may lead to low usage except by the users who were involved in the design.

It may be necessary for management, once it has checked that the system is performing well and satisfies some of the best experts, to make its use mandatory.

However, it is always better to organize regular evaluations of the system so that either constructive criticisms are made by non-users or that their 'mauvaise foi' becomes obvious and management can decide on appropriate measures.

Select the Appropriate Development Environment

This decision is also a key one, given the consequences of a bad choice: production of a lower quality product, longer time and cost of development, higher maintenance cost, and lower motivation and service to users.

It is already a great success if the concept of KB-DSS is understood. At the time of writing of this book, most large organizations have only understood the expert system concept or the spreadsheet concept and some of the DSS concepts. A better understanding of the KB-DSS concept can only be achieved through education and demonstration.

Meet User Needs and Institutionalize the System

Once a good system has been implemented the success is still not certain, if we measure success by the fact that most users will use it and consider that it helps them in making better decisions.

To achieve this goal, good training programs and assistance need to be provided, as well as opportunities for users to participate in the evolution of the system and marketing of the system.

Training Programs

The training program is needed for users other than those who took part in the design. Again, the training will be successful only if done by users involved in the design and the competence of whom is not discussed by other potential users.

The training cannot be geared only to provide familiarity with the concepts of the system, it must include cases where the users solve typical problems with the help of the system.

A well-designed training program can turn skeptic users into enthusiastic users if the training program gives them the opportunity to: work on their own problems, check that the system is easy to use, provides a better solution, will be accessible in their offices, and will give them the opportunity to improve their professional competence and career plan.

The system, however easy to use, can be a failure if it uses concepts which are too sophisticated for the users. A training program will never solve the problem of a bad design, but a well-designed system can fail due to a bad training program.

Provide On-going Assistance

Once a system has been handed over to users it is necessary to support the users. All problems cannot be dealt with during the training sessions. The users must have somebody they can call or interact with in case they need help in using the system to solve their problems. This becomes more important as the system is made compulsory. The on-going assistance should also be provided by updating user manuals, and by notes explaining the evolution of model, reports and knowledge bases. This assistance can be provided through e-mail and video conference with software such as PRO-SHARE from INTEL corporation.

Provide Opportunities to Involve Users in the Evolution of the System

In a KB-DSS application, the system will evolve with respect to the models, the reports, the knowledge base and the interface.

It is very important to have regular meetings with users to give them the opportunity to suggest improvements to the system.

Clearly, this will not solve the problem if the system is too far from users' needs, but it is by making sure that users see that their remarks and criticisms are taken into account that the institutionalization of the system will succeed. In the case of FINSIM, several user groups have been created. These user groups are either internal to a bank or are inter-bank.

A user group that is internal to a bank will discuss the problem of the knowledge base which was developed by the bank and, also, its evolution. The inter-bank user group will discuss more general questions about the KB-DSS application such as: collaboration on producing industry ratios, the definition of financial concepts used in the DSS part of FINSIM and the evolution of reports and models.

Tailor the System to People's Capabilities

One of the ideas that is found in the literature on DSS is that there are great differences among people with regard to their ability and/or propensity to use analytic techniques. When the number of users is significant it is a major problem to diagnose if the system is not used by some of them due to important differences between the decision methodology used by the designers and most users.

It is also clear that when designing the system, the experts tend to refine and improve their decision methodology. This improvement in the decision methodology may widen the gap between the experts and the more standard users.

Sell the System

It is very important to sell it to users who were not involved in the implementation. We mean here by selling, the actions which have, as their purpose, to:

- identify potential new users for the system;
- understand their interests;
- influence their choice by providing them with information;
- work with them to adapt the system to fit their needs.

The two papers describing ES failures (Coats, 1988, Gill, 1995) deal with mistakes to be avoided.

Exercises

8.1 Recall the steps in the design of a KB-DSS. Contrast it with the steps involved in standard information system development.

8.2 (a) What is the role of the normative point of view in a KB-DSS design?

(b) What is the role of the descriptive point of view?

8.3 What are the classical KB-DSS implementation problems?

8.4 How can a theory of change in organizations such as the Lewin–Schein theory, be used in improving the implementation of KB-DSS?

8.5 Define a plan for the implementation of FINSIM (described in Chapter 9) in a bank.

8.6 Define a plan to educate the users of a specific DSS. (FINSIM can be used or another system.)

8.7 Select a company that has developed a KB-DSS. Interview the person in charge of the project, a user and a manager who has users of the system under his or her authority. Describe, for each one, the implementation problems they had to face.

8.8 The learning of design methodology cannot be achieved at a purely conceptual level. The students must be confronted with the problems of designing a project and the teacher should deal with them in relation to the project. As a consequence, the following questions are related to the term projects defined in Chapters 4 and 6.

1. Use the methodology defined in this chapter to design the solution of the term project (Exercise 6.8) of a KB-DSS for personal loan evaluation.

2. Use the methodology defined in this chapter to design the solution of the term project (Exercise 6.7) of a KB-DSS to assist in the completion of a private individual's income tax returns.

3. Use the methodology defined in this chapter to design a solution for the term project (the JIIA86 case study, Exercise 4.14) of a DSS to assist the controllers of an industrial company with its branches and a foreign subsidiary.

9
Testing and Evaluation

9.1 INTRODUCTION

Building a knowledge-based system is an incremental process where the functionality of the system evolves as experience with its use is gained. When a prototype is running, design specifications are tested, revised, and new specifications are added to accomplish needs that were not initially known. Development moves through a series of cycles before the system is finally ready for operation. System development is not a linear process but can best be described as a spiral, as shown in Figure 9.1.

There are two aspects of concern in a revision cycle. Does the system work correctly and does it function well? Correctness can be tested; it is a question of right or wrong. For instance, are the conclusions drawn by the system correct? Functionality must be evaluated; it is a question of good or bad. For instance, is the man–machine interaction well designed? does the system fit well into the decision making process? what are the benefits? and so on. Is the system meeting its original intended requirements and goals?

Testing and evaluation are well-known tasks in model building and computer programming. A computer program is a model of real-world phenomena, where concepts and relationships are mapped into mathematical and logical statements. This process is a stepwise, incremental process where concepts, relationships, and operations are added successively. Before the computer program can be operational we must be sure that it works correctly – that it produces the results that it is supposed to produce, and that it has the intended effects on its environment.

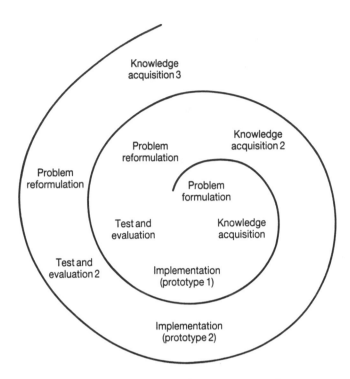

Figure 9.1 Testing and evaluation as a cyclic pattern

9.1.1 What Interesting Questions can be Asked About BANKER?

Let us take another look at BANKER, the loan evaluation system described in Section 5.10. Having implemented the system on a computer by the development tool PC-OPTRANS, what questions are relevant to ask next? Here are some:

(1) Are the conclusions given by BANKER correct?
(2) Is the system reliable and does it give consistent conclusions?
(3) Is the system robust, not missing vital concepts or concept relationships, and not entering into dead-end reasoning chains?
(4) Is the input data easily available at the precision level required by BANKER?
(5) Is the reasoning appropriate, that is, does the system ask for the right information in a natural sequence?
(6) Is the output (conclusions and reports) relevant, timely, and meaningful?

(7) Is BANKER easy to use, that is, does the system provide a user interface which is understandable and designed to conform with the user's cognitive capabilities?

(8) Does BANKER integrate successfully with the organizational setting in which it is going to be used?

A correct conclusion is an output expression, from the system, that can be interpreted as being equivalent to an expert's conclusion in the same situation. Correctness is not only dependent on the internal logic of the program, but also on valid input specifications. Thus, correctness can only be validated against observations outside the system itself.

Reliability and consistency, on the other hand, are a question of representation and logic. A reliable system will yield the same results irrespective of the sequence in which the input data is given. A consistent system behaves in a non-contradictory way. For instance, an increase in the rating of management competence from average to good should not lower the creditworthiness of the firm.

In this chapter, we shall look at a framework for testing and evaluation, how to validate data, knowledge and models, and how to assess the quality of the system. In testing and evaluating a system, we need standards or norms with which we can compare the actual behavior of the system. We have three kinds of norms (see Figure 9.2):

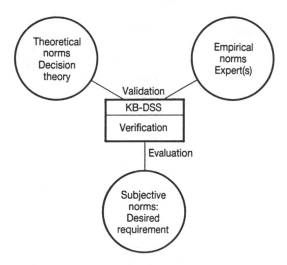

Figure 9.2 *Norms as a basis for testing evaluation*

(1) *Theoretical* norms such as norms prescribed by the normative decision theory
(2) *Empirical* norms such as the norms prescribed by the expert we model for problem solving heuristics
(3) *Subjective* norms, that is, qualitative assessments of system performance, either by the users or the experts.

When we have explicit norms, theoretical or empirical, the system can be validated. In the case of performance, system behavior is evaluated.

Testing and evaluation of models and computer programs have been dealt with in fields such as operations research, data processing and DSS. Many of the issues dealt with in these fields can be of use here. However, developing knowledge-based reasoning systems also introduces new issues. In this chapter, we shall concentrate more on the new issues created by the knowledge technology rather than the more general test and evaluation issues of traditional computer programs. In particular, we shall deal with verification and validation of knowledge-based reasoning systems. In Section 9.2 we shall present techniques to verify the logical correctness of knowledge bases including problems of completeness and consistency. In Section 9.3 we shall deal with what and how to validate. Finally, in Section 9.4, we shall discuss, in more detail, how we can evaluate performance.

Verification and validation of knowledge-based systems are tasks that are closely related to maintenance and learning. As already said, the typical building process of knowledge-based systems is incremental. New knowledge is added to existing knowledge. What is needed to increase the functionality of the system, and how does new knowledge affect existing knowledge? One of the first systems developed to assist in knowledge acquisition and knowledge base debugging was TEIRESIAS (Davis and Lenat, 1982). The idea behind TEIRESIAS is to have a system that enables the expert to interactively change a knowledge base. It was developed as a front-end system to the medical diagnosis system MYCIN.

What can we learn from this pioneering work? There are three types of knowledge that can be changed.

(1) *Inference rules* can be deleted, modified, or added to the knowledge base.
(2) *Concepts* (objects, attributes and values) can be deleted, changed, or added.
(3) *Control strategies* can be changed.

TEIRESIAS uses an explanation facility to track down the source of an error in the knowledge base. After a diagnosis is presented,

TEIRESIAS allows the expert to comment on it. If the expert does not agree with the diagnosis, a debugging process is initiated and guided by the system.

With the help of TEIRESIAS, the expert can teach the expert system new rules, expressed in terms of known concepts. But TEIRESIAS can also support the expert in teaching the expert system new concepts, and it can modify control strategies. Both of these tasks are complicated and require substantial knowledge. We shall not deal with these tasks, but refer the reader to Davis and Lenat (1982) for more details.

TEIRESIAS is a research system. It provides an interesting environment for studying many of the pertinent issues in knowledge acquisition and knowledge maintenance, in particular, for problems where the expert system development process itself is a way of explicating knowledge in a field. TEIRESIAS illustrates the problems of integrating new knowledge with existing knowledge in a knowledge base.

9.1.2 A Framework for Testing and Evaluation

Our new framework of knowledge-based decision support systems includes expert system features and DSS features under the basic paradigm of decision support. Expert systems and DSSs are different in several respects which make testing and evaluation of these two systems two different tasks.

Expert systems, although evolutionary in development, are designed for well-defined problems with predefined solution sets. This makes it possible to logically verify the knowledge base and to validate the reasoning performed by the system. As we have already seen by the TEIRESIAS example above, changes to an expert system's knowledge base are made in terms of inference rules, concepts, and control strategies. Inference rules form chains of reasoning. Rules must, therefore, be tested for incorrectness, incompleteness, and inconsistencies.

The very nature of a DSS, and the situation for which it is designed, makes it a difficult evaluation object. It becomes a moving target. Since there is no predefined solution path, and the environmental context in which it is used may change from time to time, there is no single way or prescribed way of using the system. Instead, the system is a set of resources – data and models, that are placed at the disposal of the decision maker. Thus, individual decision making behavior determines the usage of the system. A DSS may, therefore, be used in different ways by various decision makers. How can we, in these situations, evaluate the system as good or bad? First of all, there is not one single criterion by which a KB-DSS can be evaluated. Unlike expert systems, where we can use the predictive ability (conclusion success) as a measure of good or bad, such a criterion is not found in DSS. One may say that the ultimate objective is to improve the effectiveness of decision making, but when it comes to measurements it remains very much unproven. We can use the verification and validation procedures in Sections 9.2 and 9.3 to test and evaluate the knowledge-based parts of a KB-DSS.

When it comes to the decision support aspects we will lean more on the DSS literature. A review of DSS effectiveness evaluation is found in Sharda *et al.* (1988). Also, in textbooks, like Sprague and Carlson (1982) and Davis and Olson (1985) system evaluation is treated. Sprague and Carlson (1982) is more specifically devoted to DSS, while Davis and Olson (1985) treats evaluation of information systems in general.

We shall deal with performance evaluation in Section 9.4, along the following:

- system performance;
- task performance aspects;
- business opportunities;
- evolutionary aspects.

Three categories of people should be involved:

(1) the knowledge engineer (system builder),
(2) the expert,
(3) the user(s).

Figure 9.3 shows a summary of the test and evaluation framework for a KB-DSS.

9.2 KNOWLEDGE BASE VERIFICATION

9.2.1 Consistency and Completeness

In this section we describe a way of logically verifying the consistency and completeness of a knowledge base. By logic verfication we mean a systematic checking of logical statements: IF conditions and conclusions of rules and inference chains. No checking is made as to the validation of the ultimate premises, that is, the meaning of the symbolic expressions. Logic verification, therefore, means to check that a

VALIDATION
1. Data input
2. Knowledge base: concepts and relations (for example, rules)
3. Reasoning: strategies
4. Results: conclusions

SYSTEM PERFORMANCE
1. Efficiency: response time
2. Data entry
3. Output format
4. Hardware
5. Usage: how much, when
6. Man–machine interface

TASK PERFORMANCE ASPECTS
1. Decision making: time, alternatives, analysis, participants
2. Decision quality
3. User perception: trust, satisfaction, usefulness, understanding

BUSINESS OPPORTUNITIES
1. Costs: system development, operating, maintenance
2. Benefits: income, reduced costs
3. Values: service, competitive advantage, training

EVOLUTIONARY ASPECTS
1. Knowledge maintenance
2. Response time to change demands
3. Functionality of the development tool

Figure 9.3 *A framework for KB-DSS evaluation*

conclusion is logically true, and that the set of rules in an expert system logically spans, completely, the knowledge of the domain.

Logical verification of the rules can detect many potential problems that exist in a knowledge base. These potential problems can be grouped into:

(1) Consistency problems, which can be caused by redundant rules, conflicting rules, subsumed rules, unnecessary IF-conditions, and circular rules.
(2) Completeness problems, which can be caused by missing rules due to unreferenced attribute values, or missing combinations of attribute values. Completeness problems can also occur because of control faults, that is, gaps may exist in inference chains.

Logical problems of the kinds described above may not, necessarily, impose reasoning faults. Logical redundancy and subsumed rules may, for instance, not cause problems unless the system is using a scoring mechanism, for aggregating evidence for a conclusion (such as certainty factors in EMYCIN). However, there may be a potential maintenance problem when rules are revised or deleted.

Logical incompleteness occurs when legal values in the value sets of all attributes entering into the IF conditions and conclusions are only partially or not at all covered by rules. Logic completeness spans the value space of all possible combinations of legal values of the attributes of a rule set. Some combinations of legal values may not be meaningful. A rule set may, therefore, be semantically (and pragmatically) complete without being logically complete. However, logical verification will detect potential faults and allow the knowledge engineer to identify which ones represent real problems.

This description of knowledge base verification is based on two articles, Nguyen *et al.* (1987) and Suwa *et al.* (1982). Both articles also describe automated rule-checking programs with algorithms for detecting consistency and completeness problems, CHECK and ONCOCIN respectively.

9.2.2 Checking for Consistency

Redundant Rules

Two rules are redundant if they succeed in the same situation and have the same conclusions. This statement means that the condition parts of two rules are equivalent, and that one or more of the conclusions of the two rules are the same. For example, consider the two rules:

Rule 1: IF   Firm's net working capital >0, AND trend in net working capital is negative
         THEN solvency rating is low
Rule 2: IF   Trend in net working capital is not positive, AND firm's net working capital is positive
         THEN solvency rating is low.

Assuming that the attribute 'trend in net working capital' only takes the two values negative and positive, then these two rules are redundant even if the IF conditions are in different order.

Redundant rules do not necessarily cause logical problems. It may affect efficiency positively, if redundant rules are located in adequate parts of the knowledge base. However, redundant rules may create a maintenance problem. One of the redundant rules may be revised or deleted, while the others are left unchanged.

Conflicting Rules

Two rules are conflicting if they succeed in the same situation but with conflicting conclusions.

If we change the conclusion of Rule 2 to be 'solvency rating is low minus', then Rules 1 and 2 become conflicting rules. Note that it is possible that rules with equivalent conditions but different conclusions might not conflict at all. In such a case, the concluding variables belong to a multi-valued attribute, for example, a person can be allergic to many different drugs, or can apply for several different types of loans.

For instance, we may have a situation where the conclusion is an advice on which type of loan to apply for: a secured or an unsecured one. In that case, the two following rules are not in conflict even if the conclusions are different. With the given characteristics (conditions) both types of loans are eligible.

IF   Solvency rating is average, AND
        profitability rating is average
THEN apply for a secured loan

IF   Solvency rating is average, AND
        profitability rating is average
THEN apply for an unsecured loan.

Subsumed Rules

One rule is subsumed by another if the two rules have the same conclusions, but one contains additional constraints on the situation on which it will succeed. Let us define the following rule:

Rule 3: IF   Firm's net working capital >0, AND
                trend in net working capital is negative, AND
                firm's currency ratio <2
        THEN solvency rating is low.

In this case, we would say that Rule 1 is subsumed in Rule 3: Whenever Rule 3 succeeds, Rule 1 also succeeds.

Unnecessary IF Conditions

Two rules contain unnecessary IF conditions if the rules have the same conclusions, and if an IF condition in one rule is in conflict with an IF condition in the other rule, and all other IF conditions are equivalent. For instance, let us define the following rule:

Rule 4: IF   Firm's net working capital <0, AND
                trend in net working capital is negative
        THEN solvency rating is low.

In a rule set consisting of Rules 1, 2, 3 and 4, Rules 1 and 4 will contain unnecessary IF conditions.

Rule 1: Net working capital >0
Rule 4: Net working capital <0

In this case, the two rules can be combined into one:

Rule 4: IF   Trend in net working capital is negative
        THEN solvency rating is low.

A special case may occur where two rules have the same conclusion, one rule containing a single IF condition that is in conflict with an IF condition of the other rule which has two or more IF conditions. For instance:

Rule 5: IF   Firm's net working capital <0
        THEN solvency rating is low.

If Rule 5 is included in the rule set, Rule 1 should be modified to:

Rule 1 IF   Trend in net working capital is negative
        THEN solvency rating is low

(Rule 4 should be omitted).

Circular Rules

A set of rules is circular if the chaining of the rules in the set forms a cycle, for example:

Rule 6: IF   Management competence is good, AND
                financial credit rating is good
        THEN overall credit rating is good

Rule 7: IF   Overall credit rating is good, AND
                trend in profitability is very good,
        THEN management competence is good.

Here, the system will move into an infinite loop. In evaluating Rule 6 it will look for rules that conclude with 'management competence is good', it will find Rule 7, which, however, requires that the condition 'overall credit rating is good' is true. This, however, is the conclusion of Rule 6, thus completing a circular chain.

THEN

		R1	R2	R3
	R1			1
IF	R2	1		
	R3	1	1	

Figure 9.4 *Rule dependency chart*

To help detect circular rule chains one may use a dependency chart. A dependency chart is a table with rules displayed as rows and columns. An element (r_i, r_j), where i denotes a row and j denotes a column, determines a dependency if it is marked, for instance by 1. A 1 in the element (r_i, r_j) indicates that one or more IF conditions of rule r_i matches one or more conclusions of rule r_j as illustrated by the example below;

R1:   IF A and B THEN C
R2:   IF B and C THEN D
R3:   IF C and D THEN A

Here, we can see that to draw the conclusion C by R1 we need to know A and B. A is determined by R3. Thus R1 is dependent on R3 and we mark this by a 1 in the element (R1, R3). If we continue to analyze the dependencies of the small rule set above we end up with a rule dependency chart as shown in Figure 9.4.

If a dependency is marked in element (r_i, r_j) and in element (r_j, r_i) we have detected circular rules because r_i is dependent on r_j, and r_j is dependent on r_i. The circular rule chain may not always be as direct and apparent as the two rules shown above. However, an algorithm can easily be constructed to detect any implicit circular pattern among rules.

9.2.3   Checking for Completeness

Missing rules

Rules may be missing due to:

(1) *Unreferenced attribute values.* Some values in the value set of an attribute are not covered by any rule's IF conditions or conclusions. In other words, the legal values in the value set of the attribute are

| Rule number | CHARACTERISTICS | | CONCLUSIONS |
	Management competence	Financial analysis	Credit worthiness
R1 R2	High Average	High	High
R3	High	Average	Average
R4 R5	Average Marginal	High	
R6 R7	High Average	Marginal	Marginal
R8	Marginal	Marginal	Reject

Figure 9.5 *Decision table from BANKER*

only covered partially or not at all. Let us look at Figure 9.5. If the value set of creditworthiness is (High, Average, Marginal, Low or Reject), the value 'low' is unreferenced. This might indicate missing rules.

(2) *Missing combinations of condition attribute values.* In Figure 9.5 there are two attributes making up the condition parts of rules, each one having the value set (High, Average or Marginal). Two attributes with legal value sets of three elements each, lead to 3×3 possible combinations. To cover the whole set of combinations we need, therefore, nine rules. In general, for n attributes, each with a value set v where v is the number of values for attributes i, logic completeness of the entire value space requires $v_1 \times v_2 \ldots v_i \ldots \times v_n$ combinations (rules). Transferring each row of Figure 9.5 into one rule will give a total number of eight rules. A closer examination shows that there are two conflicting rules (R2 and R4) leaving a rule set of seven legal rules. Thus, two combinations must be missing in the table. A closer inspection uncovers the following missing combinations: (Average, Average) and (Marginal, Average).

The number of rules may be less than the number of possible combinations for two reasons:

(1) Disjoint conditional parts, for example:
   IF   Management competence is high *or* average AND
           financial analysis rating is high
   THEN creditworthiness is high

(2) Meaningless combinations of values. One has to be careful here. If combinations of legal values of attributes lead to meaningless conclusions we must be prepared for those combinations to be inputted. The system must, therefore, be able to detect this fault.

Illegal attribute values

If a rule refers to an attribute value that is not in the set of legal values, an error occurs.

Dead Ends

The inference tree of a production system may contain dead ends. These dead ends occur when a conclusion of a rule does not match a goal or an IF condition of another rule. Dead ends are very often caused by terminology errors, for instance, when synonyms are used.

9.3 VALIDATION

A knowledge base may be logically correct without being valid. Validation has to do with how well a model or a measurement conforms to what has been modeled or measured. Thus, validation has to do with something outside the system itself – that the symbolic expressions in the system are true representations of reality.

Three types of faults may be encountered in the validation process:

(1) *Factual* faults: An assertion does not correctly represent the fact (a property of the object studied).
(2) *Inferential* faults: A rule does not correctly represent the domain knowledge. The result is that incorrect conclusions are drawn by the system.
(3) *Control* faults: The rules are correct, but have undesirable control behavior.

The validation procedure is a three-step procedure:

(1) run the program on problems;
(2) identify faults;
(3) modify the program (rules and control strategies).

In the following, we shall first discuss validity more generally, and then describe two specific approaches to expert systems validation.

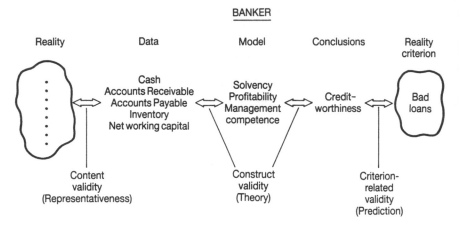

Figure 9.6   *Validity types*

9.3.1   Validity

Validity refers to relevance, meaningfulness, and correctness. A theory is valid if it is relevant and meaningful and the inferences are correctly derived from premises. A measurement is valid if it correctly measures the right property of the object. Measuring certain physical properties of objects, for instance, weight, length, or temperature, validation is no great problem. However, moving to more abstract entities like intelligence and school achievements, validation becomes more problematic. Firstly, intelligence is not directly measurable. Only through tests can we obtain a measure of intelligence. The question then arises whether the tests performed really measure intelligence. Secondly, having a measure of intelligence, is that measure a good prediction of school achievement?

As we can see, there are several kinds of validity. We shall look at three types: content, construct and criterion related. In discussing these validity types we shall draw on the theory and methods of behavioral research as described in Kerlinger (1973). To explain some of these concepts let us again return to BANKER. Figure 9.6 shows validation points related to BANKER.

Content Validity

This is the representativeness or sampling adequacy of the content – the substance, the matter and the topics – of a measuring instrument (Kerlinger, 1973, p. 458). One may ask: Does this item measure what it is supposed to measure? Another term for this concept is *face* validity. According to Kerlinger, content validation is basically judgmental. Each item must be judged for its presumed relevance to the property being measured. For instance, if net working capital is defined as an indicator, do we really measure net working capital by taking the difference of current assets and short-term liabilities from the financial statements? Content validity as it is used here, therefore, is related to data input validity.

Construct Validity

This refers to the validation of the theory behind the test (Kerlinger, 1973, p. 461). Applied to knowledge-based systems, construct validity refers to the validity of the models: the knowledge base, the reasoning strategies and the analytical relationships. For instance, are net working capital, acid ratios, and current ratios elements that will explain solvency; and are solvency, profitability, and management competence, constructs or factors that will explain creditworthiness?

A significant point about construct validity is its preoccupation with theory, theoretical constructs, and scientific empirical inquiry involving the testing of hypothesized relations (Kerlinger, 1973, p. 461). Construct validation is dependent on the way a knowledge-based system is built. If the models are built around hypothesized relationships, each relationship can be validated. If the system is built from verbal protocols, that is, we establish a theory of problem solving, then construct validation can be done by the expert's inspection (judgment) of the constructs established. One way of doing this is by a rule trace approach. Here, the system is run on a specific problem. The system behavior is traced as rules are tried, rejected, or fired. The rule trace approach is treated in more detail in Section 9.3.2.

Criterion-related Validity

This is studied by comparing test or scale scores with one or more external variables, or criteria, known or believed to measure the attribute under study (Kerlinger, 1973, p. 459). Criterion-related validity is concerned with the predictive ability of the system. When we establish a creditworthiness measure in BANKER we do this to predict the credit taker's ability to service the credit (loan) taken. One external variable, or criterion, to use is 'bad loans', that is, loans where the terms of the loans (interests and instalments) are not fulfilled according to the contract. By measuring, *ex post*, a series of loans, we can validate the predictive ability of BANKER. Criterion-related validation can be performed empirically by measuring the system's success in predicting a criterion. Statistics on overall performance (correct and incorrect conclusions) as well as on individual rules are collected. To measure the overall performance may be easy, but to identify the right and wrong behavior of individual rules is difficult. We shall look at empirical approaches to criterion-related validation in Section 9.3.3.

9.3.2   Rule Traces

Running the rules on a problem causes a search tree to be developed. The rule trace is the path through this tree. It is an account of rules that have been tried, those which did not succeed and which did. A rule trace by PC OPTRANS has been shown in Figure 5.4 above. Two types of rule trace analysis can be done: the intuitive and the analytical. In the intuitive approach a rule trace is presented to the expert who will comment on the conclusions and the reasoning. There is no explicit external reference to which the system's performance can be compared. That reference is in the expert's head. There are no systematic and controlled ways of correcting identified faults. One can only hope that changes in the program will not create significant errors in other cases, cases that may have been handled well on a previous occasion.

It is possible to perform a more formal analysis of rule traces. In the AI field, several learning programs have been developed that are based on rule traces. These programs use a more precise conceptual framework and more formal procedures to identify and correct faults. One critical point in a formal analysis is to determine which rules *should* have fired, and in what sequence. An account of this is called the *ideal trace*. Some of the learning programs take the ideal trace as input, others work it out by analysis using problem solving and inference techniques. The ideal trace is compared with the actual trace of the rules, the rule trace, to locate the first point at which the traces differ. If the actual trace differs from the ideal trace it is because the rule that fired in the actual trace, R_t, differs from that in the ideal trace, R_i. Two types of instances may occur:

(1) R_t fired incorrectly because it was insufficiently constrained (this is called an error of commission (Bundy *et al.*, 1985)).
(2) R_i was missing or R_i failed to fire because it was incorrectly constrained (this is called an error of omission (Bundy *et al.*, 1985)).

It is sufficient to concentrate on errors of commission. Correcting these errors will eventually correct errors of omission. When an error of commission is corrected, R_t no longer fires. If another rule, R_t', now causes an error of commission, this will be corrected. Eventually, R_i must be the most preferred rule (if it exists).

There are several modification techniques associated with rule trace comparisons:

● reordering of rules to correct control faults;

- adding extra conditions to the antecedent of a rule (also called specialization or discrimination);
- concept learning techniques.

A further treatment is beyond the scope of this book. For further details the reader is referred to Bundy *et al.* (1985).

9.3.3 Empirical Performance Validation

The second approach to system validation is to test the predictive ability of the system by comparing its conclusions with one or more external variables, or criteria. One external variable to use is an expert's conclusions for a set of test cases and test, empirically, how well the system's conclusions match with these.

The critical point in the rule trace approach is to have something with which the rule trace can be compared, for instance, an ideal trace. Here, the critical point is to have enough *representative* coverage for validation. In some domains, it may be possible to gather large numbers of cases for typical decision outcomes, but rare decisions always present a problem. In other domains, for instance, geological exploration, each case is more or less unique, or the cost of obtaining sample cases is very high. In PROSPECTOR, for instance, special validation techniques were used which were based on sensitivity analysis procedures.

A second critical point in this approach is that the conclusions must be precise for accurate and useful comparisons. A conclusion drawn by the system must be classified as either correct or incorrect. The credit evaluation model, BANKER, lends itself to this type of analysis. On the other hand, the financial adviser SAFIR produces a narrative output (see Figure 7.5) which is composed of several statements that are applicable to conclusions of the case. This narrative output may be difficult to force into a precise conclusion that lends itself to an accurate comparison with an expert's unconstrained narrative statements. For SAFIR, the system was validated by letting the expert inspect the system's conclusions and rule trace. Judgment substitutes statistical performance analysis.

In describing the process of empirical performance validation we shall draw on Weiss and Kulikowski (1984). The process of performance validation is described as iterations through the following steps:

(1) obtain the performance of rules on a set of stored cases;
(2) analyze the rules;
(3) revise the rules.

The first step is to produce a performance summary for all stored cases. There are several cases giving the same conclusions. Measuring the number of cases where the model's conclusions match with that of the expert, gives a performance measure called *true positive*. On the other hand, the model may also falsely infer a conclusion. This performance measure is called *false positive*. Table 9.1 shows a performance summary taken over a set of five types of diagnosis in the domain of rheumatology (taken from Weiss and Kulikowski, 1984).

Table 9.1 shows that for the diagnosis 'mixed connective tissue disease', 9 cases out of 33 were correctly diagnosed (true positives) and that no cases were misdiagnosed by the model as 'mixed connective tissue disease' (false positives). For the diagnosis 'rheumatoid arthritis', the model performs quite well (100% positive). However, there are 10 misdiagnosed cases.

This indicates that, with respect to the first diagnosis, the rules are not picking up the disease nearly as well as one would like. The antecedents should be weakened, that is, some conditions may be too strong. Weakening the antecedent conditions is called *generalization*. With respect to the second diagnosis, the opposite seems to be the situation. Here the model 'over' diagnoses this disease, 52 cases, of which 42 are correct and 10 are wrong. This calls for strengthening of the antecedent conditions of one or more rules of the inference chains leading to that diagnosis. This is called *specialization* and makes a rule's conditions more difficult to satisfy and, therefore, to execute.

In addition to the results shown above, statistics are gathered about each specific rule as shown in the example below (from Weiss and Kulikowski):

Rule 72:
43 cases: in which this rule was satisfied.
13 cases: in which the greatest certainty in a conclusion was obtained by this rule and it matched the expert's conclusion.
7 cases: in which the greatest certainty in a conclusion was obtained by this rule and it did not match the expert's conclusion.

After performance analysis, the revision of rules, also called rule refinement, is carried out. This is a process of generalizing or specializing rules.

Table 9.1 *A performance study. (Reproduced from Weiss, S. M. and Kulikowski, C. A.* A Practical Guide to Designing Expert Systems)

	True positives		False positives	
Mixed connective tissue disease	9/33	(27%)	0	(0%)
Rheumatoid arthritis	42/42	(100%)	10	(13%)
Systemic lupus erythematosus	12/18	(67%)	4	(0.4%)
Progressive systemic sclerosis	22/23	(96%)	5	(0.4%)
Polymyositis	4/5	(80%)	1	(0.1%)
Total	89/121	(74%)		

Take a situation where the system arrives at a conclusion C_s and the expert concludes with C_e. Rules leading to the conclusion C_s must have been wrongly fired (errors of commission according to Bundy *et al.* (1985)), or rules which could have led to conclusion C_e can have been incorrectly constrained (errors of omission), thus missing execution. In contrast to the approach described in Bundy *et al.* (1985), where one concentrates on errors of commission, Weiss and Kulikowski (1984) advocate a combination of the two. Errors of commission can be corrected by specialization, that is, adding constraints to the antecedents of the rules, thus limiting the situations in which it will be fired. At the same time, rules leading to the correct conclusion, C_e, could be generalized, thus being less restrictive. This is, in principle, how rule refinements are done. However, if the system now succeeds in drawing the correct conclusion for a set of cases leading to one particular conclusion, what will be the effect on other conclusions or diagnoses using parts of the same inference chains? By generalizing a rule we may increase the target ratio, that is, the number of correctly concluded cases. However, there is also a potential risk of increasing the number of misconcluded cases. On the other hand, specialization may reduce the number of misconcluded cases, but at the potential risk of reducing the target ratio.

How do we find the right rules for revision? There is no simple answer to this question. Solutions can only be found by performing experiments that incorporate changes into the rule set, and then test the modified rules on the stored cases. A system called SEEK (Politakis, 1985) has been developed to generate suggestions for specific experiments for rule refinements.

9.4 PERFORMANCE EVALUATION

9.4.1 Aspects of Evaluation

In this section, we shall look at aspects (measures) by which we can evaluate the functionality of a KB-DSS. Our ultimate goal is to improve decision making by means of a computer system – a KB-DSS. Evaluation requires an external reference to which the system can be compared. However, we have already described the difficulties in establishing such a reference for a DSS because of the evolutionary nature of these systems, the ill-structuredness of the tasks that they are applied to, and the individual decision making behavior that guides the use of these systems. Instead of being a well-defined goal, this reference point becomes a moving target. Therefore, we present categories of aspects or criteria; no one criterion is likely to be sufficient to evaluate a KB-DSS. We shall follow the categories that were presented in Figure 9.3.

- system performance,
- task performance aspects,
- business opportunities,
- evolutionary aspects.

System Performance

We can define several measures to evaluate the quality of a computer system. These include response time, availability, reliability, data entry, dialog, usage time, users, and quality of system support (documentation, training and so on). The quality of system performance is of particular importance to the acceptance of the computer program by the users. Measures on system performance can be obtained by observations, event logging, and attitude surveys (these methods are briefly described in Section 9.4.2 below).

Task Performance Aspects

These aspects are concerned with the functionality of the computer program in relation to performing the task at hand – the decision. The ideal measure for evaluating a KB-DSS that is aimed at improving decision making is the actual outcome of a decision. In an uncertain world, it is important to distinguish between decisions and outcomes. A good decision does not necessarily lead to a good outcome. The quality of a decision depends on the correctness of the actions taken by the decision maker, given information about the world. Task performance is, therefore, measured by the quality of the decision more than the quality of the outcome. Quality of decision and decision making can be measured in terms of time spent to make a decision, alternatives evaluated, and information searched. Also, some qualitative measures can be done, such as trust (confidence), satisfaction, understanding and so on.

Business Opportunities

A decision implies committing resources. The amount of resources can be measured in terms of costs, and the effects of the commitment in terms of added values: added income, reduced costs and so on. However, a KB-DSS may also lead to organizational changes, more cost-effective training, and competitive advantages. In Chapter 5 we discussed the business opportunities of expert systems in terms of cost reduction: distribution of expertise, increased productivity and so on, and also in terms of added values: better customer services, new products, competitive advantages and training.

Methods that can be used to measure business opportunities are cost/benefit analysis and value analysis.

Evolutionary Aspects

A requirement of a computer program that supports decision making in ill-structured tasks is the way that it adapts to changes in environmental factors, problem characteristics, and decision making behavior due to learning and so on. How well the system can adapt to these changes is dependent on the kind of software tool used, the availability of a system builder (knowledge engineer), and the user's own capability to make changes to the system (add data, develop models, and so on).

These measures are more qualitative than quantitative, and evaluation is, primarily, done by judgment.

9.4.2 Methods

Sprague and Carlson (1982) present seven methods that can be used to measure and evaluate the impact of a DSS. We shall briefly describe each method here. These methods are not only general with respect to the kind of information system they apply to, but also general with respect to the particular aspects that one wants to evaluate. The following briefly describes each method. They are not mutually exclusive but can be used in combination to provide a comprehensive evaluation of the system.

Event Logging

In event logging, events that might indicate KB-DSS impacts are recorded. An example is keeping a log of bad loans before and after implementation of a loan evaluation system. This is an example of a before/after evaluation. Here, care has to be taken that other external variables have not changed significantly during the measuring period. Also, the system can be evaluated on a continuous basis. For instance, which events trigger the use of the system: periodical review of loans, seeking lending opportunities, environmental events and so on? Event logging is an uninstructed method without a well-defined set of techniques. Judgment is required in selecting the events to be recorded.

Attitude Surveys

These are used to evaluate behavioral aspects, in particular, factors that have a positive or negative influence on a person's attitude towards a system. There is a huge amount of literature about users' attitudes (summarized in Christensen (1987)). Some examples of attitude indicators are:

- effect on job performance;
- perceived usefulness;
- motivation for use;
- expectations and so on.

Attitude surveys are performed by using questionnaires and interviews.

Cognitive Testing

Cognitive testing is a repertoire of methods to analyze the cognitive processes of decision makers that were developed by cognitive and social psychologists. They range from traces of decision processes to structured conceptual analysis. More specifically, we have verbal protocols, interviews, the repertory grid technique (see also the knowledge acquisition techniques in Section 7.4.3), and others.

Rating and Weighing

This is a structured method for a composite numerical evaluation. The method involves developing a set of parameters which are rated according to a given scale and weighted in terms of relative importance. However, care must be taken by the evaluator not to compute a single score by summing up the products of ratings and weights. This measure is undefined theoretically. Only when one system dominates another, that is, the ratings on all parameters are better for one system than the others, do the scores give an indisputable answer.

System Measurements

Such measurements attempt to quantify effects through measurements of performance of the task (decision making and problem solving) or of the technical system (response time and so on). The measurements may be collected automatically by the system, through questionnaires, interviews, or observations, or extracted from documents. This method of evaluation is usually made on a before/after basis. Statistical techniques may be used to analyze the data that has been collected.

Cost/benefit Analysis

This produces evaluations in economical and financial terms. Cost/benefit analysis is used more in feasibility studies (in advance) than in retrospective auditing. Care should be taken to include only those costs that are necessary to create the benefits that are measured. Cost/benefit analysis is only useful when you have clearly measurable benefits, that is, the primary objective of the system is increased efficiency. If the objective is improved effectiveness of decision making and problem solving, other methods, for instance, value analysis, should be used.

Value Analysis

This has been proposed by Keen (1981). The approach is similar to cost/benefit analysis with three important differences. Firstly, the emphasis is primarily on benefits and puts cost second. Secondly, the method attempts to reduce risk by requiring that prototyping obtains evaluation data. Thirdly, the method puts emphasis on innovative aspects more than return on investment measurements. Value analysis seems very close to the intuitive approach that many managers use to evaluate a support system.

Exercises

9.1 In the text we have made a distinction between correctness and functionality, and validation and evaluation. Discuss these concepts in relation to each other.

9.2 Explain the two concepts validation and verification. How is verification related to validation?

9.3 Describe three types of validity. How is each validity type relevant for expert systems testing?

9.4 Why is evaluation of system performance at the end of a qualitative assessment?

9.5 Given the following rule set:

(1) IF A OR B THEN D
(2) IF A THEN E
(3) IF E THEN D
(4) IF D OR E THEN B

What types of consistency problems do we encounter in this rule set?

9.6   How can you check a knowledge base for completeness?

9.7   Given the following rule:

IF return on investment is better than marginal
AND profit margin is less or equal to marginal
AND average interest rate paid on debts is between 10% and 14%
THEN profitability is marginal.

Show how this rule can be generalized and specialized respectively. What is the purpose of generalizing and specializing the rules of a knowledge base?

9.8   Discuss why a cost/benefit analysis is difficult in DSS evaluation. What kind of analysis is better for evaluating business opportunities of a DSS. Does expert system evaluation exhibit the same problems as DSS evaluation? Discuss.

9.9   Using either BANKER from Chapter 5 or FINSIM (Klein, 1989), develop a detailed plan for testing and evaluation of the system, showing which aspects should be tested and evaluated, and which methods you propose to use for the various aspects you plan to test and evaluate.

10
Knowledge-based Decision Support Systems Applications in Business

10.1 INTRODUCTION

This chapter surveys the application of knowledge-based systems to problem areas in finance and marketing. The area of finance is one of the most advanced in the use of the knowledge technology. Most problems in finance are well structured but many normative models are not in frequent practical use due to the complexity of the decision environment in which practical decision making is performed. We need prescriptive methods that are based on normative theories as well as practical judgment. This is exactly what knowledge-based systems can do.

This survey is, by no means, comprehensive. One of the major difficulties in surveying financial applications is the secrecy surrounding them. There are two reasons for this. Firstly, financial institutions do not have a tradition for research and development in technological areas. Therefore, there may be some reluctance to speak about things that are still only at an experimental stage, that is, prototypes. But even successfully-operating systems have been kept secret. The explanation for this may be that this technology is seen as a competitive tool – therefore, they want to conserve this advantage as long as possible. This, however, has changed. Since some banks are now using this technology to build an image of a progressive bank in their marketing efforts, other banks do not want to lag behind. Also, since knowledge-based systems are now appearing in the main offices, it is difficult to hide these systems from the competitors.

The sources of this survey are articles and books on expert systems as well as our own experience. These sources narrow the applications to a few well-known references appearing frequently in trade journals, as well as at fairs and conferences. In systematizing the information on applications we can use different classification schemes. We can list financial functions by objects:

- private individuals,
- corporations,
- banks and financial institutions;

For banks we can make a classification according to types of activities:

- front office,
- back office,
- services.

And for the financial industry we can make a classification according to the market served:

- retail banking,
- wholesale banking,
- merchant banking,
- securities.

Now, since financial institutions very often span more than one market, and since functions very often span more than one type of activity, we shall use a classification scheme where we differentiate among objects only, and, within each object, list the financial functions that have to be performed. Within corporations, in particular, larger ones, one may find the corporate treasurer or the accountants performing activities which are typical banking activities. These corporate activities are described under the heading of banking functions.

Corporate finance	Financial planning
	Capital budgeting
	Cash management
	Client credit analysis
	Tax planning
	Financial marketing

Personal finance	Financial planning
	Taxation
	Retirement planning
	Real estate
Banks and financial	Company credit assessment
institutions	Personal loans
	Financial advice
	Assets management
	● Assets evaluation
	● Portfolio management
	Trading
	Bank management
	● Assets and liability
	● Planning and control
	● Compliance and security
	● Branch performance analysis
	Tax regulations

10.2 CORPORATE FINANCE

Corporate finance is concerned with evaluating future potential risks and return on investments. The basic tool for this evaluation is the financial statements. All of the firm's investments and strategies, its successes and failures, are reflected in the financial statements.

Three main categories of financial decisions have given rise to DSS and KB-DSS applications:

(1) choice of investment;
(2) cash management;
(3) financial planning and financial engineering.

We shall also add a special section on financial marketing under this heading, since we have seen some interesting developments of the knowledge-based technology to this problem.

10.2.1 Choice of Investment

The first important class of decisions deals with managing the portfolio of assets of a company (investment/disinvestment). These decisions are fundamental since they explain the growth and future profitability. They contribute to the progressive development of shareholders' wealth. Such decisions require a rigorous methodology. Most financial managers admit that an acceptable investment is one which will increase shareholders' wealth. This wealth is measured by the Net Present Value (NPV) criterion.

There are a number of different ways to assess the return and to rank the relative value of investments. Normally, we will take into account the time value of money by *discounting*, that is, more value is given to money today than tomorrow. The Net Present Value (NPV) and the Internal Rate of Return (IRR) are two frequently-used techniques that take all cash flows into consideration. These methods, however, are numeric (and usually deterministic). The variables (cash flows) that go into the calculations are single values. Over- or under-estimated values result in lower or higher returns.

A DSS is well adapted to this kind of task, since it will save processing time. Thus, the decision maker will have more time to study alternative hypotheses, and to test how sensitive the NPV is to changes in some of the basic assumptions, such as the stream of cash flows and the discount rate. The choice of discount rate requires experiential knowledge. Introducing knowledge bases is, therefore, particularly helpful here. Several systems of the DSS type have been described in the literature, for instance, Raphael *et al.* (1979). More recently, knowledge-based extensions of these systems have started to appear (see, for instance, Mockler, 1989).

Not many expert systems have been reported for capital budgeting. However, in a recent article Myers (1988) reports on a system for capital budgeting programmed in LISP which runs on a Symbolics computer. The system's basic valuation tool is DCF (Discounted Cash Flow). The knowledge-based part of the system is related to three areas: problem setup and forecasting, interpreting results, and circling back. Forecasting cash flows requires a model of the project. In developing this model, knowledge and insight is required to recognize omitted factors, to cut out unimportant detail, to flush out inconsistent or unlikely assumptions, and to handle important but tricky details, such as the interaction between inflation and taxation. Interpreting results means to give qualitative statements on the basis of numeric values. Sometimes it amounts to highlighting variables or assumptions crucial to the success of the project. Results from complicated numeric calculations, such as option-pricing applications, may need deeper explanations. Finally, circling back is necessary because major decisions are rarely made in one pass. In expert hands, experimentation often generates important surprises.

When the cash flows, NPV, and IRR are calculated, the system enters into a valuation mode. Here are some of the functions available in this mode: explanation of the NPV method; impact on book earnings; and suggestions for further analysis where the following subchoices are available: analyzing the margin for error; analyzing the use of the project; valuing flexibility; and finally, analyzing the competitors' impact. The knowledge base contains rules that may be executed when one of the above functions is activated. For instance, there is a set of rules for ranking variables on their importance to project NPV. The system then reports critical values for the most imporant variables. The rules for identifying important variables are built up from common sense. A very simple example is: 'If NPV is negative, and is still negative when Sales General & Administrative (S, G & A) cost is set to zero, eliminate S, G & A cost from the sensitivity analysis'. This expert system builds a bridge between business knowledge on one side, and the numeric DCF calculations on the other. This is a system that helps and advises, as well as computes. Consequently, the system has knowledge about appropriate relationships to carry out consistency checks and to explain what it does. Furthermore, the system is taught to acquire information about basic economics of the user's business, and to feed that information back into the DCF calculations.

Another system of a similar kind is the *Financial Advisor* developed by Palladian Inc. The system helps managers make capital investment decisions using a wide range of financial techniques, and explains how it arrives at each step in an analysis. Like expert consultants, the system tests every input assumption and conclusion against an extensive knowledge of general business practices, such as the user's company policies, its accounting and management practices, its historical performance, and its competition (according to Turban (1990)).

10.2.2 Cash Management

With the rise of interest rates, cash management has received increased attention. Companies have seen their financial costs climbing and their profits declining accordingly. As a consequence, financial managers have pushed to keep a closer look at the flow of funds derived from day-to-day transactions. The management of operation dates and value dates was one of the first consequences of this closer monitoring. The option of using overdrafts or discounting letters of credit was addressed.

DSS have been developed to support stimulation of interest rates and hypotheses on cash flows. KB-DSS have appeared with new functions to suggest decisions on investments of surplus cash in various financial instruments, or disinvestment from the same. The importance of the cash management function has further increased with trading in foreign currencies, and with a treasurer who is working at a corporate level and not only at a single-entity level.

10.2.3   Financial Planning and Financial Engineering

An important acitivity in corporate finance is financial planning and financial engineering, a determination of the best financing strategy, and, hence, the best capital structure for a firm. Financial planning is concerned with forecasting and projections of the information in the financial statements. Thus, financial statement analysis is an important part of this activity. Financial statement analysis, also called financial diagnosis in the expert system's terminology, is a study of relationships within a set of financial statements at a specific point in time and with trends in these relationships over time. Financial statement analysis starts with a computation of a set of financial ratios, followed by an individual evaluation of each ratio value at a particular point in time, an evaluation of time series of a particular ratio in order to look for trends, and, sometimes cross-sectional evaluations to compare with industry ratios. When this information is combined, more can be learnt about the firm's key performance characteristics such as profitability, financial leverage, financial structure and liquidity. To perform financial planning requires a combination of computing and reasoning. Computations are performed on financial statements to calculate ratios, and analytical models are used to forecast cash positions. Many decision support systems have been developed to perform these tasks. Interactive computing facilities allow for fast responses on the consequences of alternative decision values (what-if and goal seeking).

However, in order to evaluate the meaning of the data produced by these systems and to act adequately on the information that they give, knowledge is needed, knowledge that experienced financial analysts (the experts) use in their practical performance of this task. This knowledge is not available in ordinary textbooks on corporate finance. It is, however, a target for knowledge acquisition and expert systems in corporate finance.

The class of financial tasks addressed can be broken down into a set of financial decisions:

(1) *Choice of debt/equity ratio*. In financing new investments, the financial manager must decide what percentage of the requirements should be financed with debt versus equity.
(2) *Choice of retained earnings*. How great are the funds that are available from the firm's own operations.
(3) *Choice of financial structure* (equity, debts, leasing, convertibles and so on).

These decisions, which, although presented above as separate entities, are in fact interlinked. For example, if a financial manager looks at self-financing as an investment, this will reduce the funds available to provide dividends to shareholders. DSS have been designed to support such decisions for a long time, and optimization models using modern financial concepts to integrate the investment, dividend and financing decisions, have been implemented in a DSS (Carleton, 1970a).

Many knowledge-based systems exist to perform financial planning and to support the task of evaluating a financial strategy of a company. Some of these systems are made for parties outside of the company being studied who may want to make financial evaluation of the company for various reasons. These parties include shareholders, investors and security analysts; lenders and other suppliers; customers; and government/regulatory agencies. We have already described two knowlege-based systems which can support financial diagnosis and financial planning: FINSIM and SAFIR.

In the USA, Arthur Andersen & Co. has developed a prototype called FSA – the Financial Statement Analyser – for the US Securities and Exchange Commission (SEC) in connection with its EDGAR system. EDGAR is a system that electronically receives SEC filings directly from filing companies. FSA analyses the type of financial information contained in EDGAR's filings. The purpose of FSA is to perform consistent financial analysis, despite differences among individual statements. FSA reads the relevant financial tables and footnotes of companies. The system understands a variety of captions and textual notes. It then presents the results of ratio calculations. Ratio calculations are only the first step in automating financial analysis. Once the ratios have been calculated, the results are analyzed. A combination of expert system techniques and statistical techniques is used to highlight situations such as:

- companies with ratios significantly higher or lower than average;
- companies with significant increases or decreases in the value of a ratio over a period of years;
- companies with unusual balances in particular accounts;
- companies with no line items for particular accounts.

FSA is developed in KEE and runs on a Symbolics LISP machine. Further details about the system can be found in Mui and McCarthy (1987).

Price Waterhouse has developed a knowledge based DSS called the Business Analyser. The goal of this system is to find anomalies in financial results and compute explanation for them (Hamscher, 1994).

Financial planning systems and financial analysis systems are one of the most developed areas of applications of the KB-DSS technology. Corporate financial managers need tools which enable them, not only to control the past, but also, to simulate future consequences of possible alternatives, in terms of amount and types of financing, taking into account variables such as activity level, operating expenses, amount of investment and so on. Such systems can provide the user with advice and computations. An interesting system of this kind is described in Buisine (1987).

10.2.4   Financial Marketing

Financial marketing is a term used to characterize the financial decision processes used in the marketing of products and services of such a large scale that they can have a significant impact on the customer's financial status. A customer interested in buying a high-value product is usually concerned that the financial plan being used to acquire the product is safe, and is attractive from a financial investment point of view. In such cases, financial considerations become an important part of the buying decision.

In two articles, a system called FAME (Financial Marketing Expertise) developed at IBM's Thomas J. Watson Research Center has been described (Kastner *et al*. (1986) and Mays *et al*. (1987)). FAME is an expert system that generates a financial plan. In this respect, it is different from the systems described above which are diagnostic in nature. The system employs a heuristically-guided generate-and-test problem solving procedure for *designing* an acceptable financial plan. The original prototype system consisted of over 700 OPS 5 rules. More recently, an object-oriented knowledge representation technique has been incorporated into the system.

10.3   PERSONAL FINANCIAL PLANNING

In the last decade, the financial environment has undergone tremendous changes in most countries. Deregulation of the financial industry has led to an increase in the number of performers in the market-place, and a growth in number and complexity of financial products. Also, the consumer power of people has increased, resulting in a sophisticated market-place of both the supply and demand of financial services and products.

Financial services are now provided by a multitude of financial institutions and consultant firms. Banks, for instance, have established selling places for these services, sometimes called financial supermarkets. A financial supermarket is a concept that brings together normal banking services, and services traditionally handled by other specialist institutions, with barriers to entry largely created by official regulations. Such services usually include stocks and shares brokerage, insurance, real estate finance, and brokerage services.

In this new and more complex environment, the need for counseling and guidance is also evolving. Individuals need advice on how to manage their personal income and assets. They need financial plans covering areas such as cash management, investment, credits, tax planning, retirement, real estate planning, and insurance. Good financial plans provide coordinated recommendations covering actions to be taken in these areas over time. Providing personal financial plans is a service either charged directly, or is used as a means for promoting other products.

To provide a comprehensive personal financial plan requires expert knowledge in a multitude of domains, such as investment, cash management, taxation, inheritance laws, retirement planning, insurance, real estate assets management and so on. A financial service center can either be composed of experts from different fields to whom the client can be moved, or a financial consultant can use a support system with knowledge bases of different kinds. Systems which offer advice on financial planning have been a target for expert system developers for a long time. Such a system needs certain data on the client such as age, financial status, his or her needs at various stages of the life cycle, risk profile and so on. Such a system should be able to collect data from various sources such as public wire services or company-specific files. The output is a plan providing coordinated recommendations covering actions to be taken in different areas. It should also provide an explanation of the plan, why particular actions have been selected, and how they meet the client's objectives.

Arthur D. Little has developed the Personal Financial Planning System and the Investment Manager's Assistant. The first is designed to provide personal financial plans for people with incomes between $20 000 and $70 000. It is written in LISP and runs in a Symbolics 3600 machine in batch mode, with connections to databases on an IBM mainframe (Guilfoyle and Jeffcoate, 1988). Another well-known product in this category is Plan Power provided by Applied Expert Systems (APEX). This system provides the client with a comprehensive financial plan ranging from 20 to 120 pages, plus up to 40 tabular and graphic data exhibits. The system also creates an after-planning case representing the client's situation after all recommendations have been simulated on a XEROX LISP machine (see Stansfield and Greenfeld (1987) for more details).

10.4   BANKS AND FINANCIAL INSTITUTIONS

10.4.1   Credit Assessment

Credit may be obtained in a variety of different forms, covering consumer and business lending, as well as credit cards and leasing. Many types of credit are available. Here are a few examples:

- personal loan (secured or unsecured);
- banks' overdraft facilities;
- corporate loans;
- credit card and credit card applications.

As we can understand from the list, some of the demands are high-volume, small-ticket transactions such as credit card applications, while other types of credit may be demanded far less frequently. This will affect methods for credit assessment. Credit assessment involves predicting a client's or a corporation's ability to service the debt taken on. This includes questions about solvency and profitability. Credit assessment means establishing credit-worthiness and repayment conditions on the basis of information about the client that is known at this moment, and predicting from this and other, more general, economic and market indicators, the future capability of the client to repay the debt.

The need for credit assessment has increased tremendously in the last decade or two, due to the deregulation in the financial sector in many countries. The supply and demand for credit has grown tremendously. Altogether, this has led to a level of credit in society which is higher than ever before. The ease with which credit has been made available has also led to over-consumption – people take on more credit than they can cope with. In many countries, credit institutions suffer from defaulters – people or companies who cannot fulfill their commitments. Bankruptcy is often the result, with heavy losses for the credit giver. Bad loans have been a real burden on the income statements of many commercial banks. Therefore, better procedures and better techniques for credit assessment are needed, and many developers of expert systems have seen a market for applications in this domain.

Obviously credit assessment is needed at the time credit is asked for. However, credit assessment may also be pertinent in other situations as well. Screening the credit market for low-risk credit clients is one important task of most credit institutions. Searching actively for credit clients may involve running through computer files, for instance, on companies' annual financial statements, to find prospective borrowers. In this screening process, an expert system can greatly enhance the efficiency.

Also, credit institutions need to monitor continuously their credit clients. This can be done periodically, or for particular purposes when information on key variables change. For instance, changes in interest rates or new tax regulations that affect net income, may lead to problems for the credit clients. To sum up, credit assessment is needed:

- at the time of credit giving;
- in searching and screening for new clients;
- in monitoring clients' abilities to service the credit;
- in predicting clients' problems to meet their commitments due to environmental changes in key variables, for instance, interest rate.

Corporate Loans

In the USA several systems for corporate loans have been described and we can cite the MARBLE system (Shaw and Gentry, 1988). Interestingly, the MARBLE system is akin to the heuristic method used by Cohen *et al.* (1966) as is BANKER which was described in Chapter 5. The authors also consider production rules as a good way to represent knowledge in financial analysis which was also our experience with FINSIM and SAFIR. An interesting feature of MARBLE is its knowledge acquisition and learning module. The inductive learning algorithm is used to classify the companies into different risk classes. The output of the algorithm is a set of decision rules to classify a company into a given risk class.

The two types of business lending mainly offered by commercial banks are overdraft lending and term lending. Overdraft lending is designed to meet short-term working capital fluctuations. Term loans are usually unsecured and run for a period of three to ten years, depending on the situation. Credit assessment for overdrafts requires the analysis of the current position of the company, while for term loans the analysis of future positions is required.

In Section 5.10 we described an expert system, BANKER, for credit evaluation. Credit evaluation of corporate loans involves:

- financial analysis;
- management evaluation;
- market potential of the corporation;
- general economic outlook;
- benefits for the credit institution.

Financial analysis involves analysis on historical and forecasted data where the credit has been included (pro forma financial statements).

Originally, human experts assessed credit applications using a *judgmental* method based on their own experience (heuristics) and guidelines provided by the credit institution. Carter and Cartlett (1987) have described the following drawbacks of a judgmental method.

- poor performance,
- inflexibility,
- inconsistency,
- low efficiency.

Another method, credit scoring, is one of the widely-used assessment methods.

Do knowledge-based systems perform well in this domain? It is a domain which has attracted a lot of interest in the expert system field, and many systems exist to support credit assessment in part, or as a whole. The journal *Financial Management* has a special issue (Autumn 1988) that is devoted to financial applications of expert systems. Three of the articles in this issue describe loan evaluation systems (Duchessi *et al.* (1988), Shaw and Gentry (1988) and Srinivasan and Kim (1988)).

In Chapter 5, we described the loan evaluation system BANKER in detail. BANKER classifies a corporate loan applicant's creditworthiness. But many systems have been developed for financial analysis, as we have already seen in Section 5.10.2, that can assist a credit assessor. This is also an area in which many banks have been busy. Many prototypes exist and a few systems are in operation.

In France, knowledge-based systems for company loan evaluation offered by specialized software and consulting companies are competing aggressively on the banking industry market. Due to the deregulation of financial markets, certain bank networks such as the 'Caisses d'Epargne', which, previously, were not allowed to grant loans to companies, can now do so. Because of lack of expertise, they consider expert systems to be a way to save time in the education of their employees, and, also, to make the best use of experts that they had to hire at a very high cost from competing banks.

Many banks are using such systems now on a regular basis: Crédit Agricole de Toulouse since 1987, Crédit Agricole of la Brie since 1988 and Crédit Agricole of Midi since 1989. A market for financial analysis knowledge bases has now developed around products such as FINSIM. FINSIM is now in use in more than 50 financial institutions. Also, industry-specific loan evaluation systems have now appeared on the market.

Countries in transition to a market economy are using KB-DSS technology to help their banks allocate loans more efficiently to companies and educate their credit analysts. This is the case in Slovenia where the FINBON system from the company ISPO is used by several Slovenian banks.

Professional Loans

Knowledge-based systems have also been developed for the professional market. An interesting and successful system is the SEXTAN system developed for the bank 'Crédit Agricole' by the French Company SIG to evaluate short- and long-term loans for farmers. The system has been used by about twenty 'Caisses régionales' of the Crédit Agricole for several years. This system is similar to FINSIM but uses for the historical analysis the accounting information coming from either the tax forms or the organizations in charge of dealing with the processing of the farmers' accounting information. As a result of agreements with the farmers' accounting organizations these French regional banks have constituted financial databases which are update with the farmers' accounting data and the banking data. The SEXTAN knowledge-based DSS has the same functionalities as FINSIM but several specialized functions have been added as well as the description of the type of production carried out by the farm (grapes, cereals, cattle raising, etc.);

- the system can access a specialized database of land prices or wine prices (for the farmers with vineyards);
- a knowledge base to decide on the residual long- and short-term loans which can be granted;
- the possibility to describe the private loan and assets which the farmer has obtained and which have to be consolidated with the other loans to obtain a more accurate picture of the financial and economic situation of the farm.

Two knowledge bases are used in this application. One gives a financial diagnosis of the farm. The second mixed with models provides a complete proposal in terms of short- and long-term loans as well as investment advice in case of available cash.

Credit Card Authorization

American Express has developed the expert system Authorizer's Assistant in collaboration with Inference Corp, the supplier of the expert system development tool ART. This system supports the authorizer in making decisions on charges to a card holder's account.

At American Express they have a policy of not placing a limit on the accounts as long as the card holders clear their accounts at the next billing cycle. However, this policy causes difficulties for the 300 credit authorizers who, from four different locations, may have to access up to 13 different databases in order to make credit authorization.

The authorizers' terminals communicate with an IBM mainframe. The expert system runs on a Symbolics machine which communicates with the IBM computer through a Sun workstation. The system went on line, on a trial basis, in January 1987. It is now reported to support 300 credit authorizers on a 24-hour basis. Tests from the trial period show an 11% better performance by the system over the credit authorizers, and it provides the correct decision in 96% of the cases rather than 85% before (Butler Cox, 1987).

An interesting approach to credit card assessment was taken by Carter and Cartlett (1987) at the University of Sydney. They used machine-learning techniques based on Quinlan's ID3 algorithm, which takes examples of good decisions from which it forms a general decision procedure.

10.4.2   Product Advisers

With the growing number of products and services provided by banks and financial institutions today, there is a need for an advisory system to assist sales personnel with the characteristics of the products. In this section, we shall restrict the systems to those providing information about each product – a kind of product manual. There is a considerable overlap here with financial planning systems dealt with in Section 10.3 and even more with customer support systems which are described in Section 10.4.6.

The advantages offered by product advisers include:

- providing a consistent level of information for the customers;
- covering, in detail, the full range of products on offer;
- more effective maintenance of product information at the front line;
- providing training for the bank staff.

Several banks are developing product advisers on the basis of the expert system technology. In France, the first system appeared in 1985 at Crédit Lyonnais (de Langle and Michel, 1985). Many banks are now using such systems to provide more expertise at the branch office level, for instance, Banque Populaire de Loraine (Chapuzot, 1987). Telebanking is another area where product advisers may be useful. Such systems may improve the level of service offered.

10.4.3 Assets Management

Portfolio Management

The management of investment portfolios in the form of stocks, bonds, mutual funds and so on, is a vital activity in banks and financial institutions. Given the typical magnitude of an institutional portfolio, the investment income of an institution is very sensitive to small improvements in their portfolios.

Portfolio management requires high professional financial and investment expertise. Today, the portfolio managers have access to more or less the same information networks and quantitative analytical techniques. Consequently, what distinguishes one portfolio manager from another is the judgment of economy and market developments, and the ability to couple this knowledge with quantitative analyses.

Given the current number of financial instruments, the number of possible portfolio mixes that can be composed is extremely large. To search for portfolio allocations that match the objectives and constraints of a fund manager is a laborious and time-consuming process, and a highly-skilled task. What complicates portfolio management is that the concern is with the distribution of the return on the portfolio. The characteristics of individual securities are important only in terms of their effect on the distribution of the portfolio return. There exists a highly normative theory on portfolio management which has its roots in Markowitz's (1952) research. This theory is based on probability distributions and that investors are risk averse. It is, however, advantageous to connect qualitative business knowledge to the probabilistic models of portfolio theory. Therefore, several knowledge-based systems have been developed to assist in portfolio management.

For example, the Portfolio Management Advisor developed by the Athena Group in USA is an expert system of this type. It assists professional portfolio managers in construction and maintenance of investment portfolios. The system performs portfolio analysis by making use of specific investment information provided by the portfolio manager, and internal investment analysis and portfolio construction heuristics, along with rules for implementing modern portfolio theory both quantitatively and qualitatively. The system evaluates all potential equity investments and their combinations with regard to value, risk and the investment goals and constraints. This process is facilitated by analytical models. The expert system performs asset selection, asset allocation and portfolio construction.

Another security portfolio advisory system is Le Courtier developed by the US firm Cognitive Systems Inc. for Belgium's largest bank, the Générale de Banque. The purpose is to provide high-quality investment advice to customers of the bank. While the Athena Group's system was designed for fund managers, Le Courtier is designed to be used directly by the bank's customers. The system, which accepts both conversational French and English input, offers specific recommendations about stock purchases and portfolio distribution and also answers factual questions about the Belgian stock market. Le Courtier can give detailed investment advice only if it has a detailed financial profile of the customer. It gives the customer the option of completing a brief or an in-depth financial statement questionnaire, including current investments, assets and liabilities, and cash available for investment. From this information, Le Courtier may stock portfolio recommendations or it may determine that the customer's assets are not large enough to warrant investments in the stock market. The customer may, however, override the system's recommendations.

Le Courtier differs from most other knowledge-based systems in the way it puts emphasis on natural language conversations and the combination of this with Videotex. There is a small step from using natural languages and Videotex to access a database to using the two facilities to access a knowledge base, and that is how Le Courtier was born. The database query system behaves intelligently by not only answering factual questions with facts; it may produce a recommendation along with the factual answer. For example, a customer may ask; 'Should I buy stocks in company A?' and the system may answer: 'Company A may not be a bad investment; however, company B would be a better investment.' (see Digital's management report *Europa* (June 1985) and also Turban (1990).)

Finally we shall describe an intelligent stock portfolio system developed by Lee, Chu and Kim (Lee, 1990). The system is interesting from a KB-DSS point of view because it integrates expert's knowledge, personal preferences, quadratic programming, and machine learning. A prototype, called K-FOLIO, was developed using LISP and a frame-based tool UNIK, and runs on a PC 386. A version, called BRAINS, developed for the Lucky Securities Company, a leading security corporation in Korea, has been in service since 1989.

The architecture of the system includes several interesting features. A *relational database* provides both company and industry data. A knowledge base, called the *knowledge and preference base*, consists of two components: expert knowledge and personal preferences. The expert knowledge is obtained through a knowledge acquisition system and through a machine learning system. The adopted method of machine learning is rule induction. The rules induced from historical data help predict whether the price of a stock will be up, down or remained unchanged. The personal preferences are expressed as rules to be compatible with the expert knowledge. It includes, for example, desired investment amount and/or the percentage of a certain stock.

The conclusions reached through reasoning with the knowledge and preference base make up constraints that are fed into a Markowitz quadratic programming optimization model by means of an *interpreter*. The coefficients for the optimization model is retrieved from the database except the expected return of investment which is given by the investor.

The architecture of this system is given in Figure 10.1 (from Lee, 1990).

10.4.4 Trading

The foreign exchange market is the largest financial market in the world. Approximately $150 billion in currency is traded daily on a world-wide basis. Therefore, the trading function has become a key

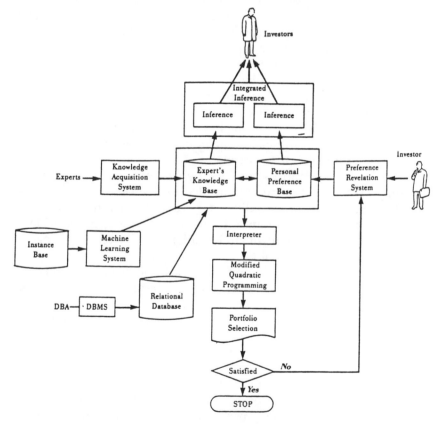

Figure 10.1 *Architecture of ISPMS (from Lee (1990))*

discipline within many financial institutions. The world's financial markets have undergone a period of radical change. As the range of tools grows, the requirements for efficient information services and decision support systems have increased. An interesting presentation of trading DSS can be found in Peziers (1986). According to this, a DSS trading should have the following features:

(1) *Versatility of data acquisition*. The system must be trained to 'read' the required information from the information vendor. This process must be reliable and easily modifiable. Indeed there are very few, if any, constraints imposed on the formats used by information contributors and the contributors may decide to change the formats at almost any time.

(2) *Possibility of respecifying static assumptions*. New tools are created every month; characteristics of old tools may change. Internal constraints (commission structure, taxes and so on) within user companies may need respecification. All these parameters must, therefore, be easily accessible and modifiable, otherwise, the software would become rapidly obsolete.

(3) *Exploratory search*. A key advantage of using a DSS or a KB-DSS is to survey a large number of alternative strategies very quickly and identify among these the best strategies that meet various classes of objectives. Thus, a cash multi-currency arbitrage system should be capable of exploring hundreds of possible arbitrage loops in a few seconds and listing the most profitable arbitrages within a class of possible transactions.

(4) *Dealing pad*. The prices supplied by vendors are for information only. They are not necessarily dealable prices or, at any rate, they may have to be adjusted by a particular user to reflect his or her own constraints. It should, therefore, be possible to override every item of information to reflect the specific circumstances of a deal.

(5) *Cash flow – monitoring*. Many strategies will have consequences spread over time or will necessitate further transactions at some future date. A dealer needs to know how and when these transactions should be carried out, and when he or she will have a chance to review the situation in the future on the basis of the current information.

Here, we shall concentrate on areas where expert systems can be applied. Front office, back office and some support functions are all potential targets, but the prospect of artificial intelligent systems advising, or in the extreme cases, performing the trading function, is the one that aroused most speculation (Guilfoyle and Jeffcoate, 1988). Such artificial intelligent systems would be high risk, and highly visible within the company. Large profits may be made by even a marginal improvement on the success ratio of trading transactions.

Buy and Sell Decisions

Price forecasting is a major, but difficult task in all trading decisions. Statistical methods have failed to provide accurate price forecasts for securities. Two principal methods are used for buy and sell decisions. They are known as fundamental analysis and technical analysis.

Fundamental analysis is made on the fundamental data of a security. For a stock, for instance, this data may include evaluations of management, product range, sales prospects, financial conditions, industry data and so on.

Technical analysis is a different way of arriving at the same result: a buy and sell signal. The assumption here is that the underlying determinants of security prices are so complicated that the best prediction of market behavior is made by empirically observing the macro behavior of the price curve, or the price action as it also is called, and other indicators.

According to Graham (1987), there are four ways in which artificial intelligence techniques can be brought to bear on technical analysis:

(1) To permit the effects of a combination of different, recognizable, buy and sell indicators to be analyzed.
(2) To allow the incorporation of non-numerical, subjective or fuzzy factors.
(3) To carry out pattern matching on price action, or point and figure charts, comparing areas of the charts with prestored templates for recognizable patterns such as head and shoulders, double bottom, flag, pennant and so on.
(4) To use data on prices and actual deals performed over a period of time to generate optimal trading rules, using some rule induction techniques.

Several systems exist in front office trading.

The Equity Trader from Arthur D. Little is designed to assist security traders by monitoring the state of the stock-market, analyzing when a trader should buy or sell, detecting orders which can be carried out without risk, and selecting a broker for a particular transaction. This system had not, apparently, proceeded beyond the prototype stage by May 1987 (Guilfoyle and Jeffcoate, 1988). A fully-developed system will accept information from on-line sources such as Reuters and Stock Exchange Automatic Quotation system.

The IF-FX (Intelligent Forecaster-Foreign Exchange) from Data Logic in Great Britain provides advice on the sterling/dollar market in the form of buy/sell recommendations based on chart forecasting techniques. The system runs on an IBM mainframe in a service bureau and is available to clients on a PC in their local environment. The system will be extended to other currencies, and to incorporate information from the New York and Tokyo markets.

Many banks and financial institutions have been active in this field. Lehman Brothers is a huge American investment bank which deals with about $15 million worth of fees for interest rate swaps on behalf of its clients. The Lehman Brothers' system, called K:Base, assists in finding the most likely candidate for the other side of the proposed swap. The system runs on IBM PCs which can be optionally connected to a Symbolics machine. Data on actual swaps is entered and the system induces decision rules which are used to query the brokers about new applications for swaps.

Option Trading

Options are contracts whose values are contingent upon the values of the underlying assets. Options can be traded for a number of reasons, two of which are speculation and hedging. Speculation occurs when one has confidence in either a rise or fall in an asset's value. Hedging occurs when trading or production activity forces the holding of futures of uncertain value. Options can be used to reduce market risks. Option trading is an interesting domain for expert system applications because traders use heuristics and special techniques widely, basing their theories on many assumptions. Furthermore, complex trading strategies are involved, and the uncertainty of future market prices presents many possibilities for large portfolios.

Graham (1987) describes an option strategy selection system for options on currency futures. It takes, as inputs user opinions on trends in the dollar and the cross rates, volatility and costs. It picks a suitable strategy and optimizes its profile in terms of strike prices, deltas and so on.

The Foreign Exchange Advisory System from the Athena group provides advice for both the initial development of a strategy in foreign currency option trading, as well as suggestions for future modifications to the option strategy as a result of currency price movements in the market-place. The system provides recommendations for a foreign currency option trading strategy based upon market outlook, expected price movements, price volatility and the investor's risk profile. It gives the following advice:

- suggested option pricing;
- selection of optimal option contract type (call and put), and option contract combination strategies (spread and so on);
- strategy choice;
- follow-up strategies based upon price movements.

The Future Dealing Room

Graham (1987) envisages the dealing room of the 1990s. Dealer work-stations are networked to information feeds and demon-driven filters. On the network there are expert systems of the types described above. These are controlled by a blackboard system which throws up advice on the dealer screens, alongside price services and price change warnings.

A blackboard system imitates a group of highly-specialized experts sitting around a blackboard in order to solve a problem. When an expert sees that he or she can contribute a new fact, for instance, to confirm or refute a hypothesis already on the board, or to add a new one. The evidence will now be available to the other experts. In this context, our experts are represented by a technical analysis system, a fundamental analysis system, an option strategy adviser and so on. Common storage, as the blackboard and the agenda, is under the control of a specialized inference program.

Furthermore, the systems are demon-driven. The most noticeable thing about a modern trading room is the large number of screens on the dealing desks. Expert systems with 'demons' can reduce the number of screens by having a ready application in the background that can make analysis of price movements, identify significant changes, direct the trader's attention to a particular information entity, and suggest an improved trading strategy.

Back Office Systems

So far most attention has been focused on front office applications. Expert systems may be employed also to back office functions of trading. Such applications include (Guilfoyle and Jeffcoate, 1988):

- processing of trades;
- difference research;
- margin questions;
- dividend and interest questions;

- auditing transactions;
- compliance to internal and external regulations;
- monitoring for fraud (insider trading).

10.4.5   Bank Management

Bank Sheet Evaluation

The banking industry has, in most countries, been a regulated activity (limitations to credit authorization, decisions on interest rates, control of international operations and so on). During the 1970s this industry experienced a substantial change in competitive conditions as a result of a deregulation movement, that first started in the USA, then moved to Great Britain, and later spread to most European countries. As a consequence, new capital markets opened which changed the traditional patterns of funding for both banks and corporations. Large percentages of bank deposits were now provided from other banks via the interbank market. Banking authorities had to define liquidity ratios, such as Cooke's ratio and structure ratio, in order to limit risk. The European Commission has defined rules for competition within the unified European Union of 1992. For example, a new set of liquidity and structure ratios have been used since 1988 to measure the capacity of banks to cope with large withdrawals made by their clients.

Several French banks have, as a consequence, developed KB-DSS to follow the evolution of these ratios, obtaining diagnoses and suggestions for actions. By the means of a data communication function of the KB-DSS, the account balance from the general ledger is transferred to the workstation on which the knowledge bases are located. The data reader of the KB-DSS is used to aggregate and sort the accounts of the general ledger. These aggregated data are downloaded to the database of the KB-DSS. A model computes a series of ratios which are presented to the financial manager in tabular or graphical forms. The expert module can be used to obtain, automatically, a diagnosis on the bank's liquidity risk. A simulation model can be used to test possible actions suggested by the expert module or the financial manager himself.

Global Analysis of Bank Risk

The system described above was implemented to follow and, also, control the liquidity of the bank. In fact, many other operations that create a risk for the bank exist: the exchange rate risk, the base rate risk and so on. The Compagnie Bancaire in France, through its subsidiary STS, has developed a DSS to analyze these kinds of risks. The structure of this system is shown in Figure 10.2.

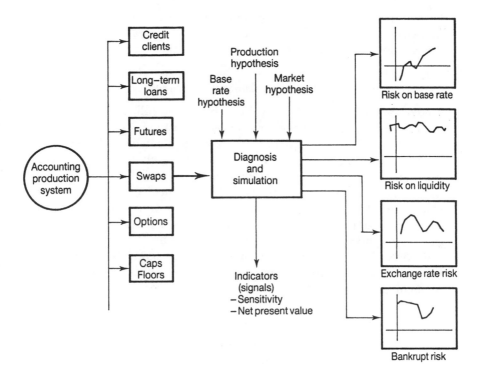

Figure 10.2 Global analysis of bank risk

The basic data used are found in th balance sheet of the bank. These data have to be sorted and aggregated by financial assets and by maturity dates to obtain the global risk. This system simulates operations on financial markets and computes risk indicators for all balance sheet items. Thus, the management obtains a picture of the risk facing the bank, as well as a simulation tool to define its strategy taking into account:

- the sensitivity of the net present value to changes in base rate;
- forecasts of commercial activities;
- changes in the base rate and so on.

Other systems have been developed to help financial institutions to make better decisions on the interest rate mixes which they offer to savers and borrowers in a highly competitive market. Singh and Cooke (1988) describe a hybrid KB-DSS which they have developed to help retail banks to determine optimal interest rates in a competitive environment. Interest rates are determined for both savings and lending products by using a knowledge base comprising the expert knowledge of a number of managers, combined with historical information and market research information.

Management Control of Branches

One of the main tasks of control in a bank is to follow the activity of each branch. A DSS has been implemented in a medium-sized French bank (50 branches). The system gives access to a database of the balance sheet of each branch. These data are automatically transferred every month from the accounting system. A model is available which enables each branch manager to simulate the balance sheet and income statement. The simulation takes into account a forecast of the commercial activity, as well as the base rate, the margins on different operations and so on. Rates and margins are common for all branches. The controller at headquarters can browse through the database to follow indicators by branch, as well as to consolidate all the branches to obtain an overall picture. The system has, recently, been extended using an expert system module to automatically display messages when certain ratios are not verified.

Compliance and Security

Compliance

Along with the tremendous growth and globalization of the financial markets, several incidents have occurred on the exchanges that have raised the issue of better surveillance and compliance. October 19, 1987, or Black Monday, and insider trading scandals on the stock-markets have triggered several studies in this area.

From October 1988, financial institutions in the United Kingdom have been legally required to ensure that their employees comply with good professional practice. The purpose of this legislation is to ensure that rules which constitute this practice are really adhered to. This means that institutions will need to monitor all business transactions made by their employees. The National Westminster Investment Bank in London is developing an automatic monitoring system using an expert system development tool called Vanilla Flavor. The details of the transactions executed by each salesman or trader are matched against a set of rules, and any breaches are brought to the attention of the compliance officer, who can then examine the records in more detail (Butler Cox, 1987).

Nixdorf has developed a system of 700 rules which advises on the import/export restriction on currency. There are 684 paragraphs covering the relevant information, yet the system can access the information required in 30 seconds. This system uses Nixdorf's expert system shell Twaice (Guilfoyle, 1988).

Also, in other countries compliance systems can be found. Banque National de Paris has built a prototype application on the rules governing foreign exchange transactions. Crédit Suisse has a prototype system developed for the Swiss brokerage rules covering the commission a broker may charge, together with their own in-house rules.

The national and international laws which govern taxation, brokerage commission and foreign exchange are rule-based systems that lend themselves to the application of the expert system technology. Such systems apply to large groups of institutions. They may be supplemented by knowledge bases that cover the internal and specific rules of an institution.

Security

Most banks and financial institutions experience losses due to intentional fraud. A distinction can be made between *internal* fraud and *external* fraud. Internal fraud refers to fraud committed by the institution's own personnel. External fraud includes bad cheques, credit card fraud, automatic teller machine-related crime, and frauds on wire transfers and loans.

Security Pacific National Bank in Los Angeles has built a fraud detection system for its bank card department. More specifically, the system deals with the problem of fraudulent use of the automated teller machine debit cards. The expert system is linked to two IMS databases residing on two different IBM mainframes. The result is an on-line bank card fraud detection system, which has been in operation since April 1988. The main advantage of the fraud detection system is that the knowledge and experience of the senior fraud investigators are made available on-line to everybody who needs it. It can analyze large amounts of financial and criminal information to prevent fraud, can detect patterns in historical transaction data to detect existing fraud activities, and can explain its decisions to the user (Lecot, 1988).

TRW Information Services has developed Discovery, an expert system to search for recurrent patterns in inquiry data and compare these patterns to daily inquiry activities to detect variances in normal use behavior. Discovery is an attempt to integrate expert system and decision support system features to provide pattern recognition, self-learning capability, and interactive features to detect unsuspected violations. TRW's goal is to review all daily inquiry activities and detect those inquiries made by potentially unauthorized individuals. The system processes 400 000 inquiries per day. A prototype was initially developed for an IBM PC-XT, but is now converted to a COBOL application on an IBM mainframe (Tener, 1988).

10.4.6 Customer Support

Banks' information systems are, traditionally, very production-oriented. They are centered around accounts or other entities which comprise the products. Information about markets in general, and customers in particular, are attributes of these accounts more than information objects in themselves.

The volatile financial markets are about to change this situation. What is needed to sell an array of financial services effectively to an increasing discerning client is an understanding of the client's full financial situation.

An approach to customer relationship management has been outlined by Alan Bond of the Santa Monica based firm Expert Software. He believes that the relationship between a financial institution and each individual customer can be modeled. It consists of five types of information:

(1) the expectations and commitments agreed between the parties;
(2) the goals of both parties;
(3) the preferences of each party;
(4) the policies which are agreed between the parties for normal situations;
(5) the history of the relationship.

This knowledge forms the basis for three types of expert systems: a product salesman, a financial adviser and a service monitor.

Another system is APEX Client Profiling from Applied Expert Systems in Cambridge, MA. It provides salesmen in the field with the expertise and analytical skills needed to sell an expanding mix of financial products effectively and uses expert systems technology to develop financial strategies for the clients. With the system, financial services firms can:

● understand client needs and match specific product offerings to those needs;
● provide tangible value to clients by offering advice that addresses their expressed needs;
● gather client information to improve customer targeting and product development.

The APEX Client Profiling sytem analyzes information regarding the customer's current financial profile–income, assets, and liabilities, in the context of his or her expressed priorities and attitudes. The system includes both a knowledge base and a product base.

10.5 FINANCIAL AND STRATEGIC ANALYSIS

Several interesting experiments have been made in France to develop knowledge-based systems in financial and economic analysis. FINSIM has been described but other systems should be mentioned, in particular the work done at the Banque de France. In 1983 two services of the Banque de France, the 'Institut de Formation' and the 'Direction des Etudes' started thinking about using AI technology for company financial analysis. A first prototype of the expert system AIDE was developed in 1985 with the assistance of the Ecole Centrale de Paris. The idea was to provide a financial and economic diagnosis service to the companies providing their accounting information to the financial database of the Banque de France called 'Centrale de Bilans'. This financial database created in 1969 is made up of about 30 000 companies which have agreed to provide the Banque de France with detailed accounting and economic information. The Centrale de Bilans is used to make global and industry studies which are based on a representative sample of the French economy. Also it is used to make individual company diagnoses. As a reward for their participation the companies which are members of the Centrale de Bilans receive a yearly detailed analysis of their financial situation. This study uses the industry statistics to position the company within its industry.

The initial goal of the AIDE knowledge-based system was to formalize a modern financial analysis methodology worked out by the experts of the 'Centrale de Bilans'. This methodology was made available to the branches of the Banque de France and at the 'Institut de Formation' in order to train the young analysts making the individual studies for the companies participating to the Centrale de Bilans. From 1985 to 1989 the AIDE system was validated internally. Many experts in the Banque de France have worked on the knowledge base of about 1000 rules. Given the success of the system internally, and maybe to recover part of its investment the Banque de France decided in 1990 to commercialize its diagnosis (not the software) to companies. The system was named GEODE. After having collected accounting information on the last four years as well as qualitative data through a dialogue with the top executives of the company the system provides a diagnosis on the strong and weak points of a company on criteria such as: competitiveness, investment policy, return, production and subcontracting policy, management policy, commercial policy, working capital requirements, financing policy, financial structure and financial strategy. The analysis is made in comparison with an industrial sector selected by the chief executive of the company. Seven hundred industry samples are available in the database. Extensions of GEODE called GEODE 2 and 3 were developed later to add the capacity to make a financial simulation. However the GEODE system does not provide to our knowledge the capacity to evaluate scenarios with a knowledge base. The Banque de France created its AI Center in 1985. Apart from the GEODE system several other systems have been developed: FIBEN for credit analysis, PREVIA for short-term forecasting, SAABA for the financial analysis of banks. In the specific domain of bank evaluation we can mention a similar system (Boniteta) developed by the Ljubjanska Banka in Slovenia. (Delidzakova E., 1988) With respect to *strategic analysis* we can mention the DSID system. This system has been developed to diagnose strong and weak points of a company. Its goal is to help a company manager to structure his or her thinking and test the coherence between external observable information of the company market, the description of the competitive mechanisms as seen by the manager and his strategic choice.

In 1994 a first international workshop was held on knowledge systems and strategic management at Åbo university in Finland.

10.6   PUBLIC FINANCE

Klein and Villedieu (1987) described a first version of a financial analysis and planning DSS called SIAD-MAIRIE which forms part of a continuous effort started in 1980 to provide French municipalities with a coherent set of knowledge-based DSS to support their financial management.

Financial management of towns raises special problems. These problems are in part due to:

- the legal and financial contraints the towns are subject to;
- the fact that they are non-profit organizations;
- the co-existence of two cultures in their management: the one of the elected politicians (mayor and city council), the one of the civil-servants (town clerk, town financial manager, etc.).

French towns are required by law to vote a balanced budget every year. This task is often a source of conflicts since the composition of the city council is usually made up of members belonging to different political groups. One group may have an absolute majority or the majority may have to be built through alliances. However French town councils are not required by law to account for the long-term consequences of their projects. But precisely for reasons related to the long-term consequences of many projects in terms of financing and induced costs and revenues, financial planning is needed. The task of planning being to balance the long-term consequences of projects with the financial resources of the town and to ensure that the timing of the projects stays acceptable.

The first system to be implemented was the financial analysis and planning DSS described in Klein and Villedieu (1987). The lessons learned from the use of this system in about forty French towns from 1985 to 1990 and the gradual improvements to the system were described in Klein *et al.* (1993c). The present system is made up of four integrated KB-DSS for (see Figure 10.4):

- financial planning and budgeting;
- project management;
- debt management;
- monthly cash management.

The financial analysis and planning DSS is there to help answer questions such as:

- Can the investments and major works planned by the city council be financed and can the towns fulfill the criteria of good financial practice?
- Is it possible to undertake a set of projects given the residual borrowing capacity of the town and to respect the legal constraints on the tax rates?
- How to keep the financial balance of the town given the hypotheses of reduction of the revenues of certain taxes and a relative reduction of the state contribution.
- What is the best financing mix to negotiate with banks to finance the program of the city council?

The main menu of the financial analysis and planning DSS is shown in the top line of Figure 10.3. The options of the report commands menu can be seen in the column on the figure. The financial manager can run a historical model and display a set of reports presenting the key criteria to make a financial analysis of the town: operating income,

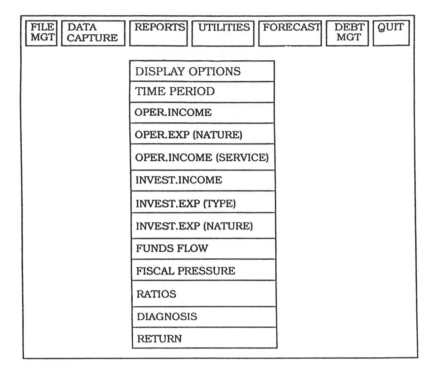

FILE MGT	DATA CAPTURE	REPORTS	UTILITIES	FORECAST	DEBT MGT	QUIT

DISPLAY OPTIONS

TIME PERIOD

OPER.INCOME

OPER.EXP (NATURE)

OPER.INCOME (SERVICE)

INVEST.INCOME

INVEST.EXP (TYPE)

INVEST.EXP (NATURE)

FUNDS FLOW

FISCAL PRESSURE

RATIOS

DIAGNOSIS

RETURN

Figure 10.3 *Main menu of financial analysis and planning DSS "SIAD MAIRIE" with Report options*

operating expenses (by nature and by each of the basic 15 services provided by a town), investment income (loans, subsidies . . .), investment expenses, fund flow analysis, fiscal pressure, key ratios, etc.

The financial manager can also compare his conclusions with the diagnosis which is provided by the expert part of the applications. This diagnosis uses a knowledge base which was developed using knowledge provided by banking experts and legal knowledge on local government from the law. The diagnosis is broken down into statements on:

- the changes in the population;
- investment policy;
- changes in revenues (fiscal taxes and other revenues) and capacity to service the debt;
- tax burden on people and companies;
- debt level;
- cash and working capital.

This knowledge base accesses a database of statistics on French towns which is updated yearly. In this way the diagnosis can be compared with other towns of similar size and type.

One of the difficulties of such a diagnosis is that most French towns of a certain size have spawned numerous organizations and the financial links between these organizations and the town are complex and not well documented. Typical such organizations are: sporting or cultural associations, low rent apartment companies, companies mixing public and private investment for managing harbors, ski-lifts, thermal spas, etc., companies providing public services (transportation, etc.).

The forescast option of the menu will let the manager access a forecasting model which will enable him or her to define scenarios corresponding to the alternatives the town council wishes to see studied. The system allows the financial manager to enter his or her hypotheses concerning any changes in the tax-bases. The evolution of the 'tax-bases' are themselves a function of the change in the population, the value of buildings, freehold land and company assets and salaries located in the town. One of the key decision variables is the level of the tax rates. These tax levels are voted by the town council and are subject to legal constraints which the simulation model should check.

The investment expense option of the forecast menu lets the user:

- use an aggregate amount for the investment each year;
- individualize the investment of the town, project by project.

In the latter case the user is in fact connected with a project management DSS. With this DSS the user will be able to define for each new project: its name, the amount of investment needed, its type (building, refurbishing, depreciation rules, etc.), the associated operating expenses and associated operating income for each period up to the time horizon.

The project management DSS will compute the cash inflows and cash outflows yearly and monthly and provide these values to the financial planning DSS and the cash management DSS as shown in Figure 10.4. The project management DSS is there to allow the financial manager to update the portfolio of important projects which are being planned, abandoned or in progress. He or she can also update the characteristics of projects with estimates coming from the various services of the town or outside contractors.

The debt management DSS is there in order to solve a problem which may be specific to the French environment. This problem is basically

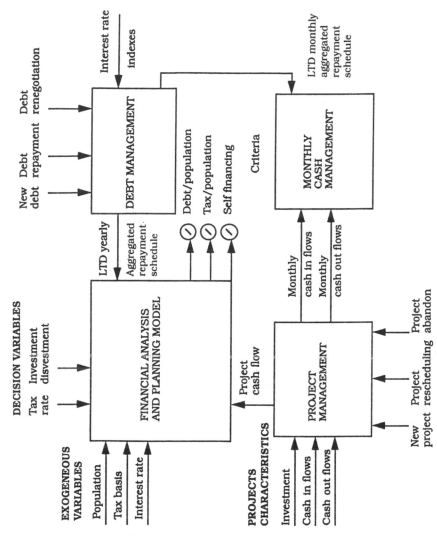

Figure 10.4 *The decision models of the DSS "SIAD-MAIRIE" and their relationship*

related to the large number of different loans taken by French towns. Indeed, the practice for a long time in French towns was to associate a loan with each project of a significant size. As a consequence even a small town of 20 000 inhabitants may have as many as 50 outstanding loans at a given time. This DSS allows the financial manager to enter the list of all outstanding loans for the town and compute an aggregate repayment schedule over the planning horizon. This schedule is computed in terms of aggregate capital repayment schedule and aggregate interest on a yearly or monthly basis. The yearly schedule is used for the financial planning DSS and the monthly schedule for the cash management DSS (see Figure 10.4).

10.7 EXPERT SYSTEM AND KB-DSS IN MARKETING

In marketing, expert systems have been developed for the purpose of sales support (McDermott, 1982), promotion planning (Keon and Bayer, 1986), advertising media selection (Mitchell, 1988) and new product introduction (Gaul and Schaer, 1988). However most of these systems have been developed using classical expert system technology and not the KB-DSS technology. We shall only present here briefly two domains of application in marketing: analysis of scanner data and advertising design. The reason for choosing advertising design is that it is a good example of a domain which is highly qualitative and where a good solution implies the integration of reasoning on qualitative concepts but where access to large quantities of information on consumers and markets is also a requirement.

With respect to the analysis of scanner data the generalization of this technology in mass distribution has generated an amount of information which is far greater than before. As a consequence it seems difficult to analyze these data for decision support without the KB-DSS technology. It is interesting to note that in their conclusion the authors referred to above point out that an important improvement would be the capacity to couple the expert system technology and database technology. Similarly they show that the modeling and expert system technology capacity which was not available in the tools they have been using, would be a valuable improvement.

In the domain of advertising design two systems have been described in some detail: ADDUCE (Burke, 1991) and ADCAD (Burke *et al.*, 1990). The goal of the ADDUCE system is to predict how consumers will respond to advertising, audience, brand and market characteristics.

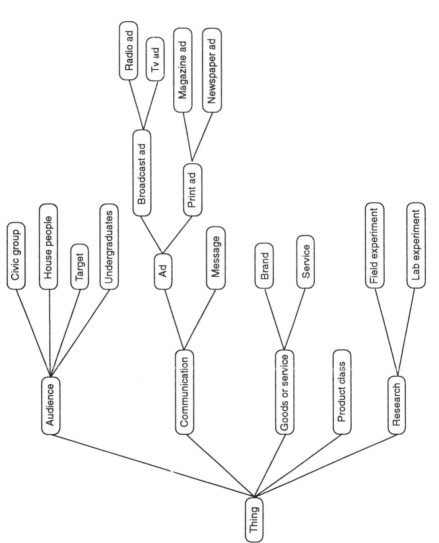

Figure 10.5 *The ADDUCE frame hierarchy from R. Burke (1991)*

Its predictions are based on a subset of advertising research discussed in Burke *et al.* (1990).

ADDUCE encodes information about objects and attributes (slots) in a frame-based representation. A segment of the ADDUCE frame hierarchy is presented in Figure 10.5.

Reasoning Strategy

The ADDUCE system reasons with theoretical and empirical relationships by deduction and by analogy respectively. Empirical reasoning consists of transferring knowledge from past experimental contexts to new situations that share significant aspects, and then by using the transferred knowledge to predict outcomes in the new situations. By extending empirical relationships to cover plausible, related situations, the author assumes that outcomes in the new situation are produced by the same process. The system first asks the user a series of background questions about the brand, advertising and target audience. This information is necessary to determine the similarity of the present situation with past experiments and to satisfy the premises of the theoretical and empirical relationships. ADDUCE then attempts to infer the audience's response by searching the knowledge base in a goal driven fashion.

Knowledge Representation

The interesting point of this system is that it shows that in the marketing domain where knowledge is more often empirical than theoretical it is important to mix different methods of knowledge representation and inference. Theoretical relationships are represented as abstract rules which are used to deduce outcomes in new situations. Empirical knowledge is represented as associations between specific objects which are generalized to analogous new situations.

The work on ADDUCE was extended by R. Burke and others into the ADCAD system. The ADCAD system uses an expert system methodology to codify and synthesize prior research, theory and expertise in a decision aid for selecting advertising objectives, creative strategy, and communication approaches. According to the authors, the system:

- improves the quality of advertising decisions;
- facilitates the accumulation of advertising knowledge;
- enhances the communication between the advertising agency and clients.

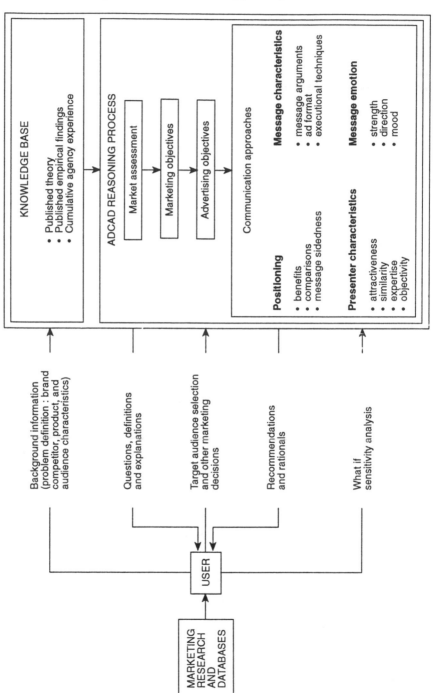

Figure 10.6 Overview of the major steps in advertising design and user-interaction with ADCAD (Burke et al., 1990)

The main stages of advertising design are according to the authors: (1) market assessment; (2) marketing strategy development; (3) segment selection; (4) selection of communication objectives for the targeted segment; (5) positioning; (6) deciding on how this positioning can best be communicated; and (7) checking that the execution is not yet preempted by a competitor.

Description of the System:

Figure 10.6 presents an overview of the stages of the advertising design process and the operation of the ADCAD system. Table 10.1 shows an example of rules for selecting marketing and advertising objectives.

We can comment on the marketing objectives which these rules translate. For new products categories (especially discontinuous innovations) and for new users of existing products categories, it is necessary to stimulate primary demand by communicating the benefits that tie the product category to consumers' needs and wants. Likewise if the product is at the maturity or decline stage of the product life-cycle and the brand has a large market share, it may be desirable

---

Table 10.1 *Example Rules for Selecting Marketing and Advertising Objectives*

Marketing Objectives (11 rules)

- IF product life-cycle stage = introduction AND innovation type = discontinuous THEN marketing objective = stimulate primary demand
- IF brand usage = none THEN marketing objective = stimulate brand trial
- IF current brand usage = some AND (brand switching = high OR product usage rate = fixed) THEN marketing objective = stimulate repeat purchase/loyalty
- IF current brand usage = some AND brand switching = low AND product usage rate = variable THEN marketing objective = increase rate of brand usage

Advertising Objectives (18 rules)

- IF marketing objective = stimulate primary demand AND product purchase motivation direction = negative THEN ad objective = convey product category information
- IF marketing objective = stimulate brand trial AND brand purchase motivation direction = positive THEN ad objective = convey brand image
- IF time of brand decision = at point of purchase AND package visibility = high AND package recognition = low THEN ad objective = increase brand recognition
- IF marketing objective = increase rate of brand usage AND new brand uses = yes THEN ad objective = convey new brand uses

to increase primary demand, as the brand will reap a large share of the increased category sales.

After having helped in deciding on the marketing and advertising objectives the ADCAD system will help select various advertising communication approaches to achieve the marketing and advertising objectives based on a consideration of consumer, product, and environmental characteristics. These approaches include brand positioning (24 rules), message and presenters characteristics (respectively 80 and 20 rules) as well as emotional tone of the advertisement (35 rules).

In their discussion of the future direction for research the authors put the emphasis on the need to link the expert system with conventional analysis tools and databases:

> 'ACAD would benefit from a direct link to databases of consumers and market information. At the present time, the user enters manually background information on the brand, competitor, product, audience characteristics. If ADCAD could extract this information directly from databases, it would reduce the number of questions in the consultation, unambiguously define the required input, insure data currency, and allow individual rather than segment-level analysis of consumer data.'

The capacity provided by a KB-DSS development environment to define applications integrating database and expert systems would be highly valuable. Also the authors point out that:

> 'The goal is to be able to develop decision models combining qualitative and quantitative reason.'

It is clear that advertising design is well suited for the KB-DSS approach we have introduced.

With respect to the use of expert system technology in studying marketing scanner data a series of interesting papers has been published in the special issue of the *International Journal of Research in Marketing* 8, 1991. This special volume is nearly entirely devoted to this topic. The paper by P. Alpar (1991) shows that it is possible to model the problem solving behavior of marketing practitioners and in particular market share analysts.

The paper by Rangaswamy, Harlam and Lodish points out that the idea that with an increase in the size of marketing data of 100 or 1000 due to scanner data the only solution is to develop an expert system which can analyze automatically this huge mass of information.

Exercises

10.1 What are the judgmental factors involved in capital budgeting and investment analysis? How can knowledge bases be embedded in a KB-DSS using discounted cash flow analysis as the basic tool?

10.2 What can a knowledge-based financial statement analyzer give in terms of added values compared to a numeric ratio calculation system?

10.3 Describe the steps required to perform a financial analysis of a company on the basis of available financial statements from an acquisition point of view.

10.4 What are the main parts and functions that a personal financial planning system should have?

10.5 When loan officers, credit analysts, and loan review committees evaluate a commercial loan application, they combine financial projections with qualitative information.

    (a) What kind of financial projections are made and on what kind of data are they based?

    (b) What kind of qualitative data are used?

    (c) How are the qualitative information combined with the financial projections to give a final credit assement?

10.6 Compare the following three systems for business loan evaluation:

    (a) CLASS (Duchessi et al., 1988);

    (b) MARBLE (Shaw and Gentry, 1988);

    (c) BANKER (Chapter 5).

Describe the similarities and differences between the features of the knowledge bases of these three systems.

10.7 How can artificial intelligence techniques be used in technical analysis for buy and sell decisions of securities?

10.8 Why is option trading an interesting domain for expert system application?

10.9 Name an expert system for foreign currency option trading. Present the main functions of this system.

10.10 Give an example of a financial problem domain where a real-time expert system is appropriate.

10.11 Discuss the problems of compliance in the financial services sector, and give examples of compliance systems.

10.12 Discuss the content of a customer support system for a bank.

10.13 A common finding in many surveys of financial management practice has been that the real-world usage of normative financial models is infrequent. It is widely recognized that this phenomenon is related to the complexity of the decision environment presented in normative models, the lack of attention to such critical details as the availability of necessary information and the difficulty of usage.

Discuss the constraints of normative models and how DSS and expert systems can overcome some of these constraints.

10.14 Develop a knowledge base for one of the following problems by interviewing an expert in the field and/or reading an article on the topic in a practice-oriented finance magazine:

(a) Financial statements analysis of a bank or an insurance company.

(b) Corporate credit management.

(c) Cash management.

(d) Assets and liabilities management.

(e) Financial restructuring of a company.

(f) Foreign exchange risk exposure for a company dealing with international business.

11
Developments and Research in Knowledge-based Decision Support Systems

11.1 INTRODUCTION

The integration of the DSS technology with expert systems, and AI technologies in general, is a recent phenomenon. Papers about a coherent knowledge-based framework for DSS were presented and discussed at the NATO Advanced Study Institute on DSS in Maratea, Italy in 1985 (the proceedings are edited by Holsapple and Whinston (1987)). At the EURO VIII Congress in Lisbon in 1986, a special session on DSS and expert systems debated the integration of DSS, experts systems and OR models. Other research, along the same lines, is the work by DSS researchers on model management systems starting at the beginning of the 1980s, and more recently, the work on intelligent decision systems. We shall return to these issues in Section 11.3.

Another line of development has been the integration of logic in database management systems. The conference on expert database systems in 1986 (Kerchberg, 1986) clearly addresses one of the fundamental problems of the KB-DSS framework: the integration of databases and expert systems. However, the perspective of this conference was not decision making and decision support.

In June 1986, a conference on multi-attribute decision making via Operation Research based expert systems was organized at the University of Passau, Germany. Several papers presented at this conference addressed the problem of integrating AI and DSS (see for instance, Jarke and Radermacher (1988), Keeney (1988), Beulens and van Neurer (1988), Richter (1988)). These papers were published in a special issue of the *DSS International Journal* under the title 'Design Issues of Advanced DSS'. In the introduction to this volume, the guest editors develop arguments in favor of the integration of classical DSSs and AI tools, and AI decision analysis methodology, to build enhanced DSSs.

In June 1991 at the NATO Advanced Study Institute on Recent Developments in DSS held at Il Ciocco, Italy an analysis of the weak points of the first generation of KB-DSS was presented and a list of priorities and research issues were presented (Klein, 1993d). Several of these issues still wait for a satisfactory solution.

In June 1992 the second conference of the International Society for DSS was held at FAW (University of Ulm) in Germany. During this very exciting conference many important issues concerning distributed KB-DSS and Intelligent DSS were discussed.

Research and development in KB-DSS is a highly interdisciplinary field, since it draws on research from a range of contributing disciplines, both basic scientific disciplines, as we have seen in Chapter 1, but also, from other areas of information systems. We do not attempt here even to summarize all of the research and development that will influence the application, design and technology of KB-DSS. However, we shall look at some improvements of the KB-DSS technology that we may expect in the coming years from what we know of the existing state-of-the-art technologies of the various components that make up a comprehensive KB-DSS development tool (as we have defined it in Chapter 6). We shall also look at what we may expect of new software development environments that not only take advantage of the new capabilities of the components, but also integrate these into a coherent and easy to use tool. Finally, as the applications of the expert systems mature, new operating environments are needed, in particular, environments where resources are distributed over several computer systems. All of the directions in improvements that we have indicated above require more demanding algorithms; as a consequence, faster machines and larger memory capacities are needed.

For example the generalization of object oriented graphical interfaces with direct manipulation of objects on the screen requires considerable central memory capacity. From these developments has arisen a new generation of KB-DSS which we have described in Chapter 6. However, much work is still needed in order to obtain satisfactory solutions to all the research issues pointed out during the Il Ciocco conference.

Research in the field of DSS and KB-DSS can be broken down into three domains:

- conceptual framework, theory, development environment;
- design methodologies;
- impact on the organizations.

As we have pointed out in Section 6.4.2 a conceptual framework cannot be evaluated in the usual scientific way; it is evaluated in terms of the usefulness of the applications it generates. We have proposed the KB-DSS framework as a higher order synthesis among DSS, ES and systems based on rational decision theory. We also would like to stress the fact that we have presented the implementation of development environments as a very important step in the research process since it is the best way to check that the framework and theory have been formulated unambiguously and precisely. It is also the only way to check the pertinence of the theory by offering users and other researchers the possibility to use new design philosophies to develop applications and study their impact on decision processes in organizations. This approach follows the tradition of Newell and Simon (1972) in the development of cognitive theories. The steps in such a research process are presented in Figure 11.1. The reader interested by the link between the methodology proposed here and theory construction should refer to Bagozzi, 1984. The process starts with a concrete decision problem. A very important step is then to move from a specific problem to a *problem class*. This is done through *abstraction*. In our case the many problems encountered where an improved solution implies a synthesis between computation and reasoning has led to a new problem class. Since this new problem could not be solved within the existing conceptual framework a new theory and conceptual framework had to be developed. In the KB-DSS case, the theory is stated as a *formal language* (including the user interface) to:

- define what is known,
- *present* what is known (directly or as the conclusion of diverse forms of rigorous reasoning with the various levels of confidence)
- define the user application *interface*.

The theory also provides algorithms for problem solving which can be implemented as *solvers*. These solvers are used to generate new facts (or knowledge). We have kept the traditional DSS constraint that the formal language should be the *same* to communicate with the users and to be executed in a machine.

The formal language used to define what is known or learnt as problem solving progresses is necessary to:

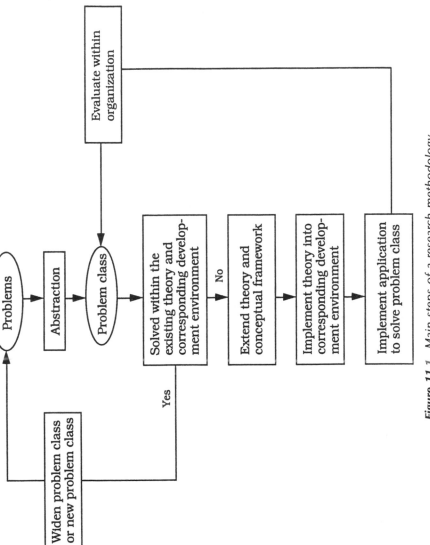

Figure 11.1   *Main steps of a research methodology*

- Describe and capture classes of elementary objects (or concepts) and their attributes observed in the world or created by our mind and useful for problem solving. These objects and their attributes are the elementary facts which will be used to build the system.
- Transform these elementary facts into aggregates (attributes and/or objects).
- Describe and validate decision models (i.e. relations among decision variables, criteria and exogenous variables). The variables of decision models being attributes of objects. We usually think of variables in decision models as quantitative but it may not be the case.
- Describe and validate knowledge which is independent from the usage of the knowledge (usage such as reasoning or explaining or acquiring) and is relevant to the problem class.
- Describe and validate the users' preferences.
- Describe the user interface of the application.

The solvers are necessary to:

- Obtain facts and new knowledge from large databases (query processor, statistical agorithms or AI algorithms for inductive learning, etc.).
- Compute criteria values (decision model solver).
- Simulate reasoning (inference engine, etc.).
- Evaluate alternatives (multi-attribute preference evaluation, multi-criteria evaluation, etc.).

The third step is to implement the above conceptual framework and theory into a development environment (i.e. software which can be used on a given computer).

The fourth step is to develop an application to solve the initial problem class. This step implies the use of design methodology for the application.

The fifth step is to evaluate the application with users in the real world.

The sixth step is to loop on the application until it is considered satisfactory by users or that they themselves pilot its evolution using the development environment.

The seventh step is to widen the problem class or move to a new problem class. For example move from an application to support credit analysis to production scheduling in a make-to-order company.

We should also remember that KB-DSS theory is a highly multi-disciplinary field. Progress can be obtained by improving functions of the KB-DSS framework but often even more by improving the integration of these functions. We shall start by describing developments which can be made using today's technology but which have not yet been implemented in KB-DSS generators. This will enable us to contrast the first generation of KB-DSS development environment available in the late eighties with the development environments available in the nineties. We shall then discuss a few selected research issues.

11.2   DEVELOPMENTS IN THE KB-DSS TECHNOLOGY

11.2.1   Data Base Management Systems

The present KB-DSS development tools integrate components which do not take advantage of the state-of-the-art technology in each component area. A new generation of development tools will emerge as the component technologies are updated. We shall now describe what we can expect of improvements in each component in the near future.

As we have seen in Chapter 4, most of the DBMS components included in today's business orientated DSS and KB-DSS are of the multi-dimensional type. The multi-dimensional type of DBMS provides, in certain situations, an easier way to deal with data structures as they are perceived by the user: lists, cubes and so on.

It is true that for management control and most financial and marketing problems the multi-dimensional data model (or the relational data model) is well adapted.

We have pointed out that the growing need to integrate the KB-DSS applications with transaction-oriented information systems has led to the development of interface with standard relational DBMS (see Section 4.4.2).

It has been pointed out that for certain applications due to the complexity of the information to deal with, an object-oriented DBMS would be more suitable. This is clearly the case in production scheduling (Lecomte *et al.*, 1993), in computer assisted design, in marketing where image or video are important information to be used in decision processes.

Four extensions to the currently applied database technology in KB-DSS will be useful:

- object orientation;
- pictorial images and multi-media;
- deductive database; and
- information discovery.

Each of these items will be discussed in more detail below.

Object-oriented Database (OODB)

OODB represents a new philosophy and implementation strategy for storing information and data. The justification of the importance of this approach for KB-DSS is due to the fact that many KB-DSS applications imply the representation of new data types (graphics, text, images, maps, etc.) which cannot be dealt with by traditional relational or multi-dimensional DBMS. In a OODBMS the object is defined by its data structure, the procedures (methods) which an object is able to execute and the messages which can activate the methods. The basic concepts of the object-oriented approach have been introduced in Section 5.5.5. For example in an object-oriented DB the class of persons could be defined as:

- *Class*: person
- *Name*: string
- *SS number*: integer
- *Photo*: bitmap
- *Date of birth*: date
- *Address*: string
- *Child*: set of (persons)

To our knowledge no full object-oriented database management system has yet been integrated as a resource in a KB-DSS development environment. Klein (1993d) presents a prototype of such a system and some of the difficulties of implementation. However in this example the link with the other resources (decision models, inference engine, etc.) was not implemented. An interesting goal is to implement a prototype where the user could at will use the multi-dimensional DBMS or the OODBMS and transfer data from one to the other when feasible.

Pictorial Images and Multi-media

We have already pointed out (Chapter 4) that many KB-DSS applications require the presentation of information which includes images and/or maps (Chapter 4). We have pointed out that the present generation of report generator let the user mix objects such as: text, tables of figures, graphics, maps and images. As a consequence the new DBMS should be able to associate with objects (entities) attributes such as: images, maps, sounds and video, which is now possible since the transfer rate between the microprocessor and the disk reaches the appropriate level.

Another consequence is the need to integrate the software to pilot color scanners to build up the images base needed by many applications. Pictorial images are extremely useful in many applications.

We already know of expert systems that advise on routes for a walk in a park. Such systems mix logical reasoning with the display of images (scenery and so on), or with maps. Some examples may illustrate the use of images in KB-DSS.

In a travel agency, a KB-DSS for supporting the selection of holiday destinations would be much enhanced if the user could be given the opportunity to see objects and maps of the places which are suggested as vacation destinations. Images and video can be displayed as the conversation between the travel agent and the client proceeds, where information about budget constraints, number of people traveling, composition of the party, preferences for locations (seaside, countryside or a mountain area) and types of activities are exchanged. An image and video processing KB-DSS can display information in much the same way as we find in the colorful catalogs in travel agents today, with the important difference that the system will help the agency to elicit preferences and guide in selecting an appropriate destination.

In a real estate agency, an expert system for selecting housing, a flat or a house should be able to display plans and pictures as the selection process progresses, to support the interaction with the client.

A KB-DSS for supporting a field engineer in charge of maintenance should be able to provide diagrams or plans of parts of the equipment.

Images are graphical objects without an explicit representation structure. They are represented as matrices which describe the pixels. To implement image processing, the pixel matrices will be stored in the database in a condensed way. Once the format of the stored data is known, it is possible to reconstruct the pixel matrices and, at the same time, transform them into forms that are appropriate for the graphics device used.

Deductive database systems

Deductive database systems are database systems with enhanced inference capabilities. Inference capabilities require a knowledge base and an inference mechanism, that is, a knowledge-based system. A typical knowledge-based system has few facts and many rules. Its knowledge base and working memory reside in main memory during reasoning. A typical database system has no rules, but many facts. These facts reside in secondary storage. In a database system, facts are retrieved or derived by a data manipulation language. In knowledge-based systems, facts are deduced by logic reasoning, a recursive process which is done by chaining in rulebased systems. Deductive database systems are, typically, built around relational database systems and logic systems.

Relational databases consist of two parts: stored relations, and data retrieval statements (for instance, written in a query language like SQL).

The drawbacks of relational database systems are, firstly that the logic that can be applied is very limited, and secondly, that they can not perform recursions because they do not accommodate rules.

Deductive databases transform 'tuples' in a relational database into facts represented as propositions in the knowledge base. By introducing rules and an inference mechanism, more complex facts can be *derived* from the stored relations.

There are two basic approaches to the design of deductive database systems (Missikoff and Widerhold, 1984). The *homogeneous* approach uses a single integrated system to manage the database, to perform fact retrieval by means of data retrieval statements, and to make inferences on the stored or retrieved facts. The *heterogeneous* approach uses a separate system to manage the relational database and another system, an inference system, to perform deductive reasoning based on retrieved facts.

In the homogeneous approach, the inference system is enhanced with data management functions. These functions manage data that is residing on external storage. Therefore, facts stored in external storage can be accessed from the inference system when needed.

The heterogeneous approach uses two separately-developed technologies, inferencing systems and database management systems, in constructing deductive database systems. The advantage of this approach is obvious. Existing DBMS and databases can be used as subsystems in a deductive database system. However, an interface allowing interaction between the two subsystems must be built.

The various architectures, tools, and techniques used to build deductive database systems draw upon aspects of knowledge-based systems and database management. Logic programming using PROLOG combined with the relational database systems SQL, is one approach. The result is known as PROSQL (Chang and Walker, 1984). Also combining production systems and relational database systems has been done. One example is RPL (the Relational Production Language). Expert systems written in RPL have direct access to conventional databases because RPL relies on a relational query language to express rules (Delcambre, 1988).

Deductive database systems make inferencing possible on large amounts of data that are currently stored in conventional databases and that, until now, have been relatively inaccessible to expert systems.

Information Discovery in Databases

Information discovery is the generation of new knowledge and detection of anomalies based on large amount of data. Any database contains knowledge in the attributes of entities.

The methods to generate this new knowledge are:

- statistical analysis;
- neural net;
- rule generation.

Statistical Analysis

Statistical analysis is the oldest method used to extract knowledge from databases. The DSS and KB-DSS framework are well suited for this type of activity since it is possible to use the tool box to submit subsets of the database to statistical analysis.

Two very well known statistical methods are used to support model building: the multiple-regression method and discriminant analysis. The multiple-regression method is a tool to test a hypothesis concerning the relation between explanatory variables and a variable to explain. Discriminant analysis uses a mathematical function (a weighted sum of a set of attributes) to predict which category a new set of observations should belong to. If we imagine each data observation as representing a point in a multi-dimensional space, then discriminant analysis can be explained as partitioning that space into regions separated by planes (the equation of which is defined by the discriminant function). This methodology has been widely used for bankruptcy prediction in financial databases.

Neural Nets

The neural modeling approach to discovery focuses on general purpose learning using neural nets. The neural net approach has several advantages over the regression (McGee, 1993):

- no function form needs to be specified;
- non-linear relationships are handled without any special effort;
- an appropriately simple neural net model will generalize new inputs without making patently absurd output estimates even for data well outside the range of values of the training set.

Neural nets as a general computational method is dealt with in Section 11.3.6 below, see also (Smith, 1993).

Rule Generation

Rule generation or discovery begins with the selection of an attribute that serves as the goal (i.e. the conclusion of the rule to be discovered).

Rules are then generated that predict the different ranges or values of the goal attribute (conclusion) based on combinations of values or ranges on other variables (the premise). Further focusing can be made by selecting the subset of attributes for possible consideration for inclusion in the premise with all other attributes being eliminated from consideration.

11.2.2 Decision Modeling Languages

Present modeling languages are efficient for definition of standard financial and economic relationships. However representing knowledge by sets of equations or equations and constraints is only a part of the modeling task of a decision situation (the modeling of the outcome). It is also necessary to model the decision situation, for this purpose decision trees and influence diagrams or belief nets (introduced in Chapter 3) are useful tools. Ideally the capacity to represent knowledge mixing influence diagrams and an equation modeling language to compute outcome node value should be available.

The KB-DSS framework integrates decision models with databases and knowledge bases. As a consequence one obvious focus of research is the integration process. It should however be clear that certain forms of integration cannot be performed seriously without first a theoretical synthesis at the conceptual level. For example in the problem diagnosis function of a KB-DSS two main approaches can be used: the probabilistic approach and the logic-based approach. These two approaches have not yet been successfully reconciled. We believe that the strength of the probabilistic approach is that it offers decision theory as a framework. The logic-based approach offers less guidance when the problem solving resources (cost of computation, cost of obtaining additional information, etc.) must be traded against the utility of finding the exact diagnosis.

Model building aids

The use of AI technology and expert systems to provide methodological knowledge in model building is an emerging issue. The user may interact with a methodology knowledge base to analyze and model a decision. A specific line of research started in the beginning of the 1980s in the DSS field addressing this issue is called *model management*. We shall return to this issue in Section 11.3.4.

An approach to decision modeling which has proved to be useful in domains characterized by great uncertainty and large consequences, is the decision analysis methodology presented in Chapter 3. This approach is based on formal decision theory and has a firm methodological basis. However, to apply decision analysis requires both time and skill. To make this methodology available for a user, a knowledge-based modeling environment has to be created. This modeling environment should support the decision analysis cycle: deterministic phase, probabilistic phase and informational phase. In agreement with this goal the decision maker should be able to find commands and corresponding procedures to:

- Generate automatic sensitivity analysis for system and decision variables.
- Encode: time preference model, multi-attribute preferences, uncertainty on stochastic variables and risk preferences.
- Compute lotteries and their certain equivalents.
- Measure stochastic sensitivity.
- Measure risk sensitivity.
- Measure economic sensitivity.

These possibilities could be introduced within a standard financial modeling language. Implementing the decision analysis approach enables us to perform *user modeling*, an aspect which is normally not found in traditional KB-DSS. They could also be introduced to support an influence diagram modeling system.

An interesting line of research is the development of knowledge-based decision analysis systems, by Holtzman (1989) called intelligent decision systems. We shall return to this concept in Section 11.3.5.

Equation reasoning

Traditional DSS have, to a large extent, been applied to domains that can be modeled by systems of simple arithmetic relationships such as finance, control and marketing. These relationships, formulated as equations, represent the structure of the domain. Values of dependent variables are computed from definitional and causal relationships. Expert systems, on the other hand, reason with domain knowledge represented as heuristic rules. The problem with a rule-based system is to make the rule set complete and general enough to handle all situations that may be encountered. Attempts at addressing this shortcoming, have resulted in systems that integrate numerical models of a problem with appropriate heuristic models.

Apté and Hong (1988) describe a general mechanism for the qualitative interpretation of simple arithmetic relations. This mechanism is based on equations and rules. The central component is an equation base where all equations are stored in an unfocused form ($x+y+z=0$). The equation base is interrogated by the equation reasoner (ER) which has general (domain-independent) qualitative knowledge (rules) about the most common arithmetic operations (addition, subtraction and so on). In a domain-specific-knowledge base the current status of the variables are stored. By means of the general knowledge in ER, and the domain knowledge in the knowledge base, a problem solver can reason qualitatively with arithmetic equations.

Qualitative reasoning can be very useful while performing financial planning and analysis. Suppose a financial planner of a corporation requires an answer to the problem: If the corporation's concern is its earning per share ratio, what criteria should be used for ranking financing alternatives? This query is passed on to the ER. Earning per share will be identified as the focused variable with the constraint 'increase'. ER will attempt to solve the earning per share ratio after having found the relevant equation in the equation base and turned it into focused form:

$$\text{Earning per share} = \frac{\text{Operating income} - \text{Taxes} - \text{Profit/loss impact}}{\text{Total Shares}}$$

By applying a particular strategy, ER will deduce a constraint on profit/loss impact to be 'decrease'. When passed back to the problem solver this can infer: If earning per share is of concern, rank alternatives by profit/loss impact.

The work of Apté and Hong is particularly devoted to domains of simple arithmetic. Research on qualitative reasoning with causal models requiring more complex mathematical representations can be found in a special issue of *Artifical Intelligence*, **24**(1–3). See also Singh (1991) and Carette (1993) for specific applications of equation reasoning in a DSS context.

Decision trees and influence diagram compilers

The best-known decision modeling tool for analysing decisions under uncertainty is the decision tree. Computer programs to describe and evaluate decision trees have been presented in Chapter 3. However, no such program has to our knowledge, been combined with an equation modeling language and embedded in a DSS to support, in a better way, both the formulation of the decision problem and the calculations necessary for the evaluation of certain parameters of the decision tree.

Influence diagrams are a generalization of decision trees which have been shown, empirically, to have considerable intuitive appeal for a wide class of decision makers, and which are a powerful communication tool for the participants in the decision process. Influence diagrams are acyclic, directed graphs representing the probabilistic, logical and informational relationships between variables in a decision model. As we have seen in Chapter 3, an influence diagram can be used to obtain optimal solutions. The possibility of formulating a problem under the form of an influence diagram and then switching to an equation mode to compute parameter values should be extremely useful in a KB-DSS environment.

A variety of software tools for building and reasoning with influence diagrams or belief nets are now available (Andersen, 1989, Arnold and Henrion, 1990).

11.2.3 Report Generation

We have seen in Chapter 6 that today report generators found in KB-DSS development environments are object oriented and support the definition by users of reports mixing text, tables of figures and images. The integration with decision models is made through variables which can be interspersed in the text. In the case of OPTRANS Object such variables will take values coming from the blackboard of the application and as a consequence from decision models, databases or user input. Important progress will be made by the possibility of using bit-maps to help present and analyze data. The map of a country is often used to convey marketing information as shown in Figure 11.2. In this hypothetical example taken from Parsaye (1993) the numbers of cars sold in each state is represented by height of the bar superimposed on the state territory. Further information is added by subdividing each bar into two pieces, representing truck sales and car sales respectively.

Clearly the key to an optimal utilization of such geographical presentation of data is the integration of the report generator with the database and the decision models. It is necessary to be able to change, for example, the product or company (the entity of which the sales data are attributes) to change the characteristics of the bar on the map. Hypermedia technology is also useful here. For example, by clicking on a city symbol the user could obtain a bar chart of sales in this city, etc.

The development environment should provide the user with the software to scan maps and images and superimpose graphics and text on these maps and images.

Further progress made possible by present day technology is the insertion of full motion video sequences as illustrations in reports. This will certainly be a revolution for KB-DSS in the domain where the

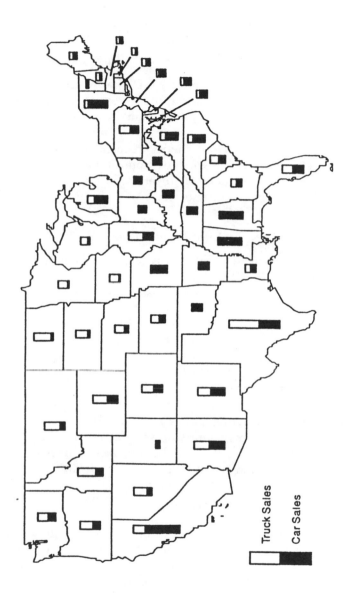

Figure 11.2 Hypothetical data on car and truck sales in the USA (Parsage, 1993)

information is well adapted to video. We have already pointed out that the domain of sales support systems for real estate or travel agencies (Chapter 5) but it will have a very high impact in marketing, advertising agencies, education and home shopping.

11.2.4 *Inference Engine & Knowledge Utilisation*

Inference engines in first generation KB-DSS were usually not the most advanced ones. Their power came more from their integration with the other resources of the system than from the most advanced characteristics in the field of expert systems. The improvements which are needed for the expert components are mainly related to the logical model used to represent knowledge (propositional calculus, predicate calculus, etc.), the treatment of uncertainty, non-monotonicity and negation, the treatment of time.

Logical model used

The propositional calculus only allows one to express links between constants. (P and $Q{\rightarrow}R$).
The predicate calculus is a formal system made of:

* constants and *variables*;
* predicates which can contain variables and can take a truth value over {true, false};
* logical operators: and, or, no,$\rightarrow$, $\leftrightarrow$;
* quantifiers: $\exists$ and $\forall$

It will be possible to write: $[\forall x, \forall y: P(x,y){\rightarrow}P(y,x)]$

For several well known kinds of KB-DSS applications the expert system should be able to use variables in rules. This is required, for instance, in production scheduling (Lecomte, 1990).

Uncertainty

Several expert systems allow for multiple approaches to dealing with uncertainty. The expert system shell Leonardo from Creative Logic in the UK provides the fuzzy set approach as well as the probability approach. The KB-DSS developing tool Guru allows several algebraic methods for dealing with uncertainty coefficients.

In the next generation of KB-DSS we may allow for several measures of uncertainty, numeric as well as non-numeric measures. In domains where the result is, at least, potentially verifiable we should use probabilities, or uncertainty coefficients that can be given a probabilistic interpretation. We could argue that most problems in finance and management control fall into this category. However, contexts in which there is 'uncertainty' concerning apparently non-verifiable statements occur frequently in AI. One type of 'uncertainty' here is impreciseness; this is illustrated by the sentence 'Mary is fairly tall'. The fuzzy set approach is often argued to be appropriate in assessing the degree to which a particular case in hand fulfills a loosely defined concept. Reasonableness is another kind of 'uncertainty', for instance, to what extent is a recommended action or conclusion reasonable. In such a case, the theory of endorsement is better suited.

For further reading on this topic, the reader is referred to the book *Uncertainty in Artificial Intelligence*, edited by Kanal and Lemmer (1986).

Non-monotonic reasoning and negation

Most of the recent research in the domain of problem solving has been restricted to systems based on logic, or, more specifically, first order predicate calculus.

Classical symbol logic lacks the tools for describing how to revise a formal theory to deal with inconsistencies caused by new information. In the world of first order predicate calculus, if we have evidence that a variable may have more than one possible value then, by some method, the contradiction must be resolved immediately and some assumption must be made to assign a value to the variable. Researchers in AI have been led to formalize systems where, as new information arises, the description of the world has to be updated and, in particular, contradictory beliefs have to be resolved. In the light of new information, if a contradiction develops, the assumptions are revised so that the consistency of the system is restored.

Inference systems allowing the withdrawals of assumptions, or the absence of knowledge, are called non-monotonic. These systems attempt to simulate the kind of reasoning in which former conclusions are re-evaluated in the light of newly acquired information. Non-monotonic logic provides a theoretical framework for updating descriptions of the world. There are several attempts to extend standard logic in order to incorporate non-monotonicity.

Few inference mechanisms are able to simulate this kind of reasoning which is, nonetheless, fundamental in management. Studies have been made by McDermott and Doyle (1980) and McDermott (1982); this approach is known as the 'Modal Approach'. Default logic, as presented in Reiter (1978), is an attempt to model the use of general rules subject to exceptions.

The treatment of negation is a complex problem. In automatic theorem proving, treatment of negation may result in combinatorial explosion. Usually, a negative answer is the result because of failure to demonstrate (negation as failure). In order to derive a negative answer within HORN clause-based logic, special rules are needed. The most popular of these special rules is called the closed world assumption introduced by Reiter (1978). This can be written: if $P \rightarrow Q$ and we have non Q then we have non P. The closed world assumption is an example of a non-monotonic inference rule.

Time representation

Time representation is a crucial aspect of many reasoning systems. Most DSS have a time dimension at the database level. In DSS many variables are time-tagged by a time variable, t. Also, it is important to be able to tell the system that a given relation is true for certain time periods or dates.

There are, basically, two approaches for handling time in logic. One is to add a time index to each predicate of the language. The other is to use temporal connectives in order to describe behavior in time. The two approaches can be combined, for example, in a formula like: $P(R(x,y))(t)$ which should read: in the past at time $t, R(x,y)$ was true. This is very useful in systems having built in time dimension with a calendar.

Some expert system shells, have a real time capability. This capability is, clearly, fundamental when decisions have to be taken in a real-time context (trade rooms, arms systems, production control and so on).

The extension of the inferencing mechanism to handle real-time situations still have to be implemented in most KB-DSS development environments.

Knowledge Representation

One clear tendency in recent research on expert systems has been that it was realized that pure rule representation is no longer considered to be sufficient either for the purpose of system construction or for that of knowledge acquisition (Wielinga, Van de Velde, Akkermans, 1993). In this sense the expert system community realizes a fact considered for long as obvious in the DSS community i.e. that quantitative models are essential knowledge representation methods in many domains of application.

For example in the KADS modeling framework, knowledge is broken down into domain knowledge, task knowledge and inference knowledge. The domain knowledge expresses relevant knowledge about the application (physical, socioeconomic . . .) that the task is about (for example knowledge in financial analysis).

The task knowledge specifies tasks. Knowledge about tasks relates to the goal of the task, as well as the activities that contribute to the achievement of that goal (for example company credit granting). The inference knowledge or problem solving knowledge specifies the way to relate task and domain knowledge in order to acheive a goal. For example the generate and test method is problem solving knowledge which can be applied to the goal of diagnosis.

Explanation

A good explanation should be as simple as possible and consistent with the key points in the demonstration of the result to be explained. Generating good explanations involves trades-off between simplicity and completeness.

The quality of explanations in expert systems can, and should still be, much improved. We have given in Chapters 5 and 6, examples of explanations provided by OPTRANS Object which can be compared to a TRACE of the work of the inference engine. As can be seen, the indentation represents the different levels of explanation. The objective in this area is to obtain more concise and easier to understand explanations for the users than of the TRACE explanation kind. A review of explanation methods in expert systems can be found in Safar (1986).

The reader can also refer for explanation related methodologies to Horvitz (1987).

Learning

When a KB-DSS is working in an environment where there is a regular updating of information then learning mechanisms may be useful. The new information may come from the database component of the system, or from the user or the expert. The toolbox of the system may include statistical learning procedures such as those which can be found in short-term forecasting algorithms. Large financial or marketing databases with frequent updating are examples of domains of application where learning can be important in management.

The most important annual conference on knowledge acquisition has been since 1986 at Banff in Canada. Most papers are reprinted in the *Journal of Man Machine Studies*.

Knowledge base verification

The problem of testing consistency and completeness in knowledge bases was discussed in Chapter 9. Many aspects of this problem are still research problems, in particular, if the rules are assigned uncertainty coefficients. Consistency and completeness verification algorithms should be added to the management functions of knowledge bases. A very good survey of the question can be found in Ayel *et al.*, 1988.

11.2.5   Man-Machine Interaction

There are several lines of development in the man-machine interface area that we can expect to see implemented in KB-DSS in the near future. We have pointed out that one key progress in the KB-DSS field has been the adoption of graphical user interface. It is true that user-interface technology and associated artifacts are continuously changing. The graphical interface is presently the dominant paradigm. We can foresee three main directions:

- speech and language based interface;
- gestural interface;
- virtual reality.

The process of generating text automatically in good natural language is difficult and may be as difficult as natural language understanding except in situations where the dialog between the computer and the user is highly predictable due to the constraints of the task.

On the contrary it is clear that users tend to avoid typing as much as possible and prefer dialog boxes when feasible rather than command inputs even in natural language.

The most current implementation of gestural interface is pen-based computing. A mark-up editor might allow the user to edit text by crossing out words with a light pen.

In virtual reality the user is emerged in a virtual world that represents the characteristics of a situation or task.

Intelligent user assistance

Assistance can be built into a KB-DSS on methodologies, at several levels. As mentioned already, we will deal with methodology knowledge bases later. However, by the use of the expert system technology we can develop intelligent help systems.

Closing the gap between conceptual and computer models of a problem

Spreadsheet programming has been a great success in promoting end-user computing for managers, despite its limitations as a full-blown DSS tool. What can we learn from this? There needs to be a close fit between the user's framing of a problem and the way the problem solving process is performed by the computer. To phrase it in another way, the conceptual model that is mapped onto the computer must fit the conceptual model of the problem as perceived by the user.

Normally, the conceptual model taken as basis for the software is more abstract than that of the user. Due to the generic character of a computer program, fewer and more abstract concepts are used. Take, for instance, the area of databases. Data modeling uses a conceptual framework, for example entity-relationships, to describe the reality. Reasoning systems may use rules and control strategies, and analytical modeling may use equation models. They are all rather abstract ways of presenting and analyzing a problem. The greater the abstraction gap is between the user and the computer language, the greater is the need for an intermediary to transform problem specifications into the language understood by the computer, unless we can design interfaces that can close this gap.

Object-oriented programming and graphical presentation techniques are areas that offer promises for closing the contextual gap discussed above. For instance, inference networks can be drawn on the screen and the system will develop the rules and the control strategies of the expert system.

Kaltenbach (1987) describes a system that allows interactive graphical description of mathematical proofs. However, one still needs to be a mathematician to use the system. The objective is to extend this system to be capable of specifying the mathematical and logical structures of the problem in non-technical terms. A substantial amount of work goes on in the area of evaluating man-machine interfaces, in view of cognitive modeling of the user (Billingsley (1982), Zoeppritz (1986) and Woods (1984)).

11.2.6 Toolbox

The present toolbox component of most KB-DSS provides three kinds of algorithms: statistical, forecasting and financial. Computerized tools like these are generally available in systems supporting decision making in areas such as finance, marketing, and management control. However, in other domains such as production, the usual required methods, such as scheduling algorithms, are lacking.

11.2.7 KB-DSS Development Environments

In 1990 during the II Ciocco seminar we gave a first description of what could be the characteristics of a new generation of KB-DSS development environments as we gave a list of research and development goals.

Some of the goals which were listed at that time have been attained. In particular:

- graphical user interface;
- the separation between the interface and the application resources (Klein, Traunmuller, 1993a, 1993b);
- an object-oriented programming of the development environment and its user interface;
- the definition of object-oriented report generators integrating text, images, graphics and maps.

At the time of writing other objectives such as integration of an object-oriented DBMS, the integration of intelligent support in the task of model building, the support of distributed versions of the development environment, the capacity to use several solvers as the modeling moves from simulation modeling to optimization modeling, etc., have not yet been achieved. Clearly the present available development environments have space for improvements. In particular the integration between the components could be improved. We shall then describe the most obvious possible advancements.

Improving Integration Between Components

DBMS-decision models

As the new DBMS (such as object-oriented DBMS) are becoming available as resources in the development environment and as new modeling paradigms are introduced (influence diagrams, etc.) the integration between these resources will have to be implemented. This means for example extending the interface with new ways of defining 'views' of the object-oriented DBMS to import values of attributes to a blackboard type structure where it is made available to the decision models.

DBMS-report generator

As images, graphics, maps, videos are made available as attributes of entities in the databases their use and transformation as objects in the report generator should be implemented. It should be possible to support the scanning of maps and the superimposition on these maps of symbols and graphics, the size of these graphics being dynamically related to decision models and/or databases' variable values.

DBMS-toolbox

The integration between statistics and the database is usually limited to elementary statistics and forecasting algorithms. The growth of the need to extract knowledge (knowledge discovery) in large financial or marketing databases implies the integration of more advanced statistical algorithms (stepwise regression, discriminant analysis, cluster analysis, etc.) with the database.

A Summary on Second Generation of KB-DSS Development Environments

We have tried to define what we believe should be available in a second generation of KB-DSS development environment. This is summarized in Figures 11.3 and 11.4. With respect to the functions available as building blocks in such a system we would like to point out:

- variety of integrated database management systems, at least multi-dimensional or relational and object-oriented;
- variety of modeling formalisms, at least: difference equations for simulation and alternative outcome computation and decision situation modeling;
- a knowledge-base management system;
- a library of statistical agorithms;
- a form generator;
- a software to scan images, maps, and drive videos sources on CD-ROM;
- a blackboard file to integrate the different sources of knowledge;
- a report generator for the presentation of reports mixing text, tables, graphics, images and videos.
- a minimum of two methodological knowledge bases: a statistical knowledge base, and a decision theory knowledge base to construct and analyze an influence diagram that responds to the specific information, and preference of a particular decision situation.
- a hypertext engine to navigate through the user manual of the system.

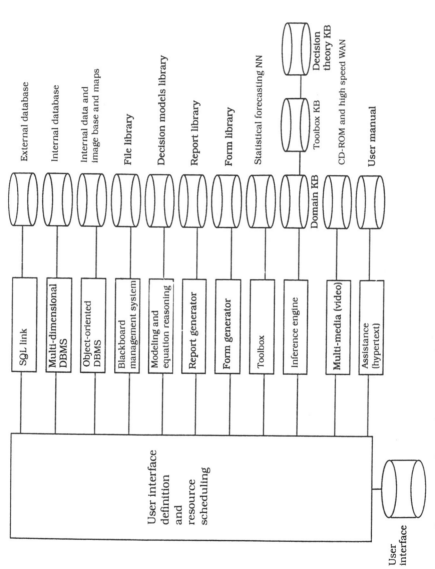

Figure 11.3   General structure of a KB-DSS development environment (2nd generation)

Components	First generation	Second generation
Database management system	Multi-dimensional or relational	Multi-dimensional and objects (including images, maps, etc.)
Decision modeling	Not available	Support of decision analysis cycle and influence diagrams
Simulation modeling	Equations	Automatic documentation and equation reasoning
Model solver	One	Library of solvers
User modeling	Not available	Multi-attribute preference functions, risk preferences
Report generator	Tables of numbers texts, graphics composite display	Object oriented: tables of numbers, texts, graphics, images, maps and video
Reasoning	Inferencing: (forward backword and mixed) No real-time capabilities	Several reasoning mode, objects have impact on reasoning, inheritance order one logic
Knowledge representation	Rules (only one knowledge representation independent from reasoning)	Rules and structured objects
Knowledge coherence	Very limited	Extended
Toolbox	Short-term forecasting Optimization Statistics	Short-term forecasting Optimization Statistics OR models
Communication	Transfer of files E-mail as separated system	Accept real-time group support and video
Distributed aspect	Limited (relation between PC and mainframe version)	Distribution of data, knowledge, models, reports
User interface	Menus Language with assistance on syntax No intelligent assistant	Intelligent assistants (methodological support for each resource)
Domain knowledge base	Yes	Yes
Methodological KB rational decision theory	Not available	Yes
Methodological KB for the toolbox	Not available	Yes

Figure 11.4 KB-DSS from first to second generation. Modified from first edition (1990)

11.3 GENERAL RESEARCH ISSUES AND EMERGING TRENDS

11.3.1 Introduction

The field of DSS is exceedingly broad, and research issues relate to a wide spectrum of disciplines, from 'hard' to 'soft' sciences, as we have already seen in Chapter 1. In the preceding section, we have dealt with technological developments that will determine the next generation of computer environments (hardware and software). Most of these developments will come from other related disciplines such as databases, expert systems, decision theory and so on. However, the DSS field itself has, in certain areas, been pushing the technology. The fast growing area of end-user computing started off in the DSS field with interactive systems needed to support ill-structured decisions where flexibility and user control were critical success factors. Also, new developments in workstation technology can be traced back to the needs for interactive computing for decision support.

However, DSS is very much an application-driven field where the focus of research has been on developing tools that can augment the decision making capabilities of the manager. The DSS research has, as its common objective, the developments of the computer technology to improve problem solving and decision making. Research issues are raised in the intersection of decision making and technology: how is a DSS used, what are the effects on the decision making, what are the requirements on the technology, how are systems built and so on?

A framework for research can be built around the three fundamental perspectives: applications, design, and technology (Hendersen, 1987).

The application perspective focuses on the use of DSS; the impacts on individual behavior; and on organizational and social issues. Also, an important part of application research is to study to what extent technological support should be given, from passive to normative support (Keen, 1986). Normative support has been advocated by researchers in the operations research and management science fields. *Decision aiding* is the term used when the DSS provides methodological computer support. We have dealt with model building aids above. Below we shall also deal with two lines of research in this area: model management systems, and intelligent decision systems.

The design perspective puts emphasis on development life-cycle methodologies and strategies which span the hold process from problem recognition and analysis, through systems specifications to computer implementation. Normative research focuses on decision modeling; behavioral research develops descriptive frameworks for studying decision making; cognitive sciences concentrates on knowledge acquisition methods and learning; and within the systems analysis tradition, issues such as adaptive design, prototyping design, and participative design are addressed.

The technology perspective has been described in the preceding sections and need not be repeated here. Much of this research focuses on man-machine interaction and developments of software environments.

In the following text, we shall deal with a few selected issues which we think may have long-term impacts on the DSS field in general, and on KB-DSS development tools, in particular. These issues are:

- knowledge level modeling;
- decision modeling systems;
- model management systems;
- intelligent decision systems;
- connectionism and neural networks.

11.3.2 Knowledge Level Modeling

In 1982 Allen Newell introduced the notion of *knowledge level* (Newell, 1982). By this notion a new perspective for research on knowledge systems as well as knowledge acquisition was established. An essential feature of this notion is that knowledge is the capacity for behavior that is distinct from whatever data structures are used to represent this behavior.

Newell viewed the knowledge level as a means to understand the behavior of all intelligent agents, including expert systems. He defined the structure of the knowledge level to include the following three abstractions: (1) the *goals* of the intelligent agent: (2) the *actions* of which the agent is capable: and (3) the *knowledge* that allows the agent to carry out actions to achieve its goals. The agent chooses actions according to the principle of rationality.

Note that the object of modeling at the knowledge level is not knowledge but behavior, i.e. observed interaction between an agent and its environment. A knowledge-level model is a model of behavior in terms of knowledge. Newell makes a distinction between various levels of descriptions. Below the knowledge level is the symbol level. Traditionally, knowledge acquisition has been concerned with extracting expert knowledge and displaying it in terms of data structures: production rules, frames, equations, etc. This is what Newell (1982) refers to as the *symbol level*. The knowledge level is a level of description above the symbol level. After Newell's article on knowledge-level systems, researchers have been more and more concerned with developing knowledge acquisition methods and tools that specify the system at the knowledge level. Defining the behaviors of an expert system at the knowledge level is an important prerequisite to implementing the system at the symbol level. *Knowledge-level analysis* is the term that refers to this modeling of intelligent systems behavior, independent of whatever symbols might ultimately be used to program those behaviors in a computer.

Most knowledge acquisition tools today specify the content of the knowledge base in terms of symbol level entities such as rules and frames, inherently ignoring the knowledge level. This is true for the landmark program TEIRESIAS (Davis and Lenat, 1982) for knowledge acquisition as well as all the knowledge base editors found in almost all expert system shells.

Researchers have begun to experiment with knowledge acquisition aids that attempt to specify knowledge in terms of the *behaviors* that are to be achieved by the target expert system. In a paper, Musen (1988) describes a taxonomy for knowledge acquisition aids that enables one to analyze to what extent the tool can assist in knowledge-level analysis. One type of conceptual models on the knowledge level is what Musen calls 'method-based conceptual models'. Here, he refers to Clancey's work on heuristic classification and shows how this model (or problem solving method) can be used in a variey of classification tasks.

Rather than incorporating models of problem solving methods, some knowledge acquisition tools instead adopt conceptual models that reflect recurring domain tasks to be performed. Defining a particular application then requires that users apply the explicit terms and relationships of a general task model to a specific task instance.

From above we see that knowledge acquisition aids can be divided into task oriented and method oriented approaches. Musen (1988) gives examples of tools of the various types. A third approach is generic or reusable models: see for instance Chandrasekaran (1986) or Gruber (1992).

Van de Velde (1993) discusses developments in knowledge-level modeling from Allen Newell's introduction of the concept until today where this concept has been turned into useful tools for the development of knowledge systems. He concludes:

'Viewing knowledge as a means of modelling behaviour (not necessarily of generating it) calls for a re-orientation of knowledge engineering. Knowledge systems are rarely problem solvers themselves. They support a process of agents interacting with the environment and building their case model of the problems and situations that they are faced with. Understanding how to support this process requires more than knowledge acquisition alone. Moreover it can be supported in other and maybe better ways than building a knowledge system. Knowledge engineering must be concerned with analysing and shaping knowledge based processes.' (Van de Velde, 1993)

Van de Velde's article gives a good update on current research on knowledge-level modeling and the developments of knowledge acquisition tools based on this concept. The reader interested in this line of research and development is referred to this article for further reading and references.

11.3.3   Decision Modeling

Decision research is a broad area attracting scientists from many different areas, as we pointed out in Chapter 1. This research could be divided into two major directions, the behavioral decision making direction as described in Chapter 2, and the normative direction in Chapter 3. New conceptual frameworks for decision modeling coming from this research will affect the way we support decision making and, thus, the design specification of a KB-DSS.

Probably the best research briefing on decision making and problem solving in more recent times is the report by a group of very distinguished decision scientists, chaired by Herbert Simon and published in *Interfaces* (Simon *et al.*, 1987). According to this group, what we need is an augmented normative theory, one that takes into account the gaps and elements of unrealism in the subjective expected utility theory by encompassing problem solving as well as choice, and demanding only the kind of knowledge, consistency and computational power that are attainable in the real world. This approach leads us to conclude that the lines of research which are needed are as follows:

- Extending empirical knowledge of actual human, cognitive processes and methods for dealing with complexity.
- Empirical studies of experts' behavior to find out how the problems that they study are solved. This should give birth to knowledge bases combining empirical knowledge and theoretical knowledge.
- Resolution of conflicts of value (individual and groups) and of inconsistencies in belief.
- Setting agendas and framing problems.

Another completely different area of research is to study the relationship between rationality and goals. Several theories give an answer to the question of what we have most reason to do. The theories we have dealt with in Chapter 3 are theories about rationality. We have pointed out, however, in the section dealing with the criticism of the rationality paradigm, that there are also moral theories. Since we defined rationality as being the ability to abide by given rules, we could equally well consider goals other than the expected utility maximization and still be rational.

11.3.4   Model Management Systems

Model management is a specific body of research within the DSS field that has focused on identifying those tasks required to build, and on using models in an interactive problem solving environment and, also on providing a high level of software support for performing these tasks (Elam and Konsynski, 1987). The term Model Management Systems (MMS) has come to denote generalized software environments that offer a wide range of models and allow for flexible access, updating, and changing of the model base.

In order to make use of the analytical capabilities contained in an MMS, the problem must be formulated and analyzed and the results interpreted. We can allocate a number of tasks to each of these functions, as shown in Figure 11.5.

Formulation Tasks
  Formulate – Formulate a new decision model if an appropriate one does not exist in the model base
  Explore – Explore ideas and analyse issues
  Choose – Choose an existing model from the model base

Analysis Tasks
  Match – Identify and test (from a base of existing model structures) the applicability of a model and its associated solution approach to a particular problem
  Expect – Detect, explain, and suggest solutions for abnormal behavior based on user-supplied expectations about model behavior and/or history of the models utility
  Plan – Determine ways to perform analyses to reach predetermined goals
  Cause – Identify causal relationships between model entities
  Recommend – Identify, evaluate, and choose among potential courses of action
  Synthesize – Synthesize new models from model fragments that prove locally successful

Interpretation Tasks
  Explain – Generate explanatory models that provide intuitively reasonable explanations for the model's results
  Interpret – Interpret the analysis solution or results in the context of the problem semantics
  Present – Select appropriate report formats for requested information

---

Figure 11.5   User-model interaction tasks – opportunities for AI application. (Reproduced from Elam J.J. and Konsynski B. (1987). Using artificial intelligence techniques to enhance the capabilities of model management systems. Decision Sciences)

To perform these tasks, human intelligence is usually required. They are, therefore, potential candidates for the application of AI techniques. According to Elam and Konsynski (1987), enhancing MMS so that they perform tasks that usually require human intelligence is, in many ways, similar to developing a knowledge-based system.

The availability of generalized MMS that support the formulation, analysis, and interpretation functions through the use of AI techniques will greatly affect the ability to deliver DSS that can be used for interactive problem solving.

More recently Blanning (1991) made an overview of research issues in Expert Modelbase System. The main areas of improvement can be identified as:

- problem formulation and model construction;
- model base integration;
- interpretation of model outputs;
- development of more convenient user/model interfaces.

We shall make some comments on these issues.

Problem Formulation and Model Building

One of the most interesting attempts to use AI in assisting model comprehension and model construction was mainly addressed by Uschold (1993). According to Uschold model comprehension is limited because models are poorly documented. The key idea of his approach is to build a domain model first, and then define the executable model in terms of it. With such an approach he is able to:

- reduce the conceptual distance between the modeling formalism and the way the user thinks;
- reduce the search in the space of possible models by structuring the modeling process;
- automatize the model documentation.

Uschold has implemented his approach into the software system ELK which is specialized for simulation modeling in ecology.

We have proposed above that the methodology of equation reasoning should be part of any modeling system in a KB-DSS. This is the way to use deep knowledge embedded in quantitative models.

A full conference has been devoted to this subject; the reader is referred to Singh (1991).

11.3.5   Intelligent Decision Systems

Intelligent Decision Systems (IDS) is the term used by Holtzman (1989) to denote a new computer-based technology for aiding decision makers in complex decision situations. The tool is built upon the discipline of decision analysis, which we have described in Chapter 3. The objective is to make the skill of expert decision analysts available by using the expert system technology. This will significantly reduce the cost, time, and level of training needed to analyze difficult decisions by the decision analysis methodology. An IDS provides both domain knowledge and methodological knowledge. Confronted with a complex decision situation there are both the generic and the unique aspects to consider. Expert systems provide help to deal with the generic aspects by means of domain knowledge. The decision analysis methodology provides help for the decision makers to understand their specific circumstances and preferences, the unique aspects of the decision situations at hand. Therefore, IDS applications can address both the generic and unique aspects of a class of decisions.

The concept of a class of decisions is central to the IDS framework. The decision analysis methodology focuses on unique aspects, specific preferences and circumstances, of a decision situation. Analyzing classes of similar decisions as a single unit can greatly reduce the overall expenses and time that are typically associated with the task of decision analysis. Holtzman gives a series of guidelines for designing a class of decisions. He points out that a rule-based system is an excellent way of implementing the analysis of a class of decisions: Analyzing a class of decisions consists of developing a domain-specific knowledge base for a rule-based system that contains a set of assertions designed to guide the analysis of *specific* decisions in a way that reflects the decision maker's unique situation (Holtzman, 1989, p. 81) (see also Figure 11.6). The rule-based system in which the decision class analysis is implemented is an expert system. This expert system, together with a powerful facility for manipulating and evaluating decision theoretic models (such as influence diagrams), constitute, according to Holtzman, an intelligent decision system.

Since the book of Holtzman it is more and more clear that the synthesis of the paradigm of expert system and rational decision analysis is one of the most promising areas of research in KB-DSS. Among the most interesting research paths are: better compilation techniques for influence diagrams, knowledge-based assistance for problem structuring, etc. The reader is referred to Henrion *et al.* (1991) for more details.

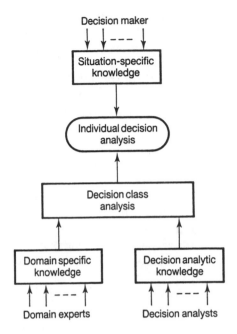

Figure 11.6 *Analyzing a class of decisions consists of designing a set of rules to guide individual decision analyses. (Reproduced from Holtzman S. (1989).* Intelligent Decision Systems)

Our position is that the KB-DSS framework is ideal to implement the IDS concept. A domain-specific knowledge base is augmented, together with a decision analysis methodology knowledge base. The decision analysis knowledge base will help the decision maker to formulate and appraise influence diagrams for the problem. An IDS provides the decision maker with several advantages over traditional expert systems which are, according to Holtzman:

- normative power;
- ease of representation and use of uncertainty;
- clarity in the acquisition of knowledge.

The normative power of an IDS arises from the maximum expected utility axiom which is the prescriptive action axiom of decision analysis. Guided by the methodology of decision analysis, an IDS can elicit important unanticipated features of the given situation. In contrast, the normative power of traditional expert systems are limited to situations that the heuristics of the knowledge base have encountered.

It has been shown that under very weak and desirable assumptions of normative decision making behavior, the representation of uncertainty must obey the axioms that define a probability measure. Non-probabilistic measures used in knowledge engineering have been developed for either or both of the following two purposes:

(1) to avoid the computational burden often associated with probabilistic calculations, and;
(2) as an attempt to automate the way humans perceive and reason with uncertainty (Holtzman, 1989, p. 94).

Intelligent decision systems address the problem of probability assessments in specific decisions.

Holtzman claims that an IDS based on decision analysis is superior to expert systems with respect to the clarity of the terms used in the knowledge acquisition process, due to a well-defined language to describe decision problems.

The knowledge base of an IDS can be divided into five components:

(1) Domain knowledge in an IDS concerns the indirect assessment of chance nodes in the decision model.
(2) Preference knowledge which is used to elicit a preference model from the decision maker;
(3) Probabilistic knowledge which guides the assessment of probability distributions for the chance nodes.
(4) User data which encompasses the set of facts that define the circumstances of the individual user.
(5) Process knowledge guides the user of an IDS through the process of decision analysis. We have called this methodological knowledge.

The IDS concept uses expert system technology and the decision analysis methodology in combination. This gives advantages in two ways:

(1) automating the skills and factual knowledge of the expertise of a few individuals, and;
(2) the normative power of decision analysis which improves the quality of the decision studied.

Figure 11.7 shows that the IDS fills an important gap in the decision making technology.

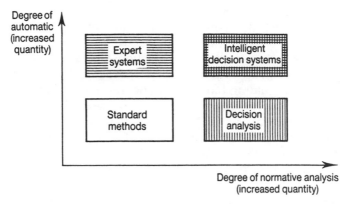

Figure 11.7 *Decision makers have a choice of four kinds of decision making technology. (Reproduced from Holtzman S. (1989).* Intelligent Decision Systems)

11.3.6 Connectionism and Neural Networks

In Chapter 2 we have described theories of cognition; in Chapter 5 we have described reasoning and how it can be implemented as computer programs like expert systems or knowledge systems; and finally, in Chapter 7 we have shown methods to elicit knowledge from experts and represent this knowledge by symbol structures that can be programmed for a computer. Common to all these descriptions is the information processing theory, also called the symbolic paradigm of cognition.

Models of the human mind based on brain analogy have, however, been around for some time. Due to limited computing power these models had limited success in the early days. With the advance of more powerful computers, brain analogy models, known as neural networks, have gained increased interest recently, not only in research environments but in practical applications as well.

The analogy with the brain lies in the way one attempts to model the functionality of the brain. In the brain, the neuron is the fundamental cellular unit. Each neuron is a simple microprocessing unit which receives and combines signals from many other neurons. There are roughly a hundred billion neurons in the human brain. Each one in the order of 1000 connections with other neurons. These connections are thought of as being either excitory or inhibitory. That is, the signal reaching a connection serves to excite (positive weights) or inhibit (negative weights) the output to a greater or lesser extent. These weights represent an encoding of knowledge. The mapping from the input to the output is determined by two functions. Firstly, there is a summation of the weighted inputs. This summation function computes the internal stimulation, or activation level, of the neuron. Based on this level, the neuron may or may not produce an output. The relationship between the internal activation level and the output may be linear or non-linear. Such relationships are expressed by a second function, an activation function. The activation function is the most important building block of the neural network architecture.

A neural network consists of many neurons (also called nodes) joined together in the above manner. Nodes are usually organized into groups called layers. A typical network consists of layers with full or random connection between successive layers. There are at least two layers: an input and output layer. Layers in between these two are called hidden layers.

There are two main phases in the operation of network–learning and recall. Learning is the process of adapting or modifying the connection weights in response to stimuli being presented at the input and the output layers. At the output layer the stimulus corresponds to a desired response to a given input. There are several modes of learning. Recall refers to how the network processes a stimulus presented at the input and creates a response at the output.

A neural network is based on the brain metaphor, as already mentioned, and it is known as the *connectionism* paradigm. The computational significance of a single neuron lies in its pattern of connections with other neurons. The computing power of connections, on the other hand, is truly impressive. The human brain for instance is capable of a huge number of operations in couple of milliseconds. For tasks such as vision, language and motor control, the brain is more powerful than 100 super computers. The human visual system, for instance, has the power of recognizing complex objects in a very short time. And yet, for simple tasks such as multiplication it is less powerful than a four-bit microprocessor (Reddy, 1988).

Connectionist theories of cognition try to stay reasonably close to the fundamental facts of the brain system. The essential features of connectionism are:

(1) *Parallelism*. The neural computational model is characterized by a massively parallel computational scheme and an iterative solution procedure. It follows an iterative procedure to estimate the unknown system parameters–the weights.
(2) *Learning*. The weights can change at the end of each iteration.
(3) *Model-free estimation*. There is no need to prespecify a model, that is the functional relationships. The neural net procedure builds its own model and learns to adjust its parameters appropriately.
(4) *Non-linear model*. A neural net creates a non-linear model of a system.

(5) *Distributed Associative Memory*. Representations do not exist explicitly, but are implicit through the connections.

Applications of neural networks, apart from vision systems, can be found to solve modeling and forecasting problems in finance and economics. One particular feature to be mentioned is the neural network's capability of dealing with non-linear relationships, relationships which are not always easy to handle by ordinary regression analysis. Other areas of applications are sensor processing, signal processing (noise filtering and data compression), and solving expert systems problems.

A number of software packages exist for building neural computing models. They fall in the same categories as expert systems shells: low-, medium-, and high-scale categories.

Several research institutions are active in the field of connectionism and neural computing. A good reference for further reading in this area is the book *Parallel Distributed Processing: Explorations in the Microstructure of Cognition*, edited by McClelland and Rumelhart (1986).

Connectionism is an alternative view on cognition to the symbolic processing view postulated in the information processing theory (IPS). A central theme in cognitive psychology is then, naturally enough, which of these two views best explains human cognition. IPS people claim that cognitive models must be compared to the symbolic level that the brain creates. Connectionists, on the other hand, do not accept that there exists such a level. They claim that what is important is to what extent the model corresponds to the biology of the brain. For further reading on this debate the reader is referred to Smolensky (1987) and Fodor (1988).

At a more pragmatic level, the two views can be seen as complementary. The choice of which one to use is a matter of the problem faced. Also, it is possible to integrate the two computing models in one system. The reasoning of the expert system can be based on a knowledge base with rule representations, while we may have available a toolbox with neural computing tools. One such system is described in Bobrow (1991). Consider a problem faced by Eaton Corporation. Eaton provides a brake-balancing service for fleets of trucks. With improper balance, 18 wheelers (very large trucks) can exhibit failures as simple as excessive brake-wear or as disastrous as the jack-knifing of trucks on the road.

Brake balancing is usually done by mechanics at a fleet maintenance shop. A rule-based expert system was developed. However, their rule-based system required as input interpretations of complex plots of the relationships of air pressure, temperature, braking force, and time, interpretations that can not be done by ordinary mechanics.

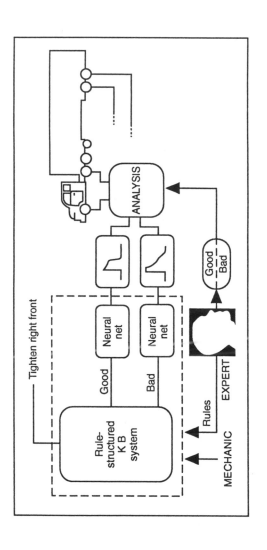

Figure 11.8 *This expert system combines a neural network and a rule-based system to support the common ground for communication to the rule-based system*

Eaton's solution to this problem was to build a system that linked the simple rule-based system to a neural network that did the interpretations of the analyzer output (see Figure 11.8). An expert trained the neural network on the analyzer graphs to produce descriptions to correspond to his own.

Exercises

11.1 What are the directions of research that are useful in the KB-DSS domain?

11.2 Select one example of industrial KB-DSS development software. Perform an analysis of the functions of each subsystem (DBMS, system modeling, user modeling, display management and knowledge management). Compare each subsystem with the functions that are expected to be available in a second-generation KB-DSS.

11.3 (a) What are the application domains that you foresee will be feasible as soon as it is possible to store pictorial images in the DBMS component of a KB-DSS?

(b) Define the specifications of an image extension of a KB-DSS. What are the extensions needed at the modeling language component level, and at the rule syntax level?

(c) Define a work plan for such an extension of a KB-DSS development environment.

11.4 (a) What are the application domains where an object extension of the DBMS component of a KB-DSS seems to be particularly useful?

(b) Define the specifications of an object extension of a first-generation KB-DSS such as OPTRANS-EXPERT. Define a work plan for implementing such an extension.

11.5 (a) Study the interest of coupling an equation modeling language (for a financial application, for example) and a decision tree compiler or, even better, an influence diagram development tool.

(b) Define the specification of such an extension.

(c) Define a work plan for implementing the extension.

11.6 Select a KB-DSS being used by several people in an organization.

(a) Define an experiment to measure:

   (i) The level of usage of the system.

   (ii) The impact of user characteristics on system usage (age, education, prior experience with DSS and prior exposure to PCs).

   (iii) The perception of the assistance given by the system.

   (iv) Objective measure of productivity.

   (v) Objective measure of decision quality.

(b) How would you organize your experiment to collect information on:

   (i) System usage by users.

   (ii) Users characteristics.

   (iii) Productivity in their tasks.

   (iv) Decision quality.

Appendix A: A Curriculum Proposal for a Course on Knowledge-based Decision Support Systems

Session Theme 2×45 minutes	Chapter References
1 **Course presentation** Course material, pedagogics, evaluation and overview	1
2 **Decision making and problem solving** The descriptive view: decision process and heuristics	2
3 **Decision making: The normative view** Basic concepts, risk, decision tree, preferences and so on	3.1–3.5
4 **Decision making: The normative view** Decision analysis cycle and criticism of normative view	3.6–3.7
5 **DSS conceptual framework** Concepts, architectures and demonstration	4.1–4.3
6 **DSS development environment** Components and functions	4.4
7 **Introduction to a development tool (part 1)** (OPTRANS): Hands-on using examples	User manual primer

Session Theme 2×45 minutes	Chapter References
8 **Introduction to a development tool (part 2)** (OPTRANS): Interface designs	User manual primer
9 **AI and Expert systems** AI techniques and knowledge representation	5.1–5.6
10 **AI and Expert systems** Concepts, architectures, opportunities and tools	5.7–5.10
11 **Knowledge-based DSS** Framework and demonstration (BANKER or FINSIM)	6.1–6.4
12 **Expert system development environment (part 1)** (OPTRANS-object) Loan example	User manual primer
13 **Introduction to a development environment Part 2** Loan example continued	User manual primer
14 **Knowledge modeling** Concepts, methods and case (SAFIR)	7
15 **Design and implementation of KB-DSS** Steps and problems	8.2–8.4
16 **Testing and evaluation**	9
17 **Application in finance** Guest lecture of a practitioner	11
18 **Applications in marketing** Guest lecture of a practitioner	11
19 **Future developments and research in KB-DSS**	12
20 **Presentation of term papers – concluding remarks**	

References

Abernathy, Bernabe, Chandler, Wilkins and Wolfe. (1985) A conceptual design of an Intelligent Front End to Scientific Application Programs. *Coupling Symbolic and Numerical Computing* Workshop 1985

Ackoff R. (1967) Management misinformation systems. *Management Science*, Dec. 1967, pp. 147–156

Ackoff R. L. (1979a) The future of operational research is past. *Journal of the Operational Research Society*

Ackoff R. L. (1979b) Resurrecting the future of operational research. *Journal of the Operational Research Society*

Alderberger O. (1976) *Simulfin, Die Finanzwirtschaft der Onternchmuig als simulations experiment.* S. Toeche-Mittles-Verlag

Alpar P. (1991) Knowledge-based modeling of marketing managers' problem solving behavior. *International Journal of Research in Marketing* 8, 5–16

Alter S. (1980) *Decision Support Systems, Current Practice and Continuing Challenges.* Reading MA: Addison-Wesley

Amsted S. M. (1983) On representing and solving decision problems. *PhD Dissertation*, Engineering-Economic Systems Department, Stanford University, Stanford, California

Andersen S. (1989) HUGIN-A Shell for Building Bayesian. Belief Universe for Expert Systems. In *Proceedings of the 11th International Joint Conference for Artificial Intelligence*, 1080–1085, Menlo Park, Calif.

Anderson J. R. and Brower G. H. (1973) *Human Associative Memory.* Washington: Winston

Anderson J. R. (1983) *The Architecture of Cognition*, Cambridge, Mass. Harvard University Press.

Anderson J. R. (1985) *Cognitive Psychology.* New York: W.H. Freeman and Company

Apté and Hong S. (1986) Using qualitative reasoning to understand financial arithmetic: in *Proceedings of the 1986 National Conference on AI*, AAAI, 1986, pp 942–948

Arkes H. R. and Freedman M. R. (1984) Demonstration of the cost and benefits of expertise in recognition memory. *Memory and Cognition*, **12**, 84–89

Arnold B. and Henrion M. (1990) *Demos Interface Manual*, Technical Report, Department of Engineering and Public Policy, Carnegie Mellon University

Arrow K. J. (1951) *Social Choice and Individual Values*. New York: Wiley

Ayel M., Chein M., Pipard E., and Rousset M. C. (1988) De la Cohérence dans les Bases de Connaissances, in Pastre (Eds): *Intelligence Artificielle*, Teknea

Bagozzi R. P. (1984) A Prospectus For Theory Construction in Marketing. *Journal of Marketing*, Winter 1984

Barr A. and Feigenbaum E. A. (1981) *The Handbook of Artificial Intelligence*. Los Altos CA: Kaufman

Bayes T. (1763) Toward solving a problem in the doctrine of chance. *Essay* (published posthumously by his friends of the Royal Society)

Bell D. E. (1979a) Consistent assessment procedures using conditional utility functions. *Operations Research*, **27**, 1054–1066

Bell D. E. (1979b) Multiattribute utility functions: decompositions using interpolation. *Management Science*, **25**, 744–753

Bernouilli D. (1738) Specimen theoriae Novae de Mensura Sortis. *Commentarii Academiae Scientiarum Imperialis Petropolitanae*, tomus V

Beulens A. J. M. and van Nunen F. A. E. E. (1988) The use of expert system technology in DSS, in design aspects of advanced DSS. *DSS International Journal*, **4**(4)

Bhatnagar R. K. and Kanal L. N. (1986) Handling uncertain information: a review of numeric and non-numeric methods. In *Uncertainty in Artificial Intelligence* (Kanal and Lemmer, eds). North-Holland

Biggs S. F. and Mock T. J. (1983) An investigation of auditor decision processes in the evaluation of internal controls and audit scope decisions. *Journal of Accounting Research*, **21**(1)

Billingsley P. (1982) Navigation through hierarchical menu structures. Does it help to have a map? In *Proc. Human Factor Society 26th Annual Meeting*, Seattle, Washington

Birtwisle G. M., Dahl O.-J., Myhrhaug B., and Nygaard K. (1973) *Simula begin*, Auerbach Press, Philadelphia

Blainbridge L. (1981) Verbal reports as evidence of the process operator's knowledge. In *Fuzzy Reasoning and its Applications* (Mamdani E. H. and Gaines B. R., eds). London: Academic Press

Blanning Robert W. (1991) Expert Modelbase Systems: Research Directions, in *Recent Developments in Decision Support Systems* (Holsapple Clyde, Whinston Andrew, eds), Springer Verlag, Computer and System Science series

Bobrow D. G. (1991) *Dimensions of Interaction*, AI MAGAZINE Fall (1991), 64–80.

Bolger F. and Wright G. (1994) Assessing the quality of expert judgment. *Decision Support Systems*, **11**, 1–24

Bonczek R. H., Holsapple C. W. and Whinston A. B. (1981) *Foundations of Decision Support Systems*. London: Academic Press

Bonini C. P. (1963) *Simulation of Information and Decision Systems in the Firm*. Englewood Cliffs NJ: Prentice-Hall

Boose J. H. (1984) Personal construct theory and the transfer of expertise. In *Proceedings of AAAI-84*, 27–33

Boose J. H. (1985) A knowledge acquisition program for expert systems based on personal construct psychology. *Int. J. Man–Machine Studies*, **23**(4)

Boudis M. and Page M. (1994) Simulation of Models Combining Quantitative and Quantitative Knowledge, Proceedings 11th European Conference on AI *AI in Finance and Business*, August 1994, Amsterdam

Bouwman M. J. (1978) Financial diagnosis: A cognitive model of the processes involved. *PhD Thesis* Carnegie-Mellon University, Pittsburg, Pennsylvania

Bouwman M. J. (1983) Human diagnostic reasoning by computer: an illustration from financial analysis. *Management Science*, **29**(6), 653–672

Bouwman M. J., Frishkoff P. A., and Frishkoff P. (1987) How do financial analysts make decisions? A process model of the investment screening decision. *Accounting, Organizations and Society*, **12**(1)

Bower R. S. and Wipern R. F. (1969) Risk, return measurement in portfolio appraisal models. *JFQA*, December 1969

Brans J. P., Vincke P. H., and Mareschal B. (1986) How to select and how to rank projects: the PROMETHEE method. *European Journal of Operational Research* **24**, 228–238. North-Holland

Breuker J. A. and Wielinga B. J. (1984) *Techniques for Knowledge Elicitation and Analysis*. Report 1.5, Esprit Project 12, University of Amsterdam

Brigg R. (1986) How a complex numerical algorithm can be transformed into a simple symbolic algorithm in *Coupling Symbolic and Numerical Computation in Expert Systems* (Kowalin J. S., ed.). North-Holland

Briys E. (1987) Etude comparative des Systemes Experts en analyse financier. In *Compte Rendus dec JIIA-87* (Noel J. L. P., ed.). 6 rue Dufrenoy, 75116 Paris

Buchanan B. G., Sutherland G. L., and Feigenbaum E. A. (1969) Heuristic DENDRAL: a program for generating explanatory hypotheses in organic chemistry. *Machine Intelligence*, Vol 4 (Meltzer B. and Michie D., eds). Edinburgh: Edinburgh Press

Buisine L. (1987) Intelligence artificielle et diagnostic d'entreprise. In *Actes de Colloque Systemes Experts et Gestion d'Entreprise*. Rue de la Gorenne, 92000 Nanterre, France

Bundy A., Silver B., and Plummer D. (1985) An analytical comparison of some rule-learning programs. *Artificial Intelligence*, **27**(2)

Burgun J. J. (1988) Presentation du système FINSIM, SOREFI de Champagne Ardenne, Direction du Development, note interne, 9 bd de la paix, 51053 Reims Cedex, France

Burke R., Rangswamy A., Wind F., and Elisshberg J. (1990) A knowledge based system for advertising design. *Marketing Science* **9**, 3, Summer

Burke R. (1991) Reasoning with empirical marketing knowledge. *International Journal of Research in Marketing*, **8**, 75–90

Butler Cox (1987) *Expert Systems in Business*. Research Report 60, Butler Cox & Partners Ltd, London

Carette P. and Singh M. (eds) (1993) Qualitative reasoning and decision technologies, *Proceedings of the IMACS International Workshop*, CINME

Carleton W. T. (1970a) An analytical model for long range financial planning. *Journal of Finance*, May 1970

Carleton W. T. (1970b) Linear programming and capital budgeting models: a new interpretation. *Journal of Finance*, December 1970

Carnap R. (1950) *Logical Foundation of Probability*, Chicago: The University of Chicago Press

Caroll D. C. and Zannetos Z. S. (1967) Toward the realization of intelligent MIS 1966. In *Information System Science and Technology* (Walter D. E., ed.), pp. 151–168. Washington DC: Thomson Book Company

Carter C. and Cartlett J. (1987) Assessing credit card applications using machine learning. *IEEE Expert*

Chambers T., Zayay J. M. E., and Pregibon D. (1981) Expert software for data analysis: an initial experiment. In *Proceedings of the 43rd Session of the International Statistics Institute*, Buenos Aires, Argentina

Chandrasekaran B. (1986) Generic tasks in knowledge-based reasoning: High level building blocks for expert system design. *IEEE Expert*, **1**, 3, 23–30

Chang C. L. and Walker A. (1984) PROSQL: A prolog programming interface with SQL/DS. In *Proc. First Int'l Workshop Expert Data Base Systems*, Kerschberg L. (ed.), Menlo Park, California: Benjamin Cummings

Chapuzot B. (1987) Un systeme expert de conseil en placement bancaire, communications. In *International Seminar on DSS and Knowledge Based DSS in Banking*, Centre HEC-1SA, F-78350 Jouy-en-Josas, France

Charniak E. and McDermott D. (1985) *Introduction to Artificial Intelligence*. Reading MA: Addison-Wesley

Charniawska B. and Wolff R. (1986) How we decide and how we act: on the assumption of Viking organization theory, Den X. *Nordiska Foretaksøkonomiske Konferanse*, NHH, Bergen, Norway

Checkland P. (1981) *System Thinking, System Practice*. Chichester: Wiley

Chi M. T. H. *et al.* (1981) Expertise in problem solving. In *Advances in the Psychology of Human Intelligence* (Sternberg R., ed.). Hillsdale NJ: Lawrence Erlbaum Associates

Christensen G. (1987) Successful implementation of decision support systems; an empirical investigation of usage intentions and behavior, *PhD Dissertation*, University of California, LA

Chomsky N. A. (1957) *Syntactic Structures*. The Hague: Morton

Chu P.-C. (1992) An object-oriented approach to modeling financial accounting systems. *Accounting, Management and Information Technology*, **2**, 1, 39–56

Clancey W. J. (1984) Knowledge acquisition for classification of expert systems. *Proc. ACM 1984 Annual Conference*, USA

Clancey W. J. (1985) Heuristic classification. *Artificial Intelligence*, **27**, 289–350

Clarkson G. P. E. (1962) *Portfolio Selection: A Simulation of Trust Investment*. Englewood Cliffs NJ: Prentice-Hall

Coats P. (1988) Why expert systems fail. *Financial Management*, **17**, 3, Autumn

Cohen K. J., Gilmore T. G., and Singer F. A. (1966) Bank procedures for analyzing business loan applications. In *Analytical Methods in Banking* (Hammer ed.) Richard Irwin

Cohen M. D., March J. G., and Olsen J. P. (1972) A garbage can model of organizational choice. *Administrative Science Quarterly*, **17**(1)

Condorcet, Marquis de (1785) *Essai sur l'application de l'analyse à la probabilité des decisions rendues à la pluralité des voix*. Paris

Cooper D. and Kornell J. (1986) Combining symbolic and numeric methods for automated induction in coupling symbolic and numeric competing in knowledge based systems

Cooper G. (1990) The computational complexity of probabilistic inference using belief networks. *Artificial Intelligence* **42**, 393–405

Crick Francis (1994) *The Astonishing Hypothesis*, Macmillan Publishing

Cyert R. M. and March J. G. (1963) *A Behavioral Theory of the Firm*. Englewood Cliffs NJ: Prentice-Hall

David J. M., Krivine J. P., and Simmons R. (eds) (1993) *Second Generation Expert Systems*. Springer

Davidson D. (1980) *Essays on Actions and Events*. Oxford University Press, 1980

Davidson D. (1982) Paradoxes of irrationality. In Frend, Wollheim, Hopkins (eds) *Philosophical Essays* Cambridge University Press, 289–305

Davis G. B. and Olson M. H. (1985) *Management Information Systems*. New York: McGraw-Hill

Davis R. and Lenat D. B. (1982) *Knowledge-Based Systems in Artificial Intelligence*. McGraw-Hill

Delcambre L. M. L. (1988) RPL: An expert system language with query power. *IEEE-Expert*

Delgrande J. P. (1987) A formal approach to learning from examples. *Int. J. Man–Machine Studies*, **26**(2)

Delidjakova-Drenik E., Mavec A., and Stariha M. (1988) *BONITETA: A knowledge Based System for Commercial Bank Credit Rating*, Eurobanking 1988, IFORS Dublin, Ireland.

De Sanctis G. and Gallupe R. B. (1987) A foundation for the study of Group Decision Support Systems, *Management Science*, **33**, 5, 589–609

Duchessi P., Shawky H., and Seagle J. P. (1988) A knowledge-engineered system for commercial loan decisions. *Financial Management*

Duda R. O., Gaschnig J. G., and Hart P. E. (1979) Model design in the PROSPECTOR consultant system for mineral exploration. In *Expert Systems in the Micro-electronic Age* (Michie D., ed.). Edinburgh: Edinburgh Press

Edwards W. (1983) Human cognitive capabilities, representativeness, and ground rules for research. In *Analyzing and Aiding Decision Processes* (Humphreys P., Svenson O. and Vari A., eds). Amsterdam: North-Holland

Elam J. J. and Konsynski B. (1987) Using artificial intelligence techniques to enhance the capabilities of model management systems. *Decision Sciences*. **18**

Eliasberg J. and Lilien G. L. (eds) (1993) Marketing in handbooks. In *Operation Research and Management Science*, North Holland

Englemore R. and Morgan T. (eds) (1989) *Blackboard Systems*. Reading, Mass.: Addison-Wesley

Ericsson K. A. and Simon H. (1984) *Protocol Analysis*. Cambridge MA: The MIT Press

Estrabaud F. and Klein M. (1995) A Decision Support System for production and Financial Planning in a Tannery. *Engineering Costs and Production Economics*, **9**, 239–247

Europa: Management Report (1985) Digital Equipment Corporation International (Europe)

Express user manual (1980) Management Decision Systems Inc, Riverside Road, Weston, Mass, 02193 USA

Feigenbaum E. (1977) The art of artificial intelligence: themes and case studies of knowledge engineering. In *Proceedings of the Fifth International Joint Conference on Artificial Intelligence*, pp 1014–1029, Cambridge MA

Feigenbaum E., Buchanan B. G., and Lederberg J. (1971) On generality and problem solving: a case study using the DENDRAL prgram. In *Machine Intelligence*, **6** (Meltzer B. and Michie D., eds). Edinburgh: Edinburgh Press

DeFinetti B. (1974) *The Theory of Probability*. London: Wiley

FINBON (1993) *Ekspertni Sistem za financno analizo poslonanja podjetja.*, ISPO, Šubičeva 2, 6100 Ljubljana, Slovenia

FINSIM-EXPERT User Manual (1994) SIG, 4 bis rue de la Libération, 78350 Jouy-en-Josas, France

Fischhoff B. *et al.* (1981) *Acceptable Risk*. Cambridge: Cambridge University Press

Fischoff B., Goitein B. P., and Shapiro B. (1982) The experienced utility of expected utility approaches. In *Expectations and Actions: Expectancy-value Models in Psychology* (Feather N., ed.). Hillsdale NJ: Erlbaum

Fodor J. A. and Pylyshyn Z. W. (1988) Connectionism and cognitive architecture: a critical analysis. *Cognition*, **28**, 3–71

Følstad H. (1984) Thinking aloud protocols and protocol analysis. An attempt to apply this to a practical case of financial analysis (in Norwegian). *Termpaper*. NHH, Bergen, Norway

Forrester J. W. (1961) *Industrial Dynamics*. Cambridge MA: The MIT Press

Fulton S. L. and Pepe C. O. (1990) An introduction to model-based reasoning. *AI Expert*, January

Galbraith J. R. (1977) *Organizational Design*. Reading MA: Addison-Wesley

Gale W. A. and Pregibon D. (1983). *Building on Expert Interface*. Technical Memorandum Bell Telephone Laboratories

Gangneux P. H. (1988) A DSS to improve the link between the sale function and the manufacturing. In *Proceedings of the 5th International Seminar on Production Economics*. Igls, Austria Elsevier

Gant W. and Schaer A. (1988) A Prolog based PC-Implementation for new-production introduction. In: *Data, Expert Knowledge and Decision* (W. Gant and A. Schaer, eds), pp. 42–53. Berlin/Heidelberg, Springer

Ganzendam H. (1993) *Variety Control Variety, On the Use of Organisation Theories in Information Theories in Information Management*. Wotters-Noordhoff

Gerrity T. P., Jr (1970) The design of man-machine decision systems. *PhD Dissertation* MIT, Cambridge MA

Gerrity T. P. Jr. (1971) The design of man-machine decision systems: an application to portfolio management. *Sloan Management Review*, **12**(2), 59–75

Gill Grandon T. (1995) Early Expert Systems: Where are they Now, *MSS Quarterly*, March 1995

Gilmore J. F. and Howard C. (1986) Expert system tool evaluation. In *Sixth International Workshop on Expert Systems*. Avignon, France

Ginzberg M. J. (1975) A process approach to management science implementation *PhD Dissertation*, MIT, Cambridge MA

Girault F. and Klein M. (1971) Le projet SCARABEE: une banque de données et de modèies pour la recherche en analyse financière et en gestion de portefeuille. *L'Analyse Financière*

Goldberg, A. and Robson D. (1983) *Smalltalk-80*. Reading, Mass.: Addison-Wesley

Gorry G. A. (1967) *A System for Computer-Aided Diagnosis*. MAC-TM-44, Project MAC, MIT, Cambridge MA

Gorry G. A. (1969) Modelling the Diagnostic Process. In *Working Paper No. 370–69*, Sloan School of Management, MIT, Cambridge MA

Graham, I. (1987) Knowledge-based systems in the dealing room. In *IBM seminar on Expert Systems in Banking and Insurance*. Jouy-en-Josas, France

de Groot M. H. (1970) *Optimal Statistical Decisions*. New York: North-Holland

Gruber T. (1992) *Ontolingua: A Mechanism to Support Portable Ontologies*. Version 3.0 Knowledge Systems Laboratory, Stanford University, CA

Guilfoyle C. and Jeffcoate J. (1988) *Expert Systems in Banking and Securities*. Ovum Ltd, London

Hamscher W. (1994) The business analyser: a second generation approach to financial decision support. In *Second Generation Expert Systems* (David, Krivine, Simmonsm, eds) Springer Verlag

Hacking I. (1975) *The Emergence of Probability*. Cambridge: Cambridge University Press

Hajek P. (1982) Applying artificial intelligence to data Analysis: GURA, in context of expert systems. In *Proc ECAI-82*, Orsay, France

Hall R. H. and Quinn R. E. (1983) *Organizational Theory and Public Policy.* Sage CA

Hapek P. and Ivanek I. (1982) *Artificial Intelligence and Data Analysis.* COMPSTAT-82, Physica-Verlag, Vienne

Harmon P. and King D. (1985) *Expert Systems: Artificial Intelligence in Business.* New York: John Wiley

Harsanyi J. C. (1977) *Rational Behavior and Bargaining Equilibrium in Games and Social Situations.* Cambridge: Cambridge University Press

Hart A. (1986) *Knowledge Acquisition for Expert Systems.* London: Kogan Page Ltd

Haugeland, J. (1985) *Artificial Intelligence: The Very Idea.* Cambridge MA: The MIT Press

Hayes-Roth B. (1985) A blackboard architecture for control. *Artificial Intelligence,* **26**, 251–321, North-Holland, Elsevier

Hayes-Roth F., Waterman D. A., and Lenat D. (eds) (1983) *Building Expert Systems.* Reading MA: Addison-Wesley

Helfert E. A. (1963) *Techniques of Financial Analysis.* Homewood Ill: Richard D. Irwin Inc

Henderson J. C. (1987) Finding synergy between decision support systems and expert systems research. *Decision Sciences,* **18**

Henrion M., Breese J., and Horvitz E. (1988) Decision theory and artificial intelligence, in *International Journal of Approximate Reasoning* special issue on uncertainty and artificial intelligence, vol 2, 247–302, Elsevier Science

Hiltz R. and Turoff M. (1978) *The Network Nation, Human Communication via Computer.* Reading MA: Addison-Wesley

Hogarth R. M. (1980) *Judgement and Choice.* New York: Wiley

Hollander A. S. (1992) A Rulke-based approach to variance analysis in O'Leary D. E. and Watkins P. R. (eds) in *Financial Application of Artificial Intelligence.* Amsterdam: North Holland

Holsapple C. W. and Whinston A. B. (1986) *Expert Systems using Guru.* Dow Jones-Irwin

Holsapple C. W. and Whinston A. B., eds (1987) *Decision Support Systems: Theory and applications.* Springer Verlag NATO ASI Series, *Computer and System Science,* **31** (This volume contains the proceeding of the NATO Advanced Study Institute on Decision Support Systems Theory and Application, which took place at Maratea, Italy in June 1985)

Holsapple C. and Whinston A. (1993) Recent developments in decision support systems, *Computer and Systems Science* vol III, Proceedings of the NATO Advance Studies Institute, II Ciocco, Springer

Holtzman S. (1989) *Intelligent Decision Systems.* Reading MA: Addison-Wesley

Howard R. A. (1968) The foundation of decision analysis, *IEEE-SSCA,* **3**

Howard R. A. (1980) An assessment of decision analysis. *Operation Research,* **28**(1), 4–27

Howard R. A. (1983) The Evolution of Decision Analysis. In *Readings on the Principles and Applications of Decision Analysis.* (Howard R. A. and Matheson J. E., eds) Vol. 1, 5–16, Strategic Decision Group, Menlo Park CA

Howard R. A. (1988) Decision analysis: practice and promise. *Management Science,* **34**(6), 679–695

Howard R. A. and Matheson J. E. (1968) An introduction to decision analysis. In *Readings on the Principles and Applications of Decision Analysis.* Decision Analysis Group, SRI International

Howard R. A. and Matheson J. E. (1983a) Influence diagrams. In *Readings on the Principles and Application of Decision Analysis* Vol II. (Howard R. A. and Matheson J. E., eds), pp. 719–762. Menlo Park CA: Strategic Decision Group

Howard R. A., James E., and Matheson E. (1983b) In *Readings on The Principles and Applications of Decision Analysis* Vols I and II. Strategic Decision Group, Menlo Park, CA

Huber G. P. and Mcdaniel R. R. Jr (1986) Exploiting information technologies to design more effective organizations. In *Managers, Micros and Mainframes* (Jarke M., ed.) New York: John Wiley

Hunt S. D. (1994) Positivism and Paradigm Dominance in Consumer research: Toward critical Pluralism and Rapprochement, *Journal of Consumer Research*, **21**, June 1994, p. 55–70

Jäger K., Peemöller N., and Mohde M. (1988) A DSS for planning chemical production in a pharmaceutical company. In *Processing of the Fifth International Seminar on Production Economics*. Elsevier

Janis I. L. and Mann L. (1977) *Decision Making: A Psychological Analysis of Conflict, Choice, and Commitment*. New York: Free Press

Jarke M. and Radermacher F. J. (1988) The AI potential of model management and its central role in decision support in design aspects of advanced DSS. *DSS International Journal*, **4**(4)

Johansen *et al.* (1974) *Group Communication through Electronic Media: Fundamental choice and Social Effects*. Education Technology

Johnson P. E. (1983) What kind of an expert should a system be? *The Journal of Medicine and Philosophy*, **8**, 77–97

Johnson P. E. (1984) The expert mind: a new challenge for the information scientist. In *Beyond Productivity: Information Systems Development for Organizational Effectiveness* (Bemelmans, ed.) Elsevier Science Publications

Johnson T. (1984) The commercial application of expert system technology. *Knowledge Engineering Review*, **1**(1), 15–25

Kahl D., Klein M., Manteau A., and Perrin J. C. (1977) *Un Système d'Information et d'Aide à la Décision pour le contrôle financier des sociétés multinationales, Modélisation et Maîtrise des Systèmes*. Editions Hommes et Techniques tome 2

Kahnemann D., Slovie P., and Tversky A. (eds) (1982) *Judgement under Uncertainty: Heuristics and Biases*. Cambridge: Cambridge University Press

Kaltenbach M. (1987) Computer representation and animation of mathematical proofs with dynaboard. *INRIA*. Le Chesnay Cedex, France

Kanal L. N. and Lemmer J. J. (eds) (1986) *Uncertainty in Artificial Intelligence*. North-Holland: Elsevier Science Publishers BV

Kastner J., Apte C., Giesmer J., Hong S. J., Karnaugh M., Mays E., and Tozawa Y. (1986) A knowledge-based consultant for financial marketing. *The AI Magazine*

Keen P. G. W. (1981) Value analysis: justifying decision support systems. *Management Information System Quarterly*, **5**(1)

Keen P. (1986) Decision support systems: the next decade. In *Decision Support Systems: A decade in Perspective* (McLean E. R. and Sol H. G., eds) North-Holland: Elsevier Science Publishers BV

Keen P. G. W. and Scott Morton M. S. (1978) *Decision Support Systems, An organizational perspective*. Reading MA: Addison-Wesley

Keeney R. (1969) *Multidimensional Utility Functions: Theory, Assessment and Application*. Technical Report No. 73, Operations Research Centre, MIT

Keeney R. (1988) Value driven expert systems for decision support, in design aspects of advanced DSS. *DSS International Journal*, **4**(4)

Keeney R. and Raiffa H. (1976) *Decisions with Multiple Objectives Preferences and Value Tradeoffs*. New York: John Wiley
Keeney R. (1993) *Value Focused Thinking*. Harvard University Press
Kelly G. (1955) *The Psychology of Personal Constructs*. Norton
Keon J. W. and Bayer J. (1986) An expert approach to sales promotion management. *Journal of Advertising Research*, **20**, 4, 19–28
Kepner C. H. and Tregoe B. B. (1981) *The New Rational Manager*. Princeton: Princeton Research Press
Kerchberg L. (1986) Expert data base systems. In *Proceedings from the first International Workshop*, Menlo Park CA: Benjamin Cummings
Kerlinger F. N. (1973) *Foundations of Behavioral Research* 2nd edn. London: Holt, Rinehart and Winston
Keynes J. M. (1921) *A Treatise on Probability*
Kim J. and Courtney J. F. (1988) A survey of knowledge acquisition techniques and their relevance to managerial problem domains. *Decision Support Systems*, **4** (3)
Kim J. and Pearl J. (1993) A computational model for causal diagnostic reasoning in inference engines. In *Proceedings of the Eighth International Joint Conference on Artificial Intelligence*, Menlo Park, California
King D. (1986) An explanation facility for decision support systems. *Sixth Journees Internationales, Les Systèmes Experts et leurs Applications*, Avignon, France
Kirkebøen G. (1992) En psykologihistorisk skisse i lys av Descartes, filosofi, *NAIM (Nordic AI Magazine)*, **7**, 2, September
Kirkwood C. W. (1982) A case history of nuclear power plant site selection. *Journal of Operational Research Society*, **33**, 353–366
Kitzmiller C. T. and Kowalik J. S. (1985) Coupling symbolic and numeric computing in knowledge-based systems. *Proceedings of the Workshop Sponsored by the AAAI*, Seattle, Washington
Klein M. (1971a) Le Projet SCARABEE: Un Système Evolutif d'Exploitation des Banques de Donnèes Financières. In *Proceedings "journeès Banques de Donnèes"*, AFCET-IRIA, Aix-en-Provence
Klein M. (1977) Systèmes question/réponse et aide à la décision en analyse financière. In *Proceedings of the International Seminar on Intelligent Question—Answering and Data Base Systems*, Bones 1977. (Simon J. C., ed.) INRIA
Klein M. (1986) Recent developments in PC-OPTRANS a KB-DSS generator. In *Euro VIII (8th European Conference on Operation Research)*. Fondation Calouste Gulbenkian, DSS and Expert System Session, (SIG)
Klein M. (1988) FINSIM Expert: a knowledge based DSS for financial analysis and planning. In *Proceedings Eurinfo '88*, North-Holland
Klein M. (1989) Experiment with FINSIM EXPERT a KB-DSS for financial analysis and planning. In *Proceedings 5th International Seminar on Production Economics*, Elsevier
Klein M. (1991) Decision support for municipality financial planning. In *Proceedings 2nd IFIP TC8 Conference on Governmental and Municipal Information System* (R. Traunmuller, ed), North Holland
Klein M. (1993c) DSS for financial decision making in public administration. In *Proceedings of the IFIP Conference Decision Support in Public Administration* (P. Bots, ed), North Holland
Klein M. (1993d) Research issues for second generation knowledge based DSS in recent development. In *Decision Support System, Proceedings NATO Advanced Studies Institute*, Il Ciocco, Italy, June 1991 (Holsapple and Winston, eds), Springer, *Coll. Computer and System Science* **101**

Klein M. (1993e) Knowledge based decision support system development environment. In *Proceedings Information Systems Architecture and Technology ISAT 93* (Bazewicz, ed) Politechnick Wroclaw, Poland

Klein M. (1994) Progress and Challenges in the Application of Decision Support Systems to Management, *13th IFIP World Computer Congress 94*, **3**. (Duncan K. and Krueger K., eds) Elsevier Science B.V.

Klein M. and Levasseur M. (1971) FINSIM: un outil d'aide à l'analyse financière. *Analyse Financière*

Klein M. and Levy J. P. (1974) SCARABEE, un langage d'aide à l'analyse financière. *01-Informatique, mensuel*

Klein M. and Manteau A. (1983) OPTRANS: a tool for implementation of decision support centers. In *Process and Tools for Decision Support* (Sol H. G., ed.)

Klein M. and Tixier V. (1971b) SCARABEE: a data and model bank for financial engineering and research. In *Proceeding IFIP World Congress*, North-Holland

Klein M. and Traunmüller R. (1993a) Architecture and user interface of knowledge based DSS development environment. In *Proceedings of the 26th Hawai International Conference on System Science* (Nunemaker, Sprague, eds), IEEE Computer Society Press

Klein M. and Traunmüller R. (1993b) User interface of knowledge based DSS development environment, some further developments. In *Proceedings of 4th International Conference DEXA*. Data Base and Expert Systems Applications, Springer, 746–755

Klein M. and Villedieu T. (1987) A KB-DSS for financial planning, application to French municipalities. *Engineering Costs and Production Economics*, **12**, North-Holland: Elsevier

Klein M., Levy J. P., and Limousin P. (1974) Projet SCARABEE. Présentation, structure du système, aspects méthodologiques. *Cahier de Recherche*, **10**, Centre HEC-ISA, Jouy-en-Josas, France

Klein M., Dussartre J. E., and Despoux F. (1987) *Introducing AI in OPTRANS a DSS Generator, in Decision Support Systems: Theory and Application* (Holsapple C. W. and Whinston A. B., eds) Springer-Verlag

Kolb D. A. and Frohman A. L. (1970) An organization development approach to consulting. *Sloan Management Review*, **12**(4), 51–65

Korsan R. J. and Matheson J. E. (1978) *Pilot Automated Influence Diagrams Decision Aid.* SRI International Technical report No. 7078 *SRI International*, Menlo Park, CA

Kosy D. and Wise B. (1984) Self explanatory financial planning models. In *Proc of the American Association for Artificial Intelligence* 1976–1981

Kraemer K. L. and King, J. L. (1988) Computer-Based Systems for Cooperative Work and Group Decision Making, ACM Computing Surveys, vol 20, June 1988, pp 115–148

Kyburg H. (1991) Normative and Descriptive Ideals, in *Philosophy and AI, Essays at the Interface* (Cummins R., Pollock J., eds) MIT Press.

de Langle C. and Michel S. (1985) Systeme Expert de placement bancaire pour les particulies. *Bancatique*, **5**

Laird J. E., Newell A., and Rosenbloom P. S. (1987) Soar: an architecture for general intelligence. *Artificial Intelligence*, **33**, 1

Laplace P. (1812) *Théorie analytique des probabilités*. Imprimerie Impériale, Paris

Larkin J. H. *et al.* (1980) Expert and novice performance in solving physics problems. *Science*, **208**, 1335–1342

Laske O. E. (1986) On competence and performance notions in expert systems design: a critique of rapid prototyping. In *Proceedings of the 6th International Workshop on Expert Systems & Their Applications*. Avignon, France

Leavitt H. J. (1965) Applied organizational change in industry: structural, technological and humanistic approaches. In *Handbook of Organizations* (March J. G., ed.). Chicago: Rand McNally

Lecomte C., Klein M., and Dejax P. (1993) Using a Knowledge Based DSS development Environment to implement a Scheduling System for a Workshop. *International Journal of Production Economics*, **30–31** 437–451. Elsevier

Lecot K. (1988) Using expert systems in banking: the case of fraud detection and prevention. *Expert Systems Review*, **1**(3) University of Southern California

Lee J. K., Chu E. C. and Kim H. S. (1990) Intelligent Stock Portfolio Management System. In *Investment Management: Decision Support and Expert Systems* (Trippi R. R. and Turban E., eds), Boyd and Fraser Publ. Comp., Boston, MA

Lee R. M. (1983) Epistemological aspects of knowledge-based decision support systems. In *Process and Tools for Decision Support* (Sol H. G., ed.), North-Holland: Elsevier

Lenat D. B. and Harris G. (1978) Designing a rule system that searches for scientific discoveries. In *Pattern-Directed Inference Systems* (Waterman D. A. and Hayes-Roth F., eds) N.Y.: Academic Press

Leong S. M. (1985) Metatheory and Metamethodology in Marketing: A Lakatosian Reconstruction. *Journal of Marketing*, **49**

Lerner E. M. and Carleton W. T. (1966) *A Theory of Financial Analysis*. Harcourt, Brace & World, Inc

Levy J. P. (1973) Automatic handling of syntax errors in SCARABEE, an interactive system. *Centre HEC-ISA, Cahier de Recherche No. 2*

Lindblom C. E. (1959) The science of muddling through. *Public Administration Review*, **19**, 78–88

Lindblom C. E. (1979) Still muddling, not yet through. *Public Administration Review*, **39**, 517–26

Little J. D. C. (1970) Models for managers: a calculus of decision. *Management Science*, **16**(8)

Little J. D. C. (1979) Decision support systems for marketing managers. *Journal of Marketing*, **43**, 9–26

Lyngstad P. B. (1987) Knowledge modeling of expertise in financial diagnostics (in Norwegian). *PhD Thesis* NHH Bergen, Norway

McCann J. (1991) Expert systems in marketing in special issue *International Journal of Research in Marketing*, April

McCarthy J. (1960) Recursive functions of symbolic expressions and their computation by machine. *Communications of the ACM*, **21**(12)

McCarthy (1984) *Private Correspondence to S. Holtzman*

McClelland J. L. and Rumelhart D. E. (eds) (1986) *Parallel Distributed Processing; Explorations in the Microstructure of Cognition*. Cambridge MA: MIT Press, Bradford Books

McDermott D. (1982) Non-monotonic logic II: non-monotonic model theories. *JACM*, 33–57

McDermott D. and Doyle J. (1980) Non-monotonic logic 1. *Artificial Intelligence*, 41–72

McDermott J. (1982a) R1: a rule-based configurer of computer systems. *Artificial Intelligence*, **19**, 39–88

McDermott J. (1982b) Xsel a computer sales person assistant, in Hayes, Michie, and Pao (eds), Machine Intelligence. Vol 20 325–338 New York: Wiley

McDermot J. and Steels L. (eds) (1994) *The Knowledge Level in Expert Systems, Conversation and Commentary*, Academic Press, Inc.

McGee V. E. and Kumar A. (1993) *Regression and Neural Networks: Time for A Change?* Amos Tuck School, Hanover, NH, USA

McNamee P. and Celona S. J. (1987) *Decision Analysis for the Professional with SUPERTREE.* Redwood City CA: Scientific Press

March J. G. (ed.) (1965) *Handbook of Organizations.* Chicago

March J. G. (1978) Bounded rationality ambiguity and the engineering of choice. *The Bell Journal of Economics,* **9**

March J. G. and Simon H. (1958) *Organizations,* New York: John Wiley

Markowitz H. (1952) Portfolio Selection. *The Journal of Finance,* 77–91

Markowitz H. (1959) *Portfolio Selection: Efficient Diversification of Investments.* New York: John Wiley

Matheson J. E. (1970) Decision analysis practice: examples and insights. In *Proceedings of the Fifth International Conference on Operational Research.* Venice and London, Tavistock Publications pp. 677–691

Mays E., Apte C., Giesmer J., and Kastner J. (1987) Organizing knowledge in a complex financial domain. *IEEE Expert*

van Melle S. and Bennett P. (1981) *The EMYCIN Manual.* Computer Science Dept. Stanford University, Stanford CA

Merkhofer M. W. and Leof E. B. (1981) A Computer-aided Decision Structuring Process—Final Report. SRI International Technical Report, Menlo Park, CA

Methlie L. B. (1982) Data management techniques for DSS. *DATA Base,* **12**(1–2)

Methlie L. B. (1983) Organizational variables influencing DSS Implementation. In *Processes and Tools for Decision Support* (Sol H. G., ed.). North-Holland

Methlie L. B. (1987) On knowledge-based decision support systems for financial diagnosis. In *Decision Support Systems: Theory and Application* (Holsapple C. W. and Whinston A. B., eds). Berlin: Springer-Verlag

Michalski R. S., Carbonell J. G., and Mitchell T. M. (1986) *Machine Learning: An Artificial Approach,* Vol. II. Los Altos, CA: Morgan Kaufman

Milanese, Mario, Vicino A., and Boradani P. (1991) Integration of modeling and AI techniques in KB-DSS generators, The EDIPLUS System, *Information and Decision Technologies,* North Holland **17**, 125–131

Miller G. A. (1956) The magical number seven, plus or minus two: some limits on our capability for processing information. *The Psychology Review,* **63**(2)

Miller G. A., Galanter E., and Pribram K. H. (1960) *Plans and the Structure of Behavior,* N.Y.: Holt, Reinhart and Winston

Mills H. D. (1971) Top down programming in large systems. In *Debugging techniques in large systems* (Rustin R., ed.), pp. 41–55. Prentice-Hall

Minsky M. (1975) A framework for representing knowledge. In *The Psychology of Computer Vision* (Winston P., ed.). New York: McGraw-Hill

Mintzberg H. (1973) *The Nature of Managerial Work.* New York: Harper & Row

Mintzberg H., Raisingani, D., and Theoret, A. (1976) The structure of the unstructured decision processes. *Administrative Science Quarterly,* **21**, 246–275

von Mises R. (1957) *Probability, Statistics and Truth.* New York: The Macmillan Corporation

Missikoff M. and Widerhold G. (1984) Towards a unified approach for expert and data base systems. In *Proc. First Int Workshop on Expert Data Base Systems* (Kerschberg L. ed.). Menlo Park CA: Benjamin Cummings

Mitchell, A. (1988) The use of alternative knowledge systems in the development of a knowledge based media planning system. *International Journal of Man–Machine Studies,* **26**, 399–412

Mockler R. J. (1989) *Knowledge-Based Systems for Management Decisions.* Englewood Cliffs, NJ: Prentice Hall

Montgomery D. B. and Urban G. L. (1969) *Management Science in Marketing*. Englewood Cliffs, NJ: Prentice-Hall

Moore E. A. and Agongino M. (1987) INFORM: an architecture for expert-directed knowledge acquisition. *Int. J. Man-Machine Studies*, **26**(2)

Mottura P. (1988) *Problem-Solving and Decision-Making in Banks and the Opportunities of Knowledge Technology*. SDA-Bocconi, Milano, Italy

Mui C. and McCarthy W. E. (1987) FSA: applying AI techniques to the familiarization phase of financial decision making. *IEEE Expert*

Murphy G. L. and Wright J. C. (1984) Changes in conceptual structure with expertise: differences between real-world experts and novices. *Journal of Experimental Psychology: Learning, Memory and Cognition*, **10**, 144–155

Musen M. A. (1988) Conceptual Models of Interactive Knowledge-Acquisition Tools, Report KSL-88-16, Knowledge Systems Laboratory, Stanford University

Myers S. C. (1988) Notes on an expert system for capital budgeting. *Financial Management*, **17**(3)

Neisser U. (1967) *Cognitive Psychology*. N.Y.: Appleton

von Neumann J. and Morgenstein O. (1944) *The Theory of Games and Economic Behavior*. Princeton: Princeton University Press

Newell A. (1990) *The Unified Theories of Cognition*, Cambridge, Mass., Harvard University Press

Newell A. and Simon H. A. (1963) GPS, a program that can simulate human thought. In *Computers and Thought* (Feigenbaum and Feldman, eds), pp. 279–296

Newell A. and Simon H. A. (1972) *Human Problem Solving*. Englewood Cliffs NJ: Prentice-Hall

Newell A. and Simon H. A. (1976) Computer science as empirical inquiry: symbols and search. *Communications of the ACM*, **19**(3)

Newell A. (1982) The knowledge level. *Artificial Intelligence*, **18**, 87–127

Nguyen T. A., Perkins W. A., Laffey T. J., and Pecora D. (1987) Knowledge base verification. *The AI-Magazine*

Olmsted, S. M. (1982) *SUPERTREE—decision tree processing program*. Menlo Park CA: Strategic Decision Group

Olson M. H. (1982) New information technology and organizational culture. *MIS Quarterly*

OPTRANS (1982) *User Manual*, SIG, 4 bis rue de la Libération, 78350 Jouy-en-Josas, France

OPTRANS Objet (1994) *User Manual, Decision Systems Research*, 4 bis rue de la Libération, 78350, Jouy-en-Josas, France.

Owen (1978) The use of influence diagrams in structuring complex decision problems. In *Readings on the Principles and Applications of Decision Analysis* Vol. 2 (1984) (Howard R. A. and Matheson J. E., eds) Menlo Park, CA, Strategic Decision Example

Page, M. (1990) *Systèmes Experts à Base de Connaissances Profondes*, Thèse de l'Institut National Polytechnique de Grenoble

Page M., Deburd S., Arrus R., and Olivier M. (1993) From Numerical Models to Knowledge Bases, in QUARDET 93: *IMACS International Workshop on Qualitative Reasoning and Decision Technologies*, Barcelona, 16–18 June 1993

Parfit D. (1986) *Reasons and Persons*. Oxford: Oxford University Press

Parnas D. L. (1972) On the criteria to be used in decomposing systems into modules. *Communications of the ACM*, **15**, 1053–1058

Parsaye K. and Chignell M. (1993) *Intelligent Database Tools & Applications*, John Wiley

Pastre D. (eds) (1988) *Intelligence Artificielle*, Actes des Journées Nationales, Teknea

PC-OPTRANS Expert User Manual. (1985) SIG, 4 bis rue de la Libération, 78350 Jouy-en-Josas

Pearl J. (1988) *Probabilistic Reasoning in Intelligent Systems*. San Mateo, California: Morgan Kaufmann

Penrose Roger (1994) *Shadows of the Mind*, Oxford University Press

Pezier J. (1986) Real time financial trading systems. *SIAD Research Seminar*, Centre HEC-ISA, 78350 Jouy-en-Josas, France

Pezier J. and Klein M. (1973) *ARBRE Manuel d'utilisation* SIG, 4 bis rue de la Libération, 78350 Jouy-en-Josas, France

Politakis P. G. (1985) *Empirical Analysis for Expert Systems*. Boston: Pitman Publishing Inc

Pople H. E. (1982) Heuristic methods for imposing structure on ill-structured problems: the structuring of medical diagnostics. In *Artificial Intelligence in Medicine* (Szolovits P., ed.) Boulder CO: Westview Press

Popper K. R. (1963) *Conjectures and Refutations Conjectures and Refutations*. London: Routledge and Kegan Paul

Popper K. R. (1965) *The Logic of Scientific Discovery*. Harper Torchbooks

Pounds W. F. (1969) The process of problem finding. *Industrial Management Review* 1–19

Pracht W. E. (1987) A visual modeling acquisition and organization. In *Proc. of the Twentieth Hawaii International Conference on Systems Sciences*, Vol. I

Prietula M. and Simon H. (1989) The experts in your midst. *Harvard Business Review*, 120–124, Jan–Feb

Quade E. S. (1975) *Analysis for Public Decisions*. New York: North-Holland

Quade E. S. (1984) *Analysis for Military Decisions*. Chicago: Rand McNally

Quinlan J. R. (1979) Discovering rules by induction from large collections of examples. In *Expert Systems in the Micro-electronic Age* (Michie D., ed.), Edinburgh: Edinburgh University Press

Raiffa H. (1968) *Decision Analysis: Introductory Lectures on Choices Under Uncertainty*. Reading MA: Addison-Wesley

Ramsey R. P. (1931) Truth and probability. In *The Foundations of Mathematics and other Classical Essays* (Braithwaite R. B., ed.). London: Kegan Paul

Rangaswamy A., Eliasberg J., Burke R., and Wind J. (1989) Developing marketing expert systems: an application to international negotiations. *Journal of Marketing* 53, 24–39

Rangaswamy A., Harlam B., and Lodish L. (1991) INFER: An expert system for automatic analysis of scanner data, In *International Journal of Research in Marketing* 8, 29–40, North Holland

Rangaswamy A. (1993) Marketing decision models: from linear programs to knowledge based systems. In *Handbooks in OR and MS*, Marketing, North Holland, 733–771

Raphael J., Klein M., and Manteau A. (1979) An investment and financial planning system for the road transport industry. *Engineering Cost and Production Economics*, 4, 193–210

Reddy R. (1988) Foundations and grand challenges of artificial intelligence. *AI-Magazine*

Reiter R. (1978) On closed world data bases. In *Logic and Data Bases* (Gallaire H. and Minker J., eds), 56–76. New York: Plenum Press

Ribe H. (1985) *A Study of Decision Processes in a Bank's Credit Department for Expert Systems Development* (in Norwegian). Arbeidsnotat nr. 8/1986, Center of Applied Research NHH, Bergen

Rich E. (1983) *Artificial Intelligence*. New York: McGraw-Hill

Rich C. and Buchanan B. (1985) Expert systems—part 1, tutorial No. 5. *IJCAI 9*

Richter M. M. (1988) AI concept and OR tools in advanced DSS, in design aspects of advanced DSS. *DSS International Journal*, 4(4)

Riesbeck G. A. and Schank R. L. (1989) *Inside Case-based Reasoning*. Hillsdale, N.J., Erlbaum

Rosch E., Mervis, C. B., Gray W. D., Johnson D. M., and Boyes-Braem P. (1976) Basic objects in natural categories. *Cognitive Psychology*, 8, 382–439

Roy B. (1973) How outranking relation helps multiple criteria decision making. In *Selected Proceedings of a Seminar on Multi-criteria Decision Making*. Chapter Hill SL: University of South Carolina Press

Roy B. and Vincke P. (1981) Multicriteria analysis: survey and new directions. *European Journal of Operation Research*, 8(3)

Roy B. and Vincke P. (1984) Relational systems of preference with one or more pseudo-criteria: some new concepts and results. *Management Science*, 30(11)

Samuelson P. A. (1947) *Foundations of Economic Analysis*. Cambridge MA: Harvard University Press

Savage L. J. (1954) *The Foundation of Statistics*. New York: Wiley

Schafer G. V. (1976) *A Mathematical Theory of Evidence*. Princeton: Princeton University Press

Schank R. C. and Abelson R. P. (1977) *Scripts, Plans, Goals, and Understanding*. Hillsdale, NJ, Erlbaum

Schoemaker P. J. H. (1980) *Experiments on Decisions Under Risk: The Expected Utility Hypothesis*. Boston: Nijhoff

Scott Morton M. S. (1971) *Management Decision Systems: Computer-based Support for Decision Making*. Cambridge, MA: Harvard Division of Research

Seaver D. A., von Winterfeld D., and Edwards, W. (1978) Eliciting subjective probability distribution on continuous variables. *Organizational Behavior and Human Performance*, 21, 379–391

Selfridge M. and Biggs S. F. (1990) The architecture of expertise: the auditor's going-concern judgement. *Expert Systems Review*, 3, 3–18

Segal R. (1970) *Research in the Design and Management Decision System*. The Moore School of Electrical Engineering

SEXTAN (1990) *User Manual*, SIG, 4 bis rue de la Libération, 78350 Jouy-en-Josas, France.

Sharda R., Barr S. H., and McDonnell J. C. (1988) Decision support systems effectiveness: a review and an empirical test. *Management Science*, 34(2)

Sharpe W. (1963) A simplified model for portfolio analysis. *Management Sciences*, 9(2), 277–293

Shaw M. J. and Gentry J. A. (1988) Using an expert system with inductive learning to evaluate business loans. *Financial Management*

Shipilberg D. *et al.* (1986) ExperTax: an expert system for corporate tax planning. *Expert Systems*, July

Schoemaker P. J. H. (1980) *Experiments on Decisions Under Risk: The Unexpected Utility Hypothesis*, Boston: Nijhoff

Shortliffe E. H. (1976) *Computer-Based Medical Consultations: MYCIN*. New York: Elsevier

Simon H. A. (1960) *The New Science of Management Decisions*. New York: Harper & Row

Simon H. A. (1969) *The Science of the Artificial*. Cambridge, MA: The MIT Press

Simon H. A. (1973) The structure of ill-structured problems. *Artificial Intelligence*, 4, 181–201

Simon H. A. (1976) *Administrative Behavior*. New York: Free Press

Simon H. A. (1982) *The Science of the Artificial*. Cambridge MA: The MIT Press

Simon H. *et al.* (1987) Decision making and problem solving. *Interfaces* 17(5)

Singh G, Madan and Cook R. (1988) Decision Support Systems for Asset and Liability Management. In *Retail Banking, Quarterly Journal of the Giro Centrale*, Austria, 1988

Singh M. and Trave-Massures (eds) (1991) Qualitative reasoning in DSS, *Proceedings of the IMACS Workshop, Toulouse*, North Holland

Slade S. (1991) Case-based reasoning: a research paradigm. *AI Magazine*, Spring

Slatter P. E. (1987) *Building Expert Systems: Cognitive Emulation*. New York: John Wiley

Smith E. E. and Medin D. L. (1981) *Categories and Concepts*. Cambridge MA: Harvard University Press

Smith J. M. (1986) Expert database systems: a database perspective. In *Expert Database Systems, Proceedings from the First International Workshop*: Menlo Park CA: Benjamin Cummings

Smith J. M. and Smith D. C. P. (1977) Database abstraction: aggregation. *Communication of the ACM*, **20**, 6, 405–413

Smith M. (1993) *Neural Networks for Statistical Modeling*, Van Nostrand Rheinhold, NY

Smolensky P. (1987) The constituent structure of connectionist mental states: a reply to Fodor and Pylyshyn. *The Southern Journal of Philosophy*, **XXVI**, 137–160

Sowa J. F. (1984) *Conceptual Structures. Information Processing in Mind and Machine*. Reading MA: Addison-Wesley

Spetzler C. S. (1968) The development of a corporate risk policy for capital investment decisions. *IEEE Transactions on System Science and Cybernetics*. SSC-4, 279–300

Spetzler C. S. and Stael von Holstein C. A. (1975) Probability encoding in decision analysis. *Management Science*, **22**, 340–352

Sprague R. H. and Carlson E. D. (1982) *Building Effective Decision Support Systems*. Englewood Cliffs NJ: Prentice-Hall

Srinivasan V. and Kim Y. H. (1988) Designing expert financial systems: a case study of corporate credit management. *Financial Management*

Stabell (1974) Individual differences in managerial decision making processes, a study of conversational computer usage. *PhD Dissertation*, MIT, Cambridge MA

Stabell C. B. (1983) A decision oriented approach to building DSS. In *Building Decision Support Systems* (Bennet J. L., ed.), Reading MA: Addison-Wesley

Stansfield J. L. and Greenfeld N. R. (1987) Plan Power—a comprehensive financial planner. *IEEE Expert*

Stephens R. G. (1980) *Uses of Financial Information in Bank Lending Decision*. Ann Arbor MI: UMI Research Press

Stillings, N. A., Feinstein M. H., Garfield J. L., Rissland E. L., Rosenbaum, D. A., Weisler S. E., and Baker-Ward L. (1987) *Cognitive Science: An Introduction*. Cambridge MA: The MIT Press

Suwa M., Scott A. C., and Shortliffe E. H. (1982) An approach to verifying completeness and consistency in a rule-based expert system. *The AI-Magazine*

Tener W. T. (1988) Expert systems for computer security. *Expert System Review*, 1(2)

Thagard P. (1988) *Computational Philosophy of Science*, Cambridge, Mass., MIT Press

Thies M. (1994) Adaptive user interface. In *13th World Computer Congress 94*, Volume 2, K. Brunnstein and E. Raubold (eds) North Holland, Elsevier

Thomas D. (1989) What is an object? *Byte*. McGraw-Hill

Tomlinson R. and Kiss I., eds (1984) *Rethinking the Process of Operational Research and System Analysis*. Oxford: Pergamon Press

Toulmin S. (1972) *Human Understanding* Vol. 1. Princeton NJ: Princeton University Press

Tribus M. (1969) *Rational Descriptions, Decisions and Design*. Oxford: Pergamon Press

Turban E. (1990) *Decision Support and Expert Systems*. New York: Macmillan

Tversky, A. and Kahneman, D. (1981) The Framing of Decision and the Psychology of Choice. *Science*, **211**, 453–458

Uschold, M. F. (1993) The use of domain information and higher order logic for model management. In *Computer and Systems Science* (Holsapple C. W., Whinston A. B., eds), Springer

Van de Velde W. (1993) Issues in knowledge level modelling. In *Second Generation Expert Systems* (David, Krivine, and Simmons, eds), Berlin: Springer, 211–231

Vincke P. (1986) Analysis of multicriteria decision aid in Europe. *European Journal of Operational Research* **25**, 160–168. North-Holland

Vincke P. (1992) *Multicriteria Decision Aids*. Chichester: John Wiley

Waddington C. H. (1973) *OR in World War 2*. London: Elek Science

Warren J. M. (1974) An operational model for securing analysis and valuation. *JFQA*

Waterman D. A. and Hayes-Roth F. (1978) *Pattern-Directed Inference Systems*. N.Y.: Academic Press

Waterman D. A. (1986) *A Guide to Expert Systems*. Reading MA: Addison-Wesley

Watson S. R. and Buede D. M. (1987) *Decision Synthesis: The Principles and Practice of Decision Analysis*. Cambridge: Cambridge University Press

Weatherford R. (1982) *Philosophical Foundation of Probability Theory*. London: Routledge and Kegan Paul

Weingartner M. H. (1963) *Mathematical Programming and the Analysis of Capital Budgeting Problems*. Englewood Cliffs NJ: Prentice-Hall

Weiss S. M. and Kulikowski C. A. (1984) *A Practical Guide to Designing Expert Systems*. Totowa NJ: Rowman & Allanheld

Welbank M. (1983) A review of knowledge acquisition techniques for expert systems. *British Telecommunications*

Wick M. R. and Slagle J. R. (1989) An explanation facility for today's expert systems. *IEEE Expert*

Wielinga B. J. and Breuker J. A. (1984) Interpretation of verbal data for knowledge acquisition. *Proc of ECA 84: Advances in Artificial Intelligence*. North-Holland: Elsevier

Wielinga B., Van de Velde W., Schreiber G., and Akkermans H. (1993) Toward a Unification of Knowledge Modelling Approaches. In *Second Generation Expert Systems* (David, J. M., Krivine, J. P., Simmons R., eds), Springer Verlag

Williamson J. P. (1970) Computerised approaches to bond switching. *Financial Analyst Journal*, July–August 1970

Winograd T. and Flores F. (1986) *Understanding Computers and Cognition*. Reading MA: Addison-Wesley

Witte E. (1972) Field research on complex decision-making processes—the phase theorem. *International Studies of Management and Organization*, 156–182

Wittgenstein L. (1953) *Philosophical Investigations*. Oxford: Basil Blackwell

Woods D. D. (1984) Visual momentum: a concept to improve the cognitive coupling of person and computers. *International Journal Man–Machine Studies*, **21**, 229–244

Yoon Y. and Guimaraes T. (1992) Developing knowledge-based systems: an object oriented organizational approach. *Information Resources Management Journal*, **5**, 3, 15–32, Summer

Zadeh L. (1965) Fuzzy Sets. *Information and Control*, **8**

Zadeh L. (1965) Fuzzy Sets as a Basis for A Theory of Possibility. *Fuzzy Sets and Systems*, **1**(1)

Zadeh L. A. (1981) Possibility theory and soft data analysis. In *Mathematical Frontiers of the Social and Policy Sciences* (Cobb L. and Thrall R. M., eds). Boulder Co: Westview Press

Zand D. E. and Sorenson R. E. (1975) Theory of change and the effective use of management science. *Administrative Science Quarterly*, **20**(4), 532–595

Zannetos Z. S. (1968) Toward intelligent management information systems. *Industrial Management Review* **9**(3), 21–38

Zeleny M. (1982) *Multiple Criteria Decision Making*. New York: McGraw-Hill

Zoeppritz A. (1986) Framework for investigating language-mediated interaction with machines. *International Journal Man–Machine Studies*, **25**, 295–315

Index